Contemporary Sociological Theory and Its Classical Roots

The Basics

THIRD EDITION

George Ritzer
University of Maryland

Connect
Learn
Succeed™

The McGraw-Hill Companies

Connect
Learn
Succeed™

Published by McGraw-Hill, an imprint of The McGraw-Hill Companies, Inc., 1221 Avenue of the Americas, New York, NY 10020. Copyright © 2010, 2007, 2003. All rights reserved. No part of this publication may be reproduced or distributed in any form or by any means, or stored in a database or retrieval system, without the prior written consent of The McGraw-Hill Companies, Inc., including, but not limited to, in any network or other electronic storage or transmission, or broadcast for distance learning.

This book is printed on acid-free paper.

1 2 3 4 5 6 7 8 9 0 DOC/DOC 0 9

ISBN: 978-0-07-340438-7
MHID: 0-07-340438-1

Editor in Chief: *Michael Ryan*
Sponsoring Editor: *Gina Boedeker*
Marketing Manager: *Pam Cooper*
Developmental Editor: *Phil Butcher*
Managing Editor: *Nicole Bridge*
Project Manager: *Michelle Gardner*
Production Service: *Laserwords Maine*
Manuscript Editor: *Tally Morgan*
Design Manager: *Margarite Reynolds*
Cover Designer: *Laurie Entringer*
Production Supervisor: *Louis Swaim*
Composition: *10/12 Palatino by Laserwords*
Printing: *45# New Era Matte Plus, R. R. Donnelley & Sons*

Cover Image: © Wetzel and Company

Credits: The credits section for this book begins on page 329 and is considered an extension of the copyright page.

Library of Congress Cataloging-in-Publication Data

Ritzer, George.
  Contemporary sociological theory and its classical roots : the basics /
George Ritzer.—3rd ed.
    p. cm.
  Includes index.
  ISBN-13: 978-0-07-340438-7
  ISBN-10: 0-07-340438-1
  1. Sociology. 2. Sociology—History. I. Title.
  HM586.R58 2010
  301.01—dc22

2009027466

The Internet addresses listed in the text were accurate at the time of publication. The inclusion of a Web site does not indicate an endorsement by the authors or McGraw-Hill, and McGraw-Hill does not guarantee the accuracy of the information presented at these sites.

www.mhhe.com

Contents

List of Boxes

About the Author

GEORGE RITZER is Distinguished University Professor at the University of Maryland. Among his awards are an Honorary Doctorate from La Trobe University, Australia, and the American Sociological Association's Distinguished Contribution to Teaching Award. He has chaired the American Sociological Association's Section on Theoretical Sociology, as well as the Section on Organizations and Occupations. His other McGraw-Hill textbooks include *Classical Sociological Theory, Modern Sociological Theory,* and *Sociological Theory.* Among his books in metatheory are *Sociology: A Multiple Paradigm Science* and *Metatheorizing in Sociology.* In the application of social theory to the social world, his books include *The McDonaldization of Society, Enchanting a Disenchanted World,* and *The Globalization of Nothing.* Sage has published two volumes of his collected works, one in theory and the other in the application of theory to the social world, especially consumption. In the latter area, he is founding editor of the *Journal of Consumer Culture.* He has edited the *Blackwell Companion to Major Social Theorists* and co-edited the *Handbook of Social Theory.* He has edited the two-volume *Encyclopedia of Social Theory* and the eleven-volume *Encyclopedia of Sociology.* His books have been translated into over 20 languages, with over a dozen translations of *The McDonaldization of Society* alone.

Preface

Compared to the second edition of this book, the fundamental structure of the third edition is unchanged. However, a number of substantial changes have been made within that overall structure and, of course, many more minor changes have been made throughout the text. The following are the changes made in this edition:

- In Chapter 5, a lengthy discussion of neo-Marxian spatial analysis, with a focus on the work of Henri Lefebvre and David Harvey, has been added (it replaces the section on Fordism and post-Fordism).
- In Chapter 6, the discussion of rational choice theory has been enhanced with much detail on the thinking of James Coleman.
- The most substantial changes are in Chapter 10, Globalization Theory. First, a detailed discussion has been added of neo-liberal economic theory, as well of the work of a major critic of that perspective, Karl Polanyi. Second, a more general discussion of political theories of globalization has been added, as has an analysis of the fate of the nation-state in the global age.
- Three new Biographical/Autobiographical Vignettes have been added: Alexis de Tocqueville (Chapter 1), C. Wright Mills (Chapter 4), and Harriet Martineau (Chapter 8)
- Additions to the Key Concepts are The Prosumer and Prosumption (Chapter 9), Globalization, and Civil Society (Chapter 10).
- The new Contemporary Applications are From Web 1.0 to Web 2.0 (Chapter 5), Domestic Violence (Chapter 9), The Death of Consumer Culture? If So, What Next?" (Chapter 9), The Great Global Economic Meltdown 2008 (Chapter 10), and Is Global Neo-Liberal Capitalism Dead? (Chapter 10). Dropped in order to make room for these were Terri Schiavo (Chapter 8), Surveillance (Chapter 9), and Al-Jazeera (Chapter 10).
- Among the lesser changes are additions to the glossary where needed, to bibliographies at the end of each chapter, a better placement of boxes closer to the relevant text and the addition of birth and death dates to the biographical/autobiographical vignettes.

Supplementary Material

Available to instructors only, this text is accompanied by an online Instructors' Manual which includes chapter outlines, chapter summaries, student exercises and discussion topics. Visit this site at **http://mhhe.com/ritzer3e.**

Acknowledgments

Once again I would like to thank Patricia Lengermann and Gillian Niebrugge for revising the material on feminist theory and, more generally, for their long-term and continuing support for this book, as well as my other theory texts with McGraw-Hill. At McGraw-Hill I would like to thank my current editor, Gina Boedeker, as well as a past editor, Phil Butcher, who came out of "retirement" to oversee the production of this edition.

I would also like to thank the reviewers of this edition for their comments and suggestions:

Martina Espinosa, *California State University;*

Rachel Hagewen, *University of Nebraska;*

Daphne Pedersen Stevens, *The University of North Dakota;*

Joy Crissy Honea, *Montana State University, Billings;*

May Takeuchi, *University of West Alabama;*

Emma Bailey, *Western New Mexico University;*

Salvador Jimenez Murguia, *California State University, San Bernardino;*

Rasby Marlene Powell, *The University of North Carolina, Pembroke;*

Jean Van Delinder, *Oklahoma State University*

CHAPTER 1

Introduction to Sociological Theory

Everyone theorizes about the social world (and many other things—natural events, supernatural possibilities) virtually all of the time. Most generally this means that people think about, speculate on, some social issue. We might think about our parents' relationship to one another or speculate about the chances that our favorite team will win the league championship or whether China will go to war with Taiwan. On the basis of such speculation we are likely to develop theories about our parents (e.g., they get along so well because they have similar personalities), our team (they will not win the league championship because they lack teamwork), or the possibility of war (China will not go to war because war would threaten China's recent economic advances). These theories deal with social realities and social relationships—for example, the personalities of our parents and how those personalities affect the way they relate to one another; teamwork and the ability to win a championship; the nature of China, and its relationship to other nations, in an era in which the global economy is increasingly tightly intertwined.

CREATING SOCIOLOGICAL THEORY

Social theorists, including those to be discussed in this book, do much the same kind of thing—they speculate, they develop theories, and their theories deal with social realities and social relationships. Of course, there are important differences between everyday theorizing and that of social theorists:

1

1. Social thinkers usually theorize in a more disciplined and self-conscious manner than do people on an everyday basis.
2. Social thinkers usually do their theorizing on the basis of the work of social thinkers who have come before them. Thus, virtually all social theorists have carefully studied the work of their forebears, while most laypeople operate largely, if not totally, on their own. To paraphrase Isaac Newton, and, more recently, the sociologist Robert Merton, if social theorists have developed better theories, it is because they have been able to build upon the ideas of those thinkers who came before them.
3. In addition, social theorists also often rely on data, either gathered by themselves or collected by others, on the social realities or relationships of interest to them. Laypeople may have some data at their disposal when they theorize, but these data are likely to be far less extensive and to be collected much less systematically.
4. Unlike laypeople, social theorists seek to publish their theories (major examples of such writings will be examined in this book) so that they can be critically analyzed, more widely disseminated, used as a basis for empirical research, and built upon by later theorists. The rigors of the review process help ensure that weak theories are weeded out before they are published or receive scant attention if they do manage to be published.
5. Most importantly, social theorists do not, at least professionally, think about specific relationships involving their parents, their favorite team, or even a particular nation. Social theorists generally think in a more inclusive manner about very broad social issues, whereas the layperson is much more likely to speculate about much narrower, even very personal, issues. Thus, in terms of the three examples already mentioned, although a layperson is likely to speculate about the relationship between her parents, the social theorist thinks about the more general issue of, for example, the changing nature of spousal relations in the early 21st century. Similarly, the layperson who thinks about the chances of success of her favorite team contrasts with the social theorist who might be concerned with such issues as the unfairness of competition between sports teams in the era of large salaries and budgets. Finally, rather than theorizing about China, a social theorist might think about the contemporary nation-state in the era of global capitalism (see Chapter 10).

Although social theorists think in general terms, this is not to say that the issues of concern to them are only of academic interest. In fact, the issues that are chosen are often of great personal interest to the theorists (and many others) and are frequently derived from issues of great import in their personal lives. Thus, the stresses and strains in their parents' marriage, or even in their own, might lead sociologists to theorize about the general issue of the modern family and the difficulties that abound within it. The best sociological theories often stem from deep personal interests of theorists.

However, this poses an immediate dilemma. If the best theory stems from powerful personal interests, isn't it likely that such theory is likely to be biased and distorted by those interests and personal experiences? The bad experiences that a theorist might have had as a child in her own home, or her own marital problems, might bias her against the nuclear family and give her a distorted view of it. This, in turn, might lead her in the direction of a theory critical of such a family. This is certainly possible, even likely, but theorists must and usually do manage to keep their personal biases in check. Yet bias is an ever-present danger that both theorists and those who read theory must keep in the forefront of their thinking.

Balancing this is the fact that feeling strongly about an issue is a powerful motivator. Sociologists with strong feelings about the family (or any other topic in sociology) are likely to do sustained work on it and to feel driven to come up with theoretical insights into the issue. As long as biases are kept in check, strong personal feelings often lead to the very best in social theory. For example, in this volume we will have a number of occasions to mention Karl Marx (1818–1883) and his pioneering work on capitalism (see Chapter 2). In many ways, Marx's theory of capitalism is one of the very best in the history of social theory, and it was motivated by Marx's strong feelings about it and the plight of the workers in it. It is true that these feelings may have blinded Marx to some of the strengths of the capitalist system, but that is counterbalanced by the fact that these feelings led to a powerful theory of the dynamics of capitalism.

One can theorize about any aspect of the social world with the result that social theorists have speculated about things we would expect them to think about (politics, the family), as well as others that we might find quite surprising (e.g., I've done work on things like fast-food restaurants, credit cards, and shopping malls). Every aspect of the social world, from the most exalted to the most mundane, can be the subject of social theory. Various social theorists find different aspects of the social world important and interesting, and it is in those areas that they are likely to devote their attention. Some might find the behavior of kings and presidents interesting, while others might be drawn to that of panhandlers and prostitutes. Furthermore, still others, often some of the best social theorists, are drawn to the relationship between highly exalted and highly debased behavior. For example, Norbert Elias (1897–1990) was concerned with the relationship (in the period between the 13th and the 19th centuries) between such mundane behaviors as picking one's nose at the dinner table, blowing one's nose, expelling wind, and changes in the king's court (see Chapter 5). In terms of mundane behaviors, he found that over time people grew less and less likely to pick their noses at the table, to stare at one's handkerchief and the results of blowing one's nose, and to noisily and publicly expel wind. This is linked to changes in the king's court that were eventually disseminated to the rest of society. Basically, the members of the king's court became dependent on a wider and wider circle of people, with the result that they became more sensitive about the impact of at least some of their behaviors (e.g., violence against others) and more circumspect about them. Eventually, these wider circles of dependence, this greater sensitivity and circumspection, made their way to the lower reaches of society, and the kinds of every-day behaviors discussed above were greatly affected by them. To put it baldly,

---

Alexis de Tocqueville (1805–1859)
A Biographical Vignette

There are several ironies associated with the work of Alexis de Tocqueville.

First, he was a French scholar, but his best-known work deals with America.

Second, he was an aristocrat, but he is famous for his work on democracy.

Third, he is most often thought of as a political scientist, but he made very important contributions to sociology and sociological theory (see, for example, the discussion of "civil society" in Chapter 10). It is Volume One of *Democracy in America* (published in 1835) that is his best-known work, but it was largely political in nature. It dealt with the American political system and how it compared to others, particularly the French political system. The second volume of that work (published in 1840) is less well-known and was less well-received, but it is far more sociological. Among other things, it deals broadly with culture, social class, "individualism" (he is often credited with having invented the term, now very popular in sociological theory), and social change.

Fourth, by the time of his later work on the French Revolution, *The Old Regime and the French Revolution* (published in 1856), Tocqueville had grown nostalgic for the aristocratic system (he wrote of the "catastrophic downfall of the monarchy") and increasingly critical of democracy and socialism. Both were seen by him as involving far too much centralization of decision-making. He felt that in his younger years aristocrats were freer and made more independent decisions. Such aristocrats served as a counter-balance to the power of centralized government. In spite of this, Tocqueville was enough of a realist to realize that there was no going back to an aristocratic system. Rather, he argued for the need for various "associations of plain citizens" to form bodies that would serve to counter the power of centralized government and protect freedom. These associations are very close to what we now think of as civil society.

---

people generally stopped (the exceptions are now quite notable) picking their noses at the dinner table or noisily expelling wind in public.

Social thinkers may focus on particular behaviors because they find them important and interesting, but they also may do so because it provides them with a point of entry into the social world. This idea is based on the perspective of Georg Simmel (1858–1918) that the social world is composed of an endless series of social relationships (see Chapter 3). Each social act, in this view, is part of a social relationship and each of those relationships, in turn, is ultimately related to every other social relationship. Thus, any given act or relationship can serve as a way of gaining a sense of the entirety of the social world, even the essential aspects and meanings of that world. Thus, Simmel chose money and relationships based on money as a specific way of gaining insight into the entirety of modern society.

Although there is a great gap between the theories to be discussed in this book and the theories we all create every day, the point is that there is *no* essential difference between professional and lay theorizing. If, after you read this book, you study previous theorizing and then theorize in a more systematic and sustained manner about general social issues, you would be a social theorist. Of course, being a social theorist does not necessarily yield high-quality theories. Your first efforts are not likely to be as good as the theories discussed in this book. In fact, the theories to be discussed in the following pages are the best of the best; and the work of many social theorists, some of them quite well known in their time, will not be discussed here because their theories have not stood the test of time well and are no longer considered important social theories. Thus, many have tried, but only a few have succeeded in creating the high quality and important theories to be discussed in this book.

DEFINING SOCIOLOGICAL THEORY

Standing the test of time is one characteristic of theories to be discussed in this book. Another is that they have a wide range of applicability. For example, they do not simply explain behavior in your family, but in a large number of similar families in the United States and perhaps even in other nations around the world. Still another is that the theories deal with centrally important social issues. Thus, the issue of globalization (see Chapter 10) and the global economy is defined by many as a key issue today and, as a result, has attracted the attention of many social theorists. Finally, the theories to be discussed in this book were created either by sociologists or by those in other fields whose work has come to be defined as important by sociologists. For example, we will devote a great deal of attention to feminist sociological theory in this book, but although some feminist theorists are sociologists (e.g., Dorothy Smith, Patricia Hill Collins), the vast majority are social thinkers from a wide variety of other fields. Whether or not theories were created by sociologists, the theories to be discussed here have been built upon by others who have refined them, expanded on them, or tested some of their basic premises in empirical research.

A more formal definition of **sociological theory** is a set of interrelated ideas that allows for the systematization of knowledge of the social world, the explanation of that world, and predictions about the future of the social world. While some of the theories to be discussed in these pages meet all of these criteria to a high degree, many others fall short on one or more of them. Nonetheless, they are all considered full-fledged sociological theories for purposes of this discussion. Whether or not they meet all the criteria, all the theories to be discussed here are considered by large numbers of sociologists (as well as those in many other fields) to be important theories. Perhaps most importantly, all of these are big ideas about issues and topics of concern to everyone in the social world.

---

sociological theory A set of interrelated ideas that allow for the systematization of knowledge of the social world, the explanation of that world, and predictions about the future of the social world.

CREATING SOCIOLOGICAL THEORY:
A MORE REALISTIC VIEW

Up to this point in this chapter, we have offered an idealized picture of sociological theory and the way it is created. In recent years a number of sociological
theorists have grown increasingly critical of this image and have sought to create a more accurate picture of theory and theory creation. They point out that at
least some theorists are quite undisciplined (if not downright casual); they don't
always study the work of their predecessors in detail; they aren't always so
careful about collecting data that bear on their theories; their work is not always
reviewed rigorously prior to publication; they allow their personal experiences
to distort their theories; and so on. Overall, the point is made that the creation
of sociological theory is far from the perfect process described previously.

    In addition to critiquing the work of individual theorists, the critics have
also attacked the general state of sociological theory. They have made the point
that the best theories are not necessarily the ones that survive, become influential, and are covered in books like this one. They contend that sociological
theory is not unlike the rest of the social world—it is affected by a wide range of
political factors. What does and does not come to be seen as important theory
(as part of the canon) is the result of a series of political processes:

1. The work of those who studied with the acknowledged masters of sociological theory, people (historically, men) who came to occupy leadership
   positions within the discipline, is likely to be seen as more important than
   the work of those who lacked notable and powerful mentors.
2. Works reflecting some political orientations are more likely to become part
   of the canon than those done from other perspectives. Thus, in the not-
   too-distant past in sociology, politically conservative theories (e.g., structural functionalism; see Chapter 4) were more likely to win acceptance than
   those that were radical from a political point of view (e.g., various theories
   done from a Marxian perspective; see, especially, Chapter 5).
3. Theories that lead to clear hypotheses that can be tested empirically are
   more likely to be accepted, at least by mainstream sociologists, than those
   that produce grand, untestable points of view.
4. Theories produced by majority group members (i.e., white males) are more
   likely to become part of the canon than those created by minorities. Thus,
   the works of black theoreticians have been highly unlikely to become part
   of the canon (for one exception, see the box on Du Bois). The same is true,
   at least until recently, of the work of female theorists (see Chapter 8). The
   theoretical ideas of those associated with cultural minorities (e.g., Chica-
   nos, homosexuals) have encountered a similar fate.

Thus sociological theory has not, in fact, always operated in anything
approaching the ideal manner that was described earlier in this chapter. However, in recent decades there has been growing awareness of the gap between
the ideal and the real. As a result, a number of perspectives that were denied
entry into the heart of sociological theory have come, in recent years, to attain

a central position within the field. Thus, Marx's theory (see Chapter 2) and a variety of neo-Marxian theories (Chapter 5) have become part of the canon. Similarly, feminist theory has become a powerful presence in sociological theory, reflected by the fact that it is not only the subject of Chapter 8, but it is also dealt with elsewhere in this book. Thus, contemporary sociological theory is now characterized by a great mix of theories, some of which fit the ideal model and others that are the product of the less idealistic, more realistic model of the way theory works. That is, those who support previously excluded theories have flexed their muscles and used their power within sociological theory to enhance the position of their perspectives. These upstarts now share center stage in sociological theory with more mainstream theories that have long occupied that position.

In order to give more substance to this discussion, in the following section we discuss a number of upstart theories that can broadly be discussed under the heading of "multicultural social theory." At least some of these theories are on their way to becoming, or have already become, part of the canon.

Multicultural Social Theory

The rise of multicultural social theory was foreshadowed by the emergence of contemporary feminist sociological theory in the 1970s. Feminists complained that sociological theory had been largely closed to women's voices; in the ensuing years, many minority groups echoed the feminists' complaints. In fact, as discussed in Chapter 8, minority women (for example, African Americans and Latinas) began to complain that feminist theory was restricted to white middle-class females and had to be more receptive to many other voices. Today, feminist theory has become far more diverse, as has sociological theory.

A good example of the increasing diversity of sociological theory is the rise of "queer" sociological theory. The silence of classical sociological theory on sexuality in general and homosexuality in particular has been now well documented. It is striking that while the classical theorists were dealing with a wide range of issues relating to modernity, they had nothing to say about the making of modern bodies and modern sexuality. Although the silence was soon to be broken, it was not until the 1970s and the work of Michel Foucault (see Chapter 9) on the relationships among power, knowledge, and sexuality that the theoretical study of sexuality in general, and homosexuality in particular, began in earnest. What emerged was the sense of homosexuality as both a subject and an identity paralleling the heterosexual self and identity.

Steven Seidman has argued, however, that what distinguishes queer theory is a rejection of any single identity, including homosexuality, and the argument that all identities are multiple or composite, unstable, and exclusionary. Thus, at any given time each of us is a composite of a series of identity components such as sexual orientation, race, class, nationality, gender, and age. These components can be combined and recombined in many different ways. As a result, Seidman rejects the homosexual–heterosexual dichotomy and seeks to move queer theory in the direction of a more general social theory.

W. E. B. Du Bois (1868–1963)
A Biographical Vignette

Unlike other black leaders (such as Booker T. Washington) and intellectuals of the late 19th and early 20th centuries, W. E. B. Du Bois was born free in the North. He attended Harvard University and obtained a doctorate from that university (he also studied at the University of Berlin). He is best known in sociology for his important contribution to urban ethnography, *The Philadelphia Negro* (1899), and to racial economic history in *Black Reconstruction in America, 1860–1880* (1935). However, Du Bois was also a polemicist and politician (traits that were also manifest in his more scholarly books), and these traits are powerfully reflected in *The Souls of Black Folks* (1903). In addition to his publications, Du Bois's accomplishments during the 20th century included being the major force opposing Booker T. Washington and his concessions to white power and being a founder of the NAACP (1909) and its principal spokesman during the second decade of the century. He also was leader of the Harlem Renaissance in the 1920s, and he received worldwide recognition as a leader of the Pan-African movement. In the 1950s he defied the U.S. government's McCarthy-like persecution of anyone thought to be a communist, and in the 1960s he settled in Ghana, where he set about to create an *Encyclopedia Africana*. Du Bois died in 1963 on the eve of the March on Washington and the ascendancy of Martin Luther King as leader of the black movement. His passionate concern for the dire implications of the "color line," especially among black Americans, continues to influence scholars, politicians, activists, and many others.

Nevertheless, queer theory is generally put forth as an example of standpoint theory: that is, a theory that looks at the social world from a particular vantage point (see Chapter 8). We can expect to see a burgeoning of such multicultural standpoint theories as the 21st century unfolds.

Multicultural theory has taken a series of diverse forms beyond that of queer theory. Examples include Afrocentric theory, Native American theory, and even theories of masculinity. Among the things that characterize multicultural theory are the following:

- It rejects universalistic theories that tend to support those in power; multicultural theories seek to empower those who lack clout.
- It seeks to be inclusive, to offer theory on the behalf of many disempowered groups.
- Multicultural theorists are not value free; they often theorize on behalf of those without power and work in the social world to change social structure, culture, and the prospects for individuals.
- Multicultural theorists seek to disrupt not only the social world but the intellectual world; they seek to make it far more open and diverse.
- No effort is made to draw a clear line between theory and other types of narratives.

- Ordinarily multicultural theory has a critical edge; it is both self-critical and critical of other theories and, most importantly, of the social world.
- Multicultural theorists recognize that their work is limited by the particular historical, social, and cultural context in which they happen to live.

Thus, multicultural theory tends to be created by atypical theorists, to focus on heretofore ignored topics, and to utilize a variety of unique approaches to theorizing. Multicultural theory in general, as well as several specific multicultural theories, is fast becoming part of the canon of sociological theory.

OVERVIEW OF THE BOOK

Although this book is primarily about contemporary sociological theory, no single date can be used to separate clearly classical sociological theory from contemporary sociological theory, nor are there characteristics that definitively separate the two. Nonetheless, we can take as the starting point of classical sociological theory the early 1800s when Auguste Comte, the French social thinker who coined the term *sociology* (in 1839), began theorizing sociologically. (By the way, thinkers long before that time, both in Western and non-Western cultures, developed idea systems that had many elements in common with sociological theory.) The 1920s and 1930s mark the close of the classical period. By that time virtually all the great classical thinkers had passed from the scene, and the new contemporary theorists were beginning to replace them. Thus, the beginnings of the contemporary theories discussed in this book can be traced back many decades, although most were produced in the last half of the 20th century and remain important, and continue to be developed, in the early years of the 21st century.

Chapters 2 and 3 deal with the major theories and theorists of sociology's classical age—roughly the late 19th and early 20th centuries. Chapter 2 covers three thinkers—Emile Durkheim, Karl Marx, and Max Weber—who are *always* acknowledged as *the* major figures in the history of sociological theory. Chapter 3 begins with a theorist—Georg Simmel—who is very often included with the other three in the pantheon of classic theorists. This chapter also deals with an American thinker (Durkheim was French; Marx, Weber, and Simmel were German)—Thorstein Veblen—who, like the others mentioned to this point, had a very broad social theory. His theorizing has received increasing recognition in recent years for the fact that while all of the above focused on issues related to production, he also concerned himself with, and foresaw, the increasing importance of consumption (especially in his famous idea of "conspicuous consumption") in the 20th and early 21st centuries. The final thinker to be discussed in the category of the great classical thinkers is another American, George Herbert Mead, who had a very different kind of theory that focused more on everyday life (although, as we will see, many of the other thinkers discussed in Chapters 2 and 3 had much to offer on this and often embedded their larger theories in ideas that related to everyday life) and less on broad social phenomena and social changes.

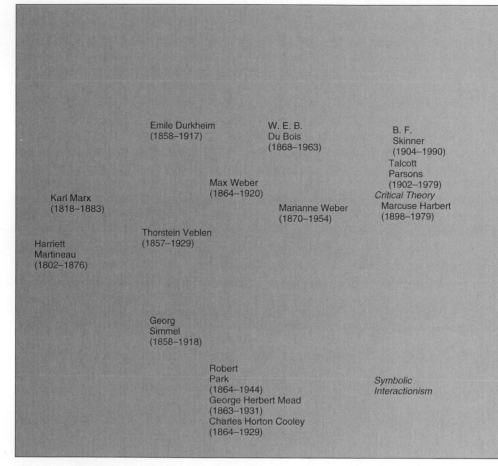

FIGURE 1.1 Sociological Theory: A Chronology

Chapters 4 and 5, indeed the rest of the book, shift the focus to our main concern with contemporary sociological theories. These two chapters deal with contemporary grand theories (as contrasted to the contemporary theories of everyday life to be discussed in Chapter 6). A **grand theory** is defined as a vast, highly ambitious effort to tell the story of a great stretch of human history and/or a large portion of the social world. In fact, all of the theorists discussed in Chapters 2 and 3 can be seen as doing grand theory. However, our focus in Chapters 4 and 5 is more contemporary grand theories. In Chapter 4 we deal with two of the best-known contemporary theories: structural functionalism and conflict theory, along with systems theory, which has enjoyed

---

grand theory   A vast, highly ambitious effort to tell the story of a great stretch of human history and/or a large portion of the social world.

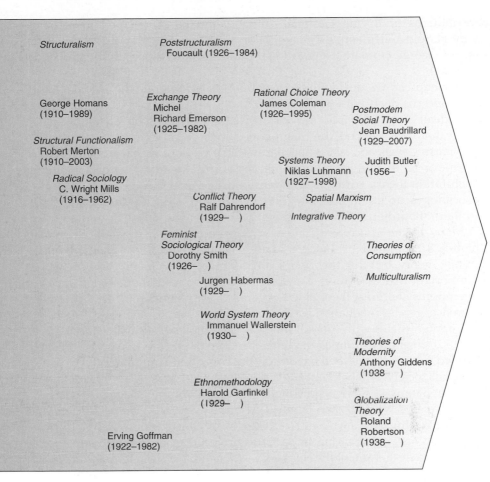

Structuralism

Poststructuralism
Foucault (1926–1984)

George Homans
(1910–1989)

Exchange Theory
Michel
Richard Emerson
(1925–1982)

Rational Choice Theory
James Coleman
(1926–1995)

Postmodem
Social Theory
Jean Baudrillard
(1929–2007)

Structural Functionalism
Robert Merton
(1910–2003)

Radical Sociology
C. Wright Mills
(1916–1962)

Systems Theory
Niklas Luhmann
(1927–1998)

Judith Butler
(1956–)

Conflict Theory
Ralf Dahrendorf
(1929–)

Spatial Marxism

Integrative Theory

Feminist
Sociological Theory
Dorothy Smith
(1926–)

Theories of
Consumption

Multiculturalism

Jurgen Habermas
(1929–)

World System Theory
Immanuel Wallerstein
(1930–)

Theories of
Modernity
Anthony Giddens
(1938–)

Ethnomethodology
Harold Garfinkel
(1929–)

Globalization
Theory
Roland
Robertson
(1938–)

Erving Goffman
(1922–1982)

a resurgence of interest lately because of the contributions of a contemporary German thinker, Niklas Luhmann. Chapter 5 deals with both another well-known contemporary theory—neo-Marxian theory—as well as three of the more specific contemporary efforts at grand theory: the civilizing process (Norbert Elias), colonizing the lifeworld (Jürgen Habermas), and the juggernaut of modernity (Anthony Giddens).

While Chapters 4 and 5 deal with grand theories dealing with large-scale structures and changes, Chapter 6 focuses on the major contemporary varieties of **theories of everyday life**: symbolic interactionism (building heavily on the work of Mead discussed in Chapter 3), dramaturgy (especially the

---

theories of everyday life Theories that focus on such everyday and seemingly mundane activities as individual thought and action, the interaction of two or more people, and the small groups that emerge from such interaction.

contributions of Erving Goffman), ethnomethodology (shaped most heavily by Harold Garfinkel), exchange theory (the focus here is on the contributions of George Homans), and rational choice theory (especially that of James Coleman).

In Chapter 7 we deal with the major efforts to integrate the kinds of large-scale concerns dealt with in Chapters 4 and 5 with the everyday (small-scale) issues dealt with in Chapter 6. We start with the efforts to create an exchange theory that goes beyond the micro-issues covered in Chapter 6 to integrate more macro-levels and issues (primarily in the work of Richard Emerson). We then move on to a series of more encompassing integrative efforts including structuration theory (Anthony Giddens' most general theoretical contribution to sociology), an attempt to integrate culture and agency (Margaret Archer), and Pierre Bourdieu's ambitious integration of what he calls habitus and field.

Many of the concerns detailed in the preceding chapter are evident in Chapter 8 (authored by Patricia Madoo Lengermann and Jill Brantley) on feminist theory, but that theory is so broad, involves so many thinkers, and is so important that it requires a chapter (at least) to itself. Four broad types of contemporary feminist theories are covered in the chapter—theories of gender difference, gender inequality, gender oppression, and structural oppression.

Chapter 9 deals with some of the most exciting theoretical developments of the late 20th century grouped under the heading of postmodern grand theories. Included here is Daniel Bell's work on the transition from industrial to post-industrial society, Michel Foucault's thinking on increasing governmentality, Zygmunt Bauman's work on postmodernity as the coming of age of modernity, the interrelated work of Jean Baudrillard on the rise of consumer society and my work on the new means (or cathedrals) of consumption, Paul Virilio on dromology or the increasing importance of speed in the postmodern world, and finally a discussion of the complex relationship between feminist and postmodern theory.

Chapter 10 deals with what is coming to be seen in the early 21st century as the most important area of new sociological (and other) theorizing—globalization theory. We begin by looking at the thinking of several important contemporary theorists on globalization—Anthony Giddens, Zygmunt Bauman, and Ulrich Beck. The remainder of the chapter is devoted to three broad types of theorizing about globalization. The first is cultural theory, which, itself, is subdivided into three subtypes. Cultural differentialism sees lasting, if not eternal, differences among cultures that are little affected by globalization. A major example of this approach is Samuel Huntington's work on civilizations. Cultural convergence focuses on areas in which cultures are growing alike. My own work on McDonaldization as a global force and the increasing globalization of "nothing" is used to exemplify this approach. Finally, cultural hybridization sees globalization as characterized by unique mixtures of the global and the local. Appadurai's work on globalization in general, and especially his thinking on disjunctures among what he calls "landscapes," is a good and important example of this approach. Second is economic theory. While there is a wide array of work under this heading, the

focus here is on neo-liberalism, as well as two neo-Marxian approaches—
Leslie Sklair on transnational capitalism and Michael Hardt and Antonio Negri
on empire—that represent critiques of neo-liberalism and alternatives to it.
Finally, we discuss political approaches to globalization with a special focus on
the decline of the nation-state in the global age.

Summary

1. We all theorize, but there are a number of characteristics that distinguish the theorizing of sociologists from that of laypeople.
2. The issues of interest to sociological theorists are usually of great personal *and* social concern.
3. Every aspect of the social world, from the most exalted to the most mundane, can be the subject of social theory.
4. Social thinkers may focus on particular behaviors because they find them important and interesting, but they also may do so because these behaviors offer them points of entry into the larger social world.
5. The theories discussed in this book have a number of characteristics in common, including having stood the test of time and having a wide range of applicability, dealing with centrally important social issues, and being created by sociologists or those who have come to be defined as important by sociologists.
6. A more formal definition of sociological theory, although few theories measure up to it fully, is: a set of interrelated ideas that allow for the systematization of knowledge of the social world, the explanation of that world, and predictions about the future of the social world.
7. Although there is an idealized image of the way in which sociological theory operates (e.g., the best ideas become part of the canon), the fact is that reality is quite different and political factors play a critical role in theory.
8. Criticisms of the ideal model and revelations about the real world of sociological theory have made it possible for a number of perspectives that were previously marginalized (e.g., Marxian, feminist, and multicultural theories) to move toward, and even become part of, the canon.
9. This book deals with contemporary sociological theory (and its classical roots) under several general headings—classical theories, grand theories (including postmodern), theories of everyday life, integrative theories, feminist theories, and theories of globalization.

Suggested Readings

CRAIG CALHOUN, et al., eds.   *Classical Sociological Theory*. Malden, MA: Blackwell, 2007. Recent collection of works in classical sociological theory.

CRAIG CALHOUN, et al., eds.   *Contemporary Sociological Theory*. Malden, MA: Blackwell 2007. Recent collection of works in contemporary sociological theory.

JAMES FARGANIS, ed.   *Readings in Social Theory*. 5th ed. New York: McGraw-Hill, 2008. One of the best collections of both classic and contemporary works in social theory.

GEORGE RITZER   *Modern Sociological Theory*. 7th ed. New York: McGraw-Hill, 2008. Deals with contemporary sociological theory much more widely and in much more detail than this volume.

GEORGE RITZER *Classical Sociological Theory.* 5th ed. New York: McGraw-Hill, 2008. Deals with classical sociological theory in greater depth than it is covered in this book and covers a much wider range of classical theorists.

GEORGE RITZER, ed. *The Blackwell Companion to Major Social Theorists.* Oxford, England, and Malden, MA: Blackwell, 2000. Twenty-five essays on leading classical and contemporary theorists authored by widely recognized scholars.

GEORGE RITZER, ed. *The Encyclopedia of Social Theory.* 2 volumes. Thousand Oaks, CA: Sage, 2005. The first full encyclopedia of social theory. It covers most of the major topics and theorists in both classical and contemporary. The entries are written by well-known experts on the topic from around the world.

GEORGE RITZER and BARRY SMART, eds. *The Handbook of Social Theory.* London: Sage, 2001. A compendium of essays dealing with many of the most important people and issues in the history of social theory.

JONATHAN TURNER *Structure of Sociological Theory.* 7th ed. Belmont, CA: Wadsworth, 2002. Latest version of a popular text in sociological theory that offers a very different perspective from the one found in this book. Turner adopts a "positivistic" perspective on theory and seeks to develop testable propositions derived from theories.

MARY ROGERS, ed. *Multicultural Experiences, Multicultural Theories.* New York: McGraw-Hill, 1996. Includes many examples of, and original contributions to, multicultural theory.

STEVEN SEIDMAN *Difference Troubles: Queering Social Theory and Sexual Politics.* Cambridge: Cambridge University Press, 1997. Book-length treatment of the topic from the leading spokesperson for queer theory.

CHARLES LEMERT "W. E. B. Du Bois." In George Ritzer, ed., *The Blackwell Companion to Major Social Theorists.* Malden, MA, and Oxford: Blackwell Publishers, 2000, pp. 345–366. Strong statement on the significance of Du Bois's work to sociology. However, Lemert goes beyond this to deal with Du Bois's importance in many different realms.

Classical Theories I

The early giants of social theory are noted for the creation of grand theories, theories that, as defined in Chapter 1, are vast, highly ambitious theoretical efforts to tell the story of great stretches of social history and large expanses of the social world. These theories of history generally culminate in the author's time with a description of a society that, while it has made progress, is beset with problems. The creators of such theories usually offer ideas about how to solve those problems and thereby to create a better society.

EMILE DURKHEIM: FROM MECHANICAL
TO ORGANIC SOLIDARITY

Emile Durkheim (1858–1917) built on the work of the French social theorist Auguste Comte, but he became a far more important figure in the history of theory than Comte. In fact, at least some observers consider him *the* most important theorist in the history of sociology. To this day, many forms of sociological theorizing bear the stamp of Durkheim's thinking.

Two Types of Solidarity

Durkheim's grand theory involves a concern for the historical transformation from more primitive mechanical societies to more modern organic societies. What differentiates these two types of society is the source of their solidarity, or what holds them together. The key here is the division of labor.

In **mechanical solidarity,** society is held together by the fact that virtually everyone does essentially the same things (gathering fruits and vegetables, hunting animals). In other words, there is little division of labor in primitive society and this fact holds society together. However, in more modern **organic solidarity** a substantial division of labor has occurred and people come to perform increasingly specialized tasks. Thus, some may make shoes, others may bake bread, and still others may raise children. Solidarity here comes from differences; that is, people need the contributions of an increasing number of people in order to function and even to survive.

Thus, Durkheim envisioned a historical transformation from mechanical to organic solidarity. This idea is clearly different from Comte's model of the change. Comte thought in terms of changes in ideas, in the way people seek to explain what transpires in the world; Durkheim dealt with changes in the material world in the way in which we divide up and do our work.

Changes in Dynamic Density

What causes the change from mechanical to organic solidarity? Durkheim's answer is that an increase in the **dynamic density** of society causes the transformation. There are two components of dynamic density. The first is simply the sheer number of people in society. However, an increased number of people is not enough to induce a change in the division of labor because individuals and small groups of people can live in relative isolation from one another and continue to be jacks of all trades. That is, even in societies with a large population, each individual can continue to do most of the required tasks. Thus, a second factor is important in order for dynamic density to increase and lead to changes in the division of labor: there must be an increase in the amount of interaction that takes place among the greater number of people in society. When an increasingly large number of people interact with greater frequency with one another, dynamic density is likely to increase to the point that a transformation from mechanical to organic solidarity occurs.

What is it about the increase in dynamic density that leads to the need for a different division of labor? With more people, there is greater competition over the use of scarce resources such as land, game, and fruits and vegetables. If everyone competes for everything, there is great disorder and conflict. With

---

mechanical solidarity   In Durkheimian theory, the idea that primitive society is held together by the fact there is little division of labor and, as a result, virtually everyone does essentially the same things.

organic solidarity   To Durkheim, the idea that because of the substantial division of labor in modern society, solidarity comes from differences; that is, people need the contributions of an increasing number of people in order to function and even to survive.

dynamic density   The number of people and their frequency of interaction. An increase in dynamic density leads to the transformation from mechanical to organic solidarity.

Emile Durkheim (1858–1917)
A Biographical Vignette

Durkheim is most often thought of today as a political conservative, and his influence within sociology certainly has been a conservative one. But in his time, he was considered a liberal. This was exemplified by the active public role he played in the defense of Alfred Dreyfus, the Jewish army captain whose court-martial for treason was felt by many to be based on anti-Semitic sentiments in some sectors of French society.

Durkheim was deeply offended by the Dreyfus affair, particularly its anti-Semitism. But Durkheim did not attribute this anti-Semitism to racism among the French people. Characteristically, he saw it as a symptom of the moral sickness confronting French society as a whole. He said:

> When society undergoes suffering, it feels the need to find someone whom it can hold responsible for its sickness, on whom it can avenge its misfortunes; and those against whom public opinion already discriminates are naturally designated for this role. These are the pariahs who serve as expiatory victims. What confirms me in this interpretation is the way in which the result of Dreyfus's trial was greeted in 1894. There was a surge of joy in the boulevards. People celebrated as a triumph what should have been a cause for public mourning. At least they knew whom to blame for the economic troubles and moral distress in which they lived. The trouble came from the Jews. The charge had been officially proved. By this very fact alone, things already seemed to be getting better and people felt consoled.

Thus, Durkheim's interest in the Dreyfus affair stemmed from his deep and lifelong interest in morality and the moral crisis confronting modern society.

To Durkheim, the answer to the Dreyfus affair and crises like it lay in ending the moral disorder in society. Because that could not be done quickly or easily, Durkheim suggested more specific actions such as severe repression of those who incite hatred of others and government efforts to show the public how it is being misled. He urged people to "have the courage to proclaim aloud what they think, and to unite together in order to achieve victory in the struggle against public madness."

---

an increased division of labor in which some people are responsible for one of these things and other people responsible for other things, there is likely to be less conflict and more harmony. Perhaps more importantly, greater specialization in performing specific tasks makes for greater efficiency and ultimately greater productivity. Thus, there will be more of everything for an expanding population with an increased division of labor. Greater peace and prosperity are the result of the increased division of labor, or at least that is what Durkheim contended.

Collective Conscience

Another important aspect of Durkheim's argument about the transition from mechanical to organic solidarity is that it is accompanied by a dramatic change in what he called the **collective conscience.** These are the ideas shared by the members of a group, a tribe, or a society. They are collective in the sense that no one individual knows or possesses all of these ideas; it is only the entire collection of individuals that knows and possesses all of them. The collective conscience in mechanical solidarity is very different from that in organic solidarity.

In mechanical solidarity and the small, undifferentiated societies associated with it, the collective conscience affects everyone and is of great significance to them. People care deeply about collective ideas. Furthermore, the ideas are very powerful and people are likely to act in accord with them. They are also quite rigid and they tend to be associated with religion.

In organic solidarity and the large, differentiated societies linked with it, fewer people are affected by the collective conscience. In other words, more people are able to evade it partially or completely. The collective conscience is not as important and most people don't seem to care about it so deeply. It is far weaker and does not exercise nearly as much control over people. The collective conscience is far more flexible and adaptable and less associated with anything we think of as religion.

For example, in primitive society with mechanical solidarity people might feel very deeply about being involved in tribal activities, including the selection of a new chief. If one member does not participate, everyone will know and difficulties will arise for that person in the tribe. However, in modern society characterized by organic solidarity, the feeling about such political participation (e.g., voting) is not nearly as strong. People are urged to vote, but there is not very much strength of conviction involved, and in any case the fact that some did not vote is likely to escape the view of their neighbors.

Law: Repressive and Restitutive

How do we know whether there has been a transition from mechanical to organic solidarity? From a strong to a weak collective conscience? Durkheim argued that we can observe these changes in a transformation in the law. Mechanical solidarity tends to be characterized by **repressive law.** This is a form of law in which offenders are likely to be severely punished for any action that is seen by the tightly integrated community as an offense against the then-powerful collective conscience. The theft of a pig might lead to cutting off the hands of the thief. Blaspheming against the community's god or gods might result in the removal of the blasphemer's tongue. Because people are

---

collective conscience   The ideas shared by the members of a collectivity such as a group, a tribe, or a society.

repressive law   Characteristic of mechanical solidarity, this is a form of law in which offenders are likely to be severely punished for any action that is seen by the tightly integrated community as an offense against the powerful collective conscience.

so involved in the moral system, an offense against it is likely to be met with swift, severe punishment. These reactions are evidence that repressive law is in place and such law is, in turn, a material reflection of the existence of a strong collective conscience and a society held together by mechanical solidarity.

As we have seen, over time mechanical solidarity gives way to organic solidarity and a progressive weakening of the collective conscience. The indicator of a weak collective conscience, of the existence of organic solidarity, is **restitutive law.** Instead of being severely punished for even seemingly minor offenses against the collective morality, individuals in this more modern type of society are likely simply to be asked to comply with the law or to repay (make restitution to) those who have been harmed by their actions. Thus, one who steals a pig might be required to work for 100 hours on the farm from which the pig was stolen, pay a fine, or repay society by spending a brief period of time in jail. This is obviously a far milder reaction than having one's hands cut off for such an offense. The reason is that the collectivity is not deeply and emotionally invested in the common morality ("thou shalt not steal") that stands behind such a law. Rather, officials (the police, court officers) are delegated the legal responsibility to be sure the law and, ultimately, the morality are enforced. The collectivity can distance itself from the whole thing with the knowledge that it is being handled by paid and/or elected officials.

More extremely, something like blaspheming against God is likely to go unnoticed and unpunished in modern societies. Having a far weaker collective conscience, believing little in religion, people in general are likely to react weakly or not all to a blasphemer. And officials, busy with far greater problems such as drug abuse, rape, and murder, are unlikely to pay any attention at all to blasphemy, even if there are laws against it.

Anomie

At one level Durkheim seems to be describing and explaining a historical change from one type of solidarity to another. The two types of solidarity merely seem to be different and one does not seem to be any better or worse than the other. Although mechanical solidarity is not problem free, the problems associated with organic solidarity and how they might be solved concern Durkheim. Several problems come into existence with organic solidarity, but the one that worries Durkheim most is what he termed *anomie.* Durkheim viewed anomie (and other problems) as a pathology, which implies that it can be cured. In other words, a social theorist like Durkheim was akin to a medical doctor, diagnosing social pathologies and dispensing cures.

---

restitutive law   Characteristic of organic solidarity and its weakened collective conscience. In this form of law offenders are likely simply to be asked to comply with the law or to repay (make restitution to) those who have been harmed by their actions.

Key Concept
Social Facts

Crucial to understanding Durkheim's thinking and the development of modern sociology is his concept of **social facts.** He developed this idea because he was struggling to separate the then-new discipline of sociology from the existing fields of psychology and philosophy. While philosophers thought about abstractions, Durkheim argued that sociologists should treat social facts as things. As such, social facts were to be studied empirically; this practice distinguished sociologists from philosophers who merely speculated about abstract issues without venturing into the real world and collecting data on concrete social phenomena.

Durkheim also argued that social facts were external to, and coercive over, individuals. This served to distinguish them from the things that psychologists studied. Psychologists were concerned with psychological facts that were internal to individuals (*not* external) and were not necessarily coercive over them.

Durkheim also distinguished between two types of social facts. The first is **material social facts.** These are social facts that are materialized in the external social world. An example is the structure of the classroom in which you are taking the course for which you are reading this book. It is a material reality (you can touch and feel the walls, desks, blackboard) and it is external to you and coercive over you. In terms of the latter, the structure of the room may encourage listening to, and taking notes on, lectures. It also serves to prevent you from, say, playing baseball in the room while a lecture is in process.

Anomie may be defined as a sense of not knowing what one is expected to do. This is traceable to the decline in the collective conscience in organic solidarity. There are few, if any, clear, strong collective ideas about things. As a result, confronted with many issues—should I take that pig that is wandering in the field? Should I blaspheme against god?—people simply do not know what they are supposed to do. More generally, people are adrift in society and lack clear and secure moorings. This contrasts strongly with mechanical solidarity, in which everyone is very clear about what the collectivity believes and what they are supposed to do in any given situation. They have clear and secure moorings; they do *not* suffer from anomie.

---

social facts   To Durkheim, social facts are the subject matter of sociology. They are to be treated as things that are external to, and coercive over, individuals and they are to be studied empirically.

material social facts   Social facts that take a material form in the external social world (e.g., architecture).

anomie   A sense, associated with organic solidarity, of not knowing what one is expected to do; of being adrift in society without any clear and secure moorings.

Key Concept—Continued

The second is **nonmaterial social facts.** These are social facts that are also external and coercive, but which do not take a material form; they are nonmaterial. The major examples of nonmaterial social facts in sociology are norms and values. Thus, we are also prevented from playing baseball while a lecture is in progress because of unwritten and widely shared rules about how one is supposed to behave in class. Furthermore, we have learned to put a high value on education, with the result that we are very reluctant to do anything that would adversely affect it.

But, although we can see how a nonmaterial social fact is coercive over us, in what sense is it also external to us? The answer is that the things like the norms and values of society are the shared possession of the collectivity. Some, perhaps most, of them are internalized in the individual during the socialization process, but no single individual possesses anything approaching all of them. The entire set of norms and values is in the sole possession of the collectivity. In this sense we can say they are external to us.

To this day, many sociologists concentrate their attention on social facts. However, we rarely use this now-antiquated term today. Rather, sociologists focus on social structures (material social facts) and social institutions (nonmaterial social facts). However, it has become clear that in his effort to distinguish sociology from psychology and philosophy, Durkheim came up with a much too limited definition of the subject matter of sociology. As we will see, many sociologists study an array of phenomena that would not be considered Durkheimian social facts.

KARL MARX:
FROM CAPITALISM TO COMMUNISM

The most important and esthetically pleasing (because analyses, conclusions, and remedies for society's ills stem seamlessly from basic premises) theory of the classical age is that of the German social thinker and political activist, Karl Marx (1818–1883). This assertion might come as a surprise to the reader who may have previously come in contact only with critical statements about Marx and his thinking. In the popular view, Marx is seen as some sort of crazed radical who developed a set of ideas that led many nations, especially the then–Soviet Union, in the direction of disastrous communist regimes. Almost all such regimes have failed or are gradually being transformed into more capitalistic societies. The failure of those societies and the abuses associated with them (e.g., the system of prison camps in the Soviet Union—the Gulag Archipelago—where millions died) have been blamed on Marx and his crazed

---

nonmaterial social facts Social facts that are external and coercive, but which do not take a material form; they are nonmaterial (e.g., norms and values).

Key Concept
Anomic (and Other Types of) Suicide

The concept of anomie played a central role in Durkheim's famous work, *Suicide*. He argued that people are more likely to kill themselves when they do not know what is expected of them. In this situation, regulation of people is low and they are largely free to run wild. This mad pursuit of anything and everything is likely to prove unsatisfying and, as a result, a higher percentage of people in such a situation are apt to commit suicide, specifically **anomic suicide.**

But what causes the rate of anomic suicide to increase? Social disruption is the main cause, but interestingly, we can see an increase in the rate of such suicide in times of both positive and negative disruption. That is, both an economic boom and economic depression can cause a rise in the rate of anomic suicide. Either positive or negative disruptions can adversely affect the ability of the collectivity to exercise control over the individual. Without such control, people are more likely to feel rootless; to not know what they are supposed to do in the changing and increasingly strange environment. The unease that this causes leads people to commit anomic suicide at a higher rate than in more stable times.

Interestingly, anomic suicide is just one of four types of suicide created by Durkheim in a broad-ranging theory of this behavior. The others are **egoistic suicide,** which occurs when people are not well integrated into the collectivity. Largely on their own, they feel a sense of futility, meaninglessness, and more of them adopt the view that they are free (morally and otherwise) to choose to do anything, including kill themselves. In **altruistic suicide,** people are too well integrated into the collectivity and kill themselves in greater numbers because the group leads them, or even forces them, to commit suicide more frequently than they otherwise would. Finally, **fatalistic suicide** occurs in situations of excessive regulation (e.g., slavery) where people are so distressed and depressed by their lack of freedom that they take their own lives more frequently than otherwise.

Thus, Durkheim offers a broad theory of suicide based on the degree to which people are regulated by, or integrated in, the collectivity.

---

anomic suicide   People are more likely to kill themselves when they do not know what is expected of them, where regulation is low, and they are largely free to run wild. This mad pursuit is likely to prove unsatisfying and, as a result, a higher percentage of people in such a situation are apt to commit this type of suicide.

egoistic suicide   When people are not well integrated into the collectivity and largely on their own, they feel a sense of futility, meaninglessness, and more of them feel that they are morally free to kill themselves.

altruistic suicide   When people are too well integrated into the collectivity, they are likely to kill themselves in greater numbers because the group leads them, or even forces them, to.

fatalistic suicide   In situations of excessive regulation (e.g., slavery) people are often so distressed and depressed by their lack of freedom that they take their own lives more frequently than otherwise.

ideas. But while the leaders of those societies invoked Marx's name and called themselves communists, the kind of societies they created would have been attacked by Marx himself for their inhumanity. The fact is that what those societies became had little in common with what Marx would have liked a communist society to be.

Human Potential

The starting point for Marx's grand theory is a set of assumptions about the potential of people in the right historical and social circumstances. In capitalistic and precapitalistic societies, people had come nowhere close to their human potential. In precapitalist societies (say, the Stone Age or the Middle Ages), people were too busy scrambling to find adequate food, shelter, and protection to develop their higher capacities. Although food, shelter, and protection were easier to come by for most people in a capitalistic society, the oppressive and exploitative nature of that system made it impossible for most people to come anywhere close to their potential.

To Marx, people, unlike lower animals, are endowed with consciousness and the ability to link that consciousness to action. Among other things, people can set themselves apart from what they are doing, plan what they are going to do, choose to act or not to act, choose a specific kind of action, be flexible if impediments get in their way, concentrate on what they are doing for long periods, and often choose to do what they are doing in concert with other people. But people do not just think; they would perish if that was all they did. They must act and often that action involves acting on nature to appropriate from it what is needed (raw materials, water, food, shelter) to survive. People appropriated things in earlier societies, but they did it so primitively and inefficiently that they were unable to develop their capacities, especially their capacities to think, to any great degree. Under capitalism, people came to care little about expressing their creative capacities in the act of appropriating nature. Rather, they focused on owning things and earning enough money to acquire those things. But capitalism was important to Marx because it provided the technological and organizational innovations needed for the creation of a communist society, where, for the first time, people would be able to express their full capacities. Under communism, people were freed from the desire merely to own things and would be able, with the help of technologies and organizations created in capitalism, to live up to their full human potential (what Marx called "species being").

Alienation

The idea that people must appropriate what they need from nature is related to the view that people, in Marx's view, need to work. Work is a positive process in which people use their creative capacities, and further extend them, in productive activities. However, the work that most people did under capitalism did not permit them to express their human potential. In other words, rather than expressing themselves in their work, people under capitalism were alienated from it.

One cannot understand what Marx meant by alienation without understanding further what he meant by human potential. In the circumstance (communism) where people achieve their human potential there is a natural interconnection between people and their productive activities, the products they produce, the fellow workers with whom they produce those things, and with what they are potentially capable of becoming. **Alienation** is the breakdown of these natural interconnections. Instead of being naturally related to all of these things, people are separated from them.

So, under capitalism, instead of choosing their productive activities, people have their activities chosen for them by the owners, the capitalists. The capitalists decide what is to be done and how it is to be done. They offer the workers (in Marx's terminology, the "proletariat") a wage and if the workers accept, they must perform the activities the way they have been designed to be performed by the capitalist. In return, they receive a wage that is supposed to provide them with all the satisfaction and gratification they need. The productive activities are controlled, even owned, by the capitalist. Thus, the workers are separated from them and unable to express themselves in them.

Second, capitalists also own the products. The workers do not choose what to produce; when the products are completed they do not belong to the workers, and the products are unlikely to be used by the workers to satisfy their basic needs. Instead, the products belong to the capitalists, who may use them, or seek to have them used, in any way they wish. Given the profit orientation that serves to define capitalism, this almost always means that they will endeavor to sell the products for a profit. Once they've made the products, the workers are completely separated from them and have absolutely no say in what happens to them. Furthermore, the workers may have very little sense of their contribution to the final product. They work on an assembly line and perform a very specific task (e.g., tightening some bolts) and may have little idea what is being produced and how what they are doing fits into the overall process and contributes to the end product.

Third, the workers are likely to be separated from their fellow workers. In Marx's view, people are inherently social and, left to their own devices, would choose to work collaboratively and cooperatively to produce what is needed to live. However, under capitalism, workers, even when they are surrounded by many other people, perform their tasks alone and repetitively. Those around them are likely to be strangers who are performing similarly isolated tasks. Often it is even worse than this: The capitalist frequently pits workers against

---

alienation   The breakdown of, the separation from, the natural interconnection between people and their productive activities, the products they produce, the fellow workers with whom they produce those things, and with what they are potentially capable of becoming.

each other to see who can produce the most for the least amount of pay. Those who succeed keep their jobs, at least for a time, while those who fail are likely to find themselves unemployed and on the street. Thus, instead of working together harmoniously, workers are pitted against one another in a life-and-death struggle for survival. Even if they are not engaged in a life-and-death struggle with one another, it is clear that workers in capitalism are separated from one another.

Finally, instead of expressing their human potential in their work, people are driven further and further from what they have the potential to be. They perform less and less like humans and are reduced to animals, beasts of burden, or inhuman machines. Consciousness is numbed and ultimately destroyed as relations with other humans and with nature are progressively severed. The result is a mass of people who are unable to express their essential human qualities, a mass of alienated workers.

Capitalism

Alienation occurs within the context of a capitalist society. As we have seen, **capitalism** is essentially a two-class system composed of capitalists and the proletariat, in which one class (capitalists) exploits the other (proletariat). The key to understanding both classes lies in what Marx called the **means of production**. As the name suggests, these are the things that are needed for production to take place. Included in the means of production are such things as tools, machinery, raw materials, and factories. Under capitalism the **capitalists** own the means of production. If the **proletariat** want to work, they must come to the capitalist, who owns the means that make most work possible. Workers need access to the means of production in order to work. They also need money in order to survive in capitalism, and the capitalists tend to have that too, as well as the ability to make more of it. The capitalists have what the proletariat needs (the means of production, money for wages), but what do the workers have to offer in return? The workers have something absolutely essential to the capitalist—labor and the time available to perform it. The capitalist cannot produce and cannot make more money and profit without the labor of the proletariat. Thus, a deal is struck. The capitalist allows the proletariat access to the means of production, and the proletariat are paid a wage (albeit a small

---

capitalism   An economic system composed mainly of capitalists and the proletariat, in which one class (capitalists) exploits the other (proletariat).

means of production   Those things that are needed for production to take place (including tools, machinery, raw materials, and factories).

capitalists   Those who own the means of production under capitalism and are therefore in a position to exploit workers.

proletariat   Those who, because they do not own means of production, must sell their labor time to the capitalists in order to get access to those means.

Karl Marx (1818–1883)
A Biographical Vignette

After graduation from the University of Berlin, Marx became a writer for a liberal-radical newspaper and within ten months had become its editor-in-chief. However, because of its political positions, the paper was closed shortly thereafter by the government. The early essays published in this period began to reflect a number of the positions that would guide Marx throughout his life. They were liberally sprinkled with democratic principles, humanism, and youthful idealism. He rejected the abstractness of philosophy, the naive dreaming of utopian communists, and those activists who were urging what he considered to be premature political action. In rejecting these activists, Marx laid the groundwork for his own life's work:

> Practical attempts, even by the masses, can be answered with a cannon as soon as they become dangerous, but ideas that have overcome our intellect and conquered our conviction, ideas to which reason has riveted our conscience, are chains from which one cannot break loose without breaking one's heart; they are demons that one can only overcome by submitting to them.

---

one, as small as the capitalist can possibly get away with). Actually the worker is paid what Marx called a **subsistence wage,** just enough for the worker to survive and to have a family and children so that when the worker falters, he can be replaced by one of his children. In exchange, the proletariat give the capitalist their labor time and all the productive abilities and capacities associated with that time.

On the surface, this seems like a fair deal: Both the capitalist and the proletariat get what they lack and what they need. However, in Marx's view this is a grossly unfair situation. Why is that so? It is traceable to another of Marx's famous ideas, the **labor theory of value.** As the words suggest, his idea is that *all* value comes from labor. The proletariat labor; the capitalist does not. The capitalist might invest, plan, manage, scheme, and so on, but to Marx this is not labor. Marx's sense of labor is the production of things out of the raw materials provided by nature. The proletariat and only the proletariat do that, although under capitalism the raw materials are provided by the capitalists and not directly by nature. To put it baldly, since the proletariat labor and the capitalists do not, the proletariat deserve virtually everything; the capitalists, almost nothing.

---

subsistence wage   The wage paid by the capitalist to the proletariat that is just enough for the worker to survive and to have a family and children so that when the worker falters, he can be replaced by one of his children.

labor theory of value   Marx's theory that *all* value comes from labor and is therefore traceable, in capitalism, to the proletariat.

Key Concept
Exploitation

To Marx, capitalism, by its very nature, leads to exploitation, particularly of the proletariat, or working class. His thinking on exploitation is derived from his labor theory of value, and more specifically the concept of **surplus value,** defined as the difference between the value of a product when it is sold and the value of the elements (including worker's labor) consumed in the production of the product. Surplus value, like all value from the perspective of the labor theory of value, comes from the worker. It should go to the worker, but in the capitalist system the lion's share of it goes to the capitalist. The degree to which the capitalist retains surplus value and uses it to his own ends (including, and especially, expansion of his capitalist business) is the degree to which capitalism is an exploitative system. In a colorful metaphor, Marx describes capitalists as "vampires" who suck the labor of the proletariat. Furthermore, the more of proletariat's "blood" the capitalist sucks, the bigger, more successful, and wealthier he will become. In capitalism, the deserving (the proletariat) grow poorer, while the undeserving (the capitalist) grow immensely wealthy.

Of course, the situation in a capitalistic society is exactly the reverse: The capitalists get the lion's share of the rewards and the workers get barely enough to subsist. Thus (and this was another of Marx's famous concepts), the proletariat are the victims of **exploitation.** Ironically, neither capitalist nor worker is conscious of this exploitation. They are both the victims of **false consciousness.** The workers think they are getting a fair day's pay. The capitalists think that they are being rewarded, not because of their exploitation of the workers, but for their cleverness, their capital investment, their manipulation of the market, and so on. The capitalists are too busy making more money, in money grubbing, ever to get a true understanding of the exploitative nature of their relationship with workers. However, the proletariat do have the capacity to achieve such an understanding, partly because eventually they are so exploited and impoverished that there is nothing to hide the reality of what is

---

surplus value The difference between the value of a product when it is sold and the value of the elements consumed in production of the product (including worker's labor).

exploitation In capitalism, the capitalists get the lion's share of the rewards and the proletariat get enough to subsist even though, based on the labor theory of value, the situation should be reversed.

false consciousness In capitalism, both the proletariat and the capitalists have an inaccurate sense of themselves, their relationship to one another, and the way in which capitalism operates.

Contemporary Applications
Does Marx's Theory Have Any Relevance to a Post-Communist World?

There are those who felt that when the Soviet Union and its allies began to fall in the late 1980s that not only had communism failed, but that Marx's theory, on which that system was ostensibly based, would finally, and once and for all, be relegated to the dustbin of disproven and dishonored theories. Indeed, in the early 1990s there was much talk of the end of Marxian theory. Yet, Marx's theory, as well as the many neo-Marxian theories that are derived from it, not only survive in the early 21st century, but there are those who argue that they are more relevant and useful than ever.

The fact is that Marx did little or no theorizing about communism. Rather, he was a theorist of capitalism and it is clear that with the demise of Soviet communism (and the transformation of Chinese communism into a very vibrant capitalist economy coexisting with a communist state), capitalism is freer than it has been in nearly 100 years (since the birth of Soviet communism in 1917), if not in its entire history, to roam the world and intrude itself into every nook and cranny of that world.

From 1917 to 1989 the expansion of capitalism was limited by communism in various ways. First, many countries in the world, including some of the biggest and most important, were communist or were allied with the communist bloc. As a result, capitalist businesses found it impossible to establish, or at least had great difficulty establishing themselves in those parts of the world. Second, the global conflict between capitalism and communism, especially the Cold War that began shortly after the close of World War II, inhibited the development and global spread of capitalism. For one thing, the huge expenditure on the military, and on military flare-ups associated with those periods in which the Cold War heated up considerably (e.g., the Korean and Vietnamese wars), sapped resources that could have been devoted to the expansion of capitalism.

With communism fast becoming a dim memory (except in Cuba, at least until Castro's death, and at least rhetorically in China), capitalism has been freed of many

---

transpiring in capitalism. In Marx's terms, the proletariat is capable of achieving **class consciousness;** the capitalists are not.

Class consciousness is a prerequisite to revolution, but the coming revolution is aided by the dynamics of capitalism. For example, capitalism grows more and more competitive, prices are slashed, and an increasing number of capitalists are driven out of business and into the proletariat. Eventually, the proletariat swells while the capitalist class is reduced to a small number who maintain their position because of their skill at exploitation. When the massive

---

class consciousness   The ability of a class, in particular the proletariat, to overcome false consciousness and attain an accurate understanding of the capitalist system.

Contemporary Applications—*Continued*

of its global restraints and is rampaging through the world. This is most obvious in the former communist countries that have become prime territory for capitalist expansionism. Western capitalists have rushed into the old Soviet bloc and established a strong presence, while in China this has not only occurred, but so has the development of a strong indigenous capitalism. Indeed, the view now is not whether China will replace the United States as the leading capitalist country, but *when* that transformation will take place.

Marx foresaw the fact that capitalism not only would, but must, become a global phenomenon. Capitalist businesses now, much more than in Marx's day, must expand or die. Thus, they must ceaselessly seek out new markets as old markets grow less able to produce ever-expanding business and profits. Marx's prediction was prevented from coming to full fruition in the 20th century because of the global conflict between communism and capitalism (as well as other factors such as two devastating world wars). However, in the last two decades the global proliferation predicted by Marx has occurred with a vengeance.

What this all means is that Marx's ideas are more relevant today than ever before to the analysis of capitalism, especially global capitalism. In fact, some of the most important works in globalization these days emanate from a Marxian perspective (see Chapter 10). That is not to say that Marx's ideas are sacrosanct. Many of them are dubious, even downright wrong, and need to be amended, adapted, or abandoned by contemporary Marxian theorists. Indeed, that is what many of those thinkers are doing. Nonetheless, they take as their starting point Marx's theoretical ideas on capitalism and build on them to cast insight into the global success of capitalism in the wake of the failure of communism.

To answer the question that is the subtitle of this box: Marx's ideas are, if anything, *more* relevant today than ever!

---

proletariat finally achieve class consciousness and decide to act, there will be no contest because the small number of capitalists are likely to be easily brushed aside, perhaps with little or no violence.

Thus, capitalism will not be destroyed and communism will not be created without the proletariat taking action. In Marx's terms, the proletariat must engage in **praxis,** or concrete action. It is not enough to think about the evils of capitalism or develop great theories of it and its demise; people must take to the streets and make it happen. This does not necessarily mean that they must behave in violent ways, but it does mean they cannot sit back and wait for capitalism to collapse on its own.

---

praxis The idea that people, especially the proletariat, must take concrete action in order to overcome capitalism.

Communism

Marx had no doubt that the dynamics of capitalism would lead to such a revolution, but he devoted little time to describing the character of the communist society that would replace capitalism. To Marx, the priority was gaining an understanding of the way capitalism worked and communicating that understanding to the proletariat, thereby helping them gain class consciousness. He was critical of the many thinkers who spent their time daydreaming about some future utopian society. The immediate goal was the overthrow of the alienating and exploitative system. What was to come next would have to be dealt with once the revolution succeeded. Some say that this lack of a plan laid the groundwork for the debacles that took place in the Soviet Union and its satellites.

Marx did have some specific things to say about the future state of communism, but we get a better sense of communism by returning to his basic assumptions about human potential. In a sense, **communism** is *the* social system that permits, for the first time, the expression of full human potential. In effect, communism is an anti-system, a world in which the system is nothing more than the social relations among the people who comprise it. Marx did discuss a transitional phase from capitalism when there would be larger structures (e.g., the dictatorship of the proletariat), but that was to be short-lived and replaced by what he considered true communism. (The experience in the Soviet Union after the 1917 revolution indicates the naivete of this view and the fact that it may be impossible to eliminate the larger structures that exploit and alienate people.)

Thus, communism is a system that permits people to express the thoughtfulness, creativity, and sociability that have always been a possibility but inhibited or destroyed by previous social systems (e.g., feudalism, capitalism). Communist society would utilize and expand upon the technological and organizational innovations of capitalism, but otherwise get out of people's way and allow them to be what they always could have been, at least potentially.

MAX WEBER:
THE RATIONALIZATION OF SOCIETY

If Karl Marx is the most important thinker from the point of view of social thought in general, as well as from the perspective of political developments of the last 100-plus years, then his fellow German theorist, Max Weber (1864–1920), is arguably (the other possibility is Emile Durkheim) the most important theorist from the perspective of sociology. Weber was a very complex thinker who made many contributions to social thought, but his best-known contribution is his theory of the increasing rationalization of the West. That theory is based on Weber's work on action, especially rational action.

---

communism   The social system that permits, for the first time, the expression of full human potential.

Social Action

For many years Max Weber's work on social action was the center of attention rather than his theory of rationalization, which is now seen as the heart of his theoretical orientation. This is traceable to the work of Talcott Parsons, who, in the 1930s, introduced classical European theory in general, and Weberian theory in particular, to a large American audience. However, he did so with a number of now widely recognized biases. One of those biases was his own action theory, which led him to accentuate the importance of Weber's thinking on action (which played a central role in the creation of Parsons's own perspective).

Behavior and Action

Weber's thinking on action is based on an important distinction in all sociologies of everyday life (see Chapter 6) between behavior and action. Both involve what people do on an everyday basis. However, **behavior** occurs with little or no thought, while **action** is the result of conscious processes. Behavior is closely tied to an approach, largely associated with psychology, known as **behaviorism,** which has played an important role in the development of many sociologies of everyday life. It focuses on situations where a stimulus is applied and a behavior results, more or less mechanically, with little or no thought processes intervening between stimulus and response. For example, you engage in behavior when you pull your hand away from a hot stove or automatically put up your umbrella when it starts raining.

Weber was *not* concerned with such behavior; his focus was on action in which thought intervened between stimulus and response. In other words, Weber was interested in situations in which people attach meaning to what they do: what they do is meaningful to them. In contrast, behavior is meaningless, at least in the sense that people simply do it without giving it much or any thought. Weber defined sociology as the study of action in terms of its subjective meaning. What matters are peoples' conscious processes. Furthermore, what people believe about a situation is more important in understanding the actions they take than the objective situation in which they find themselves.

At a theoretical level Weber was interested in the action of a single individual, but he was far more interested in the actions of two or more individuals. Sociology was to devote most of its attention to the regularities in the action of two or more individuals. In fact, Weber talked about collectivities (e.g., Calvinists, capitalists), while he argued that such collectivities must be treated solely as the result of the actions of two or more people. Only people can act and thus sociology must focus on actors, not collectivities. Sociologists' talk about collectivities is only for convenience sake. A collectivity is nothing more than a set of individual actors and actions.

---

behavior   Things that people do that require little or no thought.
action   Things that people do that are the result of conscious processes.
behaviorism   The study, largely associated with psychology, of behavior.

Max Weber (1864–1920)
A Biographical Vignette

Max Weber was born in Erfurt, Germany, on April 21, 1864, into a decidedly middle-class family. Important differences between his parents had a profound effect upon both his intellectual orientation and his psychological development. His father was a bureaucrat who rose to a relatively important political position. He was clearly a part of the political establishment and as a result eschewed any activity or idealism that would require personal sacrifice or threaten his position within the system.

In addition, the senior Weber was a man who enjoyed earthly pleasures, and in this and many other ways he stood in sharp contrast to his wife. Max Weber's mother was a devout Calvinist, a woman who sought to lead an ascetic life largely devoid of the pleasures craved by her husband. Her concerns were more otherworldly; she was disturbed by the imperfections that were signs that she was not destined for salvation. These deep differences between the parents led to marital tension, and both the differences and the tension had an immense impact on Weber.

Because it was impossible to emulate both parents, Weber was presented with a clear choice as a child. He first seemed to opt for his father's orientation to life, but later he drew closer to his mother's approach. Whatever the choice, the tension produced by the need to choose between such polar opposites negatively affected Max Weber's psyche.

During his eight years at the University of Berlin (where he obtained his doctorate and became a lawyer), Weber was financially dependent on his father, a circumstance he progressively grew to dislike. At the same time, he moved closer to his mother's values and his antipathy to his father increased. He adopted an ascetic way of life and plunged deeply into his work. During one semester as a student, his work habits were described as follows: "He continues the rigid work discipline, regulates his life by the clock, divides the daily routine into exact sections for the various subjects, saves in his way, by feeding himself evenings in his room with a pound of raw chopped beef and four fried eggs." Weber, emulating his mother, had become ascetic and diligent, a compulsive worker—in contemporary terms, a *workaholic*.

This compulsion for work led him in 1896 to a position as professor of economics at Heidelberg University. But in 1897, when Weber's academic career was blossoming, his father died following a violent argument between them. Soon after, Weber began to manifest symptoms that culminated in a nervous breakdown. Often unable to sleep or to work, Weber spent the next six or seven years in near-total collapse. After a long hiatus, some of his powers began to return in 1903, but it was not until 1904, when he delivered (in the United States) his first lecture in six and a half years, that Weber was able to begin to return to active academic life. In 1904 and 1905, he published one of his best-known works, *The Protestant Ethic and the Spirit of Capitalism*. In this work, Weber announced the ascendance, on an academic level, of his mother's religiosity. Weber devoted much of his time to the study of religion, though he was not personally religious.

Types of Action

Weber offered a now-famous distinction among four types of action. **Affectual action** (which was of little concern to Weber) is action that is the result of emotion; it is nonrational. Thus, slapping your child (or an aged parent) in a blind rage is an example of affectual action. Also nonrational is **traditional action,** in which what is done is based on the ways things have been done habitually or customarily. Crossing oneself in church is an example of traditional action. Although traditional action was of some interest to Weber (especially given its relationship to traditional authority discussed later in this chapter), he was far more interested, because of his overriding concern with rationalization, in the other two types of action, both of which are rational.

Value-rational action occurs when an actor's choice of the best means to an end is chosen on the basis of the actor's belief in some larger set of values. This may not be the optimal choice, but it is rational from the point of view of the value system in which the actor finds herself. So, if you belonged to a cult that believed in a ritual purging of one's previous meal before eating the next meal, that is what you would do, even though purging would be quite uncomfortable and delay, if not ruin, your next meal. Such action would be rational from the point of view of the value system of the cult.

Means-ends rational action involves the pursuit of ends that the actor has chosen for himself; thus, his action is not guided by some larger value system. It is, however, affected by the actor's view of the environment in which he finds himself, including the behavior of people and objects in it. This means that actors must take into account the nature of their situation when choosing the best means to an end. Thus, when you are at a party and spot someone you want to dance with, you must decide on the best way to meet that person, given the nature of the situation (it may be an all-couple party), objects (there may be a table in your path), and other people (one of whom may already be dancing with that person). Taking those things into consideration, you choose the best means of achieving your end of getting that dance.

These four types of actions are ideal types (see below). The fact is that one rarely if ever finds action that is solely within one of these four types. Rather, any given action is likely to be some combination of two or more of these ideal-typical actions.

---

affectual action Nonrational action that is the result of emotion.

traditional action Action taken on the basis of the ways things have been done habitually or customarily.

value-rational action Action that occurs when an actor's choice of the best means to an end is chosen on the basis of the actor's belief in some larger set of values. This may not be the optimal choice, but it is rational from the point of view of the value system in which the actor finds herself.

means-ends rational action The pursuit of ends that the actor has chosen for himself; that choice is affected by the actor's view of the environment in which she finds herself, including the behavior of people and objects in it.

Weber offers an approach to studying social action and the theoretical tools to study such action. Many sociologists have found this work quite useful.

Types of Rationality

While Weber's theory of action relies on the typology of action outlined above, his larger theory of rationalization rests on the typology of rationality to be outlined below. (As you will see, the two typologies overlap to some degree.)

Practical rationality is the type that we all practice on a daily basis in getting from one point to another. Given the realities of the circumstances we face, we try to deal with whatever difficulties exist and to find the most expedient way of attaining our goal. For example, our usual route to the university is blocked by a traffic accident, so we take a side road and work our way to campus using a series of back roads. People in the West are not the only ones who engage in practical rationality; all people in all societies throughout history have utilized this type of rationality.

Theoretical rationality involves an effort to master reality cognitively through the development of increasingly abstract concepts. Here the goal is to attain a rational understanding of the world rather than taking rational action within it. Thus, to continue with the example discussed above, an example of theoretical rationality as applied to traffic problems would involve the efforts of experts in the area to figure out long-term solutions to traffic bottlenecks. Like practical rationality, cognitive rationality has occurred everywhere in the world throughout history.

Substantive rationality, like practical rationality, involves action directly. Here the choice of the most expedient thing to do is guided by larger values rather than by daily experiences and practical thinking. Thus, for example, if one's tribe says that before hunting for food, one must bury a spear under a mound, then that is what one does. From the point of view of practical rationality, taking time to bury a spear is clearly not rational, but it is rational within the value system of the tribe. This means that what takes place within one tribe (or value system) is no more or less rational than what takes place in another. Thus, if in one tribe you bury a spear before hunting and in another you engage in ritual bathing, each is rational within its particular context. As with the preceding two types of rationality, substantive rationality occurs transcivilizationally and transhistorically.

---

practical rationality   On a day-to-day basis, we deal with whatever difficulties exist and find the most expedient way of attaining our goal of getting from one point to another.

theoretical rationality   An effort to master reality cognitively through the development of increasingly abstract concepts. The goal is to attain a rational understanding of the world rather than to take rational action within it.

substantive rationality   The choice of the most expedient action is guided by larger values rather than by daily experiences and practical thinking.

Finally, and most importantly to Weber, is **formal rationality,** in which the choice of the most expedient action is based on rules, regulations, and laws that apply to everyone. The classic case of this is modern bureaucracy, in which the rules of the organization dictate what is the most rational course of action. Thus, if the rules say that every action must be preceded by filling out a required form in triplicate, then that is what everyone must do. To some outside the organization this may seem inefficient and irrational, but it is rational within the context of the bureaucracy. Unlike the other types of rationality, formal rationality arose only in the Western world with the coming of industrialization.

Thus, what interested Weber was formal rationality and why it arose only in the modern West and not anywhere else at any other time. This led him to a concern for what factors expedited the development of rationalization (formal) in the West and what barriers existed to it elsewhere. Major expediting forces and barriers exist in religion.

The Protestant Ethic and the Spirit of Capitalism

In the West, Protestantism played a key role in the rise of rationalization. In this case, Weber was primarily interested in the rationalization of the economic system, and the most rational economic system is capitalism. Weber considered capitalism to be rational in a number of ways, but most importantly because of its emphasis on quantifying things, which is best represented by its development and reliance on modern bookkeeping. Thus, Weber was interested in the expediting role that Protestantism (especially the sect known as Calvinism) played in the rise of capitalism. On the other hand, other religions throughout the world (Confucianism in China, Hinduism in India) served to impede the rise of rationalization in general, and capitalism in particular, in those nations.

Weber was primarily interested in the **Protestant ethic** as it existed in Calvinism. Calvinists believed in predestination; that is, whether they were going to heaven or hell was predetermined. There was no way they could directly affect their fate. However, it was possible for them to discern signs that they were either saved or damned, and one of the major signs of salvation was success in business. Thus, the Calvinists were deeply interested in being successful in business, which meant building bigger and more profitable businesses. It also meant that instead of spending profits on frivolous personal pleasures, they had to save money and reinvest it in the business in order to make it even more successful. They were comforted in their sometimes ruthless pursuit of

---

formal rationality   The choice of the most expedient action is based on rules, regulations, and laws that apply to everyone. This form of rationality is distinctive to the modern West.

Protestant ethic   Because of their belief in predestination, the Calvinists could not know whether they were going to heaven or hell or directly affect their fate. However, it was possible for them to discern signs that they were either saved or damned, and one of the major signs of salvation was success in business.

Key Concept
Verstehen

Verstehen is a German word meaning understanding. From the point of view of action theory, *verstehen* means trying to understand the thought processes of the actor, the actor's meanings and motives, and how these factors led to the action (or interaction) under study.

Weber made clear that it was not a softer, or less scientific, method than, for example, the experimental methods employed by the behaviorist. To Weber, *verstehen* was not simply intuition, but involved a systematic and rigorous method for studying thoughts and actions. In fact, a researcher using *verstehen* has an advantage over someone who fancies herself a hard-nosed scientist using positivistic methods. The advantage lies in the fact that because subjects are fellow human beings, the social scientist can gain an understanding of what goes on in the subjects' minds and why they do what they do. A physicist studying subatomic particles has no chance of understanding those particles; in fact, the particles cannot be understood in the same way that human beings can be understood. They can only be observed from without, while thought and action can be observed from within, introspectively.

But how does this methodology, this sense of understanding actors and actions, relate to Weber's grand theory of, for example, the relationship between Calvinism and the spirit of capitalism? It could be argued (and there is some merit in it) that Weber was trying to understand what went on in the minds of individual Calvinists that led them to the kinds of actions that set the stage for the rise of the spirit of capitalism. However, another view on this is that Weber used *verstehen* as a method to put himself in the place of individual Calvinists in order to understand the cultural context in which they lived and what led them to behave in a capitalist manner (i.e., energetically seeking profits). Here the view of the researcher is outward to examine the cultural context rather than inward to examine the mental processes of the Calvinist. A third view is that *verstehen* is concerned with the relationship between individual mental processes and the larger cultural context. In fact, all three approaches have ample support. However, one valid interpretation is that *verstehen* is a method to analyze action from the perspective of individual mental processes.

---

profits by the fact that it was their ethical duty to behave in such a way. They were also provided with hard-working, conscientious workers who were similarly motivated in looking for signs of success, and being a good worker was one such sign. Finally, Calvinist businessmen did not have to agonize over the fact that they were so successful while those who worked for them were so much less successful. After all, all of this was preordained. If they weren't among the saved, they wouldn't be successful. And, if at least some of their

---

verstehen   A methodological technique involving an effort to understand the thought processes of the actor, the actor's meanings and motives, and how these factors led to the action (or interaction) under study.

employees were saved, they would prosper economically. It was a wonderfully reassuring system to those who sought and acquired wealth.

All of these beliefs about economic success among the Calvinists (and other sects) added up to the Protestant ethic. And this Weber linked to the development of another system of ideas, the **spirit of capitalism.** It was this idea system that led, in the end, to the capitalist economic system. People had been motivated to be economically successful at other times and in other parts of the world, but the difference at this time in the West was that they were not motivated by greed, but by an ethical system that emphasized economic success. The pursuit of profit was turned away from the morally suspect greed and toward a spirit that was deemed to be highly moral.

The spirit of capitalism had a number of components, including, most importantly for our purposes, the seeking of profits rationally and systematically. Other ideas associated with this spirit included frugality, punctuality, fairness, and the earning of money as a legitimate end in itself. Above all, it was people's duty to ceaselessly increase their wealth and economic prosperity. The spirit of capitalism was removed from the realm of individual ambition and made an ethical imperative.

There is a clear affinity between the Protestant ethic and the spirit of capitalism; the former helped give rise to the latter. Evidence for this was found by Weber in an examination of those European nations in which several religions coexisted. What Weber found was that the leaders of the economic system in these nations—business leaders, owners of capital, high-grade skilled labor, and more advanced technically and commercially trained personnel—were overwhelmingly Protestant. This was taken to mean that Protestantism was a significant cause in the choice of these occupations and, conversely, that other religions (for example, Roman Catholicism) failed to produce idea systems that impelled people into these vocations. In other words, Roman Catholicism did not give, and could not have given, birth to the spirit of capitalism. In fact, Roman Catholicism impeded the development of such a spirit. In this, it functioned in the West the way Confucianism and Buddhism functioned in the East.

Confucianism, Hinduism, and Capitalism

China, like the West, had the prerequisites for the development of capitalism, including a tradition of intense acquisitiveness and unscrupulous competition. There was great industry and enormous capacity for work among the Chinese. With these and other factors in its favor, why didn't China undergo rationalization in general, and more specifically why didn't capitalism develop there?

---

spirit of capitalism   In the West, unlike any other area of the world, people were motivated to be economically successful, not by greed, but by an ethical system that emphasized the ceaseless pursuit of economic success. The spirit of capitalism had a number of components including the seeking of profits rationally and systematically, frugality, punctuality, fairness, and the earning of money as a legitimate end in itself.

Although elements of capitalism were there (moneylenders, businesspeople who sought high profits), China lacked a market and other rational elements of capitalism. There were a number of reasons for the failure to develop capitalism in China, but chief among them was Confucianism and its characteristics.

Confucianism emphasized a literary education as a prerequisite to obtaining an office and acquiring status. A cultured man well-steeped in literature was valued. Also valued was the ability to be clever and witty. The Confucians devalued any kind of work and delegated it to subordinates. Although the Confucians valued wealth, it was not regarded as proper to work for it. Confucians were unconcerned with the economy and economic activities. Active engagement in a for-profit enterprise was viewed as morally dubious and unbecoming a Confucian gentleman. Furthermore, Confucians were not oriented to any kind of change, including economic change. The goal of the Confucian was to maintain the status quo. Perhaps most importantly, there was no tension between the religion of the Confucian and the world in which they lived. Therefore, they did not need to take any action to resolve it. This stands in contrast to Calvinism in which a tension between predestination and the desire to know one's fate led to the idea that success in business might be a sign of salvation and a resolution of the tension.

Hinduism in India also posed barriers to rationalization and capitalism. For example, the Hindu believed that people were born into the caste (a fixed position within a system of social stratification) that they deserved to be in by virtue of behavior in a past life. Through faithful adherence to the ritual of caste, the Hindu gains merit for the next life. Salvation was to be achieved by faithfully following the rules. Innovation, particularly in the economic sphere, could not lead to a higher caste in the next life. Activity in this world was not seen as important, because this world was merely a transient abode and an impediment to the spiritual quest of the Hindu.

Authority Structures and Rationalization

The theme of rationalization runs through many other aspects of Weber's work. Let us examine it in one other domain—authority structures. Authority is legitimate domination. The issue is: What makes it legitimate for some people to issue commands that other people are likely to obey? The three bases of authority are tradition, charisma, and rational legal. In keeping with his theory of rationalization, Weber foresaw a long-term trend in the direction of the triumph of rational-legal authority.

Traditional authority is based on the belief by followers that certain people (based on their family, or tribe, or lineage) have exercised authority since

---

traditional authority   Authority based on the belief by followers that certain people (based on their family, tribe, or lineage) have exercised sovereignty since time immemorial. The leaders claim, and the followers believe in, the sanctity of age-old rules and powers.

time immemorial. The leaders claim, and the followers believe in, the sanctity of age-old rules and powers. Various forms of traditional authority include rule by elders, rule by leaders who inherit their positions, and so on. Weber viewed feudalism as one type of traditional authority. Traditional authority structures are not rational and they impede the rationalization process. Although one still finds vestiges of traditional authority in the world today, especially in less-developed societies, it has largely disappeared or become marginalized. For example, the monarchy in England is a vestige of traditional authority, but it clearly has no power.

Charismatic authority is legitimated by a belief by the followers in the exceptional sanctity, heroism, or exemplary character of the charismatic leader. This idea obviously involves the now-famous concept of **charisma.** Although in everyday usage we now emphasize the extraordinary qualities of a person, Weber emphasized the fact that others define a person as having charisma. This leads to the important conclusion that a person need *not* have any discernible extraordinary qualities in order to be defined as a charismatic leader. To Weber, charisma is an extremely important revolutionary force. Throughout history charismatic leaders have come to the fore and overthrown traditional (and even rational-legal) authority structures.

However, it is important to remember that charismatic authority is *not* rational and therefore is ill suited to the day-to-day demands of administering a society. In fact, this becomes obvious almost immediately to the followers of a victorious charismatic leader. Soon after taking power they take steps to make their regime better able to handle the routine tasks of administering a domain. They do this through a process Weber labeled the **routinization of charisma.** In other words, they seek to recast the extraordinary and revolutionary characteristics of their regime so that it is able to handle mundane matters. They also do this in order to prepare for the day when the charismatic leader passes from the scene. If they did not take these steps, they would be out of power as soon as the leader died. However, through routinization they hope to transfer the charisma to a disciple or to the administrative organization formed by the group of disciples.

There is a terrible contradiction here. In attempting to make charisma routine, the disciples are doing what is needed to allow this form of authority to function on a daily basis and to continue in existence after the leader dies, but, if successful, they would undermine the very basis of charismatic authority—it

---

charismatic authority   Authority legitimated by a belief by the followers in the exceptional sanctity, heroism, or exemplary character of the charismatic leader.

charisma   The definition by others that a person has extraordinary qualities. A person need not actually have such qualities in order to be so defined.

routinization of charisma   Efforts by disciples to recast the extraordinary and revolutionary characteristics of the charismatic leader so that they are better able to handle mundane matters. This is also done in order to prepare for the day when the charismatic leader passes from the scene and to allow the disciples to remain in power.

Key Concept
The Ideal Type and the Ideal-Typical Bureaucracy

Weber created many important methodological ideas, but one of the most important is the **ideal type.** It is important to point out immediately that Weber did *not* mean that an ideal type is some sort of utopian, or best possible, phenomenon. It is ideal because it is a one-sided exaggeration, usually an exaggeration of the rationality of a given phenomenon. Such one-sided exaggerations become concepts that Weber used to analyze the social world in all its historical and contemporary variation. The ideal type is a measuring rod to be used in comparing various specific examples of a social phenomenon either cross-culturally or over time.

One of Weber's most famous ideal types is the **bureaucracy.** The ideal-typical bureaucracy has the following characteristics:

1. A series of official functions become offices in which the behavior of those who occupy those positions is bound by rules.
2. Each office has a specified sphere of competence.
3. Each office has obligations to perform specific functions, the authority to carry them out, and the means of compulsion to get the job done.
4. The offices are organized into a hierarchical system.
5. People need technical training in order to meet the technical qualifications for each office.
6. Those who occupy these positions are given the things they need to do the job; they do not own them.

---

would no longer be extraordinary or perceived by the followers in that way. Thus, if successful, the routinization of charisma eventually destroys charisma and the structure is en route to becoming one of Weber's other authority structures: traditional or rational-legal.

As we said, charismatic authority is a revolutionary force. It operates by changing people from within; they change their minds and opt to follow the

---

ideal type   A one-sided, exaggerated concept, usually an exaggeration of the rationality of a given phenomenon, used to analyze the social world in all its historical and contemporary variation. The ideal type is a measuring rod to be used in comparing various specific examples of a social phenomenon either cross-culturally or over time.

bureaucracy   A modern type of organization in which the behavior of officers is rule bound; each office has a specified sphere of competence and has obligations to perform specific functions, the authority to carry them out, and the means of compulsion to get the job done; the offices are organized into a hierarchical system; technical training is needed for each office; those things needed to do the job belong to the office and not the officer; the position is part of the organization and cannot be appropriated by an officer; and much of what goes on in the bureaucracy (acts, decisions, rules) is in writing.

Key Concept—Continued

7. The position is part of the organization and cannot be appropriated by an incumbent.
8. Much of what goes on in the bureaucracy (acts, decisions, rules) is in writing.

This ideal type, like all ideal types, existed nowhere in its entirety. In creating it, Weber had in mind the bureaucracy created in the modern West, but even there no specific organization had all of these characteristics and to a high degree. But Weber used this ideal type (and every ideal type) to do historical-comparative analysis, in this case, analysis of organizational forms. He did this in terms of the organizations associated with the three types of authority and found that the organizational forms associated with traditional and charismatic authority are lacking most or all of these characteristics; they are not bureaucracies and they do not function nearly as well as the bureaucratic organizations associated with rational-legal authority.

One could also use the ideal type to compare specific organizations within the modern world in terms of the degree to which they measure up to the ideal type. The researcher would use the ideal type to pinpoint divergences from the ideal type and then seek to explain them. Among the reasons why a specific organization does not measure up to the ideal type might be misinformation, strategic errors, logical fallacies, emotional factors, or, more generally, any irrationality that enters into the operation of the organization.

---

charismatic leader. Although charisma is an important revolutionary force, it pales in comparison to what Weber considered the most important revolutionary force in history—rationalization and the coming of **rational-legal authority.** The legitimacy of leaders in rational-legal authority comes from the fact that there is a series of codified rules and regulations, and leaders hold their positions as a result of those rules. Thus, for example, the president of the United States is an example of rational-legal authority, and his leadership is legitimized by the fact that he is the person who won the election, who got the most votes in the electoral college.

Although charisma changes peoples' minds—it changes them from within; rationalization changes people from without—it alters the structures in which they live. And the key structure associated with rational-legal authority is the modern bureaucracy (see the Key Concept box on the ideal type). The other forms of authority have organizations associated with them, but they do not measure up to bureaucracy and do not have nearly the effect on people that

---

rational-legal authority A type of authority in which the legitimacy of leaders is derived from the fact that there is a series of codified rules and regulations, and leaders hold their positions as a result of those rules.

bureaucracy does. Bureaucracy was so important to Weber that for him it was not only the heart of rational-legal authority, but *the* model for the rationalization process in the West. Bureaucracy was seen by Weber not only as a rational structure, but a powerful one that exercises great control over those who work within it and are even served by it. It is a kind of cage that alters the way people think and act.

More generally, Weber thought of rationalization as having cage-like qualities. There is no question that rationalization in general and rational-legal authority (and its bureaucracy) in particular bring with them numerous advantages, but Weber was very attuned to the problems associated with them. In fact, Weber was closely associated with the notion of an iron cage of rationalization—the imagery of a powerful, cage-like structure from which it is nearly impossible to escape. That was the way Weber thought of the increasing rationalization of the West. He appreciated the advances but despaired of its increasingly tight control over people. He feared that as more and more sectors of society (not just the government bureaucracy) were rationalized, people would find it increasingly difficult to escape into nonrationalized sectors of life. They would find themselves locked into an iron cage of rationalization.

Weber not only viewed rationalization as triumphant in the West, but also viewed rational-legal authority in the same way. Rational-legal authority is much more effective than traditional authority, with the result that the latter must, over time, give way to the former. Charismatic revolutions will continue to occur, but once routinized, the organization of charismatic authority is weak in comparison to the rational bureaucracy. In any case, once routinized, charisma is destroyed and the authority structure is en route to some other form. Although the new form could be traditional authority, in the modern West it is increasingly likely that charismatic authority is transformed into rational-legal authority. Furthermore, as modern charismatic movements arise, they are increasingly likely to face the iron cage of rationalization and rational-legal authority. That cage not only locks people in, but it also is increasingly impervious to external assault; it is increasingly able to keep both the charismatic leader and the rabble that follows such a leader out. The result is that in the modern world charismatic authority, as well as traditional authority, becomes increasingly inappropriate to the demands of modern society and increasingly unlikely to accede to power. Rational-legal authority, rationalization, and the iron cage of rationality are triumphant!

Summary

1. The great theories of sociology's classical age were vast, highly ambitious theoretical efforts to tell the story of great stretches of social history.
2. Emile Durkheim's theory deals with the changing division of labor and the transition from mechanical to organic solidarity.
3. The major factor in this transformation is changes in dynamic density.
4. The change from mechanical to organic solidarity is accompanied by a dramatic decline in the power of the collective conscience.

5. An indicator of that change is the transformation from the predominance of repressive to restitutive law.
6. The major pathology associated with organic solidarity and its weak collective conscience is anomie.
7. Karl Marx's theory deals with the historical roots of capitalism, capitalism itself, and the hoped-for transition to communism.
8. Marx's critique of capitalism is based on a series of assumptions about human potential. That potential is thwarted in capitalism, leading to alienation, especially among the workers.
9. Capitalism is essentially a two-class economic system in which one class (the capitalists) own the means of production and the other class (the proletariat) must sell its labor-time in order to have access to those means.
10. Marx adopts the labor theory of value—all value comes from labor—and this allows him to see that capitalists exploit the proletariat.
11. The proletariat (and the capitalists) are unable to see this reality because of false consciousness, but they are eventually capable of getting a clear picture of the way capitalism works and of achieving class consciousness.
12. To overthrow capitalism the proletariat must engage in praxis.
13. Communism is a social system that permits for the first time the full expression of human potential.
14. Max Weber distinguished among four types of rationality—practical, theoretical, substantive, and formal—but his focus was on formal rationality and the way its preeminence led to the rationalization of the West.
15. The Protestant ethic played a central role in the rationalization of the West, especially the economy. It was a key factor in the development of the spirit of capitalism and ultimately the rise of the capitalist economic system.
16. Weber was interested in the factors within Confucianism in China and Hinduism in India that prevented rationalization and capitalism.
17. Weber was concerned with the three types of authority—traditional, charismatic, and rational-legal—and the emergence of the latter as the dominant form of authority.

Suggested Readings

STEVEN LUKES   *Emile Durkheim: His Life and Work.* New York: Harper and Row, 1972. The best single book on the life and work of Emile Durkheim.

ANTHONY GIDDENS, ed.   *Emile Durkheim: Selected Writings.* Cambridge: Cambridge University Press, 1972. A nice selection of excerpts from most of Durkheim's important works.

ROBERT ALUN JONES   "Emile Durkheim." In George Ritzer, ed., *The Blackwell Companion to Major Social Theorists.* Malden, MA, and Oxford, England: Blackwell, 2000, pp. 205–250. Good coverage of Durkheim and his work with a number of unique contributions, including insights into the social and intellectual context of his work.

MUSTAFA EMIRBAYER, ed.   *Emile Durkheim: Sociologist of Modernity.* Malden, MA: Blackwell, 2003. A useful collection of some of Durkheim's most important work as well as more contemporary works that pick up on key themes in his work.

DAVID MCLELLAN   *Karl Marx: His Life and Thought.* New York: Harper Colophon, 1973. A monumental treatment of Marx's life and work.

DAVID MCLELLAN, ed.   *The Thought of Karl Marx.* New York: Harper Torchbooks. A useful compendium of excerpts from the most important of Marx's works.

ROBERT J. ANTONIO and IRA COHEN, eds.   *Marx and Modernity: Key Readings and Commentary.* Malden, MA: Blackwell, 2002. Following a lengthy and excellent introduction by Antonio, the book offers key selections from Marx's work followed by a section devoted to contemporary work on his theories.

ROBERT J. ANTONIO   "Karl Marx." In George Ritzer, ed., *The Blackwell Companion to Major Social Theorists.* Malden, MA, and Oxford, England: Blackwell, 2000, pp. 105–143. First-rate analysis of Marx's life and work.

KALBERG, STEPHEN, ed.,   *Max Weber: Readings and Commentary on Modernity.* Malden, MA: Blackwell, 2005. Key selections of Weber's work followed by contemporary work on his theories.

CHARLES CAMIC, PHILIP GORSKI and DAVID TRUBEK, eds.   *Max Weber's Economy and Society: A Critical Companion.* Stanford: Stanford University Press, 2005. Contains a series of essays on Weber's most important and all-encompassing work.

MARIANNE WEBER   *Max Weber: A Biography.* New York: Wiley, 1975. Much detail about Weber's life in a biography authored by his wife, a scholar in her own right.

ARTHUR MITZMAN   *The Iron Cage: An Historical Interpretation of Max Weber.* New York: Grosset and Dunlap, 1969. A very interesting and informative biography of Weber, with a psychoanalytic slant.

STEVEN KALBERG   "Max Weber." In George Ritzer, ed., *The Blackwell Companion to Major Social Theorists.* Malden, MA, and Oxford, England: Blackwell, 2000, pp. 144–204. Best treatment of Weber and his contributions available in the context of a lengthy essay.

FRITZ RINGER   *Max Weber: An Intellectual Biography.* Chicago: University of Chicago Press, 2004. The most recent effort to deal with Max Weber as a person, the intellectual and social context of his work, and his most important ideas. It also addresses the contemporary relevance of Weber's ideas.

CHAPTER 3

Classical Theories II

Georg Simmel: The Growing Tragedy of Culture

Thorstein Veblen: Increasing Control of Business over Industry

George Herbert Mead: Social Behaviorism

Summary

Suggested Readings

This chapter is a continuation of the last and deals with three other major classical theorists. The first, Georg Simmel, is quite a noncontroversial choice because he is increasingly included with Marx, Weber, and Durkheim as one of the founders and acknowledged masters of sociological theory. The other two selections are more atypical and controversial. Thorstein Veblen was an American and is usually thought of as an economist. However, he deserves recognition as a great classical sociological theorist because (1) his ideas were so sociological; (2) he offered a grand theory of economic change that was similar in focus and scope to those of the acknowledged masters (all of whom had much to say about the economy); and (3) he alone anticipated the great shift in the late 20th century from an economy defined by production to one that is oriented mainly to consumption. Another American, George Herbert Mead, is also a somewhat unusual choice for discussion in this context. Although Mead grappled less than the others with the big social changes and issues of his day, he did create a theory that had incomparable insights into individual consciousness (including "mind" and "self"), action, and interaction.

GEORG SIMMEL:
THE GROWING TRAGEDY OF CULTURE

Georg Simmel (1858–1918) was another important German social theorist. The big issue for Simmel was what he called the tragedy of culture. However, before we get to that issue, we need to deal with some of the building blocks of Simmel's theorizing.

Association

Although Georg Simmel had an important grand theory of the tragedy of culture, his earlier, and to some degree, continuing, fame is based on his theories of everyday life. In fact, more than any other classical thinker, Simmel was concerned with such seemingly trivial everyday behaviors as people having dinner together, asking others for directions, or dressing to please others. These forms of **association,** or interaction, serve to link people to one another. They are continually being created, worked out, dropped, and then replaced by other forms of association. To Simmel, these associations were the atoms of social life that were to be studied microscopically. This theory is clearly very different from, though not unrelated to, Simmel's grander thoughts on such things as the tragedy of culture.

Simmel, like Weber, goes so far as to define sociology as the study of everyday life: Sociology was to study society, but society is nothing more than the sum of the individual interactions that comprise it.

Forms and Types

Simmel made an important distinction between **forms** of interaction and **types** of interactants. In the real world people are confronted with a bewildering and confusing array of interactions and interactants. In order to deal with this confusion, people reduce their social world to a small number of forms of interaction and types of interactants. Think of the bewildering array of interaction taking place at a party. Someone asks you, "What brings you to a party like this?" This form of interaction could be interpreted in at least two ways: a request for information or a desire to begin a relationship. Given the nature of the party and the way the words are uttered, you might well interpret this as the form of interaction "an effort to start a relationship" rather than the form "request for information." Depending, then, on whether you are receptive to exploring a new relationship, you might say either "Why, the chance to meet someone like you," or "I came by train." The point is that because so much is always going on, we are always seeking to reduce interaction to a limited number of forms so that we are better able to understand them and deal with them.

The same thing occurs in our dealing with the large number of people that we can potentially interact with. In order to make dealing with them more manageable, we reduce them to a limited number of types of interactants. At the party, a person asks us why we are there, but since we've never met the person,

---

association   The relationships among people, or interaction.

forms   Patterns imposed on the bewildering array of events, actions, and interactions in the social world both by people in their everyday lives and by social theorists.

types   Patterns imposed on a wide range of actors by both laypeople and social scientists in order to combine a number of them into a limited number of categories.

> ## Georg Simmel (1858–1918)
> *A Biographical Vignette*
>
> Simmel was a marginal man, a "stranger," in the German academic world of his day. Even though he is now considered one of the great masters of theory, he occupied marginal academic positions throughout his life. Indeed, most of the time he did not earn a regular salary, but was dependent on student fees. He produced an impressive body of work and knew the most important intellectual figures of the day (e.g., Max Weber) and they thought highly of his work. Why, then, was he so marginal?
>
> Two reasons stand out. First, he generally did not write what were considered in his day to be legitimate academic tracts. Rather he wrote essays with popular titles often published in newspapers and magazines. He was much more comfortable with this kind of work than massive tomes (although he wrote those, too), but the administrators of German universities did not know what to make of such work.
>
> The other is that Simmel was a Jew in an academic world rife with anti-Semitism. In one report to the minister of education he was described as Jewish in the way he looked, the way he comported himself, and the way he thought. Given this view of him and the anti-Semitism of the day, it is little wonder that Simmel found it impossible to get a regular academic appointment, at least until the end of his life when he finally got such a post, albeit at a minor German university.

we do not know the particular characteristics of that person. Without knowing the person, how do we respond? The answer is that we have a series of types and we make an initial decision about the type to which the person belongs. Is the person who asked us that question a serious person or merely a flirt? Your response to the question will be shaped by your initial attempt to categorize the person. You may find later that your initial judgment was wrong and you put the person in the wrong category. Nevertheless, in a world in which we meet innumerable people, we must use such types as first approximations in order to begin (or decide to avoid) an interaction.

Simmel believed that not only do people develop forms and types on a day-to-day basis, but so must the sociologist. Thus, Simmel did many essays on forms of interaction (e.g., between superordinates and subordinates) and types of interactants (e.g., the stranger).

Consciousness

Simmel's thinking on association was related to, and shaped by, his thinking on consciousness. He operated with the assumption that people engaged in action on the basis of conscious processes. In their interaction, people have various motives, goals, and interests; they engage in creative consciousness. He also believed that people were able to confront themselves mentally, to set

---

Key Concept
Secrecy

Secrecy is defined by Simmel as the condition in which one person has the intention of hiding something while the other is seeking to reveal what is being hidden. People must know some things about other people in order to interact with them. For instance, we must know with whom we are dealing (e.g., a friend, a relative, a shopkeeper). We may come to know a great deal about other people, but we can never know them absolutely; that is, we can never know all the thoughts, moods, and so on, of other people.

In all aspects of our lives we acquire not only truth but also ignorance and error; however, it is in the interaction with other people that ignorance and error acquire a distinctive character. This relates to the inner lives of the people with whom we interact. People, in contrast to any other object of knowledge, have the capacity intentionally to reveal the truth about themselves or to lie and conceal such information.

The fact is that even if people wanted to reveal all (and they almost always do not), they could not do so because so much information would drive everybody crazy; hence, people must select the things they report to others. From the point of view of Simmel's concern with quantitative issues, we report only fragments of our inner lives to others. Furthermore, we choose which fragments to reveal and which to conceal; thus, in all interactions, we reveal only a part of ourselves, and which part we opt to show depends on how we select and arrange the fragments we choose to reveal.

The **lie** is a form of interaction in which a person intentionally hides the truth from others. With a lie, not only are others left with an erroneous conception but also the error is traceable to the fact that the liar intended that the others be deceived.

Simmel discussed the lie in terms of social geometry, specifically his ideas on distance. For example, we can better accept and come to terms with the lies of those

---

themselves apart from their own actions. In other words, people can take in external stimuli, assess them, try different courses of action, and then decide what to do. Because of these mental capacities, people are not enslaved by external stimuli or external structures. However, the mind also has the capacity to endow these stimuli or structures with a separate and real existence; in sociological terms the mind has the capacity to **reify** these phenomena. Thus, humans also have the capacity to create the conditions that constrain them. Through their mental processes people can free themselves, constrain themselves, or, more likely, do some combination of both things.

---

secrecy   As defined by Simmel, the condition in which one person has the intention of hiding something while the other is seeking to reveal that which is being hidden.

lie   A form of interaction in which a person intentionally hides the truth from others.

reify   To endow social structures, which are created by people, with a separate and real existence.

Key Concept—Continued

who are distant from us; hence, we have little difficulty learning that the politicians who habituate Washington, D.C., sometimes lie to us. In contrast, we find it unbearable if those closest to us lie. The lie of a spouse, lover, or child has a far more devastating impact on us than the lie of a government official whom we know only through the television screen.

More generally, in terms of distance, all everyday communication combines elements known to both parties with facts known only to one or the other. The existence of the latter leads to distanceness in all social relationships. Indeed, Simmel argued that social relationships require both elements that are known to the interactants and those that are unknown to one party or the other. In other words, even the most intimate relationships require both nearness and distance, reciprocal knowledge and mutual concealment; hence, secrecy is an integral part of all social relationships, although a relationship may be destroyed if the secret becomes known to the person from whom it was being kept.

In that most intimate, least secret form of association, marriage, Simmel argued that there is a temptation to reveal all to the partner, to have no secrets; however, Simmel believed this was a mistake. For one thing, all social relationships require some truth and some error. More specifically, complete self-revelation (assuming such a thing is even possible) would make a marriage matter-of-fact and remove all possibility of the unexpected. Finally, most of us have limited internal resources, and every revelation reduces the (secret) treasures that we have to offer to others. Only those few with great storehouses of personal accomplishments can afford numerous revelations to a marriage partner. All others are left denuded (and uninteresting) by excessive self-revelation.

Group Size

One of the most powerful aspects of Simmel's sociology of everyday life is the way he builds from everyday interactions to the larger structures of society. This is best seen in his famous work on the dyad and the triad. Put simply, a **dyad** is a two-person group and a **triad** is a three-person group. On first thought, there appears to be little or no difference between the two. After all, how much difference can the addition of one person make? Simmel's surprising and very important answer is that it makes an enormous difference. In fact, the crucial difference sociologically is between a two- and three-person group: No further addition to the size of the group makes nearly as much difference as the addition of one person to a dyad. Unlike all other size groups, the dyad has no meaning beyond its meaning to each of the two individuals involved.

---

dyad   A two-person group.
triad   A three-person group.

No independent group structure emerges in a dyad; it consists of two people interacting. These two separable individuals each retains a high level of individuality. Because there is no separable group, no possibility of any collective threat to the individual exists.

Of crucial importance is the fact that the addition of the third person to a dyad, the creation of a triad, makes the emergence of an independent group structure possible. Now there is the possibility of a group threat to individuality. Furthermore, with the addition of a third party, a number of new social roles become possible that were not possible before. For example, one member of the triad can take the role of mediator or arbitrator in a dispute between the other two parties. The third party can also exploit the disputes between the others to gain power. It is also possible that the other two members can compete for the favors of the third, or the third party may foster disputes between the other two, making it easier to exercise control over both. Thus, in various ways, a system of authority and a stratification system can emerge, systems that cannot exist in a dyad. The movement from dyad to triad is essential to the development of social structures that can become separate from, and dominant over, individuals. In other words, the tragedy of culture that occupies such a central place in Simmel's grand theory becomes possible only when at least a triad has developed.

Simmel offered many other insights based on group size. For example, and seemingly contradictorily, he argued that individual freedom grows with an increase in group size. A small group is likely to exert great control over an individual, who simply cannot escape the gaze and control of group members. In a large group, however, the individual is better able to become less visible and less subject to the control of the group. In large societies, especially large cities, where there are likely to be many different groups, the individual is a member of a number of them. As a result, any single group is only able to control a minute portion of an individual's behavior. However, individuals become subject to other kinds of control in large societies, as exemplified by the soon-to-be-discussed tragedy of culture. Furthermore, masses are more subject to being controlled by one idea, the simplest idea. The physical proximity of a large number of people, especially in the modern city, makes them more suggestible and more likely to follow simplistic ideas and to engage in mindless, emotional actions.

Distance and the Stranger

Along these same lines (his social geometry), Simmel was also interested in the issue of distance. For example, the social type we mentioned previously, the **stranger**, is defined by distance. The stranger is one who is neither too close nor too far. If she came too close, she would no longer be a stranger; she would be

---

stranger   One of Simmel's social types defined by distance: one who is neither too close nor too far.

Key Concept
Space

While Simmel's thinking on distance is widely known, less well-known is his broader theory of space. One of his concerns is the importance of boundaries in space. Their importance is revealed particularly when the boundaries are indefinite or indistinct. Indefinite boundaries occur when groups are not limited to their political boundaries (e.g., a mass of people in a large space). Being in the open in this way makes the group subject to impulsiveness, enthusiasm, and susceptible to manipulation. This, of course, can be related to such things as riots and the like. Indistinct space occurs when the space is unclear to a group such as when a group finds itself in pitch-black space. Among other things, this is likely to lead to increases in group fantasizing.

Some of Simmel's most interesting insights on space relate to what he has to say about the bridge and the door. For example, while the bridge always leads to connectedness, the door can lead to both connectedness (if it is open) and separation (if it is closed). Thus, he concludes that the door is much richer and has much livelier significance than the bridge. Direction makes no difference in terms of the bridge, but there are huge differences between entering through and leaving by a door.

---

a member of the group. However, if she was too far away, she would cease to have any contact with the group. Thus, to be a stranger involves a combination of closeness and distance.

The peculiar distance between the stranger and the group leads to some unusual patterns of interaction between the two. For example, the stranger can be more objective in his interaction with group members. His lack of emotional involvement allows him to be more dispassionate in his judgments of, and relationships with, members. Furthermore, because he is a stranger, other people feel more comfortable expressing confidences to him than they would to those who are close to them and members of the same group. They feel free to say things to the stranger because of the feeling that what they say will not get back to the group. (A good example of this is the fact that some people feel quite comfortable divulging very personal information to taxi drivers whom they are not likely to see again and who are unlikely to have contact with other members of their group.) On the other hand, they are reluctant to say those things to group members out of a fear that other group members will soon find out.

The stranger is not only a social type, but we can discuss strangeness as a social form of interaction. For example, a degree of strangeness, a peculiar combination of closeness and distance, enters even the most intimate relationships; thus, even the closest of marriages can have elements of distance (his poker group, her reading group). In fact, Simmel believed that successful marriages must have some degree of strangeness to keep them interesting.

Distance and Value

One of Simmel's most interesting insights on distance relates to value and the development of an alternative to Marx's labor theory of value. In terms of the issue of distance, Simmel argued that the value of things is a function of their distance from us. Things that are too close to us, too easy to obtain, are of no great value to us; thus, even though our lives depend on it, air is not very valuable to most of us most of the time because it is all around us and readily attainable. (Of course, air would be quite valuable if there was little of it [e.g., if pollution made it hard to breathe and dangerous to inhale] or it was hard to obtain [e.g., if one had emphysema].) Also, things that are too far from us, too difficult to obtain, are not of great value. Thus, a trek to the top of Mt. Everest is not very valuable to most of us because it is too far to travel, too difficult to climb the mountain, and too expensive to undertake such an adventure. In the end, what is most valuable to us are the things that are attainable but only with considerable effort.

Objective and Subjective Culture

The tragedy of culture is based on a distinction between subjective (or individual) and objective (or collective) culture. **Objective culture** involves those objects that people produce (art, science, philosophy, and so on). **Individual culture** refers to the capacity of the individual to produce, absorb, and control the elements of objective culture. The **tragedy of culture** stems from the fact that over time objective culture grows exponentially while individual culture and the ability to produce objective culture grow only marginally. Over time, peoples' ability to be creative has increased little, if at all. Yet the sum total of what they have produced has exploded.

First, the absolute size of objective culture grows. This can be seen most obviously in the case of science. Clearly, we know many more things about disease, astronomy, physics, and sociology than ever before, and with each passing day we know more and more. Second, the number of different components of objective culture increases. For example, not many years ago there was no Internet. Now it is an increasingly important part of objective culture, and there is always more and more to know about it. Finally, and perhaps most importantly, the various elements of objective culture become intertwined in

---

objective culture   The objects that people produce—art, science, philosophy, and so on—that become part of culture.

individual culture   The capacity of the individual to produce, absorb, and control the elements of objective culture.

tragedy of culture   Stems from the fact that over time objective culture grows exponentially while individual culture and the ability to produce it grow only marginally. Our meager individual capacities cannot keep pace with our cultural products. As a result, we are doomed to increasingly less understanding of the world we have created and to be increasingly controlled by that world.

ever more powerful, self-contained worlds that are increasingly beyond the comprehension, let alone control, of the actors who created them.

The tragedy of culture is that our meager individual capacities cannot keep pace with our cultural products. We are doomed to increasingly less understanding of the world we have created. More importantly, we are destined to be increasingly controlled by that world. For example, the Internet now exerts enormous control over our lives and that control is destined to grow as it becomes more important and more complex. We understand it less, but we need it more.

Division of Labor

A key factor in the tragedy of culture is the growth in the division of labor. Increased specialization leads to an increased ability to produce ever more complex and sophisticated components of the objective world. But at the same time, the highly specialized individual loses a sense of the total culture and loses the ability to control it. Thus, a person may be a highly sophisticated computer programmer; but, immersed in the details of producing a specific program, or even a minute portion of a program, the individual loses a sense of the computer technology, the Internet, or Internet culture in general. As objective culture grows, individual culture atrophies.

Of course, there are positive aspects of all of this. Specialization has led to innumerable developments that have greatly enhanced our daily lives. Given the enormous and expanding array of things available in the objective culture, we all have infinitely more choices than ever before. But all this comes at the cost of individuals feeling, and being, increasingly insignificant in comparison to the objective culture that they must confront and attempt to come to grips with on a daily basis. In that confrontation, the individual is destined to be the loser. Worse, there is no end to this process and we are destined to progressively greater insignificance in comparison to objective culture—to be increasingly controlled by it. The future inhabitants of our society are doomed to be far more tragic figures than we are.

THORSTEIN VEBLEN: INCREASING CONTROL OF BUSINESS OVER INDUSTRY

We continue this discussion of classical grand theories with the contributions of an American, Thorstein Veblen (1857–1929). Veblen's general concern throughout his career was with the conflict between business and industry. Although to our way of thinking these terms seem closely related, to Veblen there was a stark contrast, in fact an inherent conflict, between them. While the development of industry leads to greater and greater output, business interests seek to limit output in order to keep prices and profits high.

Business

Veblen detailed a historic change in the nature of business and business leaders. The early leaders tended to be entrepreneurs who were designers, builders, shop managers, and financial managers. They were more likely to have earned their income because, at least in part, it was derived from their direct contribution to production (industry). Today's business leaders are almost exclusively concerned with financial matters and therefore, at least in Veblen's view, they are not earning their income because finance makes no direct contribution to industry. (In fact, if anything, finance inhibits industry rather than enhancing it.) A further development involved the routinization of financial matters and, as a result, the handling of them by large financial organizations (e.g., investment bankers). Thus, the business leader is left as an intermediary between industry and finance with little concrete knowledge of either.

Business tended to define the world of Veblen's day, especially the interests of the upper classes. **Business** is defined by a pecuniary approach to economic processes; that is, the dominant interest is money. The focus is not on the interest of the larger community but rather on the profitability of the organization. The occupations of those with a business interest tend to involve ownership and acquisition; the leisure class tends to occupy these positions. Thus, the captains of industry as well as the captains of solvency (the investment bankers, financiers who come eventually to control the captains of industry) have a business orientation. Since it is nonproductive, Veblen viewed a business orientation as parasitic and exploitative. Instead of production, business leaders focus on such things as sharp practice, cornering the market, and sitting tight.

Veblen gave the business leader credit for increasing productive capacity, but Veblen's most distinctive contribution is his view of such leaders as being at least as much involved in disturbing production and in restricting capacity as they are in increasing it. Veblen viewed the modern corporation as a type of business. As such, its interests are in financial matters like profit and in sales and not in production and workmanship.

Industry

Industry has to do with understanding and using mechanized processes of all sorts on a large scale. An industrial orientation is associated with those involved in workmanship and production. The working classes are most likely to be involved in these activities and to have such an orientation. Unfortunately,

---

business   A pecuniary approach to economic processes in which the dominant interests are acquisition, money, and profitability rather than production and the interests of the larger community.

industry   The understanding and productive use, primarily by the working classes, of a wide variety of mechanized processes on a large scale.

Key Concepts
Conspicuous Consumption and Conspicuous Leisure

What distinguishes Veblen from every other classical theorist is that he not only developed an important theory of production, but he also created a theory of consumption. Of enduring importance is his theory of the relationship between social class and consumption. At the turn of the 20th century Veblen argued that the motivation to consume a variety of goods (services were of little interest in Veblen's day, but the same idea would apply) is not for subsistence, but to create the basis for invidious distinctions (those designed to lead to envy) between people. The possession of such goods leads to higher status for those who possess them. In other words, the leisure class engages in **conspicuous consumption**. And the conspicuous consumption of the leisure class ultimately affects everyone else in the stratification system. In deciding what goods to consume, people in every other social class ultimately emulate the behavior of the leisure class at the pinnacle of the stratification system. The tastes of that class eventually work their way down the stratification hierarchy, although most people end up emulating the acquisitions of the class immediately above them in the stratification system.

Veblen distinguished between conspicuous consumption and **conspicuous leisure**. He argued that leisure, or the nonproductive use of time, was an earlier way of making invidious distinctions between people; that is, people conspicuously wasted time in order to elevate their social status. In the modern era, people consume conspicuously (i.e., waste goods rather than time) in order to create such distinctions. Buying expensive goods when far less expensive commodities would have accomplished the same objectives is an example of waste in the realm of goods.

In the modern world, elites are more likely to engage in conspicuous consumption than conspicuous leisure because the former is more visible, and visibility is crucial if the goal is to elevate one's status and to make others envious. Driving a new Rolls Royce around one's neighborhood is far more likely to be seen than whiling away one's hours in front of one's television set.

industry is controlled by business leaders who have little or no understanding of it and only understand the "higgling of the market" and financial intrigue. The main interest of those leaders is to restrict production and restrict the free operation of the industrial system in order to keep prices (and therefore profits) high. The result is that the main task of the business leader to Veblen is to

---

conspicuous consumption   The consumption of a variety of goods, not for subsistence but for higher status for those who consume them and thereby to create the basis for invidious distinctions between people.

conspicuous leisure   The consumption of leisure; the nonproductive use of time; the waste of time as a way of creating an invidious distinction between people and elevating the social status of those able to use their time in this way.

Thorstein Veblen (1857–1929)
A Biographical Vignette

Veblen was, to put it mildly, an unusual man. For example, he could often sit for hours and contribute little or nothing to a conversation going on around him. His friends and admirers made it possible for him to become president of the American Economic Association, but he declined the offer. The following vignette offered by a bookseller gives us a bit more sense of this complex man:

> A man used to appear every six or eight weeks quite regularly, an ascetic, mysterious person with a gentle air. He wore his hair long. . . . I used to try to interest him in economics. . . . I even once tried to get him to begin with *The Theory of the Leisure Class*. I explained to him what a brilliant port of entry it is to social consciousness. He listened attentively to all I said and melted like a snow drop through the door. One day he ordered a volume of Latin hymns. "I shall have to take your name because we will order this expressly for you," I told him. "We shall not have an audience for such a book as this again in a long time, I am afraid." "My name is Thorstein Veblen," he breathed rather than said.

---

obstruct, retard, and sabotage the operation of the industrial system. Without such obstructions, the extraordinary productivity of the industrial system would drive prices and profits progressively lower.

The increasingly tightly interlocking industrial system not only lends itself to cooperative undertakings, but this characteristic makes it increasingly vulnerable to the efforts of business and national leaders to sabotage it. This may be done consciously or as a result of the business leader's increasing ignorance of industrial operations. In either case, it results in hardship to the community in the form of unemployment, idle factories, and wasted resources. Veblen even went so far as to imply that business leaders are consciously responsible for depressions: They reduce production because under certain market conditions they feel they cannot derive what they emotionally consider a reasonable profit from their goods. To Veblen, there is no such thing, from the point of view of the larger community, as overproduction. However, even with the activities of the business leaders, including the creation of depressions, the industrial system is still so effective and efficient that it allows business leaders and their investors to earn huge profits.

The modern industrial system is so productive that it yields returns far beyond that required to cover costs and to give reasonable returns to owners and investors. These additional returns are the source of what Veblen calls free income. And that free income goes to the business leaders and their investors, not to the workers (this is reminiscent of Marx's theory of exploitation). Overall, the captains of industry and the leisure class of which they are an important part, and their pecuniary orientation, are associated with waste. In encouraging such things, the leisure class tends to stand in opposition to the needs of modern, industrial society.

GEORGE HERBERT MEAD:
SOCIAL BEHAVIORISM

Perhaps the most important theorist of everyday life in the history of sociology was another American, George Herbert Mead (1863–1931). Although he taught in the philosophy department at the University of Chicago, Mead was a central figure in the development of an important contemporary sociological theory: symbolic interactionism. Just as all the grand theorists discussed previously had sociologies of everyday life, Mead also had a grand theory. However, his most important contribution to the development of sociological theory lies in his sociology of everyday life.

Interestingly, while Mead focuses on thought, action, and interaction, he emphasizes the importance of starting with the group, or, more generally, with what he calls the social. Thus, analysis is to begin with the organized group and then work its way down, rather than begin with separate individuals and work one's way up to the group. Individual thought, action, and interaction are to be explained in terms of the group and not the group by individual thought and action. The whole is prior to its individual elements.

In focusing on those individual elements, Mead found it difficult to distinguish his approach from psychological behaviorism, even though he called himself a type of behaviorist: a social behaviorist. Basically, he recognized the fact of stimulus-response, but he thought there is much more to human action than that simple model. To put it simply, the mind intervenes between the application of a stimulus and the emitting of a response; people, unlike lower animals, think before they act.

The Act

Mead comes closest to psychological behaviorism in discussing the most basic element in his theoretical system—the **act**—but he does not see people as engaging in automatic, unthinking responses. He recognizes four separable stages in the act, but each is related to all of the others and the act does not necessarily occur in the following sequence.

1. **Impulse**. The actor reacts to some external stimulus (hunger, a dangerous animal) and feels the need to do something about it (find food, run away).
2. **Perception**. The actor searches for and reacts to stimuli (through hearing, smell, taste, etc.) that relate to the impulse and to the ways of dealing with

---

act   The basic concept in Mead's theory, involving an impulse, perception of stimuli, taking action involving the object perceived, and using the object to satisfy the initial impulse.

impulse   First stage of the act, in which the actor reacts to some external stimulus and feels the need to do something about it.

perception   Second stage of the act, in which the actor consciously searches for and reacts to stimuli that relate to the impulse and the ways of dealing with it.

it. People do not simply react to stimuli; they think about them, they select among them, deciding what is important (the animal is growling) and what is unimportant (the animal has pretty eyes).

3. **Manipulation**. This involves manipulating the object once it has been perceived. This is an important phase before a response is emitted and involves two major distinctive characteristics of humans: their minds and their opposable thumbs. Thus, a hungry person can pick up a mushroom from the forest floor, examine it by rolling it around in her fingers, and think about whether it has the characteristics of a poisonous mushroom. In contrast, a hungry animal is likely to grab for the mushroom and eat it unthinkingly and without examining it.

4. **Consummation**. This involves taking action that satisfies the original impulse (eating the mushroom rather than simply manipulating and examining it, shooting the animal). The human is more likely to be successful in consummation because of his or her ability to think through the act, while the lower animal must rely on the far less efficient and effective trial and error.

Gestures

An act involves only one person or lower animal, but both people and animals interact with others. The most primitive form of interaction involves **gestures**—movements by one party that serve as stimuli to another party. People and animals make gestures and also engage in a **conversation of gestures**: Gestures by one mindlessly elicit responding gestures from the other. In a dog fight, for example, the bared teeth of one dog might automatically cause the other dog to bare its teeth. The same thing could happen in a boxing match: The cocked fist of one fighter could lead the other to raise an arm in defense. In the case of both types of fight, the reaction is instinctive and the gestures are nonsignificant because neither party thinks about its response. Although both people and animals employ nonsignificant gestures, only people employ **significant gestures**, or those that involve thought before a response is made.

---

manipulation   Third stage of the act involving manipulating the object, once it has been perceived.

consummation   Final stage of the act involving the taking of action that satisfies the original impulse.

gestures   Movements by one party (person or animal) that serve as stimuli to another party.

conversation of gestures   Gestures by one party that mindlessly elicit responding gestures from the other party.

significant gestures   Gestures that require thought before a response is made; only humans are capable of this.

Among gestures, Mead placed great importance on vocal gestures. All vocal gestures of lower animals are nonsignificant (the bark of a dog to another dog) and some human vocal gestures may be nonsignificant (snoring). However, most human vocal gestures are significant, the most important of them involving language. This system of significant gestures is responsible for the great advances (control over nature, science) of human society.

One huge difference exists between a physical and a vocal gesture. When we make a physical gesture, we cannot see what we are doing (unless we are looking in a mirror), but when we make a vocal gesture, we can hear it in the same way as the person to whom it is aimed. Thus, it affects the speaker in much the same way it affects the hearer. Furthermore, people have far better control over vocal gestures; if they don't like what they are saying (and hearing), they can stop it or alter it in midsentence. Thus, what distinguishes people from lower animals is not only their ability to think about a response before emitting it, but to control what they do.

Significant Symbols and Language

One of the most famous ideas in Mead's conceptual arsenal, and in all of sociology, is the significant symbol. **Significant symbols** are those that arouse in the person expressing them the same kind of response (it need not be identical) that they are designed to elicit from those to whom they are addressed. Physical objects can be significant symbols, but vocal gestures, especially language, are the crucial significant symbols. In a conversation of gestures, only the gestures are communicated. In a conversation involving language, gestures (the words) and, most importantly, the meaning of those words are communicated.

Language (or, more generally, significant symbols) brings out the same response in both speaker and hearer. If I were to say the word *dog* to you, both you and I would have a similar mental image of a dog. In addition, words are likely to lead us to the same or similar action. If I yelled the word *fire* in a crowded theater, we would both be driven to want to escape the theater as quickly as possible. Language allows people to stimulate their own actions as well as those of others.

Language also makes possible the critically important ability of people to think, to engage in mental processes. Thinking, as well as the **mind**, is simply defined as conversation that people have with themselves using language; this activity is like having a conversation with other people. Similarly, Mead believed that social processes precede mental processes; significant symbols and a language must exist for the mind to exist. The mind allows us to call out in ourselves

---

significant symbols Symbols that arouse in the person expressing them the same kind of response (it need not be identical) as they are designed to elicit from those to whom they are addressed.

mind To Mead, the conversations that people have with themselves using language.

not only the reactions of a single person (who, for example, shouts the word *fire* in a theater), but also the reactions of the entire community. Thus, if yelling *fire* is likely to save lives, we might think about the public recognition we would receive for doing so. On the other hand, if we contemplate yelling *fire* falsely, the anticipated reaction of the community (disapproval, imprisonment) might prevent us from taking such action. Furthermore, thinking of the reactions of the entire community leads us to come up with more organized responses than if we were to think about the reactions of a number of separate individuals.

The Self

Another crucial concept to Mead is the **self**, or the ability to take oneself as an object. The self and the mind are dialectically related to one another; neither can exist without the other. Thus, one cannot take oneself as an object (think about oneself) without a mind, and one cannot have a mind, have a conversation with oneself, without a self. Of course, it is really impossible to separate mind and self because the self is a mental process.

Basic to the self is **reflexivity**, or the ability to put ourselves in others' places: think as they think, act as they act. This ability enables people to examine themselves and what they do in the same way that others would examine them. We can adopt the same position toward ourselves as others adopt toward us. To do this, we must be able to get outside of ourselves, at least mentally, so that we can evaluate ourselves as others do. We have to adopt a specific standpoint toward ourselves that can either be the standpoint of a specific individual or of the social group as a whole. (This idea will be discussed later.)

Mead believes that the self emerges in two key stages in childhood. The first is the **play stage** in which the child plays at being someone else. The child might play at being Barney, or Sponge Bob, or Mommy. In so doing, the child learns to become both subject (who the child is) and object (who Barney is) and begins to be able to build a self. However, that self is very limited because the child can only take the role of distinct and separate others (Barney, mother). In playing at being Barney or mother, the child is able to see and evaluate herself as she imagines Barney or her mother might see and evaluate her. However, the child lacks a more general and organized sense of self.

In the next stage, the **game stage**, the child begins to develop a self in the full sense of the term. Although the child takes the role of discrete others in the play stage, in the game stage she takes the role of everyone involved in the

---

self   The ability to take oneself as an object.

reflexivity   The ability to put ourselves in others' places: think as they think, act as they act.

play stage   The first stage in the genesis of the self, in which the child plays at being someone else.

game stage   The second stage in the genesis of the self: instead of taking the role of discrete others, the child takes the role of everyone involved in a game. Each of these others plays a specific role in the overall game.

George Herbert Mead (1863–1931)
A Biographical Vignette

Most of the important theorists discussed throughout this book achieved their greatest recognition in their lifetimes for their published work. George Herbert Mead, however, was as important, at least during his lifetime, for his teaching as for his writing. His words had a powerful impact on many people who were to become important sociologists in the 20th century. One of his students said, "Conversation was his best medium; writing was a poor second." Another of his students described what Mead was like as a teacher:

> For me, the course with Professor Mead was a unique and unforgettable experience . . . Professor Mead was a large, amiable-looking man who wore a magnificent mustache and a Vandyke beard. He characteristically had a benign, rather shy smile matched with a twinkle in his eyes as if he were enjoying a secret joke he was playing on the audience . . .
>
> As he lectured—always without notes—Professor Mead would manipulate the piece of chalk and watch it intently . . . When he made a particularly subtle point in his lecture, he would glance up and throw a shy, almost apologetic smile over our heads—never looking directly at anyone. His lecture flowed and we soon learned that questions or comments from the class were not welcome. Indeed, when someone was bold enough to raise a question, there was a murmur of disapproval from the students. They objected to any interruption of the golden flow . . .
>
> His expectations of students were modest. He never gave exams. The main task for each of us students was to write as learned a paper as one could. These Professor Mead read with great care, and what he thought of your paper was your grade in the course. One might suppose that students would read materials for the paper rather than attend his lectures but that was not the case. Students always came. They couldn't get enough of Mead.

game. Each of these others plays a specific role in the overall game. Mead used the example of baseball, in which the child may play one role (say, pitcher), but must know what the other eight players are supposed to do and are going to expect from her. In order to be a pitcher, she must know what everyone else is to do. She need not have all the players in mind all the time, but at any given moment she may have the roles of three or four of them in mind. As a result of this ability to take on multiple roles simultaneously, children begin to be able to function in organized groups. They become able to better understand what is expected of them, what they are supposed to do, in the group. Although play requires only pieces of a self, the game requires a coherent self.

Another famous concept created by Mead is the **generalized other**. The generalized other is the attitude of the entire community or, in the example of the baseball game, the attitude of the entire team. A complete self is possible

---

generalized other   The attitude of the entire community or of any collectivity in which the actor is involved.

Key Concept
Definition of the Situation

W. I. Thomas (1863–1947), along with his wife Dorothy S. Thomas, created the idea of **definition of the situation**: If people define situations as real, then those definitions are real in their consequences. This means that what really matters is the way people mentally define a situation rather than what that situation is in reality. The definition, not the reality, leads people to do certain things and not others. To illustrate with the baseball example, suppose that you are playing shortstop and you define the situation as being two out when there is really only one out. The batter hits a pop fly to you and you catch it, believing in your mind that there are three outs. As a result, you jog off the field as if the inning were over. Your definition has had real consequences: You've left the field. Other real consequences may follow: Opposition runners on the bases may run around and score unmolested, your teammates may scream at you, and your manager may bench you. In many areas of our lives, how we define a situation often matters more than the reality.

---

only when the child moves beyond taking the role of individual significant others and takes the role of the generalized other. It is also important for people to be able to evaluate themselves and what they are doing from the point of view of the group as a whole and not just from that of discrete individuals. The generalized other also makes possible abstract thinking and objectivity. In terms of the latter, a person develops a more objective perspective when she relies on the generalized other rather than individual others. In sum, to have a self, a person must be a member of a community and be directed by the attitudes common to the community.

All of this, especially the generalized other, might lead one to believe that Mead's actors are conformists who lack individuality. However, Mead makes it clear that each self is unique; each develops within the context of specific biographical experiences. Furthermore, there is not one generalized other, but many generalized others because there are many groups within society. Because people belong to many different groups and have many generalized others, there are a multitude of selves. Furthermore, people need not accept the community and the generalized other as they are; they can work to change them. At times they succeed, altering the community, the generalized other, and, ultimately, the selves within that community.

I and Me

The fact that there is both conformity and individuality in the self is manifest in Mead's distinction between two phases of the self—the *I* and the *me*. Although

---

definition of the situation   The idea that if people define situations as real, then those definitions are real in their consequences (Thomas and Thomas).

Contemporary Applications
Have We Become Obsessed with the Self?

George Herbert Mead offered great insight into the nature of the self, but he might have been surprised to see the degree to which the self has been transformed, and come to be the center of attention, even an obsession, in the contemporary world. We live today in a world in which we are increasingly likely to reflect on a greater number of things. The Internet and globalization, among other things, have put us in touch with many more things and we are increasingly able (because of such developments) to reflect on them. Indeed, we need to reflect on them because so many of them (e.g., global economic changes or health threats) are likely to have a profound effect on us. And among the things that we reflect on more these days is ourselves (Mead was very interested in the relationship between the self and reflexivity).

While self-reflection occurred in the past, people were less able and likely to do so than people (at least in developed countries) are today. For one thing, people were often too busy trying to survive and provide for their daily needs to engage in all that much self-reflection. Furthermore, they lived in a culture that stressed material accomplishments and de-emphasized self-reflection and self-absorption, viewing them as excessive and not furthering the material needs of people and the larger society. However, as Anthony Giddens, a contemporary theorist, who we will discuss at several points later in this book, points out, today the self has become a project, perhaps even *the* project, for many people. For one thing, the self no longer simply emerges; it is something that we actively create. Who we are, who we think we are, are not given characteristics, or even set in childhood, but are things that we consciously and actively create throughout the course of our lives. Thus, the self is not created once and for all, but continually molded, altered, and even changed dramatically over time, and even from one time to another.

Thus, the self becomes something that we all need to watch over, monitor, and alter as needed. This makes us in many ways more flexible and adaptable. However, in many ways it is also a fearsome and difficult process. That is, a century or two ago people did not worry much about the self, but today it has become a constant source of a concern. We have become preoccupied with the self and adapting it to the changing society, our changing position in that society, and even from one situation to the next. This is not an easy task and it is one that is fraught with difficulties and tensions. There are many advantages to being in tune with the self, but there are also many costs.

---

these phases sound like things or structures of the self, in reality they are viewed by Mead as processes that are part of the larger process that is the self.

The **I** is the immediate response of the self to others. It is the incalculable, unpredictable, and creative aspect of the self. People do not know in advance what the *I* will do. Thus, in the case of a baseball game, a player does not know

---

I The immediate response of the self to others; the incalculable, unpredictable, and creative aspect of the self.

in advance what will happen—a brilliant play or an error. We are never totally aware of the *I*, with the result that we sometimes surprise ourselves with our actions. Mead stresses the importance of the *I* for four reasons. First, it is the key source of novelty in the social world. Second, it is in the *I* that our most important values lie. Third, the *I* constitutes the realization of the self and we all seek to realize the self. Because of the *I* we each develop a unique personality. Finally, Mead views a long-term evolutionary process (and here the great sociologist offers a grand theory) from primitive societies where people are dominated by *me* to contemporary society where the *I* plays a much more significant role.

The *I* reacts against the *me* within the self. The **me** is basically the individual's adoption and perception of the generalized other. Unlike the *I*, people are very cognizant of the *me*; they are very conscious of what the community wants them to do. All of us have substantial *me*, but those who are conformists are dominated by the *me*. Through the *me* society controls us. The *me* allows people to function comfortably in the social world while the *I* makes it possible for society to change. Society gets enough conformity to allow it to function, and it gets a steady infusion of innovations that prevent it from growing stagnant. Both individuals and society function better because of the mix of *I* and *me*.

Summary

1. Georg Simmel was interested in association, or interaction.
2. In order to deal with the bewildering array of interactions, sociologists and laypeople develop forms of interaction.
3. In order to deal with the bewildering array of interactants, sociologists and laypeople develop types of interactants.
4. In terms of the issue of size, there is a great difference between dyads (two-person groups) and triads (three-person groups). The existence of a third person in a triad makes possible the emergence of an independent group structure. No further additions in group size are as important as the addition of one person to a dyad.
5. The larger the group structure, the freer the individual.
6. Simmel was interested in the issue of distance. This interest was manifested in his discussion of a social type, the stranger, who is neither too close to nor too far from the group. Distance is related to a social form, strangeness, which means that a peculiar form of strangeness and distance enters all social relationships.
7. Distance is also related to Simmel's thinking on value. Those things that are valuable are neither too close nor too far.
8. Simmel's grand theory is concerned with the tragedy of culture.
9. The tragedy of culture involves the growth of objective culture and its increasing predominance over subjective culture.
10. Veblen's grand theory deals with the increasing control of business over industry and the negative effects of the former on the latter.

---

me The individual's adoption and perception of the generalized other; the conformist aspect of the self.

11. Mead was a social behaviorist interested not only in stimulus-response behavior, but in the human mind that intervenes between stimulus and response; people think before they act.
12. The four stages in the act are impulse, perception, manipulation, and consummation.
13. Although people and lower animals use gestures and engage in conversations of gestures, only people use significant gestures, significant symbols, and language.
14. The generalized other is the attitude of the entire community.
15. The self has two phases that are in constant tension: *I* (the immediate, unpredictable, creative aspect) and the *me* (the adoption of the generalized other leading to conformism).

Suggested Readings

DAVID FRISBY and MIKE FEATHERSTONE, eds. *Simmel on Culture.* London: Sage, 1997. A collection of Simmel's writings that is notable for its inclusion of Simmel's less well-known, but important, work on space.

DAVID FRISBY *Georg Simmel.* Chichester, England: Ellis Horwood, 1984. Nice, concise overview of Simmel's life and work.

DONALD LEVINE, ed. *Georg Simmel: Individuality and Social Forms.* Chicago: University of Chicago Press, 1971. Excellent collection of Simmel's most important essays and excerpts from other works.

LARRY SCAFF "Georg Simmel." In George Ritzer, ed., *The Blackwell Companion to Major Social Theorists.* Malden, MA, and Oxford, England: Blackwell, 2000, pp. 251–278. Insightful essay concentrating on Simmel's work.

JOHN PATRICK DIGGINS *Thorstein Veblen: Theorist of the Leisure Class.* Princeton: Princeton University Press, 1999. Excellent biography of Veblen with a heavy emphasis on his writings.

LOUIS PATSOURAS *Thorstein Veblen and the American Way of Life.* Montreal: Black Rose Books, 2004. Recent examination of Veblen that looks not only at his sociology and economics, but also emphasizes his politics.

GARY COOK *George Herbert Mead: The Makings of a Social Pragmatist.* Urbana: University of Illinois Press, 1993. Treatment of Mead's life and work within the context of the philosophical school of thought, pragmatism, with which he is most often associated.

J. DAVID LEWIS AND RICHARD L. SMITH *American Sociology and Pragmatism: Mead, Chicago School, and Symbolic Interactionism.* Chicago: University of Chicago Press, 1980. Controversial study of Mead's work as it relates not only to pragmatism, but also the Chicago School of sociology and symbolic interactionism.

DMITRI SHALIN "George Herbert Mead." In George Ritzer, ed., *The Blackwell Companion to Major Social Theorists.* Malden, MA, and Oxford, England: Blackwell, 2000, pp. 302–344. Rich analysis of Mead and his work.

CHAPTER 4

Contemporary Grand Theories I

In this chapter and the next we turn to several contemporary theories that, like the classical theories covered in the preceding two chapters (with the possible exception of Mead's theory), qualify as grand theories. In this chapter we deal with three closely related examples of such theories—structural functionalism, conflict theory, and general system theory. Conflict theory emerged as a reaction to the once-dominant (at least in the United States) structural functional theory and systems theory is closely associated with structural functionalism. In fact, the term "system" is often used in structural functional theory. However, the latter are now quite distinct theories as we will see in the discussion of the work of the most important contemporary system theorist, Niklas Luhmann.

STRUCTURAL FUNCTIONALISM

As the name suggests, **structural functionalism** focuses on the structures of society and their functional significance (positive or negative consequences) for other structures. In structural functionalism, the terms *structural* and *functional* need not be used together, although they are typically linked. We could study the **structures** of society, patterned social interaction and persistent social

---

structural functionalism   A sociological theory that focuses on the structures of society and their functional significance (positive or negative consequences) for other structures.

structures   In society, patterned social interaction and persistent social relationships.

relationships, without being concerned with their **functions** (consequences that can be observed and that help a particular system adapt or adjust) for other structures. Similarly, we could examine the functions of a variety of social processes (e.g., crowd behavior) that may not be structured. Still, the concern for *both* elements—structures and functions—characterizes structural functionalism. Although structural functionalism takes various forms, **societal functionalism** is the dominant approach among sociological structural functionalists and as such will be the focus of this section. The primary concern of societal functionalism is the large-scale social structures and institutions of society, their interrelationships, and their constraining effects on actors.

A structural functionalist (especially one associated with the societal version of the theory) is concerned with the relationship among the large-scale structures of society—say, the educational system and the economic system. The focus is on the functions that each provides for the other. For example, the educational system provides the trained personnel needed to fill occupational positions within the economy. The economy, in turn, provides such positions for those people who complete the educational process. This allows the educational system and its students to have an objective in mind at the end of the educational process. Although this offers an image of a positive and close-fitting relationship between social structures, it need not necessarily be that way. In the radical days of the anti–Vietnam war and student movement of the late 1960s and early 1970s, the educational system was producing large numbers of radical students who did not fit well into the occupational world then being offered to them. Although such a tension between structures often exists, structural functionalists tend to focus on the more positive, more functional relationships between structures. The following section deals with one of the most famous works in the history of structural functionalism, one that offers an intriguing and highly controversial portrait of society.

The Functional Theory of Stratification and Its Critics

The functional theory of social stratification, as articulated by Kingsley Davis and Wilbert Moore in 1945, makes it clear that stratification is regarded as both universal and necessary. They argue that no society is ever unstratified, or totally classless. Stratification is, in their view, a functional necessity. All societies need such a system and this need brings into existence a system of stratification. Davis and Moore also view a stratification system as a societal-level structure, pointing out that stratification refers not to the individuals in the stratification system but rather to a system of positions (e.g., occupations like laborer and

---

functions Consequences that can be observed and that help a particular system adapt or adjust.

societal functionalism A variety of structural functionalism that focuses on the large-scale social structures and institutions of society, their interrelationships, and their constraining effects on actors.

manager). They focus on the fact that positions within that structure carry with them varying degrees of prestige and not on how individuals come to occupy these positions; that is, the focus is on the structure of social stratification, as well as the functions it performs.

The Theory   The major issue in the Davis and Moore theory is how a society motivates and places people in their proper positions in the stratification system. This presents two problems: First, how does a society instill in the proper individuals the desire to fill certain positions? Second, once people are in the right positions, how does society then instill in them the desire to fulfill the requirements of those positions?

Proper social placement in society is a problem for three reasons. First, some positions are more pleasant to occupy than others. There is little problem getting people to occupy pleasant positions, but unpleasant ones are a different matter. In addition, some positions are more important to the survival of society than others. Although it is important to have all positions occupied, it is especially important, even necessary, that the most important ones be filled. Finally, different social positions require different abilities and talents. The problem is to find a way to be sure that the right people find their way into the right positions—that there is a satisfactory fit between individual skills and abilities and positional requirements.

Davis and Moore were concerned with the functionally most important positions in society's stratification system. The positions that rank high within the stratification system are presumed to be those that are *less* pleasant to occupy but *more* important to the survival of society and those that require the greatest ability and talent. Society must attach sufficient rewards to these positions so that an adequate number of people will seek to occupy them and the individuals who do come to occupy them will work diligently. The converse was implied by Davis and Moore but not discussed: Low-ranking positions in the stratification system are presumed to be *more* pleasant (an odd view—the position of the laborer more pleasant than that of the manager?) and *less* important and to require less ability and talent. Also, society has less need to be sure that individuals occupy these positions and perform their duties with diligence.

Thus, **social stratification** is a structure involving a hierarchy of positions that has the function of leading those people with the needed skills and abilities to do what is necessary to move into the high-ranking positions that are most important to society's functioning and survival. Davis and Moore do not argue that a society consciously develops such a stratification system in order to be sure that the high-level positions are filled, and filled adequately. Rather, they

---

social stratification   To the structural functionalist, a structure involving a hierarchy of positions that has the function of leading those people with the needed skills and abilities to do what is necessary to move into the high-ranking positions that are most important to society's functioning and survival.

make it clear that stratification is a mechanism that evolves in an unplanned way. However, it is a device that every society does, and *must*, develop if it is to survive.

In order to be sure that people occupy the higher-ranking positions, society must, in Davis and Moore's view, provide these individuals with various rewards, including great prestige, high salary, and sufficient leisure. For example, to ensure that our society has enough doctors, we need to offer them these, and many other, rewards. Davis and Moore imply that we could not expect people to undertake the burdensome and expensive process of medical education if we did not offer such rewards. The implication seems to be that people who occupy positions at the top must receive the rewards that they do. If they did not, those positions would remain understaffed or unfilled and society would suffer, if not collapse.

Criticisms The structural-functional theory of stratification has been subject to much criticism. One basic criticism is that the functional theory of stratification simply perpetuates the privileged position of those people who already have power, prestige, and money. It does this by arguing that such people deserve their rewards; indeed, they need to be offered such rewards for the good of society.

The functional theory also can be criticized for assuming that simply because a stratified social structure has existed in the past and continues to exist in the present, it must continue to exist in the future. It is possible that future societies will be organized in other nonstratified ways. Structures other than stratification could be created that would perform the same kinds of functions without having the deleterious effects (e.g., great inequality) associated with stratified systems.

In addition, it has been argued that the idea of functional positions varying in their importance to society is difficult to support. Are garbage collectors really any less important to the survival of society than advertising executives? Despite the lower pay and lower prestige of the garbage collectors, they actually may be *more* important to the survival of the society. Even in cases in which it could be said that one position serves a more important function for society, the greater rewards do not necessarily accrue to the more important position. Nurses may be much more important to society than are movie stars, but nurses have far less power, prestige, and income than movie stars have.

Is there really a scarcity of people capable of filling high-level positions? In fact, many people are prevented from obtaining the training they need to achieve prestigious positions, even though they have the ability. In the medical profession, for example, there is a persistent effort to limit the number of practicing doctors. In general, many able people never get a chance to show that they can handle high-ranking positions, even though there is a clear need for them and their contributions. Those in high-ranking positions have a vested interest in keeping their own numbers small and their power and income high.

Finally, it can be argued that we do not have to offer people power, prestige, and income to get them to want to occupy high-level positions. People can be equally motivated by the satisfaction of doing a job well or by the opportunity to be of service to others.

Thus, the structural functionalists have offered a portrait of the structure and operation of society's system of social stratification. However, it is a highly conservative and controversial portrait. There are other ways to organize society in order to motivate people to handle important social functions. In other words, it is possible to draw other kinds of portraits of social stratification, in particular, and more generally of social organization.

Talcott Parsons's Structural Functionalism

Over the course of his life, the most famous structural functionalist, Talcott Parsons, did a great deal of theoretical work. This section deals with his later structural-functional theorizing. Parsons's structural functionalism consists of the four functional imperatives for all action systems, his famous AGIL scheme. This section discusses the four functions and analyzes Parsons's ideas on structures and systems.

AGIL   In examining functions, Parsons focused on sets of activities aimed at meeting a need or the multiple needs of a system. He argued that four functions are imperatives: that is, they are necessary for (characteristic of) all systems. If they are to survive, all systems must engage in four sets of activities aimed at meeting their needs. These activities are adaptation (A), goal attainment (G), integration (I), and latency, or pattern maintenance (L). Together, these four functional imperatives are known as the AGIL scheme.

In terms of **adaptation,** a system must adjust to its environment and adjust the environment to its needs. More specifically, a system must cope with external situational dangers and contingencies. A system cannot remain long at odds with its environment. If it did, it would be in grave danger of perishing because of the lack of fit. For example, if a tribe of agriculturalists found themselves in an environment in which the soil was not conducive to raising fruits and vegetables, the tribe would not be able survive unless its members adapted to the new environment by, for example, becoming hunters and fishers rather than agriculturalists. A contemporary example is the United States, which has finally come to realize that people cannot continue to drive large gas-guzzling SUVs in a world in which there is a finite supply of oil needed for gasoline. Eventually, the United States is going to have to begin to develop alternative ways of transporting its population, thereby adapting to the external reality that fossil fuel is a limited resource.

The system can also seek to adapt its environment to its needs. The tribe discussed in the example could engage in various actions that serve to invigorate

---

adaptation   One of Parsons's four functional imperatives. A system must adjust to its environment and adjust the environment to its needs. More specifically, a system must cope with external situational dangers and contingencies.

the soil and make it more conducive to the raising of crops. In the case of the United States's dependence on limited foreign oil, it could aid other countries in finding additional stocks of oil or even help them develop alternatives to fossil fuel.

Third, and more specific, are the external dangers and contingencies to which systems must adapt. For example, during the height of the Cold War with the Soviet Union, President Ronald Reagan moved toward an antiballistic missile system designed to destroy incoming Soviet missiles before they could explode on American soil. Although such a system was never built, its mere possibility served to heighten the stakes and the costs involved in the nuclear arms race between the United States and the Soviet Union. The Soviet Union's inability to keep up was undoubtedly one of the factors (other factors included a large number of internal problems and crises such as the inability of the command economy to produce and distribute needed products) that hastened the demise of the Soviet Union. This effort to adapt to the Soviet threat helped lead to the end of that threat; it proved to be a particularly successful adaptation.

Goal attainment involves the need for a system to define and achieve its primary goals. The ultimate goal of any system is that it not only survive into the future, but that it also grow and expand. Specific social systems share this general objective, but also have a series of more specific goals. For example, the university is a system with two other basic objectives—educate its students and allow its professors to do the basic research needed to continue to enhance knowledge. Interestingly, the university, like all other systems, cannot simply define its goals once and for all and then forget about the issue. Situations change and arrangements that once allowed for goal attainment may become ineffective. Within the university, for example, the goals of educating students and doing basic research often come into conflict. If education is emphasized too much, professors are unable to devote enough time and energy to research. Similarly, if professors spend too much time doing research, the education of students suffers. Thus, the university must continually examine these two objectives and their relationships to one another in order to be able to achieve both of them to an adequate degree.

Through **integration** a system seeks to regulate the interrelationship of its component parts. Thus, if the tribe in our example succeeds in creating a viable agricultural system, it must then seek to integrate agriculture with hunting. It needs to be sure that enough time, energy, personnel, and resources are allocated to each. Similarly, within the university, administrators must be sure that research and teaching do not become totally isolated from one another. Thus, it

---

goal attainment   The second of Parsons's functional imperatives involving the need for a system to define and achieve its primary goals.

integration   The third of Parsons's functional imperatives, this one requiring that a system seek to regulate the interrelationship of its component parts. Integration also involves the management of the relationship among the other three functional imperatives (AGL).

is important that the research results obtained by professors be integrated into their classes and that students be used, where possible, in research projects. Such interrelationships help avoid the conflict between teaching and research; they make the two more integrated. Integration also involves the management of the relationship among the other three functional imperatives (AGL).

Parsons calls the fourth functional imperative latency, or pattern maintenance. **Latency** refers to the need for a system to furnish, maintain, and renew the motivation of individuals. **Pattern maintenance** refers more to the need to furnish, maintain, and renew the cultural patterns that create and sustain individual motivation.

Latency is embedded in the functional theory of stratification discussed previously; the whole structure of the system, with greater rewards to those who occupy higher-level positions within it, is designed to motivate individuals to strive to move up the stratification system and occupy the higher-level positions. This motivation must not only be created and maintained by the system, but also renewed from time to time in order to keep the system working and people striving. For example, we periodically read or hear great success stories in the media about individuals who have, through great effort or a burst of genius, vaulted quickly to the top of the system. Such stories are particularly abundant these days with the boom in the computer and the Internet and the large numbers of people whose success in it has led to a meteoric rise to the top. The best example is Bill Gates, who as a young man, and in a few years, became the richest person in the United States. Telling Gates's story, as well as those of many other computer and Internet billionaires, serves to reinforce the motivation of large numbers of people to strive to reach the pinnacle of the stratification system.

Pattern maintenance is concerned with much the same thing, but at the macro- rather than the micro-level. In order to maintain the stratification system and keep people involved in striving to the top of that system, norms and values that support such a system and such striving must be put in place and sustained. Success, especially economic success, is strongly valued in the United States, and such a value system does help to sustain the stratification system and those who seek to move up in it. However, norms and values are not static and must change in order to reflect new social realities. The norm used to be that years of striving led to a high-level position within the stratification system. But, with the coming of the so-called new economy (computers, the Internet, biotechnology), the new norm, at least in that realm of the economy, is that success should come quickly and early in one's career: the young have the mind-set and capabilities to succeed in the new economy. Such a new norm serves to sustain the new ways of reaching the top of the stratification system.

---

latency   One aspect of Parsons's fourth functional imperative involving the need for a system to furnish, maintain, and renew the motivation of individuals.

pattern maintenance   The second aspect of Parsons's fourth functional imperative involving the need to furnish, maintain, and renew the cultural patterns that create and sustain individual motivation.

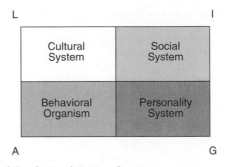

FIGURE 4.1. Structure of the General Action System

Although the AGIL scheme has been discussed both in general terms and with some specific examples, Parsons designed the AGIL scheme to be used at *all* levels in his theoretical system. This included his most general and all-inclusive sense of the four action systems: the behavioral organism, the personality system, the social system, and the cultural system. All of these relate to action, but each one is primarily involved in the performance of one of the four functional imperatives. The **behavioral organism** is the action system that handles the adaptation function by adjusting to and transforming the external world. The **personality system** performs the goal-attainment function by defining system goals and mobilizing resources to attain them. The **social system** copes with the integration function by controlling its component parts. Finally, the **cultural system** performs the latency function by providing actors with the norms and values that motivate them for action. Figure 4.1 summarizes the structure of the action system in terms of the AGIL schema.

Thus, we have already encountered two of Parsons's structural-functional portraits—the four functional imperatives and the four action systems (as well as the main function of each). Another portrait is to be found in the overall shape of Parsons's action system. Figure 4.2 gives an outline of the major levels in Parsons's schema.

The Action System   Parsons obviously had a clear notion of levels of social analysis as well as their interrelationship. The hierarchical arrangement of the

---

behavioral organism   One of Parsons's action systems, responsible for handling the adaptation function by adjusting to and transforming the external world.

personality system   The Parsonsian action system responsible for performing the goal-attainment function by defining system goals and mobilizing resources to attain them.

social system   The Parsonsian action system responsible for coping with the integration function by controlling its component parts; a number of human actors who interact with one another in a situation with a physical or environmental context.

cultural system   The Parsonsian action system that performs the latency function by providing actors with the norms and values that motivate them for action.

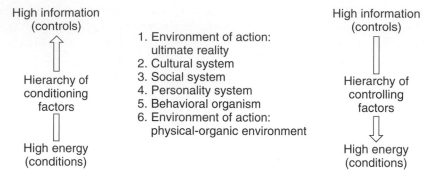

High information
(controls)

Hierarchy of
conditioning
factors

High energy
(conditions)

1. Environment of action:
   ultimate reality
2. Cultural system
3. Social system
4. Personality system
5. Behavioral organism
6. Environment of action:
   physical-organic environment

High information
(controls)

Hierarchy of
controlling
factors

High energy
(conditions)

FIGURE 4.2. Parsons's Action Schema

action system is clear, and the levels are integrated in Parsons's system in two ways: First, each of the lower levels provides the conditions, the energy, needed for the higher levels. Second, the higher levels control those below them in the hierarchy.

In terms of the environments of the action system, the lowest level, the physical and organic environment, involves the nonsymbolic aspects of the human body, its anatomy and physiology. The highest level, ultimate reality, has a metaphysical feel, but it is argued that Parsons was not really interested in the supernatural, but rather in the universal tendency for society to deal symbolically with the difficulties of human existence (e.g., uncertainty, tragedy) that represent challenges to a social organization that purports to be meaningful.

As previously discussed, the heart of Parsons's work is found in his four action systems. In the assumptions that Parsons made regarding his action systems, we encounter the problem of order that was his overwhelming concern and that has become a major source of criticism of his work. The Hobbesian problem of order—what prevents a social war of all against all—was not answered to Parsons's satisfaction by the earlier thinkers. Parsons found his answer to the problem of order in structural functionalism, which operates in his view with the following set of assumptions:

1. Systems have the property of order and interdependence of parts.
2. Systems tend toward self-maintaining order, or equilibrium.
3. The system may be static or involved in an ordered process of change.
4. The nature of one part of the system has an impact on the form that the other parts can take.
5. Systems maintain boundaries with their environments.
6. Allocation and integration are two fundamental processes necessary for a given state of equilibrium of a system.
7. Systems tend toward self-maintenance involving the maintenance of boundaries and of the relationships of parts to the whole, control of environmental variations, and control of tendencies to change the system from within.

These assumptions led Parsons to make the analysis of the ordered structure of society his first priority. In so doing, he did little with the issue of social change or the creation of a grand theory, at least until later in his career. His priority was to focus on various combinations of social variables. Only after they are described and studied is it possible to deal with how combinations of such variables change over time.

Parsons was so heavily criticized for his static orientation that he devoted more and more attention to change. However, in the view of most observers, even his work on social change tended to be highly static and structured. Actually, the key elements in Parsons's portrait of the social world do not exist in the real world but are, rather, analytical tools for thinking about and studying the real world.

Social System   Parsons's conception of the social system begins at the micro-level with interaction between ego and alter ego, defined as the most elementary form of the social system. He spent little time analyzing this level, although he did argue that features of this interaction system are present in the more complex forms taken by the social system. Parsons defined a **social system** as a number of human actors who interact with one another in a situation with a physical or environmental context. In such a situation actors are seen as seeking to optimize their gratification. Their relationship to one another, as well as to their social situations, is defined and mediated by shared cultural symbols. This definition seeks to define a social system in terms of many of the key concepts in Parsons's work—actors, interaction, environment, optimization of gratification, and culture.

Despite his commitment to viewing the social system as a system of interaction, Parsons did not take interaction as his fundamental unit in the study of the social system. Rather, he used the status-role complex as the basic unit of the social system. This is neither an aspect of actors nor an aspect of interaction, but rather a structural component of the social system. **Status** refers to a structural position within the social system, and **role** is what the actor does in such a position, seen in the context of its functional significance for the larger system. The actor is viewed not in terms of thoughts and actions but instead (at least in terms of position in the social system) as nothing more than a bundle of statuses and roles.

In his analysis of the social system, Parsons was interested primarily in its structural components. In addition to a concern with the status-role, Parsons was concerned with such large-scale components of social systems as collectivities,

---

social system   The Parsonsian action system responsible for coping with the integration function by controlling its component parts; a number of human actors who interact with one another in a situation with a physical or environmental context.

status   A structural position within the social system.

role   What an actor does in a status, seen in the context of its functional significance for the larger system.

norms, and values. In his analysis of the social system, however, Parsons was not simply a structuralist but also a functionalist. Thus, he delineated a number of the functional prerequisites of a social system (these are more specific than the four functional prerequisites [AGIL] that apply to all action systems):

1. Social systems must be structured so that they operate compatibly with other systems.
2. To survive, social systems must have the requisite support from other systems.
3. The system must meet a significant proportion of the needs of its actors.
4. The system must elicit adequate participation from its members.
5. It must have at least a minimum of control over potentially disruptive behavior.
6. If conflict becomes sufficiently disruptive, it must be controlled.
7. A social system requires a language in order to survive.

It is clear in Parsons's discussion of the functional prerequisites of the social system that his focus was large-scale systems and their relationship to one another (societal functionalism). Even when he talked about actors, it was from the point of view of the system. Also, the discussion reflects Parsons's concern with the maintenance of order within the social system.

However, Parsons did not completely ignore the issue of the relationship between actors and social structures in his discussion of the social system. Given his central concern with the social system, of key importance in this integration are the processes of internalization and socialization; Parsons was interested in the ways that the norms and values of a system are transferred to the actors within the system. In a successful socialization process these norms and values are internalized; they become part of actors' consciences. As a result, in pursuing their own interests, the actors are, in fact, serving the interests of the system as a whole. During socialization actors acquire value orientations that to a large degree fit the dominant values and the basic structure of roles within the social system.

In general, Parsons assumed that actors are usually passive recipients in the socialization process. Children learn not only how to act but also learn the norms and values, the morality, of society. Socialization is conceptualized as a conservative process in which **need-dispositions** (drives molded by society) bind children to the social system, and it provides the means by which the need dispositions can be satisfied. There is little or no room for creativity; the need for gratification ties children to the system as it exists. Parsons sees socialization as a lifelong process. Because the norms and values inculcated in childhood tend to be very general, they do not prepare children for the many specific situations that they encounter in adulthood. Thus, socialization must be supplemented throughout the life cycle with a series of more specific socializing experiences.

---

need-dispositions   To Parsons, drives that are shaped by the social setting.

Despite this need later in life, the norms and values learned in childhood tend to be stable and, with a little gentle reinforcement, tend to remain in force throughout life.

Despite the conformity induced by lifelong socialization, there is a wide range of individual variation in the system. The question is: Why is this normally not a major problem for the social system, given its need for order? For one thing, a number of social control mechanisms can be employed to induce conformity. However, as far as Parsons was concerned, social control is strictly a second line of defense. A system runs best when social control is used only sparingly. In addition, the system must be able to tolerate some variation, some deviance. A flexible social system is stronger than a brittle one that accepts no deviation. Finally, the social system should provide a wide range of role opportunities that allow different personalities to express themselves without threatening the integrity of the system.

Socialization and social control are the main mechanisms that allow the social system to maintain its equilibrium. Modest amounts of individuality and deviance are accommodated, but more extreme forms must be met by reequilibrating mechanisms. Thus, social order is built into the structure of Parsons's social system. No one deliberately planned it, but in our type of social system vicious circles of deviance that might threaten the system are forestalled by such simple and mundane efforts as approving or disapproving of an action, or rewarding some and punishing others.

Again, Parsons's main interest was the system as a whole rather than the actor in the system—how the system controls the actor, not how the actor creates and maintains the system. This interest reflects Parsons's commitment on this issue to societal functionalism.

Society   Although the idea of a social system encompasses all types of collectivities, one specific and particularly important social system is society. A **society** is a relatively self-sufficient collectivity; the members can live entirely within the framework of society and provide enough to satisfy their needs as individuals and collectivities. As a structural functionalist, Parsons distinguished among four structures, or subsystems, in society in terms of the functions (AGIL) they perform (see Figure 4.3).

- The **economy** is the subsystem that performs the function for society of adapting to the environment. On the one hand, owners, managers, and workers must adapt to their environment. For example, if no oil is available, they might shift to nuclear energy. On the other hand, they must adapt the environment to society's needs. For example, if certain types of crops are not indigenous to a society, the seeds necessary to grow them

---

society   To Parsons, a relatively self-sufficient collectivity.

economy   To Parsons, the subsystem of society that performs the function of adapting to the environment.

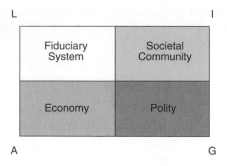

FIGURE 4.3. Society, Its Subsystems, and the Functional Imperatives

must be imported and cultivated. Through work, the economy adapts the environment to society's needs, and it helps society adapt to these external realities.

- The **polity** (or political system) performs the function of goal attainment by pursuing societal objectives and mobilizing actors and resources to that end. Thus, in 1957 the United States was shocked by the Soviet Union's *Sputnik,* the first rocket into space. A few years later President John F. Kennedy declared a dangerous space gap between the United States and the Soviet Union and successfully mobilized people and resources in order to make the United States a leader in space exploration. The goal was achieved when the United States became the first, and still the only, nation to land people on the moon.
- The **fiduciary system** (e.g., in the schools, the family) handles the pattern maintenance and latency function by transmitting culture (norms and values) to actors and seeing to it that it is internalized by them. Thus, parents and teachers socialize children into internalizing such values as economic success and such norms as getting a good education and working hard in order to achieve such success.
- Finally, the integration function is performed by the **societal community** (e.g., the law), which coordinates the various components of society. Laws that relate to the economy, the polity, and the fiduciary system serve to make sure that each functions as it should and that they relate well to one another. For example, laws about minimal levels of education required of everyone not only ensure that the educational system has ample students,

---

polity   To Parsons, the subsystem of society that performs the function of goal attainment by pursuing societal objectives and mobilizing actors and resources to that end.

fiduciary system   To Parsons, the subsystem of society that handles the pattern maintenance and latency function by transmitting culture (norms and values) to actors and seeing to it that it is internalized by them.

societal community   To Parsons, the subsystem of society that performs the integration function, coordinating the various components of society.

but they also help to make sure that people will be at least adequate workers and that they will be reasonably knowledgeable participants in political issues and debates.

As important as the structures of the social system were to Parsons, the cultural system was more important. In fact, the cultural system stood at the top of Parsons's action system, and Parsons labeled himself a cultural determinist.

Cultural System   Parsons conceived of culture as the major force binding the various elements of the social world, or, in his terms, the action system. Culture mediates interaction among actors in the social system and integrates the personality and the social systems. Culture has the peculiar capacity to become, at least in part, a component of the other systems. Thus, in the social system, culture is embodied in norms and values, and in the personality system it is internalized by the actor. But the cultural system is not simply a part of other systems; it also has a separate existence in the form of the social stock of knowledge, symbols, and ideas. These aspects of the cultural system are available to the social and personality systems, but they do not become part of them.

Parsons defined the cultural system, as he did his other systems, in terms of its relationship to the other action systems. Thus, culture is seen as a patterned, ordered system of symbols that are objects of orientation to actors, internalized aspects of the personality system, and institutionalized patterns in the social system. Because it is largely symbolic and subjective, culture is readily transmitted from one system to another. Culture can move from one social system to another through diffusion and from one personality system to another through learning and socialization. However, the symbolic (subjective) character of culture also gives it another characteristic, the ability to control Parsons's other action systems. This is one of the reasons that Parsons came to view himself as a cultural determinist.

Personality System   The personality system is controlled not only by the cultural system but also by the social system. That is not to say that Parsons did not accord some independence to the personality system. It has its own unique characteristics because of the uniqueness of peoples' life experiences. Although it is weak, the personality system is not insignificant in Parsonsian theory, although it is certainly reduced to secondary or dependent status in it.

Personality is defined as the individual actor's organized system of orientation to, and motivation for, action. The basic component of the personality, the most significant aspect of motivation, is the need-disposition. Need-dispositions should be differentiated from drives, which are innate tendencies. Because of the physiological energy associated with them, drives make action possible. In other words, drives are better seen as part of the biological organism. Need-dispositions are defined as the same tendencies, but those that are acquired

---

personality   To Parsons, the individual actor's organized system of orientation to, and motivation for, action.

socially rather than being innate. In other words, need-dispositions are drives that are shaped by the social setting.

Need-dispositions impel actors to accept or reject objects presented in the environment or to seek out new objects if the available ones do not adequately satisfy their need-dispositions. Parsons differentiated among three basic types of need-dispositions. The first type impels actors to seek love, approval, and so forth, from their social relationships. The second type includes internalized values that lead actors to observe various cultural standards. Finally, role expectations lead actors to give and get appropriate responses.

This view yields a very passive image of actors. They seem to be either impelled by drives, dominated by the culture, or, more usually, shaped by a combination of drives and culture (i.e., by need-dispositions). A passive personality system is clearly a weak link in an integrated theory, and Parsons seemed to be aware of it. On various occasions, he tried to endow the personality with some power and creativity. For example, people are capable of modifying culture in creative ways as they internalize culture. Despite views such as these, the dominant impression that emerges from Parsons's work is one of a passive personality system.

Parsons's emphasis on need-dispositions creates other problems. Because it leaves out so many other important aspects of personality, this system is impoverished. It can be argued that even when Parsons analyzed the personality system, he was not really focally interested in it. This is reflected in the various ways that Parsons linked the personality to the social system. First, actors must learn to see themselves in a way that fits with the positions they occupy in society. Second, expectations are attached to each of the roles occupied by individual actors, and actors must fulfill those expectations, at least to a high degree. Actors must also learn self-discipline, internalize value orientations, and so forth. All these forces point toward the integration of the personality system with the social system, which Parsons emphasized. He also pointed out the possibility of the malintegration of the two, which represents a problem for the system that needs to be overcome.

Another aspect of Parsons's work—his interest in internalization as the personality system's side of the socialization process—also reflects the passivity of the personality system. In emphasizing internalization and the superego, Parsons once again manifested his conception of the personality system as passive and externally controlled.

Although Parsons was willing to talk about the subjective aspects of personality in his early work, he progressively abandoned that perspective. In so doing, he limited his possible insights into the personality system. Parsons made it clear that he was shifting his attention away from the internal meanings that the actions of people may have.

Behavioral Organism   Though he included the behavioral organism as one of the four action systems, Parsons had very little to say about it. It is included because it is the source of energy for the other systems. Although it is based on

---

Talcott Parsons (1902–1979)
A Biographical Vignette

Robert Merton was one of Parsons's students when Parsons was just beginning his teaching career at Harvard. Merton, who became a noted theorist in his own right, made it clear that graduate students came to Harvard in those years not to study with Parsons but rather with Pitirim Sorokin, the senior member of the department, who was to become Parsons's archenemy:

> Of the very first generation of graduate students coming to Harvard . . . precisely none came to study with Talcott. They could scarcely have done so for the simplest of reasons: In 1931, he had no public identity whatever as a sociologist.
>
> Although we students came to study with the renowned Sorokin, a subset of us stayed to work with the unknown Parsons.

Merton's reflections on Parsons's first course in theory are interesting too, especially because the material provided the basis for one of the most influential theory books in the history of sociology:

> Long before Talcott Parsons became one of the grand old men of world sociology, he was for an early few of us its grand young man. This began with his first course in theory . . . [It] would provide him with the core of his masterwork, *The Structure of Social Action* which . . . did not appear in print until five years after its first oral publication.

Although all would not share Merton's positive evaluation of Parsons, they would acknowledge the following:

> The death of Talcott Parsons marks the end of an era in sociology. When [a new era] does begin . . . it will surely be fortified by the great tradition of sociological thought which he has left to us.

---

genetic constitution, its organization is affected by the processes of conditioning and learning that occur during the individual's life. The behavioral organism is clearly a residual system in Parsons's work, but at the minimum Parsons is to be lauded for including it as a part of his sociology, if for no other reason than that he anticipated the interest in sociobiology and the sociology of the body by some sociologists.

Thus, from his structural-functional perspective, Talcott Parsons offers several useful portraits of the social world, especially his AGIL scheme of functional prerequisites and the four action systems. We turn now to the work of Parsons's leading student, Robert Merton (1910–2003), who is best known for his outline of structural functional theory. His theory stands in contrast to that of Parsons, who offered structural-functional portraits of the social world. Merton felt that in order to do more adequate structural-functional analyses of that world, what was needed was a clearer and better sense of the nature of structural functionalism. Merton criticized some of the more extreme and indefensible aspects of structural functionalism. But equally important, his new conceptual insights helped to give structural functionalism a continuing usefulness.

Robert Merton's Structural Functionalism

Although both Merton and Parsons are associated with structural functionalism, there are important differences between them. For one thing, while Parsons advocated the creation of grand, overarching theories, Merton favored more limited **middle-range theories.** For another, Merton was more favorable toward Marxian theories than was Parsons. In fact, Merton and some of his students (especially Alvin Gouldner) can be seen as having pushed structural functionalism more to the left politically.

A Structural-Functional Model   Merton criticized what he saw as the three basic postulates of functional analysis. The first is the postulate of the functional unity of society. This postulate holds that all standardized social and cultural beliefs and practices are functional for society as a whole as well as for individuals in society. This view implies that the various parts of a social system must show a high level of integration. However, Merton maintained that although it may be true of small, primitive societies, the generalization cannot be extended to larger, more complex societies; that is, in modern societies structures may exist that are not necessarily functional for society as a whole or for individuals within society. For example, the various structures (e.g., factories, highways) that produce environmental pollution of various types are not functional for society as a whole as well as for individuals who are exposed to the pollution. Similarly, not all parts of society are highly integrated. Our poorly funded and inadequate primary and secondary school system, for example, is not well equipped to supply people with the skills needed to fit into our high-tech work world.

Universal functionalism, the second postulate, states that *all* standardized social and cultural forms and structures have positive functions. Merton argued that this idea contradicts what we find in the real world. It is clear that not every structure, custom, idea, belief, and so forth has positive functions. For example, rabid nationalism can be highly dysfunctional in a world of proliferating nuclear arms.

Third is the postulate of indispensability, which argues that all standardized aspects of society not only have positive functions but also represent indispensable parts of the working whole. This postulate leads to the idea that all structures and functions are functionally necessary for society. No other structures and functions could work quite as well as those currently found within society. Merton's criticism, following Parsons, was that we must at least be willing to admit that there are various structural and functional alternatives to be found

---

middle-range theories   Theories that seek a middle ground between trying to explain the entirety of the social world and a very minute portion of that world.

within society. Thus, it is not necessarily true that a system of social stratification is indispensable to society. A different structure could be put in place in which people are motivated to occupy high-level positions, not because of the money and power associated with them, but because of the gratification that comes from performing invaluable services for society.

Merton's position was that all these functional postulates rely on nonempirical assertions based on abstract, theoretical systems. At a minimum, the sociologist's responsibility is to examine each empirically. Merton's belief that empirical tests, not theoretical assertions, are crucial to functional analysis led him to develop his paradigm of functional analysis as a guide to the integration of such theory and research.

Merton made it clear from the outset that structural-functional analysis focuses on groups, organizations, societies, and cultures. He stated that any object that can be subjected to structural-functional analysis must be a standardized—repetitive and patterned—unit. He had in mind such things as social roles, institutional patterns, cultural patterns, social norms, group organization, social structure, and social control mechanisms. In other words, Merton was a societal functionalist.

Early structural functionalists tended to focus almost entirely on the functions of one social structure or institution for another. However, in Merton's view, early analysts tended to confuse the subjective motives of individuals with the functions of structures or institutions. The focus of the structural functionalist should be on social functions rather than on individual motives. **Functions,** according to Merton, are defined as observable consequences that help a particular system adapt or adjust. However, there is a clear ideological bias when one focuses only on adaptation or adjustment, for the consequences are always positive. It is important to note that one social structure can have negative consequences for another social structure (recall the example of pollution). To rectify this serious omission in early structural functionalism, Merton developed the idea of **dysfunctions.** Just as structures or institutions could contribute to the maintenance of other parts of the social system, they also could have negative consequences for them; they could have an adverse effect on the ability of those parts to adapt or adjust. Slavery in the southern United States, for example, clearly had positive consequences for white Southerners, such as supplying cheap labor, support for the cotton economy, and social status. It also had dysfunctions, such as making Southerners overly dependent on an agrarian economy and therefore unprepared for industrialization. The lingering disparity between the North and the South in industrialization can be traced, at least in part, to the dysfunctions of the institution of slavery in the South.

---

functions   Consequences that can be observed and that help a particular system adapt or adjust.

dysfunctions   Observable consequences that have an adverse effect on the ability of a particular system to adapt or adjust.

Robert K. Merton (1910–2003)
An Autobiographical Vignette

I wanted . . . to advance sociological theories of social structure and cultural change that will help us understand how social institutions and the character of life in society come to be as they are. That concern with theoretical sociology . . . led me to avoid the kind of subject specialization that has become (and, in my opinion, has for the most part rightly become) the order of the day in sociology, as in other evolving disciplines. For my purposes, study of a variety of sociological subjects was essential.

In that variety, only one special field—the sociology of science— . . . persistently engaged my interest. During the 1930s, I devoted myself almost entirely to the social contexts of science and technology, especially in 17th-century England, and focused on the unanticipated consequences of purposive social action. As my theoretical interests broadened, I turned, during the 1940s and afterward, to studies of the social sources of nonconforming and deviant behavior, of the workings of bureaucracy, mass persuasion, and communication in modern complex society, and to the role of the intellectual, both within bureaucracies and outside them. In the 1950s, I centered on developing a sociological theory of basic units of social structure: the role-set and status-set and the role models people select not only for emulation but also as a source of values adopted as a basis for self-appraisal (this latter being the theory of reference groups). I also undertook, with George Reader and Patricia Kendall, the first large-scale sociological study of medical education, aiming to find out how, all apart from explicit plan, different kinds of physicians are socialized in the same schools of medicine, this being linked with the distinctive character of professions as a type of occupational activity. In the 1960s and 1970s, I returned to an intensive study of the social structure of science and its interaction with cognitive structure, these two decades being the time in which the sociology of science finally came of age, with what's past being only prologue. Throughout these studies, my primary orientation was toward the connections between sociological theory, methods of inquiry, and substantive empirical research.

Source: Copyright 1981 by Robert K. Merton.

Merton also posited the idea of **nonfunctions,** which he defined as consequences that are simply irrelevant to the system under consideration. Included here might be social forms that are survivals from earlier historical times. Although they may have had positive or negative consequences in the past, they have no significant effect on contemporary society. One example, although a few might disagree, is the Women's Christian Temperance Movement. It may

---

nonfunctions   Consequences that are irrelevant to the system under consideration.

have been useful in its day in limiting alcoholism, but today it clearly has no impact on that social problem.

To help answer the question of whether positive functions outweigh dysfunctions, or vice versa, Merton developed the concept of **net balance.** However, we never can simply add up positive functions and dysfunctions and objectively determine which outweighs the other, because the issues are so complex and based on so much subjective judgment that they cannot easily be calculated and weighed. The usefulness of Merton's concept comes from the way it orients the sociologist to the question of relative significance. In the example of slavery, the question becomes whether, on balance, slavery was more functional or dysfunctional to the South. Still, this question is too broad and obscures a number of issues (e.g., that slavery was functional for groups like white slaveholders).

To cope with problems like these, Merton added the idea that there must be **levels of functional analysis.** Functionalists had generally restricted themselves to analysis of the society as a whole, but Merton made it clear that analysis also could be done on an organization, institution, group, or any standardized and repetitive social phenomenon. Returning to the issue of the functions of slavery for the South, it would be necessary to differentiate several levels of analysis and ask about the functions and dysfunctions of slavery for black families, white families, black political organizations, white political organizations, and so forth. In terms of net balance, slavery was probably more functional for certain social units and more dysfunctional for other social units. Addressing the issue at these more specific levels helps in analyzing the functionality of slavery for the South as a whole.

Merton also introduced the concepts of manifest and latent functions. These two terms have also been important additions to functional analysis. In simple terms, **manifest functions** are those that are intended, whereas **latent functions** are unintended. The manifest function of slavery was to increase the economic productivity of the South, but it had the latent function of providing a vast underclass that served to increase the social status of southern whites, both rich and poor. This idea is related to another of Merton's concepts—**unanticipated consequences.** Structures have both intended and unintended

---

net balance   The relative weight of functions and dysfunctions.

levels of functional analysis   Functional analysis can be performed on any standardized repetitive social phenomenon ranging from society as a whole, to organizations, institutions, and groups.

manifest functions   Positive consequences that are brought about consciously and purposely.

latent functions   Unintended positive consequences.

unanticipated consequences   Unexpected positive, negative, and irrelevant consequences.

Key Concepts
Social Structure and Anomie

One of the best-known contributions to structural functionalism, indeed to all of sociology, is Merton's analysis of the relationship between culture, structure, and anomie. Merton defined culture as the organized set of normative values shared by those belonging to a group or society that govern their behavior. Social structure is the organized set of social relationships in which societal or group members are involved. **Anomie** can be said to have occurred when there is a serious disconnection between social structure and culture, between structurally created abilities of people to act in accord with cultural norms and goals and the norms and goals themselves. In other words, because of their position in the social structure of society, some people are unable to act in accord with normative values. The culture calls for some type of behavior that the social structure prevents from occurring.

In American society, for example, the culture places great emphasis on material success. However, many people are prevented, by their position within the social structure, from achieving such success. If one is born into the lower socioeconomic classes and as a result is able to acquire, at best, only a high school degree, then one's chances of achieving economic success in the generally accepted way (e.g., through succeeding in the conventional work world) are slim or nonexistent. Under such circumstances (and they are widespread in contemporary American society) anomie can be said to exist, and, as a result, there is a tendency toward deviant behavior. In this context, deviance often takes the form of alternative, unacceptable, and sometimes illegal means of achieving economic success. Becoming a drug dealer or a prostitute in order to achieve economic success is an example of deviance generated by the disjunction between cultural values and social-structural means of attaining those values. This is one way in which the structural functionalist would seek to explain crime and deviance.

In this example of structural functionalism, Merton is looking at social (and cultural) structures, but he is not focally concerned with the functions of those structures. Rather, consistent with his functional paradigm, he is mainly concerned with dysfunctions, in this case, anomie. More specifically, as we have seen, Merton links anomie with deviance and thereby is arguing that disjunctions between culture and structure have the dysfunctional consequence of leading to deviance within society.

It is worth noting that implied in Merton's work on anomie is a critical attitude toward social stratification (e.g., for blocking the means of some to achieve socially desirable goals). Thus, although Davis and Moore wrote approvingly of a stratified society, Merton's work indicates that structural functionalists can be critical of a structure like social stratification.

---

anomie   To Merton, a situation in which there is a serious disconnection between social structure and culture; between structurally created abilities of people to act in accord with cultural norms and goals and the norms and goals themselves.

consequences. Slavery may have been instituted to help strengthen the South economically, but its unanticipated consequence was to slow industrialization and ultimately weaken that area from an economic point of view. Although everyone is aware of the intended consequences, sociological analysis is required to uncover the unintended consequences; indeed, to some this is the very essence of sociology. Peter Berger has called this **debunking,** or looking beyond stated intentions to real effects.

Merton made it clear that unanticipated consequences and latent functions are not the same. A latent function is one type of unanticipated consequence, one that is functional for the designated system. But there are two other types of unanticipated consequences: those that are dysfunctional and those that are irrelevant.

As further clarification of functional theory, Merton pointed out that a structure may be dysfunctional for the system as a whole and yet may continue to exist. One might make a good case that discrimination against blacks, females, and other minority groups is dysfunctional for American society; yet it continues to exist because it is functional for a part of the social system; for example, discrimination against females is generally functional for males. However, these forms of discrimination are not without some dysfunctions, even for the group for which they are functional. Males do suffer from their discrimination against females; similarly, whites are hurt by their discriminatory behavior toward blacks. One could argue that these forms of discrimination adversely affect those who discriminate by keeping vast numbers of people underproductive and by increasing the likelihood of social conflict.

Merton contended that not all structures are indispensable to the workings of the social system. Some parts of our social system *can* be eliminated. This helps functional theory overcome another of its conservative biases. By recognizing that some structures are expendable, structural functionalism opens the way for meaningful social change. Our society, for example, could continue to exist (and even be improved) by the elimination of discrimination against various minority groups.

Merton's clarifications are of great utility to sociologists who wish to perform structural-functional analyses.

CONFLICT THEORY

Conflict theory can be seen as a development that took place, at least in part, in reaction to structural functionalism. However, it should be noted that conflict theory has other roots, such as Marxian theory and Georg Simmel's work on

---

debunking   Looking beyond stated intentions to real effects.

C. Wright Mills (1916–1962)
A Biographical Vignette

C. Wright Mills was not a great neo-Marxian theorist (he made no original contributions of his own to the theory), but he was a great critic of American society (and of American sociological theory, especially the theorizing of Talcott Parsons—see above) from a Marxian, or more generally leftist, perspective. He critiqued union leaders for being insufficiently radical and did not see the labor movement and the working class as truly revolutionary forces. He critiqued white collar workers for, among other things, their great concern for elevating their personal status and their resulting disinterest in larger social change. Most importantly, he saw a "power elite" (composed of an interlocking group of corporate leaders, government officials and military leaders) emerging in American society and he worried about the control they were exercising over society. But Mills made many other kinds of contributions to sociology, especially his idea of the "sociological imagination" and the need think imaginatively about various social issues, especially the intersection between individual biography and social history, "character" and "social structure," as well as "private troubles" and "public issues."

Mills was not only a radical intellectually, but also personally. He generally refused to play the academic game according to the "gentlemanly" rules of the day (sociology was dominated by males in the mid-20th century). Beginning in graduate school, he attacked the professors in his department, and later in his career he took on senior theorists in that department (calling one a "real fool"), leaders of American sociological theory (such as Parsons), and the dominant survey research methods (and methodologists) in the field. Eventually he came to be estranged and isolated from his colleagues at Columbia University. Mills said of himself: "I am an outlander . . . down deep and good."

However, Mills did not restrict his critiques to conservative and establishment elements in the U.S. Late in his life, Mills was invited to the Soviet Union and honored as a major critic of American society. Instead of meekly accepting the award, Mills took the occasion to attack censorship in the Soviet Union with a toast to a Soviet leader who had been purged and murdered by the Stalinists: "To the day when the complete works of Leon Trotsky are published in the Soviet Union!"

social conflict. In the 1950s and 1960s, conflict theory provided an alternative to structural functionalism, but it was superseded by a variety of neo-Marxian theories (see Chapter 5). Indeed, one of the major contributions of conflict theory was the way it laid the groundwork in the United States for theories more faithful to Marx's work, theories that came to attract a wide audience in sociology. The basic problem with conflict theory is that it never succeeded in divorcing itself sufficiently from its structural-functional roots. It was more a kind of structural functionalism turned on its head than a truly critical theory of society. As such, conflict theory, like structural functionalism, offers a portrait of society, albeit one that is different in many ways.

The Work of Ralf Dahrendorf

Like functionalists, conflict theorists are oriented toward the study of social structures and institutions. Conflict theory is little more than a series of contentions that are often the direct opposites of functionalist positions. This antithesis is best exemplified by the work of Ralf Dahrendorf, in which the tenets of conflict and functional theory are juxtaposed:

- To the functionalists, society is static or, at best, in a state of moving equilibrium, but to Dahrendorf and the conflict theorists, every society at every point is subject to processes of change.
- Where functionalists emphasize the orderliness of society, conflict theorists see dissension and conflict at every point in the social system.
- Functionalists (or at least early functionalists) argue that every element in society contributes to stability; the exponents of conflict theory see many societal elements contributing to disintegration and change.
- Functionalists tend to view society as being held together informally by norms, values, and a common morality. Conflict theorists believe whatever order there is in society stems from the coercion of some members by those at the top. Whereas functionalists focus on the cohesion created by shared societal values, conflict theorists emphasize the role of power in maintaining order in society.

Dahrendorf was the major exponent of the position that society has two faces (conflict and consensus) and that sociological theory therefore should be divided into two components—conflict theory and consensus theory (one example of which is structural functionalism). Consensus theorists should examine value integration in society, and conflict theorists should examine conflicts of interest and the coercion that holds society together in the face of these stresses. Dahrendorf recognized that society could not exist without both conflict and consensus, which are prerequisites for each other; thus, we cannot have conflict unless there is some prior consensus. For example, French housewives are highly unlikely to conflict with Chilean chess players because there is no contact between them, no prior integration to serve as a basis for conflict. Conversely, conflict can lead to consensus and integration. An example is the alliance between the United States and Japan that developed after World War II.

Despite the interrelationship between consensus and conflict, Dahrendorf was not optimistic about developing a single sociological theory encompassing both processes. Eschewing a singular theory, Dahrendorf set out to construct a separate conflict theory of society.

Dahrendorf began with, and was heavily influenced by, structural functionalism. He noted that to the functionalist, the social system is held together by voluntary cooperation or general consensus or both. However, to the conflict (or coercion) theorist, society is held together by enforced constraint; thus, some positions in society are delegated power and authority over others. This fact of social life led Dahrendorf to his central thesis that systematic social conflicts are always caused by the differential distribution of authority.

Ralf Dahrendorf (1929–   )
A Biographical Vignette

Ralf Dahrendorf is best known in sociology for his conflict theory, heavily influenced by Marxian theory. He has had quite an illustrious career as a public figure, culminating in being named Baron Dahrendorf in 1993 by Queen Elizabeth II.

Born in Hamburg, Germany, Dahrendorf has had a fascinating life. As a teenager, he resisted the Nazis and was imprisoned (as his father had been) for his opposition to that regime. He was released by an SS officer from the camp where he was imprisoned in early 1945 as the Russian army approached. He studied at the University of Hamburg and earned a doctorate there, as well as another from the London School of Economics. He taught in various German universities, and later became both a public intellectual and a public figure. Among the positions he held were Member of the German Parliament, Secretary of State in the German Foreign Office, Commissioner in the European Commission in Brussels, and Director of the London School of Economics. He became a British citizen in 1988.

While his conflict theory was influenced by Marxian ideas, Dahrendorf was never a Marxist. He describes himself as a liberal. Nevertheless, he has been strongly influenced by the Marxian notion of integrating theory and practice. In fact, he has led a life in which he has developed theory and applied it to practical matters in academia and, more importantly, in the larger society.

Authority

Dahrendorf (like societal functionalists) concentrated on larger social structures. Central to his thesis is the idea that various positions within society have different amounts of authority. Authority does not reside in individuals but in positions. Dahrendorf was interested not only in the structure of these positions but also in the conflict among them. The structural origin of these conflicts is to be traced to the relationship between positions that possess authority and those that are subject to that authority. The first task of conflict analysis, to Dahrendorf, was to identify various authority roles within society. In addition to making the case for the study of large-scale structures like systems of authority roles, Dahrendorf was opposed to those who focus on the individual level. For example, he was critical of those who focus on the psychological or behavioral characteristics of the individuals who occupy such positions. He went so far as to say that those who adopted such an approach were not sociologists.

The authority attached to positions is the key element in Dahrendorf's analysis. Authority always implies both superordination and subordination. Those who occupy positions of authority are expected to control subordinates; that is, they dominate because of the expectations of those who surround them, not because of their own psychological characteristics. Like authority, these expectations are attached to positions, not people. Authority is not a generalized social phenomenon; those who are subject to control, as well as permissible spheres of control, are specified in society. Finally, because authority is legitimate, sanctions can be brought to bear against those who do not comply.

Authority is not a constant as far as Dahrendorf was concerned, because authority resides in positions and not persons. Thus, a person with authority in one setting does not necessarily hold a position of authority in another setting. Similarly, a person in a subordinate position in one group may be in a superordinate position in another. This follows from Dahrendorf's argument that society is composed of a number of units that he called **imperatively coordinated associations.** These may be seen as associations of people controlled by a hierarchy of authority positions. Since society contains many such associations, an individual can occupy a position of authority in one and a subordinate position in another.

Authority within each association is dichotomous; thus two, and only two, conflict groups can be formed within any association. Those in positions of authority and those in positions of subordination hold contrary interests. Here we encounter another key term in Dahrendorf's theory of conflict: **interests.** Groups on top and at the bottom are defined by their common concerns. Dahrendorf continued to be firm in his thinking that even these interests, which sound so psychological, are basically large-scale phenomena; that is, interests are linked to social positions and *not* to the psychological characteristics of those individuals who occupy those positions.

Within every association, those in dominant positions seek to maintain the status quo while those in subordinate positions seek change. A conflict of interest within any association is at least latent at all times, which means that the legitimacy of authority is *always* precarious. This conflict of interest need not be conscious in order for superordinates or subordinates to act on it. The interests of superordinates and subordinates are objective in the sense that they are reflected in the expectations (roles) attached to positions. Individuals do not have to internalize these expectations or even be conscious of them in order to act in accord with them. If they occupy given positions, then they will behave in the expected manner. Individuals are adjusted or adapted to their roles when they contribute to conflict between superordinates and subordinates. Dahrendorf called these unconscious concerns **latent interests. Manifest interests** are latent interests that have become conscious. Dahrendorf viewed the analysis of the connection between latent and manifest interests as a major task of conflict theory. Nevertheless, actors need not be conscious of their interests in order to act in accord with them.

---

imperatively coordinated associations   Associations of people controlled by a hierarchy of authority positions.

interests   Concerns, usually shared by groups of people.

latent interests   Unconscious interests that translate, for Dahrendorf, into objective role expectations.

manifest interests   Latent interests of which people have become conscious.

Key Concepts
The Functions of Social Conflict

While structural functionalism and conflict theory are discussed separately, and are at odds with one another in many ways, it is possible to discuss them together. In this box we do just that by discussing the functions of social conflict.

Conflict may serve to solidify a loosely structured group. In a society that seems to be disintegrating, conflict with another society may restore the integrative core. The cohesiveness of Israeli Jews might be attributed, at least in part, to the long-standing conflict with the Arab nations in the Middle East. The possible end of the conflict might well exacerbate underlying strains in Israeli society. Conflict as an agent for solidifying a society is an idea that has long been recognized by propagandists, who may construct an enemy where none exists or seek to fan antagonisms toward an inactive opponent.

Conflict with one group may serve to produce cohesion by leading to a series of alliances with other groups. For example, conflict with the Arabs has led to an alliance between the United States and Israel. Lessening of the Israeli-Arab conflict might weaken the bonds between Israel and the United States.

Within a society, conflict can bring some ordinarily isolated individuals into an active role. The protests over the Vietnam war motivated many young people to take vigorous roles in American political life for the first time. With the end of that conflict a more apathetic spirit emerged again among American youth.

Conflict also serves a communication function. Prior to conflict, groups may be unsure of their adversary's position, but as a result of conflict, positions and boundaries between groups often become clarified. Individuals therefore are better able to decide on a proper course of action in relation to their adversary. Conflict also allows the parties to get a better idea of their relative strengths and may well increase the possibility of rapprochement, or peaceful accommodation.

From a theoretical prospective, it is possible to wed functionalism and conflict theory by looking at the functions of social conflict. Still, it must be recognized that conflict also has dysfunctions.

Groups, Conflict, and Change

Next, Dahrendorf distinguished three broad types of groups. The first is the **quasi group,** or a number of individuals who occupy positions that have the same role interests. These are the recruiting grounds for the second type of group: the **interest group.** Interest groups are true groups in the sociological sense of the term, possessing not only common interests but also a structure, a

---

quasi group   A number of individuals who occupy positions that have the same role interests.

interest group   Unlike quasi groups, interest groups are true groups in the sociological sense of the term, possessing not only common interests, but also a structure, a goal, and personnel. Interest groups have the capacity to engage in group conflict.

goal, and personnel. Interest groups have the capacity to engage in group conflict. Out of all the many interest groups emerge **conflict groups,** those groups that actually engage in conflict.

Dahrendorf felt that the concepts of latent and manifest interests, of quasi groups, interest groups, and conflict groups, were basic to an explanation of social conflict. Under *ideal* conditions no other variables would be needed. However, because conditions are never ideal, many different factors do intervene in the process. Dahrendorf mentioned technical conditions such as adequate personnel, political conditions such as the overall political climate, and social conditions such as the existence of communication links. The way people are recruited into the quasi group was another social condition important to Dahrendorf. He felt that if the recruitment is random and determined by chance, then an interest group, and ultimately a conflict group, is unlikely to emerge. In contrast to Marx, Dahrendorf did not feel that the **lumpenproletariat** (the mass of people who stand below even the proletariat in the capitalist system) would ultimately form a conflict group, because people are recruited to it by chance. However, when recruitment to quasi groups is structurally determined, these groups provide fertile recruiting grounds for interest groups and, in some cases, conflict groups.

The final aspect of Dahrendorf's conflict theory is the relationship of conflict to change. Here Dahrendorf recognized the importance of Lewis Coser's work, which focused on the functions of conflict in maintaining the status quo. Dahrendorf felt, however, that the conservative function of conflict is only one part of social reality; conflict also leads to change and development.

Briefly, Dahrendorf argued that once conflict groups emerge, they engage in actions that lead to changes in social structure. When the conflict is intense, the changes that occur are radical. When it is accompanied by violence, structural change will be sudden. Whatever the nature of conflict, sociologists must be attuned to the relationship between conflict and change as well as that between conflict and the status quo. In other words, they must be sensitized to the dynamic relationships among the various elements involved in this portrait of society. Thus, theoretical portraits need not necessarily be static. This idea is even clearer in the next section on system theory.

GENERAL SYSTEM THEORY[1]

The Work of Niklas Luhmann

The most prominent system theorist in sociology was Niklas Luhmann (1927–1998). Luhmann developed a sociological approach that combined elements of Talcott Parsons's structural functionalism with general systems theory

---

conflict group   A group that actually engages in group conflict.

lumpenproletariat   The mass of people who stand below even the proletariat in the capitalist system.

and introduced concepts from cognitive biology and cybernetics. Luhmann viewed Parsons's later ideas as the only general theory complex enough to form the basis for a new sociological approach that reflects the latest findings in biological and cybernetic systems. However, he recognized two problems with Parsons's approach. First it has no place for self-reference and, according to Luhmann, society's ability to refer to itself is central to our understanding of it as a system. Second, Parsons does not recognize contingency. As a result, Parsons cannot adequately analyze modern society as it is because he does not see that it could be otherwise. To take one example from Parsons's work, the AGIL scheme should not be seen as a fact, but instead as a model of possibilities. The AGIL scheme shows that the adaptive and the goal attainment subsystems can be related in various ways; therefore the aim of analysis should be to understand why the system produced a particular relationship between these two subsystems at any given time. Luhmann addresses these two problems in Parsons's work by developing a theory that takes self-reference as central to systems and that focuses on contingency, the fact that things could be different.

System and Environment   The key to understanding what Luhmann means by a system can be found in the distinction between a system and its environment. Basically, the difference between the two is one of complexity. The system is always less complex than its environment. For example, a business, such as an automobile manufacturer, can be seen as a system that deals with a highly complex environment that includes many different types of people, a constantly changing physical environment, and many other diverse systems. However, this complexity is represented in a much simplified form within the system. When the manufacturer needs raw materials (steel, rubber, etc.), it doesn't normally care where they come from, how they are produced, and the nature of their suppliers. All of this complexity is reduced to information about the price and the quality of the raw materials. Similarly, all the diverse practices of its customers are reduced to those that directly impact whether or not they buy a car.

Simplifying complexity means being forced to select (the manufacturer cares about how raw materials are produced, but may not pay attention to the political situation in the nation in which they are produced). Being forced to select means contingency since one could always select differently (the manufacturer *could* monitor the political situation). And contingency means risk. Thus, if the manufacturer chooses not to monitor the political situation in the nation producing the raw material, the production process might be severely disrupted by a rebellion that shuts off the supply of such material.

A system simply cannot be as complex as its environment. A system that tried would bring to mind the Borges story of the king who ordered a cartographer to create a completely accurate map of his country. When the cartographer was done, the map was as big as the country and was therefore useless as a map. Maps, like systems, must reduce complexity. The cartographer must select what features are important. Different maps of the same area can be made because the selection is contingent. This is always necessary, but it is also risky since the map maker can never be sure that what is left out will not be important to the user. By the way, this point applies to all of the theories (or maps) offered in this chapter; all of them emphasize certain things but inevitably leave out other things.

Although they can never be as complex as their environment, systems develop new subsystems and establish various relations between these subsystems in order to deal effectively with their environment. If they did not, they would be overwhelmed by the complexity of the environment. For example, an automobile manufacturer could create a department of international affairs charged with monitoring political conditions in supplying nations. This new department would be responsible for keeping manufacturing apprised of potential disruptions in the supply of raw materials and for finding alternative sources in case of a disruption. Thus, paradoxically, it is only increasing complexity that can reduce complexity.

Autopoietic Systems

Luhmann is best known for his thinking on autopoiesis. This concept refers to a diversity of systems from biological cells to the entire world society. Luhmann uses the term to refer to such systems as the economy, the political system, the legal system, the scientific system, and bureaucracies, among others. **Autopoietic systems** have the following four characteristics.

1. An autopoietic system produces the basic elements that make up the system. This may seem paradoxical. How can a system produce its own elements, the very things out of which it is made? Think of a modern economic system and its basic element, money. We say money is a basic element because the value of things in the economic system can be given in terms of money, but it is very difficult to say what money itself is worth. The meaning of money, what it is worth, and what it can be used for are determined by the economic system itself. Money, as we understand that term today, did not exist before the economic system. Both the modern form of money and the economic system emerged together and they depend on each other. A modern economic system without money is difficult to imagine. Money without an economic system is just a piece of paper or metal.
2. Autopoietic systems are self-organizing in two ways: They organize their own boundaries and they organize their internal structures. They organize their own boundaries by distinguishing between what is in the system and what is in the environment. For example, the economic system counts anything that is scarce and on which a price can be set as part of the economic system. Air is everywhere in abundant supply; therefore, no price is set on it and it is not part of the economic system. Air is, however, a necessary

---

autopoietic systems   Systems that produce their own basic elements, establish their own boundaries and structures, are self-referential, and are closed.

part of the environment. What is inside or outside an autopoietic system is determined by the self-organization of the system and not, as a structural functionalist would have us believe, by the functional necessities of the system.

Other forces may try to limit the scope of autopoietic systems. For example, capitalist economic systems have always expanded their boundaries in order to include sex and illicit drugs. This occurs even though the political system passes laws aimed at keeping sex or illicit drugs from becoming economic commodities. Rather than keeping them out of the economic system, such laws instead affect the prices of sex and illicit drugs *within* the economic system. Their illegality makes their prices higher, thereby discouraging their purchase. But within the economic system, the high prices that discourage purchases also encourage sales. If a great deal of money can be made from selling sex and drugs, they will remain in the economic system. Therefore, laws that try to keep a commodity out of the economic system simply affect the way they are priced within the economic system.

Within its boundaries, an autopoietic system produces its own structures. For example, because of the existence of money, markets are structured in an impersonal way, banks are established to store and lend money, the concept of interest has developed, and so on. If the economic system did not have as its basic element such an abstract and portable entity as money, the internal structure would be entirely different. For example, if the economy were based on barter instead of money, there would be no banks, no concept of interest; and markets where goods are bought and sold would be structured in entirely different ways.

3. Autopoietic systems are self-referential. For example, the economic system uses price as a way of referring to itself. By attaching a fluctuating monetary value to shares in a company, the stock market exemplifies such self-reference within the economic system. The prices in the stock market are determined not by any individual but by the economy itself. Similarly, the legal system has laws that refer to the legal system: laws about how laws can be enacted, applied, interpreted, and so on.

4. An autopoietic system is a closed system. This means that there is no direct connection between a system and its environment. Instead, a system deals with its representations of the environment. For example, the economic system supposedly responds to the material needs and desires of people; however, those needs and desires affect the economic system only to the extent that they can be represented in terms of money. Consequently, the economic system responds well to the material needs and desires of rich people but very poorly to the needs and desires of poor people.

Another example is a bureaucracy such as the Internal Revenue Service (IRS). The IRS never really deals with its clients; it deals solely with representations of the clients. Taxpayers are represented by the forms they file and that are filed about them. The real taxpayer has an effect on the bureaucracy only by causing a disturbance in the bureaucracy's representations. Those who cause disturbances (with misfiled forms, contradictory forms, false forms) often are dealt with very harshly because they threaten the system.

Even though an autopoietic system is closed with no direct connection to the environment, the environment must be allowed to disturb its inner representations. Without such disturbances, the system would be destroyed by environmental forces that would overwhelm it. For example, the prices of stocks in the stock market fluctuate daily. The difference between the price of a company's stock from one day to the next has little to do with the real value of the company—that is, its assets or profits—and everything to do with the state of the stock market. The market may be in a boom period (a bull market) in which the prices of stocks are far higher than they should be, given the state of the companies involved. However, over the long run the price of stocks needs to reflect the actual status of the companies involved or the system will fall apart. This is what happened in the stock market crash of 1929. Because the prices of stocks had no relation to real value, the system reached a state of crisis. To function properly, the stock market as a system must periodically be disturbed by the actual condition of the companies that are part of its environment.

A closed social system is distinct from the individuals that appear to be part of it. According to Luhmann, in such systems, the individual is part of the environment. To take the example of a bureaucracy again, this means that not only are the clients part of the environment, but so are the people who work in the bureaucracy. From the perspective of the bureaucracy, the people who work in it are external sources of complexity and unpredictability. In order to be a closed system, the bureaucracy must find a way to represent even its own workers in a simplified way. Thus, instead of being seen as full-fledged human beings, one worker is seen as a manager, another as an accountant, and so on. The real, fully human worker affects the bureaucracy only as a disturbance to the bureaucracy's representations.

Differentiation

From the viewpoint of Luhmann's system theory, the principal feature of modern society is the increased process of system differentiation as a way of dealing with the complexity of its environment. **Differentiation** involves an effort to copy within a system the difference between it and the environment. This means that within a differentiated system there are two kinds of environments: one common to all subsystems and a different internal environment for each subsystem. For example, an automobile manufacturer, such as BMW, considers other manufacturers, Toyota and Nissan, as part of its environment. The international relations department (a subsystem) of BMW also considers Toyota and Nissan as outside it and part of its environment. However, the

---

differentiation The system copying within itself the difference between it and the environment.

international relations department views other subsystems within BMW (such as the human relations department [subsystem]) as outside the international relations subsystem and therefore part of its environment. Other subsystems such as the human relations department are internal to the organizational system as a whole, but are in the environment of the international relations subsystem, hence an internal environment. Similarly, the human relations subsystem considers other manufacturers as part of its environment, but in addition views other subsystems (this time including the international relations subsystem) as part of its environment. Therefore, each of the subsystems has a different view of the internal environment of the system, which creates a highly complex and dynamic internal environment.

Differentiation within a system is a way of dealing with changes in the environment. Each system must maintain its boundary in relation to the environment. Otherwise, it would be overwhelmed by the complexity of its environment, break down, and cease to exist. In order to survive, the system must be able to deal with environmental variations. For instance, it is well known that any large-scale organization as a system adjusts slowly to alterations in its environment (e.g., concrete demands by the public, political changes, or even technological changes such as the availability of personal computers). However, organizations do develop; they evolve by creating differentiation within the system. In other words, an environmental change will be translated into the structure of the organization. An example is the creation by the automobile manufacturer of a new department to deal with a new situation such as the presence of personal computers in the workplace. New workers will be hired; they will be trained to handle the new technology; a manager will be selected; and so forth.

The differentiation process is a means of increasing the complexity of the system, since each subsystem can make different connections with other subsystems. It allows for more variation within the system in order to respond to variation in the environment. In the previous example, the new department is, like every other department of the bureaucratic system, an environment for other departments, but the new one increases organizational complexity because new and additional relations between departments are made possible. A new department created to service workers' computers will be better able to respond to further changes in computer technologies and to help the entire organization to integrate these new capabilities. In addition, it may provide for new connections between existing departments, such as allowing general accounting to be centralized or salespeople to access inventory directly.

More variation caused by differentiation not only allows for better responses to the environment, but also allows for faster evolution. **Evolution** is a process of selection from variation. The more variation that is available, the better the selection. However, Luhmann argues that only a few forms of internal differentiation have developed. He calls these segmentation, stratification,

---

evolution   The process of selection from variation.

center-periphery, and functional differentiation. These differentiations increase the complexity of the system through the repetition of the differentiation between system and environment within the system. In terms of their evolutionary potential, these forms of differentiation have a different ability to produce variability and therefore provide for more selectivity for evolutionary processes. The more complex forms of differentiation have the potential to accelerate the evolution of the system.

Segmentary Differentiation   **Segmentary differentiation** divides parts of the system on the basis of the need to fulfill identical functions over and over. For instance, an automobile manufacturer has functionally similar factories for the production of cars at many different locations. Every location is organized in much the same way; each has the same structure and fulfills the same function—producing cars.

Stratificatory Differentiation   **Stratificatory differentiation** is a vertical differentiation according to rank or status in a system conceived as a hierarchy. Every rank fulfills a particular and distinct function in the system. In the automobile firm, we find different ranks. The manager of the new department of international relations occupies the top rank within the hierarchy of that department. The manager has the function of using power to direct the operations of that department. A variety of lower-ranking workers within the department handle a variety of specific functions (e.g., word processing). In addition, the manager of the department of international relations has a position within the stratificatory system of the automobile manufacturer. The president of the company has a higher-ranking position than that of the manager of international relations and is in a position to issue orders to the latter.

In segmentary differentiation, inequality results from accidental variations in environments (such as more cars being sold in one geographic area than another), but it has no systemic function. In stratificatory differentiation, inequality is essential to the system. More correctly, we see the interplay of equality and inequality. All members in the same ranks (e.g., all the word processors) are basically equal, while different ranks are distinguished by their inequality. The higher ranks (e.g., department managers) have more access to resources and greater ability to become the subject of influential communications. Consequently, a stratified system is more concerned with the well-being of those in the upper ranks and generally is concerned about the lower ranks only if they threaten the higher ranks. However, both ranks depend on one another and the social system can survive only if all ranks, including the lowest, successfully realize their functions.

---

segmentary differentiation   The division of parts of the system on the basis of the need to fulfill identical functions over and over.

stratificatory differentiation   Vertical differentiation according to rank or status in a system conceived as a hierarchy.

Niklas Luhmann (1927–1998)
A Biographical Vignette

As a system theorist, Niklas Luhmann's name is almost always closely tied to that of Talcott Parsons. As we saw earlier in this chapter, Parsons wrote a great deal about systems and his ideas influenced the later thinking of Luhmann. Furthermore, Luhmann got to know Parsons when he studied public administration at Harvard in 1960–1961.This inevitably led to an assumed linkage between Luhmann and structural functionalism (the theory for which Parsons was most famous). Since structural functionalism fell out of favor by the late 1960s, Luhmann's linkage to it led him to have less influence than he otherwise might have had, especially in the United States. However, in recent years it has become clear that while Luhmann is a system theorist, he is *not* a structural functionalist and, among other things, has a very different sense of structure than Parsons and rejects Parsons's focus on such things as value consensus in society and social order. As it is increasingly freed of its linkages to structural functionalism, Luhmann's system theory has an increasing influence on social theory around the world.

The importance of the lower ranks and yet their difficulty in becoming the subject of influential communication create a structural problem that limits the complexity of the system. When those directing the system become too removed from the lowest ranks, the system tends to collapse because the important functions of the lowest ranks are not being properly performed. In order to have an effect on the system, the lower ranks must resort to conflict.

Center-Periphery Differentiation   The third type of differentiation, **center-periphery differentiation,** is a link between segmentary and stratificatory differentiation. For instance, some automobile firms have built factories in other countries; nevertheless, the headquarters of the company remains the center, ruling and, to some extent, controlling the peripheral factories.

Differentiations of Functional Systems   **Functional differentiation** is the most complex form of differentiation and the form that dominates modern society. Every function within a system is ascribed to a particular unit. For instance, an automobile manufacturer has functionally differentiated departments such as production, administration, accounting, planning, and personnel.

Functional differentiation is more flexible than stratificatory differentiation, but, if one system fails to fulfill its task, the whole system will have great trouble surviving. However, as long as each unit fulfills its function, the

---

center-periphery differentiation   Differentiation between the core of a system and its peripheral elements.

functional differentiation   The most complex form of differentiation and the form that dominates modern society. Every function within a system is ascribed to a particular unit.

different units can attain a high degree of independence. In fact, functionally differentiated systems are a complex mixture of interdependence and independence. For instance, although the planning division is dependent upon the accounting division for economic data, as long as the figures are accurate, the planning division can be blissfully ignorant of exactly how the accountants produced the data.

This indicates a further difference between the forms of differentiation. In the case of segmentary differentiation, if a segment fails to fulfill its function (e.g., one of the automobile manufacturer's factories cannot produce cars because of a labor strike), it does not threaten the system. However, in the case of the more complex forms of differentiation such as functional differentiation, failure will cause a problem for the social system, possibly leading to its breakdown. On the one hand, the growth of complexity increases the abilities of a system to deal with its environment. On the other hand, complexity increases the risk of a system breakdown if a function is not properly fulfilled.

In most cases, this increased vulnerability is a necessary price to pay for the increase in possible relations between different subsystems. Having more types of possible relations between the subsystems means more variation to use to select structural responses to changes in the environment. In a segmentary system, the relations between different subsystems are not structurally different. For example, the relations that any two factories have with each other are all basically the same. In a stratified system, the relations between ranks are basically different from those within the rank. For example, the relations that a factory has with headquarters is different from those that it has with another factory. In functionally differentiated systems, the different relations multiply. The accounting and production departments have a different relationship with each other than that between accounting and research, which is, in turn, different from the relationship between production and research. Functional differentiation gives the automobile manufacturer greater flexibility. Thus, in an environment in which technical advances are providing opportunities for economic advantage, the company can be led by research, but in an environment in which economic advantage is found in doing the same old thing, only cheaper, the company can be led by accounting.

We should note that the more complex forms of differentiation do not exclude the less complex forms, and, in fact, they may require the less complex forms. For example, an automobile manufacturer is stratified, but it still contains individual factories that are a segmentary form. This is important, since we usually speak of functionally differentiated systems within modern society to describe its dominant mode of differentiation; nevertheless, the other forms continue to exist.

Code   A **code** is a way to distinguish elements of a system from elements that do not belong to the system. A code is the basic language of a functional system.

---

code   A way of distinguishing elements of a system from elements that do not belong to the system; the basic language of a functional system.

Contemporary Applications
Is the "War on Terror" Functional?

In the aftermath of September 11, the United States embarked on a so-called war on terror. As a social phenomenon, that "war" is analyzable from a variety of theoretical perspectives, including the structural-functional perspective discussed in this chapter. It qualifies for such analysis because it is a structure that is both repetitive and patterned. This is best exemplified by the Department of Homeland Security, but it applies as well to the many places and ways in which that "war" is being fought.

The first issue to be addressed is the "functions" of this war, the ways in which it has helped the United States adjust and adapt to the reality that there are external enemies able and willing to inflict significant damage on the country. Among the things that can be mentioned here is that Osama bin Laden (the al-Qaeda leader behind the 9/11 attacks) has been hounded, forced into hiding, and apparently largely neutralized; Saddam Hussein (falsely presumed to be an ally and supporter of al-Qaeda) was forced from power and executed; all sorts of security measures have been put in place in and around the United States; and perhaps most important of all, there have been no additional terror incidents in the United States (such incidents have occurred elsewhere, notably the Madrid and London train bombings) since 9/11 and there is some evidence that several have been warded off.

However, there are also a number of "dysfunctions" associated with the war on terror. Among them is the high economic cost of fighting this war, especially in the occupation of Iraq and in fighting those who opposed the American presence there. Of course, the economic cost is small in comparison with the loss of human lives in Iraq. Then there are the enemies that the United States has made as a result of its military actions in Iraq and Afghanistan, as well as other actions such as the capture and abduction of thousands of people and their incarceration in Guantanamo Bay, Cuba, and elsewhere. There are many seemingly tangential dysfunctions such as that poppy growing in Afghanistan has grown dramatically since the fundamentalist and repressive Taliban were forced from power, thereby increasing the source of cocaine for illegal sale in many countries, including the United States. In the United States, many programs—social welfare, spending on infrastructure—are being starved for funds because the money is being spent elsewhere.

The big question in terms of net balance becomes: Do the functions of this war outweigh the dysfunctions, or vice versa? For some groups, it is certainly functional (e.g., defense contractors) and for others it is dysfunctional (most Iraqis, American welfare recipients), but what of the United States as a whole? A systematic analysis of the functions and dysfunctions of the war on terror does not yield a ready and simple answer for the nation as a whole, but it does offer a systematic way of trying to think through what such an answer would look like.

Codes are, for instance, truth (versus nontruth) for the science system, payment (versus nonpayment) for the economic system, and legality (versus illegality) for the legal system. Every communication using a particular code is a part of the system whose code reference is being used.

A code is used to limit the kind of permissible communication. Every communication that does not use the code is not a communication belonging to the system under consideration. Thus, within the scientific system we will usually find only communications with reference to the code of truth. For instance, if the head of NASA (National Aeronautics and Space Administration) and the head of NIH (National Institutes of Health) met to discuss what facts had been discovered about aging in John Glenn's 1998 space flight, the matter would be part of the scientific system using the code of truth or nontruth. If these same people met to discuss who will pay for what part of the research conducted on that space flight, the matter would be in the economic system using the code of payment or nonpayment.

In Luhmann's system theory, no system uses and understands the code of another system. There is no way to translate the code of one system into the code of another system. Because the systems are closed, they can react only to things happening in their environment (if what happens makes enough noise to be noticed by the system). But the system must describe the noise in the environment in relation to its own code. This is the only way to make sense of what is happening, the only way to give it meaning. For example, an economic system views a scientific system only in terms of what makes money (makes future payments possible) or requires investments (requires initial payments before it can be repaid).

Summary

1. Structural functionalism is a theory that focuses on the structures of society and their functional significance (positive and negative consequences) for other structures.
2. One type of structural functionalism is societal functionalism, which focuses on the large-scale social structures and institutions of society, their interrelationships, and their constraining effects on actors.
3. To structural functionalists, stratification is a functional necessity. All societies need such a system, and this need brings into existence a system of stratification. The stratification system is viewed as a societal-level structure, referring not to the individuals in the stratification system but rather to a system of positions (e.g., occupations like laborer and manager).
4. People must be offered great rewards in order to do what is necessary to occupy the high-ranking and crucially important positions in the stratification system.
5. The functional theory of stratification has come under great attack. The key point is that there are ways to motivate people to do things other than offering them inordinate benefits.
6. To Parsons any system is faced with four functional imperatives: adaptation, goal attainment, integration, and pattern maintenance (or latency).
7. The four action systems in order of their control over the system below them are cultural, social, personality, and behavioral organism.
8. Robert Merton developed a sophisticated model of a structural-functional approach involving a focus not only on functions, but also dysfunctions, nonfunctions, net balance, levels of functional analysis, manifest and latent functions, and unanticipated consequences.

9. Conflict theory developed in reaction to structural functionalism and is in many ways its mirror image, focusing on change (rather than equilibrium), dissension and conflict (rather than order), forces that contribute to disintegration (rather than integration), and the coercion that holds society together (rather than norms and values).

10. Dahrendorf's focus was on authority, which always implies superordination and subordination. The organizations in which authority positions are found are called imperatively coordinated associations.

11. Groups within these associations are defined by their interests; superordinate and subordinate groups each have common interests.

12. Three types of groups are formed in imperatively coordinated associations, especially among those in subordinate positions. The quasi group is a number of individuals who occupy positions that have the same role interests. These are the recruiting grounds for interest groups that have the capacity to engage in group conflict. Out of all the many interest groups emerge conflict groups, or those groups that actually engage in conflict.

13. Conflict has the capacity to lead to change.

14. Key to understanding Luhmann's distinction between system and environment is the fact that the system is always less complex than the environment.

15. Although a system can never be as complex as its environment, it develops new subsystems and relationships among them to deal with the environment and its complexity.

16. Autopoietic systems have several basic characteristics: They produce the elements that make them up, they are self-organizing in terms of boundaries and internal structures, they are self-referential, and they are closed.

17. Differentiation is the effort to copy within a system the difference between itself and the environment; this leads to increasing complexity.

18. The four types of differentiation are segmentary, stratificatory, center-periphery, and functional.

19. Functional differentiation is the most complex form and the one that dominates society.

20. Code is the language that makes it possible to distinguish elements of a system from those that do not belong to it.

Suggested Readings

MARK ABRAHAMSON *Functionalism*. Englewood Cliffs, NJ: Prentice Hall, 1978. Interesting brief introduction to structural functionalism.

MELVIN TUMIN "Some Principles of Stratification: A Critical Analysis." *American Sociological Theory* 18, 1953: 387–394. The classic critique of the structural functional theory of stratification.

VICTOR LIDZ "Talcott Parsons." In George Ritzer, ed., *The Blackwell Companion to Major Social Theorists*. Malden, MA, and Oxford, England: Blackwell, 2000, pp. 388–431. Overview of the life and work of Talcott Parsons authored by one of his former students.

RICHARD MUNCH "Talcott Parsons." In George Ritzer, ed., *The Encyclopedia of Social Theory*, 2 volumes. Thousand Oaks, CA: Sage, 2005, pp. 550–555. Overview of some of Parsons's most important ideas by a leading German disciple.

PIOTR SZTOMPKA *Robert K. Merton: An Intellectual Profile.* London and New York: Macmillan and St. Martin's Press, 1986. Book-length treatment of Merton's life and work.

PIOTR SZTOMPKA "Robert Merton." In George Ritzer, ed., *The Blackwell Companion to Major Social Theorists.* Malden, MA, and Oxford, England: Blackwell, 2000, pp. 435–456. Updated treatment of Merton's contributions to sociological theory.

PIOTR SZTOMPKA "Robert Merton." In George Ritzer, ed., *The Encyclopedia of Social Theory,* 2 volumes. Thousand Oaks, CA: Sage, 2005, pp. 499–500. A brief sketch of Merton's perspective that is barely able to scratch the surface on Merton's many contributions to social theory. The author is an intellectual biographer and disciple of Merton.

RANDALL COLLINS *Conflict Sociology: Toward an Explanatory Science.* New York: Academic Press, 1975. Important, more contemporary, and micro-oriented contribution to conflict theory.

LEWIS COSER *The Functions of Social Conflict.* New York: Free Press. Classic effort to integrate conflict theory and structural functionalism.

JONATHAN TURNER "Conflict Theory." In George Ritzer, ed., *The Encyclopedia of Social Theory,* 2 volumes. Thousand Oaks, CA: Sage, 2005, pp. 134–138. Nice overview of some of the major types of conflict theory by an important contributor to that theory and to social theory in general.

NIKLAS LUHMANN "Modern Systems Theory and the Theory of Society." In V. Meja, D. Misgeld, and N. Stehr, eds., *Modern German Sociology.* New York: Columbia University Press, 1987, pp. 173–186. Early but comparatively readable rendition of some of Luhmann's basic ideas on systems theory.

GERD NOLLMANN "Niklas Luhmann." In George Ritzer, ed., *The Encyclopedia of Social Theory,* 2 volumes. Thousand Oaks, CA: Sage, 2005, pp. 454–457. Brief overview of Luhmann's ideas with particular attention to the relationship between his ideas and those of Parsons.

KENNETH BAILEY "General Systems Theory." In George Ritzer, ed., *The Encyclopedia of Social Theory,* 2 volumes. Thousand Oaks, CA: Sage, 2005, pp. 309–315. A prominent systems theorist offers a broad overview of this theory that puts Luhmann's contribution in the context of the work of other theorists and theoretical ideas.

Endnote

[1]This section was co-authored by Douglas Goodman and Matthias Junge.

CHAPTER 5

Contemporary Grand Theories II

This chapter deals with four more important modern grand theories. We begin with neo-Marxian theory, which encompasses such a broad range of theories that we are able to focus on only two of its main varieties—critical theory and theories of the nature of space is the contemporary world. We then turn to grand theories closely associated with contemporary theorists—Norbert Elias's civilizing process, Jürgen Habermas's (a later critical theorist) colonization of the lifeworld, and Anthony Giddens's juggernaut of modernity. The theories covered here and in the previous chapter constitute only a small sample of the wide range of contemporary grand theories.

NEO-MARXIAN THEORY

Many theorists followed Marx and over the years took his theories in many different directions; there are a number of neo-Marxian theories. It is worth noting that not all neo-Marxian theories offer grand narratives, but several, including the two to be discussed here, do closely follow Marx in the sense of offering theories of great sweep.

Critical Theory and the Emergence of the Culture Industry

Critical theory was founded in 1923 at the Institute of Social Research in Frankfurt, Germany. However, in the 1930s the Institute was taken over by the Nazis and the theorists associated with it were forced to flee, many of them to the United States. Many of critical theory's most important ideas were formulated in the United States, but with the end of World War II many of its practitioners gradually returned to Germany.

As the name suggests, the critical theorists were social (and intellectual) critics. In this they were following Marx, who was a critic of capitalism. The focus of Marx's work was on the economy because in the era in which he lived (the height of the Industrial Revolution) the economy was of overwhelming importance. However, critical theory is based on the idea that in the half century or so between Marx's *Capital* and the heyday of the critical school, capitalism had undergone a dramatic change. The most important aspect of society was in the process of shifting from the economy to the culture; people were more and more likely to be controlled by the culture rather than the economy. Thus, the critical school had to focus its critical gaze not on the economy (where Marx and many of his followers, even to this day, concentrated), but rather on the culture.

Marx, and those who followed immediately in his wake, tended to think of culture, along with the state, as a **superstructure** erected on an economic **base.** In other words, the economy is of prime importance and everything else in society is based on it. The capitalist economy was seen as especially powerful and it played a central role in determining and controlling culture and the state. Both tended to be seen as mechanisms manipulated by the capitalists in order to further their own economic interests. What the critical theorists argued was that culture, as well as those who lead and control it, has achieved significant autonomy from the capitalists. In this and in their focus on the culture industry, the critical theorists took a position radically different from virtually all Marxists who had come before them.

Culture   At the most general level, the critical theorists were most concerned with what they called the **culture industry** and its increasing domination of society in general and of individuals in particular. The critical theorists were sensitized to the rise of what has come to be called **mass culture.** In their day, the major disseminators of culture to the masses were newspapers, magazines, and the relatively new movies and radio broadcasts. Those media continue to be important today, but we now have newer and far more powerful disseminators of mass culture, most notably television and the Internet. Although it is clear that if the critical theorists were right in their day to be interested in the culture industry, there is far more reason to be concerned with it today.

---

superstructure   To Marx, secondary social phenomena, like the state and culture, that are erected on an economic base that serves to define them. Most extremely, the economy determines the superstructure.

base   To Marx, the economy, which conditions, if not determines, the nature of everything else in society.

culture industry   To the critical theorists, industries such as movies and radio that were serving to make culture a more important factor in society than the economy.

mass culture   The culture (e.g., radio quiz shows) that had been made available to, and popular among, the masses.

Why were the critical theorists so concerned about culture? For one thing, the impact of culture is more pervasive than that of work. Work largely affects people while they are on the job, but the impact of culture is felt around-the-clock, seven days a week. Another reason is that culture's impact is far more insidious—gradually working its way into people's consciousness and altering the way they think, feel, and act. Third, at work people know that they are being dominated. This is quite clear when they are given orders, when they are being forced to do certain things over and over again by technologies like the assembly line, and when they are laid off or fired. In the case of culture, control is largely invisible. In fact, people crave more and more mass culture (more radio and TV shows, and today, more time on the Internet) without realizing the way it exercises domination over them. In a sense, the critical theorists came to the realization that people had come to seek out their own domination.

Culture came to dominate people in various ways. The most important was what Marx called an opiate of the masses. Lulled into semiconsciousness by the culture industry, the proletariat would not be receptive to revolutionary messages. This was a very pleasant kind of control. Rather than being controlled at gun point, or by the whip, the masses were controlled in the 1930s, for example, by a steady diet of Hollywood B-movies that did not elevate their tastes, but reduced them to the lowest common denominator. In addition, there was the string of nightly radio programs with listeners tuned in for hours to low-brow comedies, dramas, and contests of one kind or another. Radio also served to bring mass sports into people's homes so that additional hours could be spent listening to the exploits of one's favorite professional and college teams. People entertained for many hours a week were likely to lose whatever hostility they might have had to the capitalist system. Furthermore, the sheer amount of time listening to the radio or going to the movies, combined with the hours spent at work, left little time for revolutionary reading and thinking, let alone action.

Today, of course, other media play the central role in narcotizing the masses. Television is a key player, with endless soap operas during the day followed by one reality show after another at night. The latter are, at least for the moment, among the most watched programs on network television. Millions of viewers devote several hours a week to watching people compete with one another to win the money they need, without having to work for it or to be players in the capitalist economic system. Instead of rebelling against the capitalist system, viewers are left to daydream about what they would do with all that money.

But the culture industry of the 1930s, 1940s, and today has played a much more direct role in the maintenance of capitalism by turning more and more people into consumers. As mass consumers, people came to play another central role (the other was as worker) in the capitalist system. Their consumption served as an important motor of capitalist production. In the early 1900s that ultimate capitalist Henry Ford recognized this by paying his workers an adequate enough wage to buy his products as well as those of other capitalist enterprises. Of course, the key development was the growing magnitude and sophistication of the advertising industry. Radio was a wonderful new medium for advertising, while the mass magazines and newspapers (especially the tabloids) were a more traditional medium for advertisers. Spurred on by these advertisements, people spent more and more time shopping; once again, time was not being used to think about and undertake social revolution. Furthermore, the burgeoning needs of consumers meant that they had to work as much as they could, seek as much overtime as possible, and even work second jobs, in order to be able to afford all those goodies being advertised everywhere. Working not only further reduced the amount of time for revolutionary activities, but the additional time at work and the energy expended working meant that the proletariat had even less energy for revolution. They had just about enough strength left at the end of the workday or workweek to drag themselves home, switch on the radio, and doze off during lulls in the action.

If this was true of America in the 1930s, it is far more true of America in the early years of the 21st century. However, in the interim the culture industry has grown far more powerful and infinitely more sophisticated. Few of us switch on the radio at night, but virtually all of us turn on the television set, often for many hours. We still go the movies on occasion, but with the advent of DVDs and on-demand movies we no longer need to go out to see a movie. Magazines are more numerous and more spectacular than their predecessors. Newspapers are less prevalent, but those that remain are emulating *USA Today* and becoming more attractive and seductive. Then there are the home computer and the Internet. Although they are wonderful tools for education, most people use them for online social networking (e.g., Facebook, Twitter), entertainment (especially video games) and, increasingly, to shop 24 hours a day, 365 days a year. Because shopping is the favorite leisure activity of Americans, they spend many long hours after work and on weekends at the shopping mall (or, at least they did before the onset of the recession which began in late 2007). Vacation is likely to be spent consuming services and goods in places like a Las Vegas casino-hotel, a cruise ship, or Disney World. Today's opiates are far more numerous, ever-present, and sophisticated than those the critical theorists were so concerned about. The tools at the disposal of advertisers are much more sophisticated and their ability to manipulate us into consuming is much greater. And there is infinitely more time available for shopping and many more venues, both real and virtual, in which we can do our shopping. All of this means, of course, that there is much less interest in and time for revolutionary thinking and action. In fact, there is virtually no sign in the contemporary United States of any interest in revolution. As the critical theorists might put it, people are too anesthetized by the mass media, too busy shopping and working to afford what they buy when they shop, to think very much about revolution, let alone to act on such thoughts.

It seems clear that an even better argument could be made today that the major source of domination over people is the culture and not the economic system. Work has come to play a less important role in people's lives, while culture, the consumption of it, and the wares associated with it have grown dramatically in importance. To put it succinctly, the shopping mall is now far more important than the factory (especially in developed nations such as the United States), and the fully enclosed shopping mall (which did not exist

---

Herbert Marcuse (1898–1979)
A Biographical Vignette

Herbert Marcuse was a member of the Critical School and a major contributor to critical theory. He became a major public intellectual in the United States and in Europe in the 1960s and 1970s because his ideas resonated well with the revolutionaries, especially students, who were protesting the Vietnam War and oppression in its various forms. Marcuse was a critic of repression wherever he found it, but especially in advanced capitalist society, and its negative effects on people. This theme is apparent in his best-known book, *One-Dimensional Man* (1964), published just before the advent of the revolutionary movements of the late 1960s and a powerful influence on them. Among other things, Marcuse singled out modern technology, especially television (were he alive today he might have said many of the same things about the computer and the Internet), for advances in repression, especially its ability to make repression seem so pleasant. Television, and other contemporary technologies, invade individuals and serve to whittle them down. As a result people become "one-dimensional." They become more-or-less what these repressive, but oh so pleasant, technologies tell them to be. In the process they lose a key dimension—the ability to think critically and negatively about many things, including the society and technologies that are repressing them. The answer, for Marcuse, is not the elimination of modern technologies (they are here to stay and will only increase), but the wresting of control of them away from oppressive forces and putting them in the hands of free people. Clearly, such a critique and political program were attractive to student (and other) radicals of the late 1960s and, to some, they remain attractive today in light of continuing advances in television technology and the development of new technologies (e.g., iPod, Xbox) that make repression even more ubiquitous and deeply implicated in our everyday lives.

---

during the heyday of the critical school) is one of the centers of contemporary mass culture. Inside a megamall like Mall of America, outside Minneapolis, is an amusement park; in addition, the mall encompasses shops that push the latest fashions, movie theaters, video rental stores, Walt Disney stores, play centers for children, fast-food and theme restaurants, educational centers, religious sites, and on and on. A visit to a shopping mall is a visit to many of the elements of contemporary mass culture. One rarely sees any revolutionary consciousness expressed, or revolutionary action undertaken, in a shopping mall.

Modern Technology   Implicit in the critique of the culture industry is the critical school's attack on modern technology. Obviously, many of today's key elements of the culture industry—television, computers, the Internet—are the result of technological advances that occurred after the heyday of the critical school. But the critical school itself confronted new technologies (e.g., the radio) that it saw as creating major problems for, and sources of control over, people.

Rather than being controlled by people, these technologies controlled people. However, the main thrust of the work of the critical school was to argue that it was not technology per se that was the problem, but the way technology was deployed and employed in capitalism. Thus, the capitalists used technology to control people, deaden their critical capacities, and greatly limit their ability to revolt against this inherently exploitative system. Critical theorists believed that in another economic system, say, socialism, technology could be used to make people more conscious, more critical, and resistant to exploitative systems like capitalism. Thus, instead of offering mediocre programs designed mainly to help sell things, radio programs could be truly stimulating and educational.

Focusing on the role of technology, one critical theorist, Herbert Marcuse, argued that it was being used to create what he called a **one-dimensional society.** In an ideal world Marcuse, like Marx and many other Marxists, saw a dialectical relationship between people and the larger structures, like technology, that they created. In other words, people should be fulfilling their needs and expressing their abilities as they create, employ, and alter technologies. In this way, both people and technology would flourish. However, in capitalism this is transformed into a one-sided relationship. People create technology, but it is owned and controlled by the capitalists and it is used by them to their own advantage to control and exploit workers. Thus, instead of expressing themselves through the use of technology, people are impoverished by the control exerted over them by technology. Individuality is suppressed as everyone conforms to the demands of technology. Gradually, individual freedom and creativity dwindle away into nothingness. As a result, people lose the capacity to think critically and negatively not only about technology but the society that controls and oppresses them. Without that ability, people are unable to revolt against and overthrow the capitalist system. The answer to this problem from Marcuse's perspective is the creation of a society in which people (i.e., the proletariat) control technology rather than being controlled by it.

The technologies employed by the capitalists, such as the assembly line, tend to be highly rationalized; this fact relates to another central concern of the critical theorists. Strongly influenced not only by Karl Marx but also Max Weber, they tended to argue that society was growing increasingly rationalized. Like Weber, some of them even came to see that increasing rationalization, rather than capitalism, was the central problem of their day. This rationalization undergirded not only the technologies being put into place but also the culture industry; both were growing increasingly rationalized.

---

one-dimensional society   To Herbert Marcuse, the breakdown in the dialectical relationship between people and the larger structures so that people are largely controlled by such structures. Lost is the ability of people to create and to be actively involved in those structures. Gradually, individual freedom and creativity dwindle away into nothingness, and people lose the capacity to think critically and negatively about the structures that control and oppress them.

In their view, increasing rationality tends to lead to **technocratic thinking.** That is, people grow concerned with being efficient, with simply finding the best means to an end without reflecting on either the means or the end. An example is the Nazis associated with the concentration camps (given their origins in Germany, many observers feel that the critical theorists anticipated the horrors associated with Nazism), who focused all of their attention and energies on the goal of killing the greatest number of Jews using the most efficient means (e.g., the gas chambers) possible. Such thinking serves the interests of those in power.

In the case of capitalism, both the capitalists and the proletariat were dominated by this kind of thinking. However, the critical theorists were most interested in and concerned about the proletariat. For example, an assembly line worker is led, even forced, to concentrate on working as efficiently as possible. The continual pressure of the assembly line leaves workers little or no time to reflect on how they are doing the work and how tiring and debilitating it is to do one thing over and over. Furthermore, it leaves them even less time and energy to think about the ends of the production process, say, the automobiles that roll off the assembly line and the fact that they kill and maim many thousands of people each year, pollute the air, use up valuable natural resources, and so on.

What is lost in the process is the alternative to technocratic thinking, **reason,** which assesses means to ends in terms of ultimate human values such as justice, freedom, and happiness. Reason, to critical thinkers, is the hope for humanity. Auschwitz, for example, was a very rational place, but it was certainly not reasonable. If the Nazis had employed reason rather than technocratic thinking, the Holocaust would never have occurred because the actions associated with it flew in the face of all human values. Much the same could be said of capitalism: It is very rational but not very reasonable. To the critical theorists the hope for society was the creation of a society dominated by reason rather than technocratic thinking, where human values take precedence over efficiency.

In other words, despite the seeming rationality of capitalism, it is a system rife with irrationality. This is the notion of the **irrationality of rationality;** rational systems inevitably spawn a series of irrationalities. In the rational world of capitalism, it is irrational that such a system is destructive of individuals and their needs and abilities; that technology makes them one-dimensional; that the culture industry controls them rather than helping them to express their finest aspirations and abilities; and that despite the existence of more than sufficient wealth, many people remain impoverished, repressed, exploited, and unable to fulfill themselves.

---

technocratic thinking   Concern with being efficient, with simply finding the best means to an end without reflecting on either the means or the end.

reason   People assess the choice of means to ends in terms of ultimate human values such as justice, freedom, and happiness.

irrationality of rationality   The idea that rational systems inevitably spawn a series of irrationalities.

Key Concept
Knowledge Industry

Another sector of society that came under attack by the critical school was what they called the **knowledge industry.** Paralleling the idea of the culture industry, this term refers to those entities in society concerned with knowledge production and dissemination, especially research institutes and universities. Like the culture industry, these settings achieved a large measure of autonomy within society, which allowed them to redefine themselves. Instead of serving the interests of society as a whole, they have come to focus on their own interests; this means that they are intent on expanding their influence over society. Research institutes help to turn out the technologies needed by the culture industry, the state, and the capitalists and, in so doing, help to strengthen their position in, and influence over, society. Universities come to serve a similar series of interests, but perhaps more importantly serve to foster technocratic thinking and, in the process, help to suppress reason. Universities are dominated by technocratic administrators who run the university much like any bureaucracy and who impose rules on professors and students alike. Furthermore, the universities become increasingly dominated, not by the liberal arts that might encourage reason, but by the business, professional, and technical schools that are dominated by technocratic thinking. Furthermore, instead of challenging students to think, universities become more like factories for the manufacture of hordes of students. The focus is not on making them reasonable human beings, but on processing as many students as possible in the most efficient way. Universities come to turn out students in much the same way that factories turn out automobiles or sausages.

Pessimism about the Future   All of this, but especially the focus on increasing rationalization, leads the critical theorists, unlike Marx and most Marxists, to a very pessimistic view of the future. Instead of the overthrow of the capitalists by the proletariat, the critical theorists envision continued and expanding rationalization. This is true within the culture, technology, and the knowledge industry (see Key Concept box). However, each of these was likely not only to grow increasingly rational, but each was expected to grow more important in its own right. Thus, the future is seen as a kind of iron cage composed of increasingly rational cultural, technological, and educational systems that interpenetrate to control people and make them increasingly one-dimensional. This kind

---

knowledge industry   To the critical theorists, those entities in society concerned with knowledge production and dissemination, especially research institutes and universities. Like the culture industry, these settings achieved a large measure of autonomy within society, which allowed them to redefine themselves. Instead of serving the interests of society as a whole, they have come to focus on their own interests; this means that they are intent on expanding their influence over society.

Contemporary Applications
From Web 1.0 to Web 2.0

Critical theorists tended to see technology as controlling individuals. However, a dramatic change has taken place on the Internet that has given much greater control to individuals. In its early years the Internet could be described as Web 1.0, but in recent years many examples of Web 2.0 have taken their place alongside continuing examples of Web 1.0. While Web 1.0 continues to exist on the Internet and to demonstrate technological control over individuals, the individual exercises far more power in Web 2.0.

Examples of Web 1.0 include:

- Switchboard.com and YellowPages.com, which dictate how users are supposed to find people and businesses through the framework of the sites.
- The Apple Store and other shopping sites that dictate the content and users' browsing (and shopping).
- Yahoo's website, which offers the user a preset set of options (although they can now be altered by the user).

On Web 1.0 sites, many opinions are presented, often by those who are, or at least claim to be, experts. For instance, the creators of Fodors.com use their own tastemakers to point tourists to various hotels, restaurants, activities, and so forth. (This site, like many associated originally with Web 1.0, now allows users to choose between the experts, *à la* Web 1.0, or to read community opinions, *à la* Web 2.0.) More general information is searched for on sites like about.com, whose creators employ "experts" to help users find information. The author of this volume is also Editor of the *Blackwell Encyclopedia of Sociology Online* (www.sociologyencyclopediaonline.com/public/) where the reader finds almost 2000 entries written by experts in the field.

Web 2.0 accords far less power to the creators of these systems and much more to their users; Web 2.0 sites are, to a large extent, user-generated. In addition to the Web 1.0 experience of reading, browsing, and consuming online content, Web 2.0 also allows for writing and producing content. One way of describing this is to see the implosion of the consumer and the producer on Web 2.0 into the "prosumer" (see Key Concepts box in Chapter 9). Because of this user-generated content, sites on Web 2.0 are always in a state of flux.

of thinking has far more in common with the pessimistic views of Max Weber than the optimistic perspectives of Marx and most other neo-Marxists.

This kind of pessimistic thinking about the future did not endear the critical theorists to other Marxists. After all, Marxists were not supposed to be merely thinkers, but also people of action intent on relating their theories to revolutionary movements. The pessimism of the critical theorists seemed to foreclose the possibility of action, let alone revolution. The proletariat were left to await their inevitable fate—imprisonment in the iron cage of rationality being put in place by the various elements of the culture industry. From the point of view of the critical theorists, the masses did not view this as an unpleasant fate. In fact, the iron cage has been made as pleasant and comfortable as possible. It is

---

Contemporary Applications—Continued

Major examples of Web 2.0, and of the centrality of user-generation on them, include:

- Wikipedia, where users generate articles and constantly edit, update, and comment on them (compare to the *Blackwell Encyclopedia of Sociology Online*);
- Facebook, MySpace and other social networking websites, where users create profiles composed of videos, photos, and text, interact with one another, and build communities;
- Second Life, where users create the characters, communities, and entire virtual environment;
- The blogosphere, blogs (web logs) and the comments on them;
- eBay and Craigslist, where consumers rather than retailers create the market;
- YouTube and Flickr, where mostly amateur photographers upload and download videos and photographs;
- Current TV, where viewers create much of the programming, submit it via the Internet, and decide which submissions are aired;
- Linux, a free, collaboratively-built open-source operating system, and open-source software applications;
- Amazon.com, whose consumers do all the work involved in ordering products and write the product reviews;
- The GeoWeb, which consists of online maps that users are increasingly creating and augmenting with Google, Microsoft, and Yahoo tools. Google Maps users, for example, can fix errors, add the locations of their businesses, upload photos, and blog about their experiences with, or reviews of, places on the map, thereby creating social communities.

This explosion of user-generated content has massively transformed the Internet. There has been dramatic shift from Web 1.0, where the user experience was best characterized as "looking stuff up" preset by others, to a Web 2.0 experience of production, networking, and collaborating. In contrast to thinking of the critical theorists, on Web 2.0 it is people who, to a large degree, are controlling the technology rather than being controlled by it.

---

nicely padded and furnished. It is loaded with amenities like *People* magazine and *USA Today*; labor-saving devices like dishwashers and microwave ovens; televisions, TiVos, DVDs, and all the tapes and disks one could ever want; computers with free and continuous access to video games, movies, Facebook, and shopping sites on the Internet, and so on. People have come to love their cages and they are eager to fill them with more of the goodies being churned out by the capitalist system. However, this situation is precisely the problem. In love with their cages and the consumer toys that crowd them, people see no need to revolt; indeed, they are no longer even able to see that there are such problems as exploitation and control. In the end, these attractive and pleasant methods of control are far more effective than the oppressive actions of the capitalists and their lackeys that characterized the early years of capitalism.

Neo-Marxian Spatial Analysis

There have been a number of notable contributions by neo-Marxian theorists to spatial analysis and to the role of space in the social world. And this is only part of a broader resurgence of interest in space in sociology and social theory.

A starting point for the growth in interest in space in neo-Marxian theory (and elsewhere) is the work of Michel Foucault (see Chapter 9), who pointed out that many theories, but especially Marxian theories, had emphasized time over space (e.g., the focus on Marxian theory in the historical transitions from feudalism to capitalism and ultimately to communism), viewing space as "dead" while time was seen as alive. The implication is that space should, along with time, be given its due in social analyses.

Henri Lefebvre on Space.   It is Henri Lefebvre who did the pathbreaking work in the neo-Marxian theory of space. Lefebvre argues for the need for Marxian theory to shift its focus from things in space (for example, means of production such as factories) and the production that takes place there to the actual production of space itself. Marxian theory needs to broaden its concerns from capitalist industrial production to the way that a system reproduces itself in space. Space serves in various ways to reproduce the capitalist system, the class structure within that economic system, and so on. For example, the rich live in elegant gated communities while the poor live in slums far removed from those wealthy communities. Thus, any revolt against the capitalist system must concern itself not only with changing the structure of production, but also with restructuring space so that it reflects a more egalitarian class structure.

Lefebvre begins his analysis with **spatial practice,** which for him involves the actions (including and especially the actions of the masses) that produce and continually reproduce space. For example, by meekly remaining in their slums or accepting the fact that they may not enter rich gated communities, the poor reproduce those spatial arrangements on a daily basis.

Overlying and ultimately dominating spatial practice are **representations of space,** or space as it is conceived by societal elites such as urban planners and architects. Elites think of this as "true space" and it is used by them and others to achieve and maintain dominance. Thus, for example, urban planners and architects conceived the once popular program of "urban renewal" that was designed, theoretically, to tear down the dilapidated slum housing of the poor and replace it with far better and more modern housing. However, urban renewal came to be known as "urban removal." The poor were moved out to make room for new housing, but when that housing was built, it was more often for the middle and upper classes interested in gentrifying the city.

Spatial practice   involves the actions (including and especially the actions of the masses) that produce and continually reproduce space.

Representations of space   involve space as it is conceived by societal elites such as urban planners and architects; it overlies and ultimately dominates spatial practice.

Frequently, the poor had to move to new areas, often finding themselves in housing little, if at all, better than what they had left. They also were forced to adapt to new areas, communities, and neighbors. Thus, the "spatial practices" of the poor (e.g., where they lived and shopped) were radically altered by the "representations of space" of those who supported, created, and implemented urban renewal.

Representations of space are dominant not only over spatial practices but also over representational spaces. While representations of space are the creations of dominant groups, **representational spaces** are ideas about, representations of, space that flow from the lived experiences of people, especially from those who are poor, silent, underground, or clandestine. While, as we have seen, representations of space are considered "true space" by those in power, representations of space yield the "truth of space." That is, they reflect what "really" happens in lived experience rather than being an abstract truth created by someone such as an urban planner in order to achieve dominance. However, in the contemporary world, representational spaces like spatial practices, suffer because of the dominance of representations of space. In fact, representational space tends to become subordinated to, to get lost in, representations of space. Thus, a major problem for Lefebvre is the predominance of the representations of space of the "haves" over the spatial practices and silent representational spaces of the "have-nots." Furthermore, it is out of representational spaces that new and potentially revolutionary ideas flow, but if those spaces are subordinated and suppressed, how is the hegemony of elites ever to be contested, let alone threatened?

The preceding is a way of addressing space that emphasizes ideas and representations, but Lefebvre offers a second set of distinctions that addresses space in more material—and more optimistic—terms. Lefebvre begins with what he calls **absolute spaces,** or natural spaces (e.g., "green" areas) that are not colonized, rendered inauthentic, or smashed by elite economic and political forces. Lefebvre spends little time on absolute space; it serves as a basic assumption on which his other ideas are based. Just as Marx devoted most of his attention to critiquing capitalism, Lefebvre is interested in critically analyzing what he calls **abstract space,** which, like representations of space, is space from the point of view of a theoretician such as an urban planner or an architect. But abstract space is not just about ideas; it involves real, material spaces that actually

---

Representational spaces are ideas about, representations of, space that flow from the lived experiences of people, especially from those who are poor, silent, underground, or clandestine.

Absolute spaces are natural spaces (e.g., "green" areas) that are not colonized, rendered inauthentic, or smashed by elite economic and political forces.

Abstract space. This is space from the point of view of a theoretician such as an urban planner or an architect, but it is not just about ideas; it involves real, material spaces that actually replace historical spaces (which are erected on the base of absolute spaces).

replace historical spaces (which are erected on the base of absolute spaces). An example of an abstract space is a public housing project. Such a space is characterized largely by the absence of that which is associated with absolute space (trees, clean air, and so on). It is a dominated, occupied, controlled, authoritarian (even brutal and violent), and repressive space. Lefebvre emphasizes the role of the state, more than economic forces, in exercising power over abstract space, although that exercise of power is often hidden. Thus, abstract space can be seen, and is used, as a tool of power. That is, not only is power exercised in it, but the abstraction of space is itself a form of power. While those in power have always sought to control space, what is new here is that the ruling class uses abstract space as a tool to gain control over increasingly large spaces. While Lefebvre de-emphasizes economic factors and forces, he does recognize that power of and over abstract space does generate profit. That is, it is not just the factory that generates profits, but also the bus routes, railway lines, and highways that provide routes into the factory for raw materials and out of the factory for finished products. Further, elites gain from owning and speculating on property in areas in which the poor live.

As a good Marxian theorist, Lefebvre emphasizes contradictions. While abstract space serves to smother contradictions, it simultaneously generates them, including those that have the potential to tear apart such space, and the larger society. Although he wonders why people accept, and are silent about, the kind of control exerted over them by abstract spaces, they eventually will be spurred to action by these contradictions. Indeed, as in Marx's analysis of contradictions in capitalism, Lefebvre argues that the seeds of a new kind of space can be glimpsed within the contradictions of abstract space.

That new kind of space, the third of the types of space to be discussed here, is **differential space.** While abstract space (e.g., in public housing projects) seeks to control and homogenize everyone and everything, differential space accentuates difference and freedom from control. While abstract space breaks up the natural unity that exists in the world, differential space restores that unity. A differential space would, for example, be one where rich and poor live together, or one in which people are immersed in their natural environment (trees, clean air), rather than having it denied them.

Lefebvre argues that space can play a variety of roles in the socioeconomic world. First, it can be one of many forces of productions (other, more traditional such forces are factories, tools, and machines). For example, more farm land can be used to produce larger quantities of corn to be turned into ethanol to be used, instead of gasoline, to power automobiles. Second, space itself can be a vast commodity that is consumed for pleasure (as, for example, by a tourist visiting Disneyland), or it can be consumed productively (for example, the land on which a factory is built). Third, it is politically instrumental, facilitating control of the system (building roads to facilitate troop movements to put

---

Differential space.   A hoped-for space that accentuates difference and freedom from control; it would restore the natural unity that is broken by abstract space.

down rebellions). Fourth, space underpins the reproduction of productive and property relations (for example, those expensive gated communities for the capitalists and slums for the poor). Fifth, space can take the form of a superstructure that, for example, seems neutral but conceals the economic base that gives rise to it and that is far from neutral. Thus, a highway system may seem neutral but really advantages capitalistic enterprises that are allowed to move raw materials and finished products easily and cheaply. Finally, there is always positive potential in space, such as the creation of truly human and creative works in it, as well as the possibility of reappropriating space on behalf of those who are being controlled and exploited.

The production of space occupies two positions in Lefebvre's work. First, as discussed above, it constitutes a new focus of analysis and critique. That is, our attention should shift from the means of production to the production of space. Second, Lefebvre puts this all in terms of a desired direction for social change. That is, we live in a world characterized by a particular mode of *production in space.* This is a world of domination in which control is exercised by the state, the capitalist, and the bourgeoisie. It is a closed, sterile world, one that is being emptied out of contents (e.g., highways replacing and destroying local communities).

Lefebvre argues that we need instead a world characterized by the *production of space* where, instead of domination, we would have a world in which appropriation is predominant. That is, in concert with others, people would work in and with space to produce what they need to survive and prosper. In other words, they modify natural space in order to serve their collective needs. Thus, Lefebvre's goal is the production of space that is a product and reflection of the human beings. It would be planet-wide space that would serve as the basis for transforming everyday life. Needless to say, state and private ownership of the means of production that control the mode of production would wither away under such a system. Thus, the production of space is not only Lefebvre's analytic focus but also his political objective in much the same way that communism is Marx's political goal.

David Harvey on Space.   One aspect of David Harvey's complex body of work that is particularly relevant to this discussion of neo-Marxian theory is his analysis and critique of the geographical arguments made by Karl Marx and Friedrich Engels in the *Communist Manifesto* (1868). Harvey sees what he calls the "spatial fix" as central to the argument made in the *Manifesto.* That is, the need to create ever-higher profits means that capitalist firms must, among other things, continually seek new geographic areas (and markets) to exploit *and* find more ways of exploiting more intensively the areas in which they already operate. While such geographical arguments occupy an important place in the *Manifesto,* they characteristically are subordinated, as Foucault argued, to a perspective that prioritizes time and history (e.g., the history of class struggles, especially proletariat vs. capitalists) at the expense of space and geography.

Harvey wants to see more attention paid to the way the world, including capitalism, is organized geographically. Thus, for example, it is not enough to say that the state is controlled by the capitalists; the way a territorially defined state is organized and administered is also of great importance. For example, loosely connected provinces have to be brought together to form the nation. However, territories do not remain set in stone once they have been transformed into states. All sorts of things alter territorial configurations, including revolutions in transportation and communication, differences in resources, and the uneven outcomes of class struggle. Furthermore, boundaries between territories are always porous and products, money, and workers flow through them rather easily. Thus, territories are being redefined and reorganized continually, with the result that any model that envisions a final formation of the state on a territorial basis is overly simplistic. The implication is that we need to be attuned continuously to territorial changes in a world dominated by capitalism (as well as any other economic system).

Another of the spatial arguments made in the *Communist Manifesto* is that capitalism (e.g., its factories, offices) tends to become concentrated in the cities. This, in turn, leads to the concentration of the proletariat in those cities (they were formerly scattered throughout the countryside). Instead of conflict between isolated workers and capitalists, it becomes more likely that a collectivity of workers will confront capitalists, who are themselves now more likely to be organized into a collectivity. Thus, the nature and likelihood of class struggle is strongly affected by spatial changes.

There is much more to be said about the relationship between space and class struggle, and this is amply demonstrated in the more recent history of capitalism. For example, capitalists in the late nineteenth century dispersed factories from the cities to the suburbs and small towns in an effort, at least in part, to limit the concentration of workers and their power. And in the late twentieth century we witnessed the dispersal of factories to remote areas of the world in order not only to reduce labor costs, but as a further effort to weaken the proletariat and to strengthen the capitalists. Most generally, capitalism itself has grown ever-more widespread throughout the world; it has become increasingly global (see Chapter 10).

Harvey also points out that the *Manifesto* tended to focus on the urban proletariat and thereby largely ignored rural areas, as well as agricultural workers and peasants. Of course, the latter groups have over the years proved to be very active in revolutionary movements. Furthermore, Marx and Engels tended to homogenize the world's workers, to argue that they have no country and that national differences are disappearing in the development of a homogeneous proletariat. Harvey notes that not only do national (spatial) differences persist, but capitalism itself produces national (and other) differences among workers. In addition, labor plays a role here in sustaining spatial distinctions by, for example, using organizations based in given territories to mobilize workers and creating loyalties rooted in those places. Finally, Harvey notes the famous call in the *Manifesto* for workers of the world to unite and argues that given the increasingly global character of capitalism, such an exhortation is more relevant and more important than ever. An ever more global capitalism makes a reaction, even a revolution, against it increasingly likely to be global in scope.

Key Concept
The Modern World-System

Immanuel Wallerstein (1930–) chose a unit of analysis unlike those used by most Marxian thinkers. He did not look at workers, classes, or even states, because he found most of these too narrow for his purposes. Instead, he looked at a broad economic entity with a division of labor not circumscribed by political or cultural boundaries. He found that unit in his concept of the **world-system,** a largely self-contained social system with a set of boundaries and a definable life span (i.e., it does not last forever). It is composed internally of a variety of social structures and member groups. He viewed the system as being held together by a variety of forces in inherent tension. These forces always have the potential for tearing the system apart.

Wallerstein argued that thus far we have had only two types of world-systems: One was the world empire, of which ancient Rome was an example; the other is the modern capitalist world-economy. A world empire was based on political (and military) domination, whereas a capitalist world-economy relies on economic domination. A capitalist world-economy is seen as more stable than a world empire for several reasons. It has a broader base because it encompasses many states, and it has a built-in process of economic stabilization. The separate political entities within the capitalist world-economy absorb whatever losses occur, while economic gain is distributed to private hands. Wallerstein foresaw the possibility of a third world-system, a socialist world government. Whereas the capitalist world-economy separates the political from the economic sector, a socialist world-economy reintegrates them.

Within the capitalist world-economy, the **core** geographical area is dominant and exploits the rest of the system. The **periphery** consists of those areas that provide raw materials to the core and are heavily exploited by it. The **semiperiphery** is a residual category that encompasses a set of regions somewhere between the exploiting and the exploited. To Wallerstein the international division of exploitation is defined not by state borders but by the economic division of labor in the world.

In addition to critiquing the ideas of the *Communist Manifesto,* Harvey develops many of his own ideas under the heading of "spaces of hope." With this perspective, he wishes to counter what he perceives to be a pervasive pessimism among scholars today. He wants to acknowledge that there are spaces in which

---

world-system   A broad economic entity with a division of labor that is not circumscribed by political or cultural boundaries. It is a social system, composed internally of a variety of social structures and member groups, that is largely self-contained, has a set of boundaries, and has a definable life span.

core   The geographical area that dominates the capitalist world-economy and exploits the rest of the system.

periphery   Those areas of the capitalist world-economy that provide raw materials to the core and are heavily exploited by it.

semiperiphery   A residual category in the capitalist world-economy that encompasses a set of regions somewhere between the exploiting and the exploited.

political struggle exist and, as a result, there is hope for society as a whole. Finally, he describes a utopian space of the future that offers hope to those concerned about the oppressiveness of today's spaces.

Thus, in these and many other ways, Harvey builds on Marx's (and in this case Engels's) limited insights into space and capitalism to develop a richer and more contemporary perspective on their relationship to each other. In that sense, what Harvey is doing here is a model of neo-Marxian spatial analysis.

THE CIVILIZING PROCESS

Norbert Elias's (1897–1990) life work was the study of a long-term historical development he called the **civilizing process.** He arbitrarily chose as his starting point Europe in the Middle Ages, and he was interested in changes in everyday behaviors. The source of much of Elias's information was books on manners written between the 13th and the 19th centuries. What he found was a long-term change in manners as they relate to daily behavior. Everyday behaviors that were once acceptable have, over time, become increasingly unacceptable. We are more likely to observe the everyday behaviors of others, to be sensitive to them, to understand them better, and, perhaps, most importantly, to find an increasing number of them embarrassing. What we once found quite acceptable now embarrasses us enormously. As a result, what was once quite public is now hidden from view. Because others are likely to find certain mundane behaviors offensive, we are more likely to engage in those behaviors out of public view.

Examples of the Civilizing Process

Take some examples from eating at the table. In the 13th century most people found it acceptable to gnaw on the bones of animals and then put them back in the serving dish. They became self-conscious about it only when others commented on it and brought their attention to the offensive nature of the behavior. Most people also had to be told that it was unacceptable to pick their noses while eating. The need to warn people about such behaviors makes it clear that many were accustomed to engaging in them. They were not embarrassed by them; they did know that they were uncivilized. However, as the decades and centuries passed, the lessons were learned and increasing attention was

---

civilizing process   The long-term change in the West in manners as they relate to daily behavior. Everyday behaviors once acceptable have, over time, become increasingly unacceptable. We are more likely to observe the everyday behaviors of others, to be sensitive to them, to understand them better, and, perhaps most importantly, to find an increasing number of them embarrassing. What we once found quite acceptable now embarrasses us enormously. As a result, what was once quite public is now hidden from view.

given in books on manners to such things as picking one's nose at the table. When nose picking finally became a behind-the-scenes behavior (except for very young children), attention turned to other, less egregious violations. For example, a 16th century document warned against such things as licking one's fingers at the table or stirring sauce with one's fingers. Such behaviors have now been eliminated from the table.

A similar trend is found in various natural functions such as expelling wind. A 14th century book for schoolchildren had various pieces of advice about such behavior:

- It is best to expel wind without a sound.
- However, better to expel it with a noise than to hold it back.
- To avoid offending others with the sound, press your buttocks firmly together.
- A cough is an excellent way of concealing the sound of wind being expelled.

Again, the point is that the need to offer advice about such things makes it clear that the public expelling of wind, often quite noisily, was very common. Clearly, in the more civilized 21st century there would be no need for such a document or such admonitions. Few people today expel wind noisily in public, unless they cannot avoid it or they think no one is nearby. As Elias puts it, the frontier of embarrassment has moved to encompass the expelling of wind.

The blowing of one's nose followed the same trajectory. In the 15th century readers of books on manners were warned about blowing their noses with the same hand that held their meat. In the 16th century there was an admonishment about opening one's handkerchief after blowing one's nose and admiring the results. However, although by the 18th century advice was still being offered about blowing one's nose, the kinds of behaviors discussed had largely disappeared behind the shame frontier.

Sexual relations experienced a similar fate. In the Middle Ages it was not uncommon for men and women, who may have been little more than acquaintances, to spend the night in the same room and to sleep naked. On a couple's wedding night in the Middle Ages, a procession accompanied the bride and groom to their bed. Bridesmaids undressed the bride. For a marriage to be considered valid, the bed had to be mounted by the couple in the presence of others. Bride and groom had to be laid together. All of this, of course, has now passed behind the shame frontier and bride and groom spend their wedding nights only in one another's presence.

Explaining the Changes: Lengthening Dependency Chains

Elias described historical changes in mundane behaviors. However, how did he explain these changes? Although Elias explained changes in everyday life, that which explains those changes occurs, at least at first, at the macro-level of the state. A crucial development was the emergence of a strong head of state, a

---

Norbert Elias (1897–1990)
A Biographical Vignette

Norbert Elias had an interesting and instructive career. He produced his most important work in the 1930s, but it was largely ignored at the time and for many years thereafter. During World War II, and for almost a decade after, Elias bounced around with no secure employment and remained marginal to British academic circles. However, in 1954 Elias was offered two academic positions and he accepted one at Leicester. Thus, Elias *began* his formal academic career at the age of 57! Elias's career blossomed at Leicester and a number of important publications followed. However, Elias was disappointed with his tenure at Leicester because he failed in his effort to institutionalize a developmental approach that could stand as an alternative to the kind of static approaches (of Talcott Parsons and others) that were then pre-eminent in sociology. He was also disappointed that few students adopted his approach; he continued to be a voice in the wilderness at Leicester, where students tended to regard him as an eccentric voice from the past. Reflective of this feeling of being on the outside was a recurrent dream reported by Elias during those years in which a voice on the telephone repeated, "Can you speak louder? I can't hear you." Throughout Elias's years at Leicester *none* of his books was translated into English and few English sociologists of the day were fluent in German.

However, on the Continent, especially in the Netherlands and Germany, Elias's work began to be rediscovered in the 1950s and 1960s. In the 1970s Elias began to receive not only academic, but public, recognition in Europe. Throughout the rest of his life Elias received a number of significant awards.

---

king. With the king emerged a stable central government in control of taxes and warfare. Around the king a court developed, in which power was relatively equally divided. The court was central to Elias's argument.

Prior to the emergence of a court, warriors were pre-eminent and they were able to engage in violence because they had what Elias called short **dependency chains.** Relatively few people were dependent on them and they were dependent on a small number of other people. Thus, when warriors engaged in violent behavior, their behavior affected those against whom the violence was aimed, as well as a relatively small number of other people. In a sense, warriors were free to engage in violence because it did not affect or disrupt too large a portion of society. In contrast, the court nobles developed long dependency chains, which served to prevent violence. They became dependent on those who provided them with the goods and services they desired (warriors had far fewer such needs and desires), and others depended on the nobles for that business. In this case, violence engaged in by nobles affected large numbers of people, perhaps the society as a whole. Long dependency chains forced nobles to become increasingly

---

dependency chains   The chain of relationships involving those people that a person is dependent on as well as those people's dependency on the person.

Key Concept
Figurations

Elias was involved in an effort to overcome the tendency of sociologists to distinguish between individuals and society. In order to help achieve his integrative goal (see Chapter 7), Elias proposed the concept of figuration, an idea that makes it possible to overcome our inability to think of people as both individuals and societies.

Figurations can be seen, above all, as processes. In fact, later in his life Elias came to prefer the term *process sociology* to describe his work. **Figurations** are social processes involving the interweaving of people. They are *not* structures external to and coercive of relationships between people; they are those interrelationships. Individuals are seen as open and interdependent; figurations are made up of such individuals. Power is central to social figurations and they are, as a result, constantly in flux. Figurations emerge and develop, but in largely unseen and unplanned ways.

Central to this discussion is the fact that the idea of a figuration applies to every social phenomenon between small groups and societies, even China with well over a billion people.

Elias refuses to deal with the relationship between individual and society. In other words, both individuals and societies (and every social phenomenon in between) involve people—human relationships. The idea of chains of interdependence is as good an image as any of what Elias means by figurations and what constitutes the focus of his sociology. He is interested in how people are linked together and why that linkage occurs.

Elias's notion of figuration is linked to the idea that individuals are open to, and interrelated with, other individuals. He argues that most sociologists operate with a sense of single individuals totally independent of all other human beings. Such an image does not lend itself to a theory of figurations; an image of open, interdependent actors is needed for figurational sociology.

---

sensitive to the needs and expectations of others. Sensitized to others, the nobles were disinclined to commit violence against them. They were even less likely to engage in violence against others that might offend those involved in their dependency chains. Another factor serving to inhibit the nobles from engaging in violence was the fact that the king not only controlled the money needed to buy weapons, but the weapons themselves.

Now the issue is: What does the change at the top of society (among the nobles and their dependency chains) have to do with picking one's nose and expelling wind? The answer is that the situation confronting, and the behavior engaged in by, the nobles came to be the reality for more and more people throughout society. Dependency chains grew progressively longer for more

---

figurations   Social processes involving the interweaving of people who are seen as open and interdependent. Power is central to social figurations; they are constantly in flux. Figurations emerge and develop, but in largely unseen and unplanned ways.

and more people. As a result, the majority of people, like the nobles, grew more sensitive to those around them and they had to be sensitive to the needs of more people. The longer dependency chains meant that engaging in untoward behaviors would not just be known to, and affect, a few people in the immediate environment, but also large numbers of people far removed along the dependency chain. Thus, if one picked one's nose at the table or expelled wind at a party, large numbers of people would eventually come to know of these behaviors. Knowledge of this new reality and increasing sensitivity to it led people to be increasingly circumspect about expelling gas or picking their noses in public.

Over time people have grown more concerned about, and better able to control, their baser instincts. We might think that this is all to the good. After all, aren't we all better off when people are likely to be less violent or less likely to expel wind in our presence? Life has grown less dangerous, less base, less unpredictable; but it has also grown less exciting, less interesting. Unable to act out various behaviors, people are likely to become increasingly repressed, bored, and restless.

A Case Study: Fox Hunting

In addition to looking at great expanses of history, Elias also applied his ideas to more specific arenas such as sports in general and fox hunting in particular. Following the general line of his argument, we have witnessed a general decline in the violence associated with sports. In the early years, fox hunting was quite vicious, dominated by humans killing and eating the fox. However, over the years fox hunting has become increasingly civilized (in 2005, Great Britain legally banned fox hunting). For example, instead of people doing the killing, the hounds do it. Furthermore, it is no longer the norm for people to eat the fox. However, with such "sportization" comes boredom; fox hunting and many other sports are just not as interesting or exciting as they once were. The need for more excitement is reflected in the violence that frequently erupts at European, especially British, soccer matches. Furthermore, violence has certainly not disappeared. It is found regularly in the taverns, on the streets, and in skirmishes and open warfare between nations. Perhaps if we allowed more violence in sport, if sport were less civilized, then we might have somewhat less violence elsewhere in the world. More generally, Elias does not think that civilization is necessarily a good thing. Less civilized societies had many advantages over more civilized ones, and increasing civilization has meant the loss of various things that are important to people.

THE COLONIZATION OF THE LIFEWORLD

Jürgen Habermas is a neo-Marxian theorist; in fact, in his early years as a scholar he was associated directly with the critical school. Although he made important contributions to critical theory, over the years he has fused Marxian theory with many other theoretical inputs to produce a very distinctive set of theoretical ideas. One is his grand theory of the increasing colonization of the lifeworld.

An understanding of what Habermas means by the colonization of the lifeworld requires a prior understanding of what he means by lifeworld, as well as of what is doing the colonizing, the system.

Lifeworld, System, and Colonization

The **lifeworld** is a concept used by Alfred Schutz (and others associated with phenomenology and phenomenological sociology) to refer to the world of everyday life. Schutz was primarily concerned with intersubjective relations within the lifeworld, but Habermas has a different interest within the lifeworld. Habermas is primarily concerned with the interpersonal communication that takes place within the lifeworld. Ideally, that communication would be free and open, with no constraints. To Habermas free and open communication means the rationalization of communication within the lifeworld. Although the concept of rationalization has been used in a negative sense, and in another context Habermas will use it that way, within the confines of the lifeworld and communication, rationalization takes on a positive connotation. Those who interact with one another will be rationally motivated to achieve free and open communication, leading to mutual understanding. Rational methods will be employed to achieve consensus. Consensus will be arrived at, and understanding achieved, when the better argument wins the day. In other words, external forces like the greater power of one party should play no role in achieving consensus. People debate issues and the consensus reached is based solely on what is the best argument.

The **system** has its source within the lifeworld, but it comes to develop its own distinctive structures, such as the family, the legal system, the state, and the economy. As these structures develop, they grow increasingly distant and separated from the lifeworld. Like the lifeworld, the system and its structures undergo progressive rationalization. However, the rationalization of the system takes a different form than the rationalization of the lifeworld. Rationalization here means that the system and its structures grow increasingly differentiated, complex, and self-sufficient. Most importantly, the power of the system and its structures grows and with it their ability to direct and control what transpires in the lifeworld. This has a number of ominous implications for the lifeworld;

---

lifeworld To Schutz, the commonsense world, the world of everyday life, the mundane world; that world in which intersubjectivity takes place. Habermas is more concerned with interpersonal communication in the lifeworld.

system To Habermas, the structures (such as the family, the legal system, the state, and the economy) that have their source within the lifeworld, but which come to develop their own distinctive existence and to grow increasingly distant and separated from the lifeworld.

Jürgen Habermas (1929–)
A Biographical Vignette

In 1956 Habermas arrived at the Institute for Social Research in Frankfurt and became associated with the Frankfurt school. He became research assistant to one of the most illustrious members of that school, Theodor Adorno, as well as an associate of the institute. Although the Frankfurt school is often thought of as highly coherent, that was not Habermas's view:

> For me there was never a consistent theory. Adorno wrote essays on the critique of culture and also gave seminars on Hegel. He presented a certain Marxist background—and that was it.

Although he was associated with the Institute for Social Research, Habermas demonstrated from the beginning an independent intellectual orientation. A 1957 article by Habermas got him into trouble with the leader of the institute, Max Horkheimer. Habermas urged critical thought and practical action, but Horkheimer was afraid that such a position would jeopardize the publicly funded institute. Horkheimer strongly recommended that Habermas be dismissed from the Institute. Horkheimer said of Habermas, "He probably has a good, or even brilliant, career as a writer in front of him, but he would only cause the Institute immense damage." The article was eventually published, but not under the auspices of the institute and with virtually no reference to it. Eventually, Horkheimer enforced impossible conditions on Habermas's work and the latter resigned.

---

most importantly it colonizes (intrudes upon) the lifeworld. This **colonization of the lifeworld** takes many forms, but none is more important than the fact that the system imposes itself on communication in the lifeworld and serves to limit the ability of actors to argue things through and achieve consensus within it. In other words, the rational structures of the system, instead of enhancing the capacity to communicate and reach understanding and consensus, threaten those processes through the exertion of external control over them.

For example, a group of close friends may meet in order to decide through free and open discussion how they might go about pooling their resources in order to earn more money in the future. They may want to use knowledge derived from the fact that they are all well-placed officers of important companies to form a stock club in order to invest in the stocks of some of those companies. However, they are prevented from doing so, and even prevented from getting very far in discussing it, by laws that forbid insider trading. An officer of one company is prohibited from sharing with other members of the group information about upcoming developments that might affect the company's share prices. Thus, the law prohibits free and open discussion of this way

---

colonization of the lifeworld   As the system and its structures grow increasingly differentiated, complex, and self-sufficient, their power grows and with it their ability to direct and control what transpires in the lifeworld.

Key Concept
Ideal Speech Situation

Underlying much of Habermas's thinking is his notion of free and open communication (in the lifeworld), or what he calls the "ideal speech situation." In most cases, power determines which argument wins out over all of the others. However, for Habermas, the **ideal speech situation** is one that is free of all distorting influences, especially power. It is one in which the better argument wins out rather than the one that is backed by the most powerful individual or group. The better argument is the one that, for example, has the most evidence behind it and that is made most convincingly. A consensus arises out of this contest of ideas as to what is the truth. Thus, the truth arises from consensus and not because it is a copy of reality.

The problem in the contemporary world is that very little communication is undistorted. It is especially the case that power affects virtually all communication with the result that not only is all communication distorted, but there is a general failure to arrive at a true consensus and, therefore, at the truth. Given his Marxian orientation, there is a set of practical and political implications to this diagnosis of contemporary ills. That is, the barriers to free and open communication, especially the power that so distorts it, need to be removed so that people can freely arrive at consensus and the truth.

---

of acquiring wealth within the lifeworld of this group. We might think that insider trading should be banned, but the fact remains that the law in this case prohibits the achieving of consensus through free and open communication.

Given these views on the lifeworld and the system, Habermas is arguing that while they stem from the same roots, they have been decoupled from one another. Once they are separated, it is possible for the system to colonize the lifeworld. This colonization has a destructive effect on the lifeworld in general and especially on communication within it. Communication becomes increasingly rigidified, impoverished, and fragmented; the lifeworld itself is pushed to the brink of dissolution. However, even when colonization is quite extensive, the lifeworld continues.

Rationalization of System and Lifeworld

The problem for Habermas is that the system and the rationalization characteristic of it have gained ascendancy over the lifeworld and its distinctive form of rationalization. The solution to this problem for Habermas lies in the

---

ideal speech situation   A speech situation that is free of all distorting influences, especially power; one in which the better argument wins out rather than the one that is backed by the most powerful individual or group. A consensus arises out of this contest of ideas as to what is the truth; truth arises from consensus and not because it is a copy of reality.

rationalization, each in their own way, of *both* lifeworld and system. The system and its structures need to be allowed to grow more differentiated and complex, while the lifeworld needs to be refined so that free communication is possible and the better argument is permitted to emerge victorious. The full rationalization of both would permit the lifeworld and the system to be recoupled in such a way that each enhances, rather than negatively affects, the other. A more rational system should be used to enhance rational argumentation in the lifeworld; that argumentation should, in turn, be used to figure out ways of further rationalizing the system. In this way the two systems would be mutually enriching rather than, as in the present situation, the system deforming the lifeworld.

For example, a more rationalized system might permit groups of people to discuss exchanges of certain types of information that heretofore would have been considered insider trading. For their part, such groups through free and open communication might come up with better guidelines on what should and should not be considered insider trading. In a world in which both system and lifeworld were rationalized, these views on new guidelines would be fed back into the system and lead to changes there and to a more refined sense of what is and is not insider trading.

THE JUGGERNAUT OF MODERNITY

Anthony Giddens considers himself a modern social theorist and argues that we continue to exist in a modern world, albeit one that is in its advanced stages. He does not reject the idea that we may at some time move into a postmodern world, but his ideas about such a world are very different from those who associate themselves with postmodern social theory (see Chapter 9). Although a modernist, Giddens has a very different view of the modern world than classical theorists of modernity like Marx and Weber.

The Juggernaut

Giddens sees modernity as a **juggernaut,** a massive force that moves forward inexorably riding roughshod over everything in its path. Imagine a trailer truck the size of *Titanic* careening down a busy city street. People steer this juggernaut but, given its size and bulk, they cannot totally control the path it takes and the speed at which it travels. There is the ever-present possibility that they could lose control and the juggernaut, and everyone in it or nearby, could be destroyed. For those who control it, as well as those in its path, the juggernaut can bring great rewards (the huge truck may be bringing a great supply of new

---

juggernaut   Giddens's metaphor for the modern world as a massive force that moves forward inexorably riding roughshod over everything in its path. People steer the juggernaut, but it always has the possibility of careening out of control.

drugs needed by the population), but also great dangers, including a constant anxiety that those who drive it might at any moment lose control, threatening the lives of many people.

The notion of a juggernaut is quite abstract. What, more specifically, does Giddens have in mind with this metaphor and the dangers posed by it? Take the specific example of the trailer truck delivering medical supplies. The truck could be delivering drugs that seem to be worthwhile, but that, in the future, cause more harm than good. This was the case with Fen Phen, a weight-control drug that was very popular for a time but was taken off the market when it was learned that many who took it developed heart valve problems. Other concrete examples of human creations that appear worthwhile, but could turn out disastrously, include nuclear technology (e.g., power plants) and genetic research. All are produced by humans who are also in day-to-day control of them. However, that control is tenuous and there is the ever-present possibility of disasters such as the meltdown of a nuclear reactor (as occurred at Chernobyl), or the unleashing of genetic mutations that threaten the future of humankind.

Space and Time

Our ability to control the various components of the modern juggernaut is complicated by the fact that they have tended to grow quite distant from us in space and time (Giddens calls this **distanciation**). Whereas in a premodern society, or even in early modern societies, such components tended to be physically close to us, they are now spread out across the globe. A nuclear submarine with enormous capacity for destruction may be half a world away from those who direct its activities. The nuclear disaster at Chernobyl affected people thousands of miles away. The same point can be made about time. Things that were created long ago (the nuclear waste that has been accumulating for more than a half century) can have disastrous effects on us. Similarly, things that we are in the process of creating (e.g., genetic technology) can have adverse effects well into the future.

Because of these changes in time and space, those who live in the modern world are forced to develop a sense of trust in both systems and the people who control and operate them. For example, we need to trust that the captain of a nuclear submarine will not take it upon himself to launch a multiwarhead nuclear attack, or that those doing genetic research will take the precautions needed to protect future generations. In other words, the nature of the modern world requires that we place our trust in a variety of experts.

Reflexivity

People in the modern world, however, are not content simply to leave things to the experts. People are reflexive, constantly examining big issues like nuclear

---

distanciation   The tendency for various components of the modern juggernaut to grow quite distant from us in space and time.

Anthony Giddens (1938–   )
A Biographical Vignette

As a theorist, Giddens has been highly influential in the United States, as well as many other parts of the world. Interestingly, his work has often been less well received in his home country of Great Britain than in many other parts of the world. This lack of acceptance at home may be attributable, in part, to the fact that Giddens has succeeded in winning the worldwide theoretical following that many other British social theorists sought and failed to achieve: "Giddens has perhaps realized the fantasies of many of us who committed ourselves to sociology during the period of intense and exciting debate out of which structuration theory developed."

Giddens's career took a series of interesting turns in the 1990s. Several years of his undergoing therapy led him to a greater interest in personal life and books such as *Modernity and Self-Identity* and *The Transformation of Intimacy*. Therapy also gave him the confidence to take on a more public role and to become an advisor to British Prime Minister Tony Blair. In 1997 he became director of the highly prestigious London School of Economics (LSE). He moved to strengthen the scholarly reputation of LSE as well as to increase its voice in public discourse in Great Britain and around the world. Some believe that all this has had an adverse effect on Giddens's scholarly work (his recent books lack the depth and sophistication of his earlier works).

---

technology and genetic research, as well as the most mundane of their everyday activities. Although reexamination of the big issues may have little effect on them, it does leave people with a constant sense of uneasiness about them and their implications for their lives. More importantly, by our constantly examining and reforming our own actions, we have an even greater degree of uneasiness. Few things are ever done once and for all. Rather, everything is constantly open to reexamination and to a revision or modification of actions taken. We not only reflect on our actions, but we reflect on our thinking about those actions. This succeeds in leaving us with an even more pervasive sense of uneasiness than our reflection on things like the dangers of nuclear technology.

Insecurity and Risks

In what Giddens calls high modernity, we are all faced with great insecurity about life. The insecurity is made manageable by childhood socialization that leaves us with the ability to trust not only our parents but also authority figures in general. In addition, we all follow a set of daily routines that make it seem as if our lives are safe. However, we remain painfully aware of the risks that surround us. These risks are global in nature and involve not only the things previously discussed, but also things like increasing global economic interdependence and the likelihood that an economic crisis in one part of the world could bring the entire global economy crashing down around us. We

---

Key Concept
Risk Society

While the idea of risk is important to Giddens, it lies at the center of the work of a contemporary German theorist, Ulrich Beck (1944–), as reflected in the title of his best-known book, *Risk Society* (1992). Beck sees society today as being defined by risk and the ways in which it can be prevented, minimized, or channeled. Thus, instead of finding solidarity the way previous generations did in the pursuit of such great positive goals as greater equality, what unifies people today is the largely negative goal of being spared the dangers associated with various risks.

Many of today's risks stem from modern industry, but what makes them unique is not just that they are more dangerous than ever before (an accident at a nuclear power plant is far more dangerous than one in a conventional power plant), but that they are not restricted by place or time. For example, a nuclear accident, such as the one at Chernobyl in 1986, was not restricted to the geographic area around the plant, but affected many parts of the world, some quite remote from the original site. Furthermore, its impact was not restricted to the time at which the accident occurred, but its effects have lingered as the site and its environs remain dangerous to this day and, more importantly, people continue to suffer the ill effects of radiation exposure with some experiencing new symptoms or developing symptoms for the first time.

Risk, like many other things in the social world, is stratified. Rich nations and the upper classes in every nation are less likely to experience risk than poor nations and the lower classes. Risks are much more likely to exist in poor nations than rich (and the latter export risks to the former) and in areas where the lower rather than the upper classes live. Nevertheless, even the upper classes cannot be free from risk in the contemporary world. One reason is the **boomerang effect** whereby risks strike back on the upper classes and rich nations most responsible for their production. Thus, rich nations and upper classes seek to place factories that adversely affect the environment as far away from them as possible, but many of those risks find their way back to them in the form of polluted air and water, a widening hole in the ozone layer, global warming, and the like. Thus, in many ways, there is no way for anyone to hide from, or escape, the risk society.

---

also know that while we generally trust the experts, they cannot fully control the juggernaut. The actions they take can cause crises and the actions they take to deal with those crises can easily serve to worsen them.

Why the risks? Or, to put it another way, why is the juggernaut always threatening to rush out of control? Giddens offers four answers:

1. Those who designed the juggernaut and its various components made mistakes; the juggernaut has design faults. For example, those involved in the

---

boomerang effect   Risks strike back on the upper classes and rich nations most responsible for their production.

design and creation of Chernobyl (and undoubtedly other nuclear reactors around the world) made a number of mistakes that led to the meltdown.

2. Those who run the juggernaut (its operators) made mistakes; the juggernaut is subject to operator failure. Thus, the meltdown at Chernobyl may have been caused by fatal errors made by those who ran the plant on a daily basis. In fact, the meltdown was undoubtedly the result of some combination of operator failure and design faults.

3. We cannot always foresee accurately the consequences of modifying the juggernaut or creating new components for it; such actions often have unintended consequences. For example, we are at present at the beginning of a genetic revolution, but we cannot foresee all of the consequences of the genetic changes we are now undertaking. Similarly, the manufacturers of Fen Phen had no idea that it would lead to heart valve defects in patients who took the drug.

4. People in general, and experts in particular, are constantly reflecting on the juggernaut and, in the process, creating new knowledge about it. Such new knowledge applied to the juggernaut makes it likely that it will move at a different pace and/or direction. However, this new pace or direction may bring with it a series of negative consequences. For example, at times the Federal Reserve system increases interest rates in order to keep inflation under control. However, rising interest rates bring with them the possibility of an economic recession; the economy could slow down too much.

Summary

1. Critical theory is focally interested in the culture industry and the increasing control of culture over people. Key to this control is mass culture, especially that disseminated by the mass media.

2. Critical theorists are critical of technology, especially the way it is used in capitalism.

3. The predominance of technology is producing a one-dimensional society in which people lose their ability to think creatively and critically.

4. Critical theorists are concerned with the effect of technology on thinking: People seek only the best means to an end without reflecting on the means or end. People lose the capacity for reason; this is part of the irrationality of rational systems.

5. Unlike most Marxists, critical theorists have a pessimistic view of the future, seeing only increasing technological control and rationalization.

6. Some neo-Marxists have shifted their attention to spatial analysis, especially the way space reproduces capitalist class relationships and the need to restructure space in a more egalitarian manner.

7. Lefebvre focuses on the relationship between spatial practices, representations of space and representational spaces, as well as absolute, abstract, and differential space.

8. Lefebvre wants to see a transition from production in space to production of space.

9. David Harvey reanalyzes *The Communist Manifesto* in order to uncover its spatial implications and the weaknesses in its spatial arguments. He also uses this analysis to develop a more positive image of the future in terms of "spaces of hope."

10. Norbert Elias's grand theory deals with the civilizing process whereby a number of once visible behaviors have come to be seen as uncivilized and have disappeared from public view.

11. A key factor in this change was the emergence of the court with its long dependency chains and, more generally, the lengthening dependency chains of more and more people.

12. Jürgen Habermas's grand theory deals with the colonization of the lifeworld by the system and the prevention of free and open communication.

13. The lifeworld, to Habermas, is the realm of everyday communication.

14. The system, to Habermas, has its origin in the lifeworld, but comes to develop its own structures (e.g., the family, the state) that grow more distant and separate from the lifeworld.

15. Anthony Giddens's grand theory deals with the juggernaut of modernity, a massive force, which, although it is steered by people, always has the possibility of lurching out of control.

16. Among the factors that can cause the juggernaut of modernity to rush out of control are design faults, operator error, unintended consequences, and the use of new knowledge that sends the juggernaut in unanticipated directions.

Suggested Readings

MARTIN JAY   *The Dialectical Imagination.* Boston: Little Brown, 1973. Important overview of neo-Marxian theory, especially as it relates to the critical school.

ROLF WIGGERSHAUS   *The Frankfurt School: Its History, Theories, and Political Significance.* Cambridge, MA: MIT Press, 1994.

DOUGLAS KELLNER   "Frankfurt School." In George Ritzer, ed., *The Encyclopedia of Social Theory*, 2 volumes. Thousand Oaks, CA: Sage, 2005, pp. 290–293. Concise summary of the importance of this school, also known as critical theory, by an important contemporary exponent of this approach.

ANDY MERRIFIELD   *Henri Lefebvre: A Critical Introduction.* London, Routledge, 2006.

RICHARD KILMINSTER and STEPHEN MENNELL   "Norbert Elias." In George Ritzer, ed., *The Blackwell Companion to Major Social Theorists.* Malden, MA, and Oxford, England: Blackwell, 2000, pp. 601–629. Recent and reasonably brief overview of Elias's life and work.

STEPHEN MENNELL   *Norbert Elias: An Introduction.* Dublin: University College Dublin Press, 1998. For those who crave more detail about Elias's perspective.

JOHN RUNDELL   "Norbert Elias." In George Ritzer, ed., *The Encyclopedia of Social Theory*, 2 volumes. Thousand Oaks, CA: Sage, 2005, pp. 239–245. Recent overview of Elias's work focusing on his most important theoretical ideas.

WILLIAM OUTHWAITE   "Jürgen Habermas." In George Ritzer, ed., *The Blackwell Companion to Major Social Theorists.* Malden, MA, and Oxford, England: Blackwell, 2000, pp. 651–670. A brief overview of Habermas's perspective.

WILLIAM OUTHWAITE   *Habermas: A Critical Introduction.* Cambridge: Polity Press, 1994. For those who want greater detail—in this case, on Habermas's work.

ROB STONES   "Anthony Giddens." In George Ritzer, ed., *The Encyclopedia of Social Theory*, 2 volumes. Thousand Oaks, CA: Sage, 2005, pp. 321–327. Broad overview of Giddens's theoretical work with special attention to his later theorizing.

CHRISTOPHER G. A. BRYANT and DAVID JARY   "Anthony Giddens." In George Ritzer, ed., *The Blackwell Companion to Major Social Theorists.* Malden, MA, and Oxford, England: Blackwell, 2000, pp. 670–695. Handy, brief overview of Giddens's contributions.

STJEPAN G. MESTROVIC   *Anthony Giddens: The Last Modernist.* London and New York: Routledge, 1998. Interesting for its critiques (often outrageous) of Giddens's work.

GERD NOLLMAN   "Jürgen Habermas." In George Ritzer, ed., *The Encyclopedia of Social Theory*, 2 volumes. Thousand Oaks, CA: Sage, 2005, pp. 351–352. Brief look at just a few of the highlights of Habermas's theoretical contributions.

CHAPTER 6

Contemporary Theories of Everyday Life

Symbolic Interactionism
Dramaturgy
Ethnomethodology and Conversation Analysis
Exchange Theory
Rational Choice Theory
Summary
Suggested Readings

The preceding two chapters dealt with contemporary grand theories of large-scale changes in the social world. In this chapter we remain focused on contemporary theories, but this time those that are oriented to a variety of small-scale phenomena associated with everyday life. We begin with symbolic interactionism, a theory strongly influenced by the thinking of George Herbert Mead (see Chapter 3). This is followed by an examination of dramaturgy that sees much of social life as analogous to a theatrical performance. Ethnomethodology is concerned with the methods we all use regularly to accomplish our lives on a daily basis. Next is exchange theory that looks at social relationships in terms of rewards and costs and argues, among other things, that we are likely to continue in relationships that are rewarding and discontinue those that are costly. Finally, we discuss rational choice theory that focuses on actors making choices that maximize the satisfaction of their needs and wants.

SYMBOLIC INTERACTIONISM

The focus of **symbolic interactionism,** like the other theories discussed in this chapter, is on everyday life. Its distinctive focus, as its name suggests, is on

---

symbolic interactionism The school of sociology that, following Mead, focused on symbolic interaction.

interaction (as well as action and people as agents) and the symbols (and their meanings) that are deeply implicated in it. We can get a handle on this theory by enumerating some of its most fundamental assumptions and principles.

First, people act toward things, but they do so on the basis of the meanings those things have for them. Thus, we act toward the American flag, say by saluting it, based on the meaning that flag has for us (our homeland) and not simply on its physical characteristics. This also means that others can act toward it in other ways (say, by burning or defacing it) because it has other meanings (a symbol of U.S. imperialism) for them.

Second, these meanings stem from our interactions with other people. Thus, we may have learned about the flag as a positive symbol through interactions at school while enemies of the United States may have learned theirs through interactions with groups of revolutionaries.

Third, people do not simply internalize the meanings that they learn through social interaction, but they are also able to modify them through an interpretive process. Thus, while one may have learned to see the flag as a positive symbol, dissatisfaction with, say, America's foreign policies might lead one to reinterpret the flag and to feel a bit less positive toward, or even develop negative sentiments about, it and what it stands for. Conversely, those who develop negative views in a revolutionary cell, may become more positive about the flag and what it symbolizes as a result of U.S. actions that satisfy some of the revolutionaries' demands.

Fourth, people, in contrast to other animals, are unique in their ability to use and rely on symbols. While other animals react directly or blindly to stimuli, people are able to give them meaning (turn them into symbols) and then act on the basis of that meaning. To put this another way, other animals react instinctively to objects, while we think through their meaning. Thus, a hungry animal might eat a poison mushroom, but we would be able to think through the fact that we had better not eat it because it might be poisonous.

Fifth, people become human through social interaction, especially in the early years with family members and then in school. We are born with the capacities to become human, but that potential can only be realized through human interaction. Thus, feral children—those raised in the wild by animals (e.g., wolves)—cannot become human, but begin to become human when they are rescued and begin to interact with other humans.

Sixth, as George Herbert Mead made clear (see Chapter 3), people are conscious, capable of reflecting on themselves and what they do, and therefore capable of shaping their actions and interactions. In Mead's terms, then, people have both a "mind" and a "self." Particularly important is our ability to interact with ourselves in order to decide how to interact with objects in our world. This gives us a large measure of autonomy in our actions, but we certainly are not totally free to do as we wish—there are many external constraints on our actions.

Seventh, people have purposes when they act in, as well as toward, situations. We define situations, give them meaning, and then act toward them. We

Key Concepts
The Conceptual Contributions of Charles Horton Cooley

Charles Horton Cooley (1864–1929) is best known for his concept of the **looking-glass self.** We form our sense of ourselves by looking in some sort of mirror. That mirror is the other people with whom we interact. We use others as mirrors to assess who we are and how we are doing. We look at their eyes and their body language and we listen to their words. Looking in that mirror, we determine whether we are who we want to be and whether our actions are having the desired effect. If we see what we expect to see, if people evaluate us the way we hope, if they do what we want them to do, then the mirror confirms ourselves and we continue on as we have been thinking and acting. However, if the reverse occurs, then we may need to reassess our actions and even our sense of who we are. If the looking glass continues to show us a reflection that is different from what we think we are, then we may need to re-evaluate our sense of who we are, in other words, re-evaluate our self-images. The looking-glass self reflects Cooley's interest, like that of others associated with symbolic interactionism, in the mind, self, and interaction.

Another key concept associated with Cooley is the **primary group,** an intimate face-to-face group that plays a crucial role in linking the individual to the larger society. Of special importance are the primary groups of the young, mainly the family and friendship groups, within which the individual grows into a social being. It is mainly within the primary group that the looking-glass self develops and the child makes the transition from thinking mainly about himself to taking others into consideration. As a result of this transformation, the child begins to develop the capabilities that will enable him to become a contributing member of society.

Cooley also made an important methodological contribution arguing for the need for sociologists to put themselves in the place of the actors they were studying (usually in the real world) in order to better understand the operation of their mental processes. Cooley called this **sympathetic introspection**—putting oneself in the places and the minds of those being studied, doing so in a way that is sympathetic to who they are and what they are thinking, and trying to understand the meanings and the motives that lie at the base of their behavior. This method continues to be one of the cornerstones of the study of everyday life, at least for some sociologists.

---

looking-glass self   The idea that we form our sense of ourselves by using others, and their reactions to us, as mirrors to assess who we are and how we are doing.

primary group   An intimate face-to-face group that plays a crucial role in linking the individual to the larger society. Of special importance are the primary groups of the young, mainly the family and friendship groups.

sympathetic introspection   The methodology of putting oneself in the places and the minds of those being studied. Researchers do so in a way that is sympathetic to who others are and what they are thinking, and they try to understand the meanings and the motives that lie at the base of peoples' behavior.

Robert E. Park (1864–1944)
A Biographical Vignette

Robert Park did not follow the typical career route of an academic sociologist: college, graduate school, professorship. Instead, he led a varied career before he became a sociologist late in life. Despite his late start, Park had a profound effect on sociology in general and on theory in particular. Park's varied experiences gave him an unusual orientation to life; this view helped to shape the Chicago school, symbolic interactionism, and, ultimately, a good portion of sociology.

Park was born in Harveyville, Pennsylvania, on February 14, 1864. As a student at the University of Michigan, he was exposed to a number of great thinkers, such as John Dewey. Although he was excited by ideas, Park felt a strong need to work in the real world. Park said, "I made up my mind to go in for experience for its own sake, to gather into my soul . . . 'all the joys and sorrows of the world.'" Upon graduation, he began a career as a journalist, which gave him this real-world opportunity. He particularly liked to explore (hunting down gambling houses and opium dens). He wrote about city life in vivid detail. He would go into the field, observe and analyze, and finally write up his observations. Essentially, he was already doing the kind of research (scientific reporting) that came to be one of the hallmarks of Chicago sociology: urban ethnology using observation techniques.

Although the accurate description of social life remained one of his passions, Park grew dissatisfied with newspaper work because it did not fulfill his familial or, more important, his intellectual needs. Furthermore, it did not seem to contribute to the improvement of the world, and Park had a deep interest in social reform. In 1898, at age 34, Park left newspaper work and enrolled at Harvard.

---

choose ends and then act toward them (although not always successfully or in a linear manner since we may encounter all sorts of barriers and roadblocks).

Eighth, we can see society as consisting of people engaging in social interaction. Thus, society is not some macro-level entity separable from people. People produce society; society is the joint action of people.

There is, of course, much more to symbolic interactionism than this, but this brief overview, as well as the earlier, more detailed discussion of Mead's ideas, should give the reader a sense of this theoretical perspective.

However, one more basic point needs to be made before we move on. Symbolic interactionists are inclined to do social research rather than to develop abstract theories. This means they often go out and study people and get at their meanings from their point of view. To do so means they must often venture into the real world and observe and interact with people.

A key figure in this tradition of social research in the real world is Robert E. Park (1864–1944). Park had been a reporter before becoming a sociologist, and as a reporter he was accustomed to collecting data on and observing whatever social reality he was writing about. When he became a sociologist, Park urged his students as well as colleagues to do much the same thing. In one sense, he was encouraging them to do what has come to be known as **fieldwork:** that is, venturing into the field to observe and collect relevant data. More specifically, as a result of the urging of Park (and others), the key method of symbolic interactionists became **observation.** The attraction of being an observer is that researchers can both engage in sympathetic introspection and put themselves in the place of actors to try to understand their meanings and motives and observe the various actions that people take. Thus, observation was a perfect way for those associated with symbolic interactionism to study the thought processes, the actions, and the interactions of everyday life.

DRAMATURGY

The concept of self is very important to, and lies at the heart of, symbolic interactionism. Herbert Blumer defined the self in extremely simple terms as the fact that people can be the objects of their own actions: that is, people have the ability to act not only toward others, but also toward themselves (e.g., by admonishing themselves for saying something foolish). Both types of actions are based on the kinds of objects people are to themselves (e.g., whether they look upon themselves in a positive or negative light). Being able to do this, to act toward themselves, allows people to act in a conscious manner rather than merely reacting to external stimuli. People actually interact with themselves to point out the things toward which they are acting and the meaning of those things. They interpret the meaning of things and alter those interpretations on the basis of the situation they are in and what they hope to accomplish.

The most important work on the self in symbolic interactionism is *Presentation of Self in Everyday Life* by Erving Goffman. Goffman's conception of the self is deeply indebted to Mead's (see Chapter 3) ideas, in particular his discussion of the tension between *I*, the spontaneous self, and *me*, social constraints within the self. This tension is mirrored in Goffman's work on what to him was a critical discrepancy between our all-too-human selves on the one hand and our socialized selves on the other. The tension results from the difference between what we may want to do spontaneously and what people expect us to do. We are confronted with demands to do what is expected of us; moreover, we are not

---

fieldwork   A methodology used by symbolic interactionists and other sociologists that involves venturing into the field (the day-to-day social world) to observe and collect relevant data.

observation   A methodology closely related to fieldwork, in which the symbolic interactionist (and other sociologists) studies the social world by observing what is transpiring in it. In the case of symbolic interactionism, this enables researchers to engage in sympathetic introspection and put themselves in the place of actors in order to understand meanings and motives and to observe the various actions that people take.

supposed to waver. In order to cope with this tension and to maintain a stable self-image, people perform for their social audiences. As a result of this interest in performance, Goffman focused on **dramaturgy,** or a view of social life as a series of dramatic performances akin to those performed in the theater.

Dramaturgy

Goffman's sense of the self was shaped by his dramaturgical approach. To Goffman (and to most other symbolic interactionists), the self is not a possession of the actor but rather the product of the dramatic interaction between actor and audience. In other words, the **self** is a sense of who one is that is a dramatic effect emerging from the immediate scene being presented. Because the self is a product of dramatic interaction, it is vulnerable to disruption during the performance. Much of Goffman's dramaturgy is concerned with the processes by which such disturbances are prevented or dealt with. Although the bulk of his discussion focuses on these dramaturgical contingencies, Goffman pointed out that most performances are successful. The result is that in ordinary circumstances a firm self is accorded to performers, and it appears to emanate from the performers.

Goffman assumed that when individuals interact, they want to present a certain sense of self that will be accepted by others. However, even as they present that self, actors are aware that members of the audience can disturb their performance. For that reason actors are attuned to the need to control the audience, especially those members of it who might be disruptive. The actors hope that the sense of self that they present to the audience will be strong enough for the audience to define the actors as the actors want to be defined. The actors also hope that this will cause the audience to act voluntarily as the actors want them to. Goffman characterized this central interest as **impression management.** It involves techniques actors use to maintain certain impressions in the face of problems they are likely to encounter and methods they use to cope with these problems.

Front Stage   Following the theatrical analogy, Goffman spoke of a **front stage,** that part of the performance that generally functions in rather fixed and general

---

dramaturgy   A view of social life as a series of dramatic performances akin to those that take place in the theater.

self   To Goffman, a sense of who one is that is a dramatic effect emerging from the immediate dramaturgical scene being presented.

impression management   The techniques actors use to maintain certain impressions in the face of problems they are likely to encounter and the methods they use to cope with these problems.

front stage   That part of a dramaturgical performance that generally functions in rather fixed and general ways to define the situation for those who observe the performance.

ways to define the situation for those who observe the performance. A professor lecturing to a class may be said to be in her front stage, as would a student at a fraternity party. Within the front stage, Goffman further differentiated between the setting and the personal front. The **setting** refers to the physical scene that ordinarily must be there if the actors are to perform. Without it, the actors usually cannot perform. For example, a surgeon generally requires an operating room, a taxi driver a cab, and an ice skater an ice rink. The **personal front** consists of those items of expressive equipment that the audience identifies with the performers and expects them to carry with them into the setting. A surgeon, for instance, is expected to dress in a medical gown, have certain instruments, and so on.

Goffman subdivided the personal front into appearance and manner. **Appearance** includes those items that tell us the performer's social status (e.g., the taxi driver's license). **Manner** (e.g., the expression of confidence on the surgeon's face) tells the audience what sort of role the performer expects to play in the situation. A brusque manner and a meek manner indicate quite different kinds of performances. In general, we expect appearance and manner to be consistent.

Although Goffman approached the front and other aspects of his system as a symbolic interactionist, he did discuss their structural character. He argued that fronts tend to become institutionalized, so collective representations arise about what is to go on in a certain front. Very often when actors take on established roles, they find particular fronts already established for such performances. The professor who appears before a class has a front that has been established by many professors and students who have come before her. The result, Goffman argued, is that fronts tend to be selected, not created. This idea conveys a much more structural image than we would receive from most symbolic interactionists.

Despite such a structural view, Goffman's most interesting insights lie in the domain of interaction. He argued that because people generally try to present an idealized picture of themselves in their front-stage performances, inevitably they feel that they must hide things in their performances:

1. Actors may want to conceal secret pleasures engaged in prior to the performance (e.g., the professor who consumed alcohol just before entering class) or in past lives (e.g., physicians who had been drug addicts but had overcome their addiction) that are incompatible with their performance.

---

setting   The physical scene that ordinarily must be there if the actors are to engage in a dramaturgical performance.

personal front   Those items of expressive equipment that the audience identifies with the performers and expects them to carry with them into the setting.

appearance   The way the actor looks to the audience; especially those items that indicate the performer's social status.

manner   The way an actor conducts himself; tells the audience what sort of role the actor expects to play in the situation.

Key Concept
Role Distance

Another of Goffman's interests was the degree to which an individual embraces a given role. In his view, because of the large number of roles, few people get completely involved in any given role. **Role distance** deals with the degree to which individuals separate themselves from the roles they are in. For example, if older children ride on a merry-go-round, they are likely to be aware that they are really too old to enjoy such an experience. One way of coping with this feeling is to demonstrate distance from the role by, in a careless, lackadaisical way, performing seemingly dangerous acts while on the merry-go-round. In performing such acts, the older children are really explaining to the audience that they are not as immersed in the activity as small children might be or that if they are, it is because of the special things they are doing.

One of Goffman's key insights is that role distance is a function of one's social status. High-status people often manifest role distance for reasons other than those of people in low-status positions. For example, a high-status surgeon may manifest role distance in the operating room to relieve the tension of the operating team. People in low-status positions usually manifest more defensiveness in exhibiting role distance. For instance, people who clean toilets may do so in a lackadaisical and uninterested manner. They may be trying to tell their audience that they are too good for such work.

---

2. Actors may want to conceal errors made in the preparation of the performance as well as steps taken to correct these errors. For example, a surgeon may seek to hide the fact that he prepared to do an appendectomy when, in fact, he was scheduled to do open heart surgery. A professor who brings the wrong notes to class may be forced to improvise during the class period in order to conceal that fact.
3. Actors may find it necessary to show only end products and to conceal the process involved in producing them. For example, professors may spend several hours preparing a lecture, but they may want to act as if they have always known the material.
4. It may be necessary for actors to conceal from the audience that dirty work was involved in the making of the end products. Dirty work may include doing things that are immoral, illegal, or degrading. For example, a manufacturer of peanut butter may seek to conceal from government inspectors the fact that an inordinate number of rodent droppings and rodent hairs found their way into the finished product.
5. In giving a certain performance, actors may have to let other standards slide. For example, in order to keep up with a busy surgical schedule, the

---

role distance   The degree to which individuals separate themselves from the roles they are in.

surgeon may not be able to find the time to do enough reading to keep up with recent developments in his field.

6. Finally, actors probably find it necessary to hide any insults, humiliations, or deals made so that the performance could go on. A surgeon may well want to hide the fact that he has been admonished by his superiors for not keeping up with recent developments and that he will be suspended if he does not demonstrate that he is reducing his surgical schedule so that he has time to do so.

Generally, actors have a vested interest in hiding all of the facts discussed from their audience.

Another aspect of dramaturgy in the front stage is that actors often try to convey the impression that they are closer to the audience than they actually are. Actors may try to foster the impression that the performance in which they are engaged at the moment is their only performance or at least their most important one. Thus, a physician must try to convey the impression to every patient that he or she is *the* most important patient and the object of her undivided attention. To do this, actors have to be sure that their audiences are segregated so that the falsity of the performance is not discovered. The physician's patients would be upset to learn that an effort is made by the doctor to make each one of them feel as if he or she is the most important patient. Even if it is discovered, Goffman argued, the audiences themselves may try to cope with the falsity, to avoid shattering their idealized image of the actor. Thus, patients may console themselves with the fact that that's the way doctors are and, in any case, the doctor does excellent work. This reveals the interactional character of performances. A successful performance depends on the involvement of all the parties.

Another example of this kind of impression management is an actor's attempt to convey the idea that there is something unique about this performance as well as his or her relationship to the audience. Thus, a car salesperson may seek to convey the idea that he really likes a particular customer and is giving her a far better deal than he would give anyone else. The audience, too, wants to feel that it is the recipient of a unique performance. Car buyers want to feel that their salesperson is not giving them the same old spiel and that they have a special relationship with the salesperson.

Actors try to make sure that all the parts of any performance blend together. A priest might seek to ensure consistency and continuity among his Sunday sermons. In some cases, a single discordant aspect can disrupt a performance. However, performances vary in the amount of consistency required. A slip by a priest on a sacred occasion would be terribly disruptive, but if a taxi driver made one wrong turn, it would not be likely to damage the overall performance greatly.

Another technique employed by performers is **mystification.** Actors often tend to confound their audience by restricting the contact between themselves

---

mystification   An effort by actors to confound their audience by restricting the contact between themselves and the audience, concealing the mundane things that go into their performance.

and the audience. They do not want the audience to see the very mundane things that go into a performance. Thus, a professor may prepare a lecture by simply reading a textbook not being used in a particular class, but she will certainly conceal this fact and attempt to act as if she has known this material and much else for a long time. By generating social distance between themselves and the audience, actors try to create a sense of awe in the audience. Students are supposed to be awed by how much a professor knows and how effortlessly a mass of information can be brought to bear on a particular lecture. This awe, in turn, keeps the audience from questioning the performance. Goffman pointed out that the audience is involved in this process and often seeks to maintain the credibility of the performance by keeping its distance from the performer. In the case being discussed here, students would not want to know how the professor prepares for class because it would demystify the whole process.

Goffman also had an interest in teams. To Goffman, as a symbolic interactionist, a focus on individual actors obscured important facts about interaction. Thus, Goffman's basic unit of analysis was not the individual but the team. A **team** is any set of individuals who cooperate in staging a single routine. The preceding discussion of the relationship between the performer and audience is really about teams. Each member is reliant on the others because all can disrupt the performance and all are aware that an act is being put on. Goffman concluded that a team is a kind of secret society. A class is such a secret society and class members cooperate with the professor in making each class a credible performance. Of course, at times a professor makes so many slips, or reveals so many weaknesses, that the students can no longer ignore them and the performance is disrupted, if not destroyed. However, this a rarity and something students and professors, audiences and performers, seek to avoid at all costs.

Back Stage and Outside   Goffman also discussed a **back stage,** where facts suppressed in the front stage or various kinds of informal actions may appear. A back stage is usually adjacent to the front stage, but it is also cut off from it. Performers can reliably expect no members of their front audience to appear in the back. Furthermore, they engage in various types of impression management to make sure of this. A performance is likely to become difficult when actors are unable to prevent the audience from entering the back stage. The doctors' lounge is the back stage relative to the office where physicians interact with patients. Safely in the back stage lounge, doctors can say things about their patients, their expertise, or their performance that they would never say to patients in the front stage. A doctor would rarely, if ever, tell a patient that she dislikes him, has no idea what ails him, or what to do about it.

---

team   Any set of individuals who cooperate in staging a single performance.

back stage   Where facts suppressed in the front stage or various kinds of informal actions may appear. A back stage is usually adjacent to the front stage, but it is also cut off from it. Performers can reliably expect no members of their front audience to appear in the back.

Key Concept
Stigma

Goffman was interested in *stigma,* or the gap between what a person ought to be, **virtual social identity,** and what a person actually is, **actual social identity. Stigma** involves a gap between virtual and actual social identity. Goffman focuses on the dramaturgical interaction between stigmatized people and normals. The nature of that interaction depends on which of two types of stigma an individual has. In the case of **discredited stigma,** the actor assumes that the differences are known by the audience members or are evident to them (e.g., a paraplegic or someone who has lost a limb). A **discreditable stigma** is one in which the differences are neither known by audience members nor perceivable by them (e.g., a person who has had a colostomy or a homosexual passing as straight). For someone with a discredited stigma, the basic dramaturgical problem is managing the tension produced by the fact that people know of the problem. For someone with a discreditable stigma, the dramaturgical problem is managing information so that the stigma remains unknown to the audience.

Most of the text of Goffman's *Stigma* is devoted to people with obvious, often grotesque, stigmas (e.g., the loss of a nose). However, as the book unfolds, the reader realizes that Goffman is really saying that we are all stigmatized at some time or other, or in some setting or other. His examples include the Jew passing in a predominantly Christian community, the fat person in a group of people of normal weight, and the individual who has lied about his past and constantly must be sure that the audience does not learn of this deception.

A third, residual domain is the **outside,** which is neither front nor back. For example, a brothel is (usually) outside, relative to the doctor's office and lounge. However, it is possible that a brothel could become a back stage if it is visited by doctors or patients who then bend the ear of the hooker by complaining about each other.

The latter illustrates the idea that *no* area is *always* one of these three domains. Also, a given area can occupy all three domains at different times. A professor's office is front stage when a student visits, back stage when the student leaves, and outside when the professor is at a university basketball game.

---

virtual social identity   What a person ought to be.

actual social identity   What a person actually is.

stigma   A gap between virtual and actual social identity.

discredited stigma   The actor assumes that the stigma is known by the audience members or is evident to them.

discreditable stigma   The stigma is neither known by audience members nor discernible by them.

outside   Neither front nor back; literally outside the realm of the performance.

Erving Goffman (1922–1982)
A Biographical Vignette

Erving Goffman died in 1982 at the peak of his fame. He had long been regarded as a cult figure in sociological theory. This status was achieved in spite of the fact that he had been professor in the prestigious sociology department at the University of California, Berkeley, and later held an endowed chair at the Ivy League's University of Pennsylvania.

By the 1980s he had emerged as a centrally important theorist. He had been elected president of the American Sociological Association in the year he died but was unable to give his presidential address because of advanced illness. Given Goffman's maverick status, Randall Collins says of his address: "Everyone wondered what he would do for his presidential address: a straight, traditional presentation seemed unthinkable for Goffman with his reputation as an iconoclast . . . we got a far more dramatic message: presidential address cancelled, Goffman dying. It was an appropriately Goffmanian way to go out."

Impression Management

In general, impression management is oriented to guarding against a series of unexpected actions, such as unintended gestures, inopportune intrusions, and *faux pas*, as well as intended actions, such as making a scene. Goffman was interested in the various methods of dealing with such problems.

1. One set of methods involves actions aimed at producing dramaturgical loyalty by, for example, fostering high in-group loyalty, preventing team members from identifying with those outside the performance, and changing audiences periodically so that they do not become too knowledgeable about the performers.
2. Goffman suggested various forms of dramaturgical discipline, such as having the presence of mind to avoid slips, maintain self-control, and manage the facial expressions and verbal tone of one's performance.
3. He identified various types of dramaturgical circumspection, such as determining in advance how a performance should go, planning for emergencies, selecting loyal teammates, selecting good audiences, being involved in small teams where dissension is less likely, making only brief appearances, preventing audience access to private information, and settling on a complete agenda to prevent unforeseen occurrences.

The audience also has a stake in successful impression management by the actor or actors. The audience often acts to save the show through such devices as giving great interest and attention to it, avoiding emotional outbursts, not noticing slips, and giving special consideration to neophyte performers.

One thing that many critics of Goffman's thinking on dramaturgy have pointed out is his cynical view of actors. He believed that actors are putting on performances and they are well aware of that fact. They cynically manipulate

---

Contemporary Applications
September 11, 2001, and the Stigmatization of Muslims

Prior to the 9/11 attacks on the World Trade Center and the Pentagon, relatively little hostility was aimed at Muslims in the United States. They were simply yet another group of immigrants who had integrated, or were integrating, into the United States. It was other groups—mainly Blacks and Mexican immigrants (especially those here illegally)—that were often stigmatized; Muslims largely escaped this process. However, the heinous acts of September 11—planned and committed largely, if not exclusively, by Muslims associated with Osama bin Laden and al-Qaeda—changed all that. There is an increasing and palpable tendency for many Americans to stigmatize Muslims both in and out of the United States. Some Muslims have a discredited stigma since their physical appearance, accent, mode of dress, and so on, make it clear to others (or seem to) that they are Muslims. Other Muslims whose appearance, accent, and way of dressing are not dissimilar from most other Americans are more likely to confront the stresses and strains of a discreditable stigma. Because of this, others who are mistakenly thought to be Muslim are also stigmatized.

One indicator of the increasing stigmatization of Muslims is the growing tendency for movies and television shows to depict the villains as Muslims. This was the case, for example, in the 2004–2005 season of the TV series *24* in which a group of ruthless Muslims (one of whom was willing to kill his own son and wife for the cause) were depicted as intent on death and destruction in the United States by, for example, causing a meltdown of nuclear reactors throughout the country. The stigmatization of Muslims was so blatant that the show had to issue disclaimers. At one point, the show's star, Kiefer Sutherland, appeared in a spot in which he claimed that the stigmatization of Muslims was *not* the intent of the show and that many Muslims were good Americans. In one episode, two clearly Muslim shop owners were depicted allying themselves with Jack Bauer (Sutherland's character on the show) and taking up arms against a private army employed by a ruthless defense contractor. Such disclaimers and actions did little to counter the stigmatization of Muslims on the show . . . and increasingly in the larger society.

---

their performances or the impressions they seek to make in order to accomplish their objectives. They are generally quite aware that some aspects of what they say and do are false, but they persevere nonetheless.

ETHNOMETHODOLOGY AND CONVERSATION ANALYSIS

Given its Greek roots, the term *ethnomethodology* literally means the methods that people use on a daily basis to accomplish their everyday lives. To put it slightly differently, the world is seen as an ongoing practical accomplishment. People are viewed as rational, but they use practical reasoning, not formal logic, in accomplishing their everyday lives.

Defining Ethnomethodology

The definition of **ethnomethodology** is the study of ordinary members of society in the everyday situations in which they find themselves and the ways in which they use commonsense knowledge, procedures, and considerations to gain an understanding of, navigate in, and act on those situations.

We can gain insight into the nature of ethnomethodology by examining efforts by its founder, Harold Garfinkel (1917–), to define it. Like Durkheim (see Chapter 2), Garfinkel considers social facts to be the fundamental sociological phenomenon. However, Garfinkel's social facts are very different from Durkheim's social facts. For Durkheim, social facts are external to and coercive of individuals. Those who adopt such a focus tend to see actors as constrained or determined by social structures and institutions and able to exercise little or no independent judgment. In the acerbic terms of the ethnomethodologists, such sociologists tended to treat actors like judgmental dopes.

In contrast, ethnomethodology treats the objectivity of social facts as the accomplishment of members (see below)—as a product of members' methodological activities. In other words, ethnomethodology is concerned with the organization of everyday, ordinary life. To the ethnomethodologist, the ways in which we go about organizing our ordinary, day-to-day lives are extraordinary.

Ethnomethodology is certainly not a macrosociology in the sense intended by Durkheim and his concept of a social fact, but its adherents do not see it as a microsociology either. Thus, while ethnomethodologists refuse to treat actors as judgmental dopes, they do not believe that people are continually thinking about themselves and what they ought to do in every situation that presents itself. Rather, they recognize that most often action is routine and relatively unreflective. Ethnomethodologists do not focus on actors or individuals, but rather on members. However, members are viewed not as individuals, but rather as membership activities, or the artful practices through which people produce what are *for them* both large-scale structures (e.g., bureaucracy, society) and the structures of everyday life (e.g., patterns of day-to-day interaction). In sum, ethnomethodologists are interested in *neither* microstructures *nor* macrostructures; they are concerned with the artful practices that produce people's sense of *both* types of structures. What Garfinkel and the ethnomethodologists have sought is a new way of getting at the traditional concern of sociology with objective structures, both small- and large-scale.

---

ethnomethodology   The study of ordinary members of society in the everyday situations in which they find themselves and the ways in which they use commonsense knowledge, procedures, and considerations to gain an understanding of, navigate in, and act on those situations.

Accounts

One of Garfinkel's key points about ethnomethods is that they are reflexively accountable. **Accounts** are the ways in which actors explain (describe, criticize, and idealize) specific situations. **Accounting** is the process by which people offer accounts in order to make sense of the world. Ethnomethodologists devote a lot of attention to analyzing people's accounts, as well as to the ways in which accounts are offered and accepted (or rejected) by others. This is one of the reasons that ethnomethodologists are preoccupied with analyzing conversations. For example, when a student explains to her professor why she failed to take an examination, she is offering an account. The student is trying to make sense out of an event for her professor. Ethnomethodologists are interested in the nature of that account but more generally in the **accounting practices** by which the student offers the account and the professor accepts or rejects it. In analyzing accounts, ethnomethodologists adopt a stance of ethnomethodological indifference. They do not judge the nature of the accounts but rather analyze them in terms of how they are used in practical action. They are concerned with the accounts as well as the methods needed by both speaker and listener to proffer, understand, and accept or reject accounts.

Extending the idea of accounts, ethnomethodologists take great pains to point out that sociologists, like everyone else, offer accounts. Reports of sociological studies can be seen as accounts, and they can be analyzed by ethnomethodologists in the same way that all other accounts can be studied. This perspective on sociology serves to demystify the work of sociologists, indeed, all scientists. A good deal of sociology (indeed, all sciences) involves commonsense interpretations. Ethnomethodologists can study the accounts of the sociologist in the same way that they can study the accounts of the layperson. Thus, the everyday practices of sociologists and all scientists come under the scrutiny of the ethnomethodologist.

We can say that accounts are reflexive in the sense that they enter into the constitution of the state of affairs they make observable and are intended to deal with. When we offer an account of a situation that we are in, we are in the process altering the nature of that situation. If I am interacting with someone, realize that I have just made a faux pas, and seek to explain (account for) that mistake, in doing so I am changing the nature of that interaction. This is as true for sociologists as it is for laypeople. In studying and reporting on social life, sociologists are, in the process, changing what they are studying; subjects alter

---

accounts   The ways in which actors explain (describe, criticize, and idealize) specific situations.

accounting   The process by which people offer accounts in order to make sense of the world.

accounting practices   The ways in which one person offers an account and another person accepts or rejects that account.

Harold Garfinkel (1917–   )
A Biographical Vignette

Harold Garfinkel was drafted in 1942 and entered the air force. Eventually he was given the task of training troops in tank warfare on a golf course on Miami beach in the complete absence of tanks. Garfinkel had only pictures of tanks from *Life Magazine*. The real tanks were all in combat. The man who would insist on concrete empirical detail in lieu of theorized accounts was teaching real troops who were about to enter live combat to fight against imagined tanks in situations where things like the proximity of the troops to the imagined tank could make the difference between life and death. The impact of this on the development of his views can only be imagined. He had to train troops to throw explosives into the tracks of imaginary tanks; and to keep imaginary tanks from seeing them by directing fire at imaginary tank ports. This task posed, in a new and very concrete way, the problems of the adequate description of action and accountability that Garfinkel would take up as theoretical issues.

their behavior as a result of being the subject of scrutiny and in response to descriptions of that behavior.

Some Examples

Ethnomethodology has gained much notoriety through its research.

Breaching Experiments   In **breaching experiments,** social reality is violated in order to shed light on the methods by which people construct social reality. The assumption behind this research is not only that the methodical production of social life occurs all the time but also that the participants are unaware that they are engaging in such actions. The objective of the breaching experiment is to disrupt normal procedures so that the process by which the everyday world is constructed or reconstructed can be observed and studied.

Lynch offers the following example (Figure 6.1) of breaching, derived from earlier work by Garfinkel. This, of course, is a game of tic-tac-toe. The rules allow participants in the game to place a mark *within* each of the cells, but the rules have been breached in this case and a mark has been placed by player 1 *between* two cells. If this breach were to occur in a real game of tic-tac-toe, the other player (player 2) would likely insist on its being erased and placed correctly. If such a new placement did not occur, player 2 would try to explain (offer an account of) why player 1 had taken such an extraordinary action. The actions of player 2 would be studied by the ethnomethodologist to see how the everyday world of tic-tac-toe is reconstructed.

---

breaching experiments   Experiments in which social reality is violated in order to shed light on the methods by which people construct social reality.

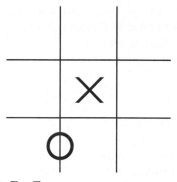

FIGURE 6.1. Breaching in Tic-Tac-Toe.
Source: Michael Lynch, 1991. "Pictures of Nothing? Visual Constructs in Social Theory."
Sociological Theory 9:15.

In another experiment, Garfinkel asked his students to spend between 15 minutes and an hour in their own homes imagining that they were boarders and then acting on the basis of that assumption. They were told to behave in ways that are usually not found in a family situation. For example, they were instructed to be polite, cautious, impersonal, and formal; they were to speak only when family members spoke to them. In the vast majority of cases, family members were dumbfounded and outraged by such behavior. The students reported (offered accounts of) family members who expressed astonishment, bewilderment, shock, anxiety, embarrassment, and anger. Family members charged that the students who engaged in these behaviors were mean, inconsiderate, selfish, nasty, or impolite. These reactions indicate how important it is that people act in accord with the commonsense assumptions about how they are supposed to behave.

What most interested Garfinkel was how the family members sought in commonsense ways to cope with such a breach. They demanded explanations from the students for their behavior. In the questions they asked of students, they often implied an explanation of the aberrant behavior. They asked whether the students were ill, had been fired, were out of their minds, or were just stupid.

Family members also sought to explain the behaviors to themselves in terms of previously understood motives. For example, a student was thought to be behaving oddly because she was working too hard or had had a fight with her fiancè. Such explanations are important to participants—the other family members, in this case—because the explanations help them feel that under normal circumstances interaction would occur as it always had.

If the student did not acknowledge the validity of such explanations, family members were likely to withdraw and to seek to isolate, denounce, or retaliate against the culprit. Deep emotions were aroused because the effort to restore order through explanation was rejected by the student. The other family members felt that more intense statements and actions were necessary to restore the equilibrium. In one case, the student was told that if he did not stop behaving in this way, he had better move out. In the end, the students explained the experiment to their families, and in most situations harmony was restored. However, in some instances hard feelings lingered.

Breaching experiments are undertaken to illustrate the way people order their everyday lives. These experiments reveal the resilience of social reality, since the subjects (or victims) move quickly to normalize the breach—that is, to render the situation accountable in familiar terms. It is assumed that the way people handle these breaches tells us much about how they handle their everyday lives. Although these experiments seem innocent enough, they often lead to highly emotional reactions. These extreme reactions reflect how important it is to people to engage in routine, commonsense activities. Reactions to breaches are sometimes so extreme that ethnomethodologists have been warned in more recent years not to perform the kinds of breaching experiments performed by Garfinkel.

Accomplishing Gender

It seems incontrovertible that one's gender—male or female—is biologically based. People are seen as simply manifesting the behaviors that are an outgrowth of their biological makeup. People are not usually thought of as accomplishing their gender. In contrast, sexiness is clearly an accomplishment; people need to speak and act in certain ways in order to be seen as sexy. However, it is generally assumed that one does not have to do or say *anything* to be seen as a man or a woman. Ethnomethodology has investigated the issue of gender, with some very unusual results.

The ethnomethodological view is traceable to one of Harold Garfinkel's now classic demonstrations of the utility of this orientation. In the 1950s Garfinkel met a person named Agnes, who seemed unquestionably a woman. Not only did she have the figure of a woman, but it was virtually a perfect figure with an ideal set of measurements. She also had a pretty face, good complexion, no facial hair, and plucked eyebrows—and she wore lipstick. This was clearly a woman, or was it? Garfinkel discovered that Agnes had not always appeared to be a woman. In fact, at the time he met her, Agnes was trying, eventually successfully, to convince physicians that she needed an operation to remove her male genitalia and create a vagina.

Agnes was defined as a male at birth. In fact, she was by all accounts a boy until she was 16 years of age. At that age, sensing something was awry, Agnes ran away from home and started to dress like a girl. She soon discovered that dressing like a woman was not enough; she had to *learn to act* like (to pass as) a woman if she was to be accepted as one. She did learn the accepted practices and as a result came to be defined, and to define herself, as a woman. Garfinkel was interested in the passing practices that allowed Agnes to function like a woman in society. The more general point here is that we are not simply born men or women; we all also learn and routinely use the commonplace practices that allow us to pass as men or women. Only in learning these practices do we come to be, in a sociological sense, a man or a woman. Thus, even a category like gender, which is thought to be an ascribed status, can be understood as an accomplishment of a set of situated practices.

EXCHANGE THEORY

Another theory of everyday behavior is exchange theory. Although there are a number of varieties of exchange theory in sociology, the focus here is on the work of George Homans.

The Exchange Theory of George Homans

Although there are a variety of inputs into George Homans's development of exchange theory, perhaps the most important is the psychological theory known as behaviorism. The behavioral sociologist is concerned with the relationship between the effects of an actor's behavior on the environment and the impact on the actor's later behavior. This relationship is basic to **operant conditioning,** or the learning process by which the consequences of behavior serve to modify that behavior. One might almost think of this behavior, at least initially in the infant, as a random behavior. The environment in which the behavior exists, whether social or physical, is affected by the behavior and in turn acts back in various ways. That reaction—positive, negative, or neutral—affects the actor's later behavior. If the reaction has been rewarding to the actor, the same behavior is likely to be emitted in the future in similar situations. If the reaction has been painful or punishing, the behavior is less likely to occur in the future. The behavioral sociologist is interested in the relationship between the history of environmental reactions or consequences and the nature of present behavior. Past consequences of a given behavior govern its present state. By knowing what elicited a certain behavior in the past, we can predict whether an actor will produce the same behavior in the present situation.

The heart of George Homans's exchange theory lies in a set of fundamental propositions powerfully influenced by behaviorism. Although some of Homans's propositions deal with at least two interacting individuals, he was careful to point out that these propositions are based on psychological principles. According to Homans, they are psychological for two reasons: (1) They are usually the province of psychologists and (2) they deal with individual behavior rather than large-scale structures like groups or societies. As a result of this position, Homans admitted to being a psychological reductionist. To Homans, reductionism involves showing that the propositions of one science (in this case sociology) are derived from the more general propositions of another science (in this case, psychology).

---

operant conditioning   The learning process by which the consequences of behavior serve to modify that behavior.

Although Homans made the case for psychological principles, he did not think of individuals as isolated. He recognized that people are social and spend a considerable portion of their time interacting with other people. He attempted to explain social behavior with psychological principles. In other words, the principles that apply to the relationship between human beings and the physical environment are the same as those that relate to instances where the environment is made up of other human beings. Homans did not deny the Durkheimian position of emergence—that something new emerges from inter-action. Instead, he argued that those emergent properties can be explained by psychological principles; there is no need for new sociological propositions to explain social facts. He used the basic sociological concept of a norm as illustra-tion. Homans does not doubt that norms exist and that they lead to conformity. However, people do not conform automatically. They do so because they see it as an advantage to conform to those norms.

Homans detailed a program to bring men back into sociology, but he also tried to develop a theory that focuses on psychology, people, and the elemen-tary forms of social life. In terms of the latter, he focused on social behavior involving at least two people in the exchange of tangible and intangible activi-ties. Such behavior would vary in terms of the degree to which it was reward-ing or costly to the people involved.

For example, Homans sought to explain the development of power-driven machinery in the textile industry, and thereby the Industrial Revolution, through the psychological principle that people are likely to act in such a way as to increase their rewards. More generally, in his version of exchange theory, he sought to explain elementary social behavior in terms of rewards and costs. Homans set for himself the task of developing propositions that focus on the psychological level; these form the groundwork of exchange theory.

Roots in Behaviorism In *Social Behavior: Its Elementary Forms,* Homans acknowledged that his exchange theory was derived, in large part, from behavioral psychology. In fact, Homans regretted that his theory was labeled exchange theory because he viewed it as behavioral psychology applied to spe-cific situations. Homans began with a discussion of the work of the leading fig-ure in psychological behaviorism, B. F. Skinner—in particular, Skinner's study of pigeons born with the ability to explore their environments by pecking at the things that confronted them. Placed in an experimental cage, pigeons begin to peck and eventually peck at a target placed there by the researcher. When the pigeon does so, it is rewarded with a bit of grain. Since the pigeon has been rewarded for pecking the target, the chances are good that it will do so again. In formal, behaviorist terms, the pecking at the target is the operant, that operant has been reinforced, and the reinforcer was the bit of grain. Thus, the pigeon has undergone a process of operant conditioning: The pigeon has learned to peck the target because it has been rewarded for doing so.

Skinner was interested in this instance in pigeons; Homans's concern was humans. According to Homans, Skinner's pigeons are not engaged in a true exchange relationship with the psychologist. The pigeon is engaged in a

George Caspar Homans (1910–1989)
An Autobiographical Vignette

I had long known Professor Talcott Parsons and was now closely associated with him in the Department of Social Relations. The sociological profession looked upon him as its leading theorist. I decided that what he called theories were only conceptual schemes, and that a theory was not a theory unless it contained at least a few propositions. I became confident that this view was correct by reading several books on the philosophy of science.

Nor was it enough that a theory should contain propositions. A theory of a phenomenon was an explanation of it. Explanation consisted in showing that one or more propositions of a low order of generality followed in logic from more general propositions applied to what were variously called given or boundary conditions or parameters. I stated my position on this issue in my little book *The Nature of Social Science* (1967).

I then asked myself what general propositions I could use in this way to explain the empirical propositions I had stated in *The Human Group* and other propositions brought to my attention by later reading of field and experimental studies in social psychology. The general propositions would have to meet only one condition: In accordance with my original insight, they should apply to individual human beings as members of a species.

Such propositions were already at hand—luckily, for I could not have invented them for myself. They were the propositions of behavioral psychology as stated by my old friend B. F. Skinner and others. They held good of persons both when acting alone in the physical environment and when in interaction with other persons. In the two editions of my book *Social Behavior* (1961 and revised in 1974), I used these propositions to try to explain how, under appropriate given conditions, relatively enduring social structures could arise from, and be maintained by, the actions of individuals, who need not have intended to create the structures. This I conceive to be the central intellectual problem of sociology.

---

one-sided exchange relationship, whereas human exchanges are at least two-sided. The pigeon is being reinforced by the grain, but the psychologist is not truly being reinforced by the pecks of the pigeon. The pigeon is carrying on the same sort of relationship with the psychologist as it would with the physical environment. Because there is no reciprocity, Homans defined this as individual behavior. He seemed to relegate the study of this sort of behavior to the psychologist, whereas he urged the sociologist to study social behavior in which the activities of two (or more) human beings reinforce (or punish) the activities of the other. In other words, Homans is interested in behavior in which each person influences the other. However, it is significant that, according to Homans, *no new propositions* are needed to explain social behavior as opposed to individual behavior. The laws of individual behavior as developed by Skinner in his study of pigeons explain social behavior as long as we take into account the complications of mutual reinforcement.

Homans admitted that he might ultimately have to go beyond the principles derived by Skinner, but only reluctantly.

In his theoretical work, Homans restricted himself to everyday social interaction. It is clear, however, that he believed that a sociology built on his principles would ultimately be able to explain all social behavior. Homans used the case of two office workers to exemplify the kind of exchange relationships he was interested in. According to office rules, each person was to do his job on his own. If help was needed, a supervisor was to be consulted. However, suppose one of the workers (worker A) had trouble completing his work from time to time, but he could do it better and more quickly with help. According to the rules, he should consult his supervisor, but to do so would make his incompetence clear to the supervisor and adversely affect his future with the organization. It is far safer to ask his colleague (worker B) for help, especially if she has more experience and greater capacity to do the work. It is also assumed that such a consultation will not come to the supervisor's attention. One worker gives the needed assistance and the other offers thanks and approval. In other words, an exchange has occurred between them—help in exchange for approval.

Basic Propositions

Focusing on this sort of situation, and basing his ideas on Skinner's findings, Homans developed several propositions.

1. The *success proposition* states that the more often a person is rewarded for a particular action, the more likely the person is to perform the rewarded action. In terms of the office situation example, this proposition means that worker A is more likely to ask others for advice if he has been rewarded in the past with useful advice. Furthermore, the more often a person received useful advice in the past, the more often he or she will request advice in the future. Similarly, the other person (worker B) will be more willing to give advice and give it more frequently if he or she often has been rewarded with approval in the past. Generally, behavior in accord with the success proposition involves three stages: first, a person's action; next, a rewarded result; and finally, a repetition of the original action or at minimum one similar in at least some respects.

   Homans specified a number of things about the success proposition. First, although it is generally true that increasingly frequent rewards lead to increasingly frequent actions, this reciprocation cannot go on indefinitely. At some point individuals simply cannot act that way as frequently. Second, the shorter the interval between behavior and reward, the more likely a person is to repeat the behavior. Conversely, long intervals between behavior and reward lower the likelihood of repeat behavior. Finally, it was Homans's view that intermittent rewards are more likely to elicit repeat behavior than regular rewards. Regular rewards lead to boredom and satiation, whereas rewards at irregular intervals (as in gambling) are very likely to elicit repeat behaviors.

2. The *stimulus proposition* asserts that if in the past a person's action has been rewarded as a result of responding to a particular stimulus, or set of stimuli, then the person is more likely to perform the same action (or something similar) when stimuli are applied that are similar to those in the past. In the office worker example, if, in the past, the two workers in question found the giving and getting of advice rewarding, then they are likely to engage in similar actions in similar situations in the future. Homans offered an even more down-to-earth example when he argued that those who catch fish in dark pools are more likely to fish in such pools in the future.

   Homans was interested in the process of **generalization,** the tendency to extend behavior to similar circumstances. In the fishing example, one aspect of generalization is to move from fishing in dark pools to fishing in any pool with any degree of shadiness. Similarly, success in catching fish is likely to lead from one kind of fishing to another (e.g., freshwater to saltwater) or even from fishing to hunting. However, the process of **discrimination** is also important. The actor may fish only under the specific circumstances that proved successful in the past. For one thing, if the conditions under which success occurred were too complicated, then similar conditions may not stimulate behavior. If the crucial stimulus occurs too long before behavior is required, then it may not actually stimulate that behavior. An actor can become oversensitized to stimuli, especially if they are very valuable to the actor. In fact, the actor could respond to irrelevant stimuli, at least until the situation is corrected by repeated failures. All this is affected by the individual's alertness or attentiveness to stimuli.

3. The *value proposition* states that the more valuable people find the results of their action, the more likely they are to perform that action. In the office worker example, if the rewards each worker offers to the other are considered valuable, the workers are more likely to perform the desired behaviors than if the rewards are not seen as valuable. At this point, Homans introduced the concepts of rewards and punishments. **Rewards** are actions with positive values; an increase in rewards is more likely to elicit the desired behavior. **Punishments** are actions with negative values; an increase in punishment means that the actor is less likely to manifest undesired behaviors. Homans found punishments to be an inefficient means of getting people to change their behavior, because people may react in undesirable ways to the punishment. It is preferable simply not to reward undesirable behavior (e.g., anger); then such behavior eventually becomes

---

generalization   The tendency to extend behavior to similar circumstances.

discrimination   The tendency to manifest behavior only under the specific circumstances that proved successful in the past.

rewards   Actions with positive values; an increase in such actions is more likely to elicit the desired behavior.

punishments   Actions with negative values; an increase in such actions means that the actor is less likely to manifest undesired behaviors.

extinguished. Rewards are clearly to be preferred, but they may be in short supply. Homans did make it clear that his is not simply a hedonistic theory; rewards can be either materialistic (e.g., money) or altruistic (helping others).

4. The *deprivation-satiation proposition* contends that the more often in the recent past people have received a particular reward, the less valuable will be future rewards of that type. In the office example, the two workers may reward each other so often for giving and getting advice that the rewards cease to be valuable to each other. Time is crucial here; people are less likely to become satiated if particular rewards are stretched over a long period of time.

At this point, Homans defined two other critical concepts: cost and profit. The **cost** of any behavior is defined as the rewards lost in forgoing alternative lines of action. **Profit** in social exchange is seen as the greater number of rewards gained over costs incurred. The latter led Homans to recast the deprivation-satiation proposition as the greater the profits people receive as a result of particular actions, the more likely they are to perform those actions.

5. There are two *aggression-approval propositions*. In Proposition 5A Homans argues that when people do not receive expected rewards for their actions, or they receive unanticipated punishment, they become angry, more likely to act aggressively, and to find the results of such aggressive behavior more valuable.

In the office worker example, if worker A does not get the advice he or she expects and worker B does not receive the praise he or she anticipates, both are likely to be angry. We are surprised to find the concepts of frustration and anger in Homans's work, because they would seem to refer to mental states. Purists in behaviorism would not deal with such states of mind. Homans went on to argue that frustration of such expectations need *not* refer only to an internal state. It can also refer to wholly external events, observable not just by worker A but also by outsiders.

Proposition 5A on aggression-approval refers only to negative emotions, whereas Proposition 5B deals with more positive emotions and argues that people will be pleased when they receive an expected reward, especially one that is greater than expected; they will, as a result, be more likely to perform the behavior that has received approval and the results of that behavior will become of increasing value. For example, in the office worker example, when worker A gets the advice that he or she expects and worker B gets the praise that he or she expects, both are pleased and more likely to get or give advice. Advice and praise become more valuable to each.

6. In the *rationality proposition* people are seen as choosing from the available alternatives, the action for which, given the person's perception at the time, there are greater rewards and greater probability of getting those rewards.

---

cost   Rewards lost in adopting a specific action and, as a result, in forgoing alternative lines of action.

profit   The greater number of rewards gained over costs incurred in social exchange.

Although the earlier propositions rely heavily on behaviorism, the rationality proposition demonstrates most clearly the influence of rational choice theory (see the next section) on Homans's approach. In economic terms, actors who act in accord with the rationality proposition are maximizing their **utilities.**

Basically, people examine and make calculations about the various alternative actions open to them. They compare the amount of rewards associated with each course of action. They also calculate the likelihood that they will actually receive the rewards. Highly valued rewards are devalued if the actors think it unlikely that they will obtain them. On the other hand, lesser-valued rewards will be enhanced if they are seen as highly attainable. Thus, there is an interaction between the value of the reward and the likelihood of attainment. The most desirable rewards are those that are *both* very valuable *and* highly attainable. The least desirable rewards are those that are not very valuable and difficult to attain.

Homans related the rationality proposition to the success, stimulus, and value propositions. The rationality proposition tells us that whether or not people perform an action depends on their perceptions of the probability of success. But what determines this perception? Homans argued that perceptions of whether chances of success are high or low are shaped by past successes and the similarity of the present situation to past successful situations. The rationality proposition also does not tell us why an actor values one reward more than another; for this we need the value proposition. In these ways, Homans linked his rationality principle to his more behavioristic propositions.

In the end, Homans's theory can be condensed to a view of the actor as a rational profit seeker. However, Homans's theory was weak on mental states and large-scale structures. For example, on the subject of consciousness Homans admitted the need for a more fully developed psychology.

Despite such weaknesses, Homans remained a behaviorist who worked resolutely at the level of individual behavior. He argued that large-scale structures can be understood if we adequately understand elementary social behavior. He contended that exchange processes are identical at the individual and societal levels, although he granted that at the societal level there is greater complexity to the ways in which fundamental processes are put together to form large-scale phenomena.

RATIONAL CHOICE THEORY

Although it influenced the development of exchange theory, rational choice theory was generally marginal to mainstream sociological theory. Largely through the efforts of one man, James S. Coleman, rational choice theory has

---

utilities   Actor's preferences, or values.

become one of the "hot" theories in contemporary sociology. For one thing, in 1989 Coleman founded a journal, *Rationality and Society*, devoted to the dissemination of work from a rational choice perspective. For another, Coleman published an enormously influential book, *Foundations of Social Theory*, based on this perspective. Finally, Coleman became president of the American Sociological Association in 1992 and used that forum to push rational choice theory and to present an address entitled "The Rational Reconstruction of Society."

A Skeletal Model

The basic principles of rational choice theory are derived from neoclassical economics (as well as utilitarianism and game theory). Based on a variety of different models, it is possible to piece together what can be described as a skeletal model of rational choice theory.

The focus in rational choice theory is on actors. Actors are seen as being purposive, or as having intentionality; that is, actors have ends or goals toward which their actions are aimed. Actors are also seen as having preferences (or values, utilities). Rational choice theory is unconcerned with what these preferences, or their sources, are. Of importance is the fact that action is undertaken to achieve objectives consistent with an actor's preference hierarchy.

Although rational choice theory starts with actors' purposes or intentions, it must take into consideration at least two major constraints on action. The first is the scarcity of resources. Actors have different resources as well as differential access to other resources. For those with lots of resources, the achievement of ends may be relatively easy. However, for those with few, if any, resources, the attainment of ends may be difficult or impossible.

Related to scarcity of resources is the idea of **opportunity costs.** In pursuing a given end, actors must keep an eye on the costs of forgoing their next most attractive action. An actor may choose not to pursue the most highly valued end if her resources are negligible, if, as a result, the chances of achieving that end are slim, and if in striving to achieve that end she jeopardizes her chances of achieving her next most valued end. Actors are seen as trying to maximize their benefits; that goal may involve assessing the relationship between the chances of achieving a primary end and what that achievement does for chances for attaining the second most valuable objective.

A second source of constraints on individual action is social institutions. Such constraint occurs throughout the life course and is manifest through schools and their rules, the policies of employing organizations, and the laws of society. These all serve to restrict choices available to actors and, thereby, the outcome of actions. These institutional constraints provide both positive and negative sanctions that serve to encourage certain actions and to discourage others.

---

opportunity costs   The costs of forgoing the next most attractive action when an actor chooses an action aimed at achieving a given end.

It is possible to enumerate two other ideas that can be seen as basic to rational choice theory. The first is an aggregation mechanism whereby a variety of individual actions are combined to form a social outcome. The second is the importance of information in making rational choices. At one time, it was assumed that actors had perfect, or at least sufficient, information to make purposive choices among the alternative courses of action open to them. However, there is a growing recognition that the quantity or quality of available information is highly variable and that variability has a profound effect on actors' choices.

In his introductory comments to the first issue of *Rationality and Society*, Coleman made it clear that he gave allegiance to rational choice theory not only because of the strengths of the theory itself, but also because it is the only theory capable of producing a more integrative sociological approach. He views rational choice theory as providing the micro-level base for the explanation of macro-level phenomena. Beyond such academic concerns, Coleman wants work done from a rational choice perspective to have practical relevance to our changing social world. For example, the issue of public policies aimed at AIDS prevention has been studied from a rational choice perspective.

Foundations of Social Theory

Coleman argues that sociology should focus on social systems, but that such macro-phenomena must be explained by factors internal to them, ideally, individuals. He favors working at the individual level for several reasons, including the fact that data are usually gathered at that level and then aggregated or composed to yield the system level. Among the other reasons for favoring a focus on the individual level is that this is where interventions are ordinarily made to create social changes. Central to Coleman's perspective is the idea that social theory is not merely an academic exercise but should affect the social world through such interventions.

Given his focus on the individual, Coleman recognizes that he is a methodological individualist, although he views his particular perspective as a special variant of that orientation. His view is special in the sense that it accepts the idea of emergence and that while it focuses on factors internal to the system, those factors are not necessarily individual actions and orientations. Micro-level phenomena other than individuals can be the focus of his analysis.

Coleman's rational choice orientation is clear in his basic idea that people act toward goals in a purposive manner and both goals and actions are shaped by values (or preferences). But Coleman then goes on to argue that for most theoretical purposes, he will need a more precise conceptualization of the rational actor derived from economics, one that sees the actors choosing those actions that will maximize utility, or the satisfaction of their needs and wants.

The two key elements in his theory are actors and resources. Resources are those things over which actors have control and in which they have some interest. Given these two elements, Coleman details how their interaction leads to the system level. This is based on the fact that actors have resources and those resources are of interest to others. As a result, actors engage in actions

James S. Coleman (1926–1995)
A Biographical Vignette

Looking back from the vantage point of the mid-1990s, Coleman found that his macro-level approach had changed. For example, with respect to his work on social simulation games at Johns Hopkins in the 1960s, he said that they "led me to change my theoretical orientation from one in which properties of the system are not only determinants of action (à la Emile Durkheim's *Suicide* study), to one in which they are also consequences of actions sometimes intended, sometimes unintended." Coleman needed a theory of action, and he chose, in common with most economists,

> the simplest such foundation, that of rational, or if you prefer, purposive action. The most formidable task of sociology is the development of a theory that will move from the micro-level of action to the macro-level of norms, social values, status distribution, and social conflict.

This interest explains why Coleman is drawn to economics:

> What distinguishes economics from the other social sciences is not its use of rational choice but its use of a mode of analysis that allows moving between the level of individual action and the level of system functioning. By making two assumptions, that persons act rationally and that markets are perfect with full communication, economic analysis is able to link the macro-level of system functioning with the micro-level of individual actions.

> Another aspect of Coleman's vision for sociology, consistent with his early work on schools, is that it be applicable to social policy. Of theory he says, "One of the criteria for judging work in social theory is its potential usefulness for informing social policy."

that involve others and a system of action, a structure, emerges among them. In other words, interdependent actors, each seeking to maximize interests, form a social system.

Given his orientation to individual rational action, it follows that Coleman's focus in terms of the micro-macro issue (see, especially, Chapter 7) is the micro-to-macro linkage, or how the combination of individual actions creates the larger system. While he accords priority to this issue, Coleman is also interested in the macro-to-micro linkage, or how the macro-system constrains the orientations of actors. Finally, he is interested in the micro-micro aspect of the relationship, or the impact of individual behavior on the behavior of other individuals.

In spite of this seeming balance, there are at least three major weaknesses in Coleman's approach. First, he accords overwhelming priority to the micro-to-macro issue, thereby giving short shrift to the other relationships (macro-micro, micro-micro). Second, he ignores the macro-macro issue. Finally, his causal arrows go mainly in one direction (macro to micro); in other words, he ignores the ongoing reciprocal relationship among and between micro and macro phenomena.

Utilizing his rational choice approach and starting at the micro-level of rational individual behavior, Coleman seeks to explain a series of macro-level phenomena including collective behavior, norms, and the corporate actor.

Collective Behavior. Coleman (and other rational choice theorists) chooses to deal with collective behavior (of, for example, a crowd) because its often disorderly and unstable character is thought to be difficult to analyze from a rational choice perspective. But Coleman's view is that rational choice theory *can* explain all types of macro phenomena, not just those that are orderly and stable. What is involved in collective behavior is the unilateral transfer by rational actors of control over their actions to others (e.g., crowd organizers or leaders). They do this in an attempt to maximize their utility. Normally, such maximization involves a balancing of control among several actors; this balance produces equilibrium within society. However, in the case of collective behavior, because there is a unilateral transfer of control, individual maximization creates an imbalance and does not necessarily lead to system equilibrium. Instead, there is the disequilibrium characteristic of collective behavior such as in the case of an unruly crowd.

Norms. Another macro-level phenomenon that comes under Coleman's scrutiny is norms. Unlike collective behavior, norms are not only quite stable but they serve to produce order in society. While most sociologists take norms as given and invoke them to explain individual behavior, they do not explain why and how norms come into existence. Coleman wonders how, in a group of rational actors, norms emerge and are maintained. He argues that norms are created and maintained by some people who see benefits resulting from norms that control group behavior and see harm stemming from the violation of those norms. Thus, norms against smoking in public places have emerged because they protect nonsmokers (likely those who helped create the norms) from second-hand smoke and violation of such norms would lead to higher rates of lung cancer among them. People are willing to give up some control over their own behavior (others decide whether smoking in public places is permissible), but in the process they gain some individual and collective control (through norms) over the behavior of others (preventing them from smoking in such settings). Once again, people are seen as maximizing their utility by partially surrendering rights of control over themselves and gaining some control over others. Because the transfer of control is mutual, it is *not* unilateral as it is in the case of collective behavior, there is equilibrium in the case of norms.

Norms often act to the advantage of some people (e.g., nonsmokers) and to the disadvantage of others (smokers). In some cases (including smoking in public places), actors surrender the right to control their own actions to those who initiate and maintain the norms. Such norms become effective when a consensus emerges that some people have the right to control (through norms) the actions of other people. Furthermore, the effectiveness of norms depends on the ability to enforce that consensus (e.g., forcing violators to extinguish their cigarettes in public places). This consensus and enforcement are other factors that prevent the kind of disequilibrium characteristic of collective behavior.

Coleman recognizes that norms become interrelated (bans on smoking on airplanes and in airports), but he sees such a macro-macro (norm-norm) issue as beyond the scope of his work on the foundations of social systems. However, he is willing to take on the macro-to-micro issue of the internalization of norms. He sees the internalization of norms as the establishment of an internal sanctioning system; people sanction themselves when they violate a norm. Coleman looks at this in terms of the idea of one actor or set of actors endeavoring to control others by having norms internalized in them. Thus, it is in the interests of one set of actors to have another set of people internalize norms and be controlled by them.

The Corporate Actor.   Within such a collectivity as a corporation or a state, individual actors may not make choices among actions in terms of their self-interest but often must choose on the basis of the interest of the collectivity. Thus, a U.S. President might choose not to run for a second term even though it would be in his self-interest to do so. Rather, he chooses that option because it is in the interest of his political party, the nation, and its citizens.

There are various rules and mechanisms for moving from individual choice to collective (social) choice. The simplest is the case of voting and the procedures for tabulating the individual votes and coming up with a collective decision. This is the micro-to-macro dimension, while such things as the slate of candidates proposed by the collectivity involve the macro-to-micro linkage.

Coleman argues that both corporate actors and human actors have purposes. Furthermore, within a corporate structure such as an organization, human actors may pursue purposes of their own that are at variance with corporate purposes. This conflict of interest helps us understand the sources of revolts against corporate authority. The micro-to-macro linkage here involves the ways in which people divest authority from the corporate structure and vest legitimacy in those engaged in the revolt. But there is also a macro-to-micro linkage in that certain macro-level conditions lead people to such acts of divestment and investment.

As a rational choice theorist, Coleman starts with the individual and with the idea that is where all rights and resources exist. It is the interests of individuals that should determine the course of events. However, this is often not the case, especially in modern society, where many rights, significant resources, and even sovereignty reside in corporate actors. In the modern world corporate actors have taken on increasing importance. The corporate actor may act to the benefit or the harm of the individual. How are we to judge the corporate actor in this regard? Coleman contends that we need to do this on the basis of the assumption that it is individual persons who are sovereign and the social system must be evaluated on the basis of how well it serves individual sovereignty.

Coleman differentiates between traditional structures based on the family, such as neighborhoods and religious groups, and purposive structures, such as economic organizations and the government. There have always been corporate actors, but the traditional ones, such as the family, are steadily being replaced by new, purposively constructed, free-standing corporate actors. He sees a progressive "unbundling" of the activities that once were tied together within, for example, the family. Such traditional structures are "unraveling" as their functions are dispersed and taken over by a range of corporate actors (e.g., child care centers in the case of the family). Coleman is concerned about this unraveling as well as about the fact that we are now forced to deal with positions in purposive structures (e.g., managers) rather than with the people who populated traditional structures. The existence of these new corporate actors raises the issue of how to ensure that they are socially responsible. Coleman suggests that we can do this by instituting internal reforms or by changing the external structure, such as the laws affecting such corporate actors or the agencies that regulate them.

The ultimate goal of Coleman's work is the creation of a new social structure as the traditional one upon which people depended disappears. The passing of traditional structures and their replacement by purposive structures have left a series of voids that have not been filled adequately by the new social organizations. Social theory and the social sciences more generally are made necessary by the need to reconstruct a new society. The goal is not to destroy purposive structures but rather to realize the possibilities, and to avoid the problems, of such structures.

An overview of the field confirms Coleman's views on rational choice theory. Work continues on many of the macro-issues identified by Coleman (e.g., collective behavior), but it has also expanded not only into other macro-areas (e.g., social stratification), but also to micro-areas (e.g., emotions) that one would not immediately think of as being amenable to rational choice analysis.

Although he has faith in rational choice theory, Coleman does not believe that this perspective, at least as yet, has all the answers. But it is clear that he believes that it can move in that direction. His hope is that work in rational choice theory will, over time, reduce the issues that cannot be dealt with by that theory.

Coleman recognizes that in the real world people do not always behave rationally, but he believes that this makes little difference in his theory; the same theoretical predictions would be made whether or not people behave rationally.

Summary

1. Symbolic interactionism, like the other theories discussed in this chapter, focuses on everyday life, especially interaction (as well as action and people as agents) and the symbols (and their meanings) that are deeply implicated in it.
2. Symbolic interactionism is defined by a set of fundamental assumptions:
   a. People act toward things on the basis of the meanings those things have for them and these meanings stem from their interactions with other people.
   b. People do not simply internalize the meanings that they learn through social interaction, but they are also able to modify them through an interpretive process.

     c. People, in contrast to other animals, are unique in their ability to use and rely on symbols.

     d. People become human through social interaction, especially in the early years with family members and then in school.

     e. People are conscious, capable of reflecting on themselves and what they do, and therefore capable of shaping their actions and interactions.

     f. People have purposes when they act in, as well as toward, situations.

     g. Society consists of people engaging in social interaction.

3. To Erving Goffman, dramaturgy views social life as a series of dramatic performances akin to those performed in the theater.

4. From a dramaturgical perspective, the self is a sense of who one is that is a dramatic effect that emerges from the immediate scene being presented.

5. Impression management involves techniques actors use to maintain certain impressions in the face of problems they are likely to encounter, and methods they use to cope with these problems.

6. The front stage is that part of dramaturgical performance that generally functions in rather fixed and general ways to define the situation for those who observe the performance.

7. The back stage is where facts suppressed in the front stage or various kinds of informal actions may appear.

8. Role distance deals with the degree to which individuals separate themselves from the roles they are in.

9. Stigma involves a gap between virtual (what a person ought to be) and actual (what a person actually is) social identity.

10. A discredited stigma occurs when the actor assumes that the differences are known by the audience members, or are evident to them, while a discreditable stigma is one in which the differences are neither known by audience members nor perceivable by them.

11. Ethnomethodology is the study of ordinary members of society in the everyday situations in which they find themselves and the ways in which they use commonsense knowledge, procedures, and considerations to gain an understanding of, navigate in, and act on those situations.

12. Ethnomethodologists are concerned with accounts, accounting, and accounting practices.

13. Breaching experiments violate social reality in order to shed light on the methods by which people construct social reality.

14. George Homans's exchange theory is based primarily on behaviorist principles.

15. The heart of Homans's exchange theory lies in the following propositions:

     a. The more often a person is rewarded for a particular action, the more likely the person is to perform the rewarded action.

     b. If in the past a person's action has been rewarded as a result of responding to a particular stimulus, or set of stimuli, then the person is more likely to perform the same action (or something similar) when stimuli are applied that are similar to those in the past.

     c. The more valuable people find the results of their action, the more likely they are to perform that action.

     d. The more often in the recent past people have received a particular reward, the less valuable will be future rewards of that type.

e. When people do not receive expected rewards for their actions, or they receive unanticipated punishment, they become angry and are more likely to act aggressively and to find the results of such aggressive behavior more valuable.

f. People are pleased when they receive an expected reward, especially one that is greater than expected; and they will, as a result, be more likely to perform the behavior that has received approval and the results of that behavior will become of increasing value.

g. People choose from the available alternatives the action for which, given the person's perception at the time, there are greater rewards and greater probability of getting those rewards.

16. The focus in rational choice theory is on actors.

17. Actors are seen as being purposive, or as having intentionality; that is, actors have ends or goals toward which their actions are aimed.

18. Actors are also seen as having preferences (or values, utilities). Rational choice theory is unconcerned with what these preferences, or their sources, are. Of importance is the fact that action is undertaken to achieve objectives consistent with an actor's preference hierarchy.

19. In addition, rational choice theory must take into account scarcity of resources and opportunity costs, or the costs of forgoing their next most attractive action, as well as the constraints imposed by social institutions.

20. Utilizing a rational choice approach and starting at the micro-level of rational individual behavior, Coleman seeks to explain a series of macro-level phenomena, including collective behavior, norms, and the corporate actor.

Suggested Readings

Kent Sandstrom and Sherryl Kleinman "Symbolic Interaction." In George Ritzer, ed., *The Encyclopedia of Social Theory*, 2 volumes. Thousand Oaks, CA: Sage, 2005, pp. 821–826. Nice overview of the basic principles of symbolic interactionism as well as of current trends and future directions.

Erving Goffman *The Presentation of Self in Everyday Life*. Garden City, NY: Anchor, 1959. Goffman's works tend to be quite readable. This is the best source on dramaturgy.

Erving Goffman *Stigma: Notes on the Management of Spoiled Identity*. Englewood Cliffs, NJ: Prentice Hall, 1963. One of Goffman's most interesting and insightful works.

Gary Alan Fine and Philip Manning "Erving Goffman." In George Ritzer, ed., *The Blackwell Companion to Major Social Theorists*. Malden, MA, and Oxford, England: Blackwell, 2000, pp. 457–485. Good, concise overview of Goffman and his work.

Philip Manning "Dramaturgy." In George Ritzer, ed., *The Encyclopedia of Social Theory*, 2 volumes. Thousand Oaks, CA: Sage, 2005, pp. 210–213. A look at dramaturgy focusing on the contributions of Erving Goffman, although it also includes a look at the perspective after Goffman as well as some of the basic criticisms of it.

Anne Rawls "Harold Garfinkel." In George Ritzer, ed., *The Blackwell Companion to Major Social Theorists*. Malden, MA, and Oxford, England: Blackwell, 2000, pp. 545–576. Rare personal glimpse into Garfinkel's life and work.

Richard Hilbert "Ethnomethodology." In George Ritzer, ed., *The Encyclopedia of Social Theory*, 2 volumes. Thousand Oaks, CA: Sage, 2005, pp. 253–257. Informative look at some of the background of ethnomethodology, its relationship to the social sciences, its terminology, and some of its basic studies. Also includes a brief discussion of conversation analysis.

ANNE RAWLS   "Conversation Analysis." In George Ritzer, ed., *The Encyclopedia of Social Theory*, 2 volumes. Thousand Oaks, CA: Sage, 2005, pp. 145–149. More detailed examination of conversation analysis, including its ties to ethnomethodology.

GEORGE HOMANS   *Coming to My Senses: The Autobiography of a Sociologist*. New Brunswick, NJ: Transaction Books, 1984. The title is self-explanatory.

JON CLARK, ed.   *James S. Coleman*. London: Falmer Press, 1996. Excellent collection of essays on Coleman's contributions to sociology and sociological theory.

SIEGWART LINDENBERG   "James Coleman." In George Ritzer, ed., *The Blackwell Companion to Major Social Theorists*. Malden, MA, and Oxford, England: Blackwell, 2000, pp. 513–544. Brief overview of Coleman's contributions. Especially strong on his work on schools.

DOUGLAS HECKATHORN   "Rational Choice." In George Ritzer, ed., *The Encyclopedia of Social Theory*, 2 volumes. Thousand Oaks, CA: Sage, 2005, pp. 620–624. Overview of the varieties of rational choice theory authored by one of the important contributors to that theory.

CHAPTER 7

Contemporary
Integrative Theories

In previous chapters we have dealt with a variety of contemporary theories that focus either on the large-scale structures and institutions of society (Chapters 4 and 5) or on the micro-levels we associate with everyday life (Chapter 6). In this chapter we deal with theoretical efforts that have sought to deal with the full range of micro-macro issues in a more integrative fashion.

A MORE INTEGRATED EXCHANGE THEORY

While George Homans was involved in an effort to create a microreductionistic exchange theory, Richard Emerson sought to create a more integrated version of that theory. He published two related essays written in 1972 that had a profound effect on the development of exchange theory. Three basic factors served as the impetus for this new body of work. First, Emerson was interested in exchange theory as a broader framework for his earlier interest in power and dependence. It seemed clear to Emerson that power was central to the exchange theory perspective. Second, Emerson felt that he could use behaviorism (operant psychology) as the base of his exchange theory but avoid some of the problems that had befallen Homans. Homans and other exchange theorists had been accused of assuming an overly rational image of human beings, but Emerson felt he could use behaviorism without assuming a rational actor. In addition, Emerson felt he could avoid the charge of reductionism (one that Homans reveled in) by being able to develop an exchange perspective capable of explaining macro-level phenomena. Third, Emerson wanted to deal with social structure and social change by analyzing social relations and social networks and using them as foundations that could be employed from the most microscopic levels of analysis to the most macroscopic. In addition, the actors in Emerson's system could be either individuals or larger corporate structures (albeit, structures working through agents). Thus, Emerson used the principles of operant psychology to develop a theory of social structure.

In his two essays published in 1972, Emerson developed the basis of his integrative exchange theory. In the first essay Emerson dealt with the psychological basis for social exchange, while in the second he turned to the macro-level and exchange relations and network structures. Later, Emerson made the micro-macro linkage more explicit, and the linkage between micro- and macro-levels of analysis was exchange network structures. Karen Cook, Emerson's most important disciple, pointed out that it is the idea of exchange network structures that is central to the micro-macro linkage; it can link single individuals and two-person groups to larger collectivities such as organizations and political parties.

Both Emerson and Cook accept and begin with the basic, micro-level premises of exchange theory, especially the rewards that people get from, and contribute to, social interaction. More specifically, Emerson accepts behavioristic principles as his starting point. Emerson outlines three core assumptions of exchange theory: (1) When people are engaged in situations that they find rewarding, they will act rationally and, as a result, the situations will occur; (2) as people become satiated with the rewards they obtain from situations, those situations will be of declining importance to them; (3) benefits obtained depend on benefits provided in exchange. Therefore, exchange theory focuses on the flow of rewards (and costs) in social interaction. All this is quite familiar, but Emerson begins to point behavioristically oriented exchange theory in a different direction at the close of his first micro-oriented 1972 essay by arguing that he wants to move on to dealing with more complex situations than those usually dealt with by behaviorism.

This theme opens the second 1972 essay in which Emerson makes it clear that he wants to include social structure as a dependent variable in exchange theory. Whereas in the first 1972 essay Emerson was concerned with a single actor involved in an exchange relation with his or her environment (e.g., a person fishing in a lake), in the second essay Emerson turns to social-exchange relationships as well as to exchange networks.

Exchange Relationships and Networks

The actors in Emerson's macro-level exchange theory can be either individuals or collectivities. Emerson is concerned with the exchange relationship among

---

Richard Emerson (1925–1982)
A Biographical Vignette

Richard Emerson was born in Salt Lake City, Utah, in 1925. Raised near mountains, he never seemed to stray too far away from rivers, mountain peaks, and glaciers. One of his most prized personal accomplishments was his participation in the successful ascent of Mt. Everest in 1963. Aspects of this experience are captured in his publication "Everest Traverse" in the December 1963 edition of the *Sierra Club Annual Bulletin* and in an article published in *Sociometry* in 1966. He received a grant from the National Science Foundation to study group performance under prolonged stress on this climb. This project earned him the Hubbard Medal, presented to him by President Kennedy on behalf of the National Geographic Society in July 1963.

His love of mountains and the rural social life of the mountain villages of Pakistan became a constant source of sociological inspiration for Richard Emerson during his career. His studies of interpersonal behavior, group performance, power, and social influence were often driven by his close personal encounters with expedition teams for which the intensity of cooperation and competition were exacerbated by environmental stress.

Source: This biographical vignette was written by Karen Cook.

---

actors. An **exchange network** has the several components. First, such a web of social relationships involves a number of either individual or collective actors. Second, the various actors have a variety of valued resources. All actors, individual and collective, in the network have exchange opportunities and exchange relations with one another. Finally, a number of these exchange relations exist and interrelate with one another to form a single network structure; thus, at least two exchange relations between actors can be seen as forming a social structure.

The connection between exchange relations is of great importance and is critical to linking exchange between two actors (dyadic exchange) to more macro-level phenomena. What is crucial is the contingent relationship between dyadic exchanges. We may say that two dyadic-exchange relations, *A-B* and *A-C*, form a minimal network (*A-B-C*) when exchange in one is contingent on exchange (or nonexchange) in the other. It is *not* enough for *A*, *B*, and *C* to have a common membership for an exchange network to develop; there must be a contingent relationship between exchanges in *A-B* and *B-C*.

---

exchange network   A web of social relationships involving a number of either individual or collective actors and the various actors have a variety of valued resources as well as exchange opportunities and exchange relations with one another. A number of these exchange relations exist and interrelate with one another to form a single network structure.

Each exchange relation is embedded within a larger exchange network consisting of two or more such relationships. If the exchange in one relationship affects exchange in another, they can be said to be connected. That connection can be positive when the exchange in one positively affects the exchange in another (e.g., the money obtained from one is used to gain social status in another); negative when one serves to inhibit the exchange in the other (e.g., time spent earning money in one relationship reduces the ability to spend time with friends in another); or it can be mixed.

Power-Dependence

Emerson defined **power** as the potential cost that one actor can induce another to accept. **Dependence** involves the potential cost that an actor is willing to tolerate within a relationship. These definitions lead to Emerson's power-dependence theory, which can be summarized by saying that in an exchange relationship the power of one actor over another is a function of that actor's dependence on the other actor. Unequal power and dependence lead to imbalances in relationships, but over time these move toward a more balanced power-dependence relationship.

Actors' dependence on one another is critical in Emerson's work. Among other things, this mutual dependence determines the nature of their interaction and the amount of power they exercise over one another. A sense of dependence is linked to Emerson's definition of power. Thus, the power of actor A over actor B is equal to and based on actor B's dependence on actor A. There is balance in the relationship between actor A and actor B when the dependence of A on B equals the dependence of B on A. Where there is an imbalance in the dependencies, the actor with less dependence has an advantage in terms of power; thus, power is a potential built into the structure of the relationship between A and B. Power can also be used to acquire rewards from the relationship. Even in balanced relationships, power exists, albeit in a kind of equilibrium.

Power-dependence studies have focused on positive outcomes—the ability to reward others. However, in a series of studies, Linda Molm has emphasized the role of negative outcomes—punishment power—in power-dependence relationships; power can be derived from both the ability to reward and the ability to punish others. In general, Molm has found that punishment power is weaker than reward power, in part because acts of punishment are likely to elicit negative reactions. However, in one of her recent studies, Molm has suggested that the relative weakness of punishment power may arise because it is not widely used and not because it is inherently less effective than reward

---

power   To Emerson, the potential cost that one actor can induce another to accept.

dependence   The potential cost that an actor will be willing to tolerate within a relationship.

power. Molm and her coauthors found that the use of punishment power is more likely to be perceived as fair when it is used by those who also have the power to reward.

A More Integrative Exchange Theory

In explaining power dependence, exchange theory focuses on the dyadic relation between actors. In order to move away from the dyadic approach of exchange theory and toward a focus on the power of a position within a structure, Cook and Emerson argue that the determination of the power of a position is based on the amount of dependence of the entire structure on that position. Such systemwide dependence will, in their view, be a function of *both* the structural centrality of the position and the nature of power-dependence relationships. They are adopting a vulnerability approach in an effort to raise power-dependence theory from a microscopic to a more macroscopic level of analysis. Vulnerability involves the networkwide dependence on a particular structural position.

Cook, Jodi O'Brien, and Peter Kollock define exchange theory in inherently integrative terms as being concerned with exchanges at various levels of analysis, including those among interconnected individuals, corporations, and nation-states. They identify two strands of work in the history of exchange—one at the micro-level, focusing on social behavior as exchange, and the other at the more macro-level, viewing social structure as exchange. They see the strength of exchange theory in micro-macro integration, since the basic propositions of this theory apply to individuals and collectivities. In addition, it is explicitly concerned with the impact that changes at one level have on other levels of analysis.

Cook, O'Brien, and Kollock identify three contemporary trends, all of which point toward a more integrative exchange theory: One is the increasing use of field research focusing on more macroscopic issues, which can complement the traditional use of the laboratory experiment to study microscopic issues. Second, they note the shift, discussed earlier, in substantive work away from a focus on dyads and toward larger networks of exchange. Third, and most important, is the ongoing effort to synthesize exchange theory and structural sociologies. There are a number of recent examples of efforts by exchange theorists to synthesize their approach with other theoretical orientations.

STRUCTURATION THEORY

In creating one of the most satisfying efforts to develop an integrated theory that we will encounter in this chapter, Anthony Giddens began by surveying a wide range of theories that begin with either the individual/agent (e.g., symbolic interactionism) or the society/structure (e.g., structural functionalism) and rejected both of these polar alternatives. Rather, Giddens argues that we must begin with recurrent social practices. Thus, to structuration theory, the focus is neither on large-scale structures nor everyday actions and interactions, but social practices that recur in a patterned way. As in much of his theory, time and space are significant to Giddens's conception of these practices: They recur and are ordered over time; they not only occurred yesterday, and are occurring today, but are apt to recur tomorrow, next week, next year, and in the next century. Similarly, they recur and are ordered across space so that patterned social practices found in New York are also found in Chicago, Tokyo, and London, among other places.

At its core Giddens's structuration theory, with its focus on social practices, is a theory of the relationship between agency and structure. What is thought of in the United States as the micro-macro issue is the agency-structure issue in Europe. Although there are some important differences between them, for the purposes of this discussion we will treat micro-macro and agency-structure as all but identical continua.

To Giddens, agency and structure cannot be conceived of apart from one another; they are two sides of the same coin. In Giddens's terms, they are a **duality** (the next section discusses Archer's critique of this orientation). All social action involves structure, and all structure involves social action. Agency and structure are inextricably interwoven in ongoing human activity or practice.

As pointed out earlier, Giddens's analytical starting point is human practices, but he insists that they be seen as **recursive.** This means several things: (1) Social practices are not created mentally (or any other way) by actors; (2) they are not created by the structural social conditions in which actors find themselves; (3) most importantly, as people are expressing themselves as human actors, they are creating their consciousness and the structural conditions that make these practices possible. Practices, consciousness, and structure are being created simultaneously by the actor. Activities are not produced by consciousness, by the social construction of reality, nor are they produced by social structure. Rather, in expressing themselves as actors, people are engaging in practice, and it is through that practice that *both* consciousness and structure are produced. Giddens is concerned with consciousness, or reflexivity. However, in being reflexive, the human actor is not merely self-conscious but is also engaged in the monitoring of the ongoing flow of activities and structural conditions. Most generally, it can be argued that Giddens is concerned

---

duality   All social action involves structure and all structure involves social action. Agency and structure are inextricably interwoven in ongoing human activity or practice.

recursive   The idea that social practices are neither created mentally (or any other way) by actors, nor are they created by the structural social conditions in which actors find themselves. Rather, as people are expressing themselves as human actors, they are creating their consciousness and the structural conditions that make these practices possible; practices, consciousness, and structure are created simultaneously by the actor.

with the dialectical process in which practice, structure, and consciousness are produced. Thus, Giddens deals with the agency-structure issue in a historical, processual, and dynamic way.

Not only are social actors reflexive, but so are the social researchers who are studying them. This led Giddens to his well-known ideas on the **double hermeneutic.** Both social actors and sociologists use language. Actors use language to account (here Giddens draws on ethnomethodology) for what they do, and sociologists, in turn, use language to account for the actions of social actors. Thus, we need to be concerned with the relationship between lay and scientific language. We particularly need to be aware of the fact that the social scientist's understanding of the social world may have an impact on the understandings of the actors being studied. In that way, social researchers can alter the world they are studying and thus lead to distorted findings and conclusions.

Elements of Structuration Theory

Giddens's structuration theory includes his thoughts on agents, who, as discussed previously, continuously monitor their own thoughts and activities as well as their physical and social contexts. In their search for a sense of security, actors rationalize their world. By **rationalization** Giddens means the development of routines that not only give actors a sense of security, but enable them to deal efficiently with their social lives. Actors also have motivations to act and these motivations involve the wants and desires that prompt action. Thus, although rationalization and reflexivity are continuously involved in action, motivations are more appropriately thought of as potentials for action. Motivations provide overall plans for action, but most of our action, in Giddens's view, is not directly motivated. Although such action is not motivated and our motivations are generally unconscious, motivations play a significant role in human conduct.

Also within the realm of consciousness, Giddens makes a (permeable) distinction between discursive and practical consciousness. **Discursive consciousness** entails the ability to describe our actions in words. **Practical consciousness** involves actions that the actors take for granted, without being able to express in words what they are doing. The latter type of consciousness is particularly important to structuration theory, reflecting a primary interest in what is done rather than what is said.

---

double hermeneutic   The social scientist's understanding of the social world may have an impact on the understandings of the actors being studied, with the result that social researchers can alter the world they are studying and thus lead to distorted findings and conclusions.

rationalization   To Giddens, this means the development of routines that not only give actors a sense of security but enable them to deal efficiently with their social lives.

discursive consciousness   The ability to describe our actions in words.

practical consciousness   Involves actions that the actors take for granted, without being able to express in words what they are doing.

This focus on practical consciousness provides a smooth transition from agents to agency, the things that agents actually do. Thus, **agency** involves actions that are perpetrated by actors; that is, what occurs would not have occurred in that way were it not for the fact that the actor intervened and took the action in question. Thus, Giddens gives great (his critics say too much) weight to the importance of agency. He takes great pains to separate agency from intentions because he wants to make the point that actions often end up being different from what was intended; in other words, intentional acts often have unanticipated consequences. The idea of unintended consequences plays a great role in Giddens's theory and is especially important in getting us from agency to the social-system level.

Consistent with his emphasis on agency, Giddens accorded the agent great power. Giddens's **agents** have the ability to make a difference in the social world. Even more strongly, the notion of an agent makes no sense without according her power; that is, an actor ceases to be an agent if she loses the capacity to make a difference. Giddens certainly recognizes that there are constraints on actors, but this does not mean that actors have no choices and make no difference. To Giddens, power is logically prior to consciousness because action involves power, or the ability to transform the situation. Thus, Giddens's structuration theory accords power to the actor and action and is in opposition to theories that are disinclined to such an orientation and instead grant great importance either to the intent of the actor (phenomenology) or to the external structure (structural functionalism).

The conceptual core of structuration theory lies in the ideas of structure, system, and duality of structure. **Structure** is defined unconventionally as the structuring properties (specifically, rules and resources) that give similar social practices a systemic form. More specifically, it is what allows those social practices to exist across widely varying expanses of both time and space; thus, structure is made possible by the existence of rules and resources. Structures themselves do not exist in time and space. Rather, social phenomena have the capacity to become structured. Only through the activities of human actors can structure exist. Giddens offers a definition of structure that does *not* follow the Durkheimian pattern of viewing structures as external to and coercive of actors. He takes pains to avoid the impression that structure is outside or external to human action. Structure gives shape and form to social life, but it is not itself either that form or shape.

---

agency   Actions that are perpetrated by actors; what occurs would not have occurred in that way were it not for the fact that the actor intervened and took the action in question.

agents   Actors who have the ability to make a difference in the social world; they have power.

structure   To Giddens, the structuring properties (specifically, rules and resources) that give similar social practices a systemic form.

Giddens does not deny the fact that structure can be constraining on action, but he feels that sociologists have exaggerated the importance of this constraint. Furthermore, they have failed to emphasize the fact that structure is capable of both constraining and enabling action. Structures often allow agents to do things they would not otherwise be able to do. Although Giddens de-emphasizes structural constraint, he recognizes that actors can lose control over the structured properties of social systems as they stretch away in time and space. However, he is careful to avoid Weberian iron-cage imagery and notes that such a loss of control is *not* inevitable.

The conventional sociological sense of structure is closer to Giddens's concept of social system. To Giddens, **social systems** are reproduced social practices, or relations between actors or collectivities that are reproduced, becoming regular social practices. The idea of social system is derived from Giddens's focal concern with practice. Social systems do *not* have structures, but they do exhibit structural properties. Structures do not themselves exist in time and space, but they do become manifested in social systems in the form of reproduced practices. Although some social systems may be the product of intentional action, Giddens places greater emphasis on the fact that such systems are often the unanticipated consequences of human action. These unanticipated consequences may become unrecognized conditions of action and feed back into it. These conditions may elude efforts to bring them under control, but, nevertheless actors continue in their efforts to exert such control.

Thus structures are instantiated in social systems. In addition, they are also manifest in the memories of individual agents. As a result, rules and resources manifest themselves at both the macro-level of social systems and the micro-level of human consciousness.

The concept of **structuration** is premised on the idea, discussed previously, that agents and structures are a duality (not a dualism); they are *not* independent of one another. Instead, they are interrelated to such an extent that at the moment they produce action, people produce and reproduce the structures in which they exist. It is clear that structuration involves the dialectical relationship between structure and agency. Structure and agency are a duality; neither can exist without the other.

As previously indicated, time and space are crucial variables in Giddens's theory. Both depend on whether other people are present temporally or spatially. The primordial condition is face-to-face interaction, in which others are present at the same time and in the same space. However, social systems extend

---

social system(s)   Reproduced social practices, or relations between actors or collectivities, that are reproduced, becoming regular social practices.

structuration   Agents and structures are interrelated to such an extent that at the moment they produce action, people produce and reproduce the structures in which they exist; the dialectical relationship between structure and agency. Structure and agency are a duality; neither can exist without the other.

in time and space, so others may no longer be present. Such distancing in terms of time and space is made increasingly possible in the modern world by new forms of communication and transportation. The central sociological issue of social order depends on how well social systems are integrated over time and across space. One of Giddens's most widely recognized achievements in social theory is his effort to bring the issues of time and space to the fore.

CULTURE AND AGENCY

Margaret Archer has moved the issue of agency-structure in another direction by focusing on the linkage between agency and culture. One key difference between Giddens and Archer is Giddens's case for dualities as opposed to Archer's critique of Giddens's devotion to dualities and her case for the utility of using (analytic) dualisms for analyzing the social world. In her view, as a **dualism** structure (and culture) and agency are analytically distinct, although they are intertwined in social life. Archer argued that Giddens (and others) are too eager to examine both sides of the coin simultaneously. In doing so, they are prevented from examining the interrelationship between one side and the other, between agency and structure. She thought it was necessary that theorists resist any theory that prevents study of this interrelationship because it will then be impossible to unravel the relationship between the two sides.

In our view, both dualities and dualisms have a role to play in analyzing the social world. In some cases it may be useful to separate structure and action, or micro and macro, in order to look at the way in which they relate to one another. In other cases, it may help to look at structure and action (micro and macro) as inseparable—as a duality. In fact, it may well be that the degree to which the social world is characterized by dualities or dualisms is an empirical question. In one case the social setting might better be analyzed using dualities, while in another case it might be better to use dualisms. Similar points could also be made about different moments in time. We should be able to study and measure the degree of dualities and dualisms in any social setting at any given time.

A second major criticism of Giddens is that in his structuration theory the problem of structure and agency has overshadowed the issue of culture and agency. Archer sees, as do most sociologists, a distinction between structure and culture. However, the distinction is a conceptual one because structure and culture are obviously intertwined in the real world. Although structure is the realm of material phenomena and interests, culture involves nonmaterial phenomena and ideas. Not only are structure and culture substantively different, but they are also relatively autonomous. In Archer's view, structure and culture must be dealt with as relatively autonomous, not lumped together under

---

dualism   Structure (and culture) and agency can be distinguished for analytic purposes, although they are intertwined in social life.

the heading of structure. However, in spite of the revival of cultural sociology, cultural analysis lags far behind structural analysis.

HABITUS AND FIELD

Pierre Bourdieu's theory is animated by the desire to overcome what he considers to be the false opposition between objectivism and subjectivism, or between the individual and society.

He places Durkheim and his study of social facts (see Chapter 2) within the objectivist camp. Durkheimians are criticized for focusing on objective structures and ignoring the process of social construction by which actors perceive, think about, and construct these structures and then proceed to act on that basis. Objectivists ignore agency and the agent, whereas Bourdieu favors a position that is structuralist without losing sight of the agent, or real-life actor.

Bridging Subjectivism and Objectivism

The goal of bridging subjectivism and objectivism moves Bourdieu in the direction of a subjectivist position, one that is associated with symbolic interactionism (Chapter 6). The latter is viewed by Bourdieu as an example of subjectivism because of its focus on the way agents think about, account for, or represent the social world while largely ignoring the large-scale structures in which those processes exist. Bourdieu views theories such as symbolic interactionism as largely concentrating on agency and ignoring structure.

Bourdieu, on the other hand, focuses on the dialectical relationship between objective structures and subjective phenomena. For their part, objective structures constrain thought, action, and interaction, as well as the way people represent the world. However, those representations cannot be ignored because they ultimately affect objective structures.

To sidestep the objectivist-subjectivist dilemma, Bourdieu focuses on **practice,** which he views as the outcome of the dialectical relationship between structure and agency. Practices are not objectively determined, nor are they the product of free will. Reflecting his interest in the dialectic between structure and the way people construct social reality, Bourdieu labels his own orientation constructivist structuralism, structuralist constructivism, or genetic structuralism. Bourdieu defines **genetic structuralism** as the study of objective structures that cannot be

---

practice   To Bourdieu, actions that are the outcome of the dialectical relationship between structure and agency. Practices are not objectively determined, nor are they the product of free will.

genetic structuralism   Bourdieu's approach, which involves the study of objective structures that cannot be separated from mental structures that, themselves, involve the internalization of objective structures.

Pierre Bourdieu (1930–2002)
A Biographical Vignette

In the early 1950s, Pierre Bourdieu attended, and received a degree from, a prestigious teaching college in Paris, École Normale Superiéur. However, he refused to write a thesis, in part because he objected to the mediocre quality of his education and to the authoritarian structure of the school. He was offended by, and was active in the opposition against, the strong communist, especially Stalinist, orientation of the school.

Bourdieu taught briefly in a provincial school but was drafted in 1956 and spent two years in Algeria with the French army. He wrote a book about his experiences and remained in Algeria for two years after his army tenure was over. He returned to France in 1960 and worked for a year as an assistant at the University of Paris. He attended the lectures of the anthropologist Claude Lévi-Strauss at College de France and worked as an assistant to the sociologist Raymond Aron. Bourdieu moved to the University of Lille for three years and then returned to the powerful position of Director of Studies at L'École Practique des Hautes Études in 1964.

In the succeeding years Bourdieu became a major figure in Parisian, French, and ultimately world intellectual circles. His work has had an impact on a number of different fields, including education, anthropology, and sociology. He gathered a group of disciples around him in the 1960s, and his followers collaborated with him and made intellectual contributions of their own. In 1968 the Centre de Sociologie Européenne was founded and Bourdieu was named its director. Associated with the center was a unique publishing venture, Actes de la Recherche en Sciences Sociales, which has been an important outlet for the work of Bourdieu and his supporters.

When Raymond Aron retired in 1981, the chair at College de France became open, and most of the leading French sociologists (including Raymond Boudon and Alain Touraine) were in competition for it. However, the chair was awarded to Bourdieu. After that Bourdieu was, if anything, a more prolific author than he had been before, and his reputation continued to grow.

separated from mental structures that, themselves, involve the internalization of objective structures.

He clearly subscribes, at least in part, to a **structuralist perspective,** but it is one that is different from that of most traditional structuralists. Although they focused on structures in language and culture, Bourdieu argues that structures also exist in the social world itself. Bourdieu sees a social world composed of objective structures that are independent of actors, but that can guide and constrain their thoughts and practices. However, what truly differentiates

---

structuralist perspective   The view that there are hidden or underlying structures that determine what transpires in the social world.

Bourdieu from structuralists is the fact that he simultaneously adopts a **constructivist perspective** that allows him to deal with the genesis of schemes of perception, thought, and action as well as of social structures.

Although Bourdieu seeks to bridge structuralism and constructivism, and he succeeds to some degree, there is a bias in his work in the direction of structuralism. For this reason he is thought of as a **poststructuralist.** There is more continuity in his work with structuralism than there is with constructivism. Unlike the approach of most others (e.g., phenomenologists, symbolic interactionists), Bourdieu's constructivism ignores subjectivity and intentionality. He does think it important to include within his sociology the way people, on the basis of their position in social space, perceive and construct the social world. However, the perception and construction that take place in the social world are both animated and constrained by structures. What he is interested in is the relationship between mental structures and social structures. Some microsociologists would be uncomfortable with Bourdieu's perspective and would see it as little more than a more fully adequate structuralism. They would be particularly upset by his unwillingness and inability to deal with subjectivity. Yet there is a dynamic actor in Bourdieu's theory, an actor capable of invention and improvisation. However, these are very limited in his work: The invention is intentionless; the improvisation is regulated by structures. The heart of Bourdieu's work, and of his effort to bridge subjectivism and objectivism, lies in his concepts of habitus and field, as well as their dialectical relationship to one another. While habitus exists in the minds of actors, fields exist outside their minds.

Habitus

Bourdieu is most famous for his concept of habitus. **Habitus** is the mental or cognitive structure through which people deal with the social world. People are endowed with a series of internalized schemes through which they perceive, understand, appreciate, and evaluate the social world. Through such schemes people both produce their practices and perceive and evaluate them.

Dialectically, habitus is the product of the internalization of the structures of the social world. We can think of habitus as social structures that have been internalized; it is embodied social structures. It reflects objective divisions in the class structure, such as age groups, genders, and social classes. A habitus is acquired as a result of long-term occupation of a position within the social

---

constructivist perspective   The view that schemes of perception, thought, and action create structures.

poststructuralist   A theorist, like Bourdieu, who has been influenced by a structuralist perspective but has moved beyond it to synthesize it with other theoretical ideas and perspectives.

habitus   The mental or cognitive structures through which people deal with the social world.

world. Thus, habitus varies depending on the nature of one's position in that world; not everyone has the same habitus. However, those who occupy the same position within the social world tend to have a similar habitus.

In this sense, habitus can also be a collective phenomenon. The habitus allows an actor to make sense out of the social world, but the existence of a multitude of habitus means that the social world and its structures do not impose themselves uniformly on all actors.

A habitus available at any given time has been created over the course of collective history. The habitus manifested in any given individual is acquired over the individual life course and is a function of the particular point in social history in which it occurs. Habitus is both durable and transposable—that is, transferable from one field to another. However, it is possible for people to have an inappropriate habitus, to suffer from what Bourdieu calls **hysteresis.** A good example is someone who is uprooted from an agrarian existence in a contemporary precapitalist society and put to work on Wall Street. The habitus acquired in a precapitalist society would not allow one to cope very well with life on Wall Street.

The habitus both produces and is produced by the social world. On the one hand, habitus is a structuring structure, a structure that structures the social world. On the other hand, it is a structured structure; that is, it is a structure that is structured by the social world. In other words, the habitus involves a double-sided dialectic: It involves the internalization of external structures, but also there is the externalization of things internal to the individual. The concept of habitus allows Bourdieu to escape from having to choose between subjectivism and objectivism.

Practice mediates between habitus and the social world. On the one hand, through practice the habitus is created; on the other, as a result of practice the social world is created. Although practice tends to shape habitus, habitus, in turn, serves to both unify and generate practice.

Although habitus is an internalized structure that constrains thought and choice of action, it does *not* determine them. This lack of determinism is one of the main things that distinguishes Bourdieu's position from that of traditional structuralists. The habitus merely suggests what people should think and what they should choose to do. People engage in a conscious deliberation of options, although this decision-making process reflects the operation of the habitus. The habitus provides the principles by which people make choices and choose the strategies that they will employ in the social world. As a result, people, to Bourdieu, as to Garfinkel and the ethnomethodologists, are not judgmental dopes. However, people are not fully rational either (Bourdieu has disdain for rational choice theory); they act in a reasonable manner—they have practical sense. There is a logic to what people do—the logic of practice.

Practical logic is polythetic; that is, our practical logic can sustain a number of confused and seemingly illogical (from the point of view of formal logic) means. This is important not only because it underscores the difference between

---

hysteresis   The condition that results from having a habitus that is not appropriate for the situation in which one lives.

Key Concept
Reflexive Sociology

Pierre Bourdieu calls for a **reflexive sociology** in which sociologists use their own tools to better understand their discipline. Sociologists, who spend their careers turning aspects of the social world into objects of study, ought to spend some time objectivizing their own practices. Using his own terminology, Bourdieu would favor examining the habitus and practices of sociologists within the fields of sociology as a discipline and the academic world, as well as the relationship between those fields and the fields of stratification and politics. He would also be concerned with the strategies of individual sociologists, as well as of the discipline itself, to achieve distinction. For example, individual sociologists might use jargon to achieve high status in the field, and sociology might wrap itself in a cloak of science so that it could achieve distinction vis-à-vis the world of practice. In fact, Bourdieu has claimed that the scientific claims of sociology and other social sciences are really assertions of power. Of course, this position has uncomfortable implications for Bourdieu's own work. He has sought to maintain his own symbolic power while at the same time criticizing the scientific approach that lies at the base of his own work.

Bourdieu makes an interesting case for metatheorizing when he argues that practicing sociologists need to avoid being toys of social forces that play on them and their work. The only way to avoid such a fate is to understand the nature of the forces acting upon the sociologist at a given point in history. Such forces can be understood only via metatheoretical analysis, or what Bourdieu calls socioanalysis. Once sociologists understand the nature of the forces (especially external-social and external-intellectual) operating on them, they will be in a better position to control their impact on their work. Bourdieu, himself, seeks always to use sociology to cleanse his work of social determinants.

---

practical logic and rationality (formal logic), but also because it reminds us of Bourdieu's relationism. The latter is important in this context because it leads us to recognize that habitus is *not* an unchanging, fixed structure, but rather is adapted by individuals who are constantly changing in the face of the contradictory situations in which they find themselves.

The habitus is neither conscious nor are we able to articulate linguistically the ways in which it functions. We cannot scrutinize it introspectively, nor are we able to control it through acts of will. Although we are not conscious of habitus and its operation, it manifests itself in our most practical activities, such as the way we eat, walk, talk, and even blow our noses. The habitus operates as a structure, but people do not simply respond mechanically to it or to external structures that are operating on them. Thus, in Bourdieu's approach we avoid the extremes of unpredictable novelty and total determinism.

---

reflexive sociology The use by sociologists of their own theoretical and empirical tools to better understand their discipline.

Field

Bourdieu thinks of the concept of field relationally rather than structurally. The **field** is a network of relations among the objective positions within it. These relations exist apart from individual consciousness and will. They are *not* interactions or intersubjective ties among individuals. The occupants of positions may be either agents or institutions, and they are constrained by the structure of the field. The social world has a number of semi-autonomous fields (e.g., art, religion, higher education), all with their own specific logics and all generating among actors a belief about the things that are at stake in a field.

Bourdieu views the field, by definition, as an arena of struggle and battle with people occupying positions within fields and oriented, either as individuals or collectivities, to defending their present position or to improving it. The structure of the field both lies at the base of, and guides, the strategies used to safeguard or improve positions. The field is a type of competitive marketplace in which various kinds of capital (economic, cultural, social, symbolic) are employed and deployed. However, the field of power (of politics) is of the utmost importance; the hierarchy of power relationships within the political field serves to structure all the other fields.

Bourdieu lays out a three-step process for the analysis of a field. The first step, reflecting the primacy of the field of power, is to trace out the relationship of any specific field to the political field. The second step is to map out the objective structure of the relations among positions within the field. Finally, the analyst should seek to determine the nature of the habitus of the agents who occupy the various types of positions within the field.

The positions of various agents in the field are determined by the amount and relative weight of the capital they possess. Bourdieu even uses military imagery (emplacements, fortresses) to describe the field and the struggles that take place within it. Capital allows one to control one's own fate as well as the fate of others. Bourdieu usually discusses four types of capital. The idea is, of course, drawn from the economic sphere and the meaning of **economic capital** is obvious. **Cultural capital** involves various kinds of legitimate knowledge; **social capital** consists of valued social relations between people; **symbolic capital** stems from one's honor and prestige.

Occupants of positions within the field employ a variety of strategies. This idea shows, once again, that Bourdieu's actors have at least some freedom. However, strategies are not conscious or preplanned. Rather, they are structured and are structurally patterned and regular. The strategies deployed by actors depend upon their habitus and the nature of their position within the field.

---

field　A network of relations among the objective positions.

economic capital　The economic resources possessed by an actor.

cultural capital　The various kinds of legitimate knowledge possessed by an actor.

social capital　The extent of the valued social relations possessed by an actor.

symbolic capital　The amount of honor and prestige possessed by an actor.

Bourdieu views the state as the site of the struggle over the monopoly of what he calls **symbolic violence.** This is a soft form of violence because the agent against whom it is practiced is complicit in its practice. Symbolic violence is practiced indirectly, largely through cultural mechanisms, and stands in contrast to the more direct forms of social control that sociologists often focus on. The educational system is the major institution through which symbolic violence is practiced on people. The language, the meanings, the symbolic system of those in power are imposed on the rest of the population. This serves to buttress the position of those in power by, among other things, obscuring what they are doing from the rest of society and getting subordinates to accept the legitimacy of that which dominates them. More generally, Bourdieu views the educational system as deeply implicated in reproducing existing power and class relations. In his ideas on symbolic violence, the political aspect of Bourdieu's work is clearest. Bourdieu is interested in the emancipation of people from this violence and, more generally, from class and political domination. Yet Bourdieu is no naive utopian; a better description of his position might be reasoned utopianism.

In underscoring the importance of *both* habitus and field, Bourdieu is rejecting the split between **methodological individualists** and **methodological holists** and adopting a position that has been termed **methodological relationism,** that is, he is focally concerned with the relationship between habitus and field. He sees this as operating in two main ways. On the one hand, the field conditions the habitus; on the other, the habitus constitutes the field as something that is meaningful, that has sense and value, and that is worth the investment of energy.

Applying Habitus and Field: Distinction   Bourdieu does not simply seek to develop an abstract theoretical system; he also relates it to a series of empirical concerns and thereby avoids the trap of pure intellectualism. The application of his theoretical approach is illustrated in his empirical study *Distinction,* which examines the aesthetic preferences of different groups throughout society.

In this work, Bourdieu attempts, among other things, to demonstrate that culture can be a legitimate object of scientific study. He is attempting to reintegrate culture in the sense of high culture (e.g., preferences for classical music) with the anthropological sense of culture, which looks at all its forms, both high

---

symbolic violence   A soft form of violence (the agent against whom it is practiced is complicit in its practice) that is practiced indirectly, largely through cultural mechanisms.

methodological individualists   Those social scientists who focus on the micro-level and view it as determining the macro-level.

methodological holists   Those social scientists who focus on the macro-level and view it as determining the micro-level.

methodological relationism   The position of social scientists who focus on the relationship between macro- and micro-level phenomena.

and low (e.g., country or rap music). More specifically, in this work Bourdieu links taste for refined objects like fine foods with taste for the most basic food such as burgers and fries.

Because of structural invariants, especially field and habitus, the cultural preferences of the various groups within society (especially classes and fractions of classes) constitute coherent systems. Bourdieu is focally concerned with variations in aesthetic taste, the acquired disposition to differentiate among the various cultural objects of aesthetic enjoyment and to appreciate them differentially. Taste is also practice that serves, among other things, to give an individual, as well as others, a sense of his or her place in the social order. Taste serves to unify those with similar preferences *and* to differentiate them from those with different tastes. Through the practical applications and implications of taste, people classify objects and, in the process, classify themselves. We are able to categorize people by the tastes they manifest, for example, by their preferences for different types of music or movies. These practices, like all others, need to be seen in the context of all mutual relationships, that is, within the totality. Thus, seemingly isolated tastes for art or movies are related to preferences in food, sports, or hairstyles.

Two interrelated fields are involved in Bourdieu's study of taste: class relationships (especially within fractions of the dominant class) and cultural relationships. He sees these fields as a series of positions in which a variety of games are undertaken. The actions taken by the agents (individual or collective) who occupy specific positions are governed by the structure of the field, the nature of the positions, and the interests associated with them. However, this game also involves self-positioning and use of a wide range of strategies to allow one to excel at the game. Taste is an opportunity both to experience and to assert one's position within the field. But the field of social class has a profound effect on one's ability to play this game; those in the higher classes are far better able to have their tastes accepted and to oppose the tastes of those in the lower classes. Thus, the world of cultural works is related to the hierarchical world of social class and is itself both hierarchical and hierarchizing.

Needless to say, Bourdieu also links taste to his other major concept, habitus. Tastes are shaped far more by these deep-rooted and long-standing dispositions than they are by surface opinions and verbalizations. People's preferences for even such mundane aspects of culture as clothing, furniture, or cooking are shaped by the habitus. And these dispositions serve to unify classes, albeit unconsciously. To put it another way, taste is a matchmaker. Through taste one habitus indicates its compatibility with another habitus. Dialectically, of course, it is the structure of the class that shapes the habitus.

Although both field and habitus are important to Bourdieu, their dialectical relationship is of utmost importance and significance; field and habitus mutually define one another. Out of the dialectical relationship between habitus and field, practices, cultural practices in particular, are established.

Bourdieu views culture as a kind of economy, or marketplace. In this marketplace people utilize cultural rather than economic capital. This capital is largely a result of people's social class origin and their educational experience.

In the marketplace, people accrue more or less capital and either expend it to improve their position or lose it, thereby causing their position within the economy to deteriorate.

People pursue distinction in a range of cultural fields—the beverages they drink (Perrier or cola), the automobiles they drive (Mercedes Benz or Kia), the newspapers they read (*The New York Times* or *USA Today*), or the resorts they visit (the French Riviera or Disney World). Relationships of distinction are objectively inscribed in these products and reactivated each time they are appropriated. In fact, when one looks at all of the fields taken together, there is an almost inexhaustible set of possible fields in which to pursue distinction. The appropriation of certain cultural goods (e.g., a Mercedes Benz) yields profit, while appropriation of others (a Kia) yields no gain, or even a loss.

Bourdieu takes pains to make it clear that he is not simply arguing, following Thorstein Veblen's famous theory of conspicuous consumption (see Chapter 3), that the motor force of human behavior is the search for distinction. Rather, he contends that his main point is that to occupy a position within a field is to differ from those who occupy neighboring positions—to be different. Through tastes people demonstrate differences from others. Thus, for example, one who chooses to own a grand piano is different from one who opts for an accordion. That one choice (the grand piano) is seen as worthy of high status, while another (the accordion) is considered vulgar is a result of the dominance of one point of view and the symbolic violence practiced against those who adopt another viewpoint.

A dialectic exists between the nature of the cultural products and tastes. Changes in cultural goods lead to alterations in taste, but changes in taste are also likely to result in transformations in cultural products. The structure of the field not only conditions the desires of the consumers of cultural goods but also structures what the producers create in order to satisfy those demands.

Changes in taste (and Bourdieu sees all fields temporally) result from the struggle between opposing forces in both the cultural (e.g., the supporters of old versus new fashions) and the class (the dominant versus the dominated fractions within the dominant class) arenas. However, the heart of the struggle lies within the class system, and the cultural struggle between artists and intellectuals, for example, is a reflection of the interminable struggle between the different factions of the dominant class to define culture, indeed the entire social world. Oppositions within the class structure condition oppositions in taste and in habitus. Although Bourdieu gives great importance to social class, he refuses to reduce it merely to economic matters or to the relations of production but sees class as defined by habitus as well.

Bourdieu offers a distinctive theory of the relationship between agency and structure within the context of a concern for the dialectical relationship between habitus and field. His theory is also distinguished by its focus on practice (in the preceding case, aesthetic practice) and its refusal to engage in arid intellectualism. In that sense it represents a return to the Marxian concern for the relationship between theory and practice.

Contemporary Applications
The "Field" of American Higher Education Today

Higher education in the United States in the early 21st century is certainly a field in the sense of the term as it is used by Bourdieu. It is a network of relations among objective positions within it. Among those positions are universities and colleges, a wide range of academic departments, chancellors and deans, professors of various ranks, graduate students, undergraduate students, staff, and so on. Like other fields, it can be looked at as a kind of vast military battlefield in which a variety of struggles to improve or protect positions are taking place. Among the ongoing struggles are the following:

1. *Elite universities versus those that aspire to that status.* There are a relatively small number of elite universities in the United States (e.g., Harvard, Stanford) that have a disproportionate share of the best-known and most productive scholars and produce the vast majority of PhDs. There are many other lesser universities (most state universities) that would like to achieve elite status, but almost always find it impossible to do so. The elite universities often undercut their efforts by, for example, hiring away their best professors.
2. *Department versus department.* Within any university there is a status hierarchy among departments with, for example, the hard sciences (e.g., physics, chemistry) almost always ranking above the social sciences (economics, sociology), with arts and humanities (history, English) ranking even lower. This hierarchy is reflected in, among other ways, the relative funding of departments and the average salaries of faculty in them. Lower-ranking departments frequently struggle to move up the hierarchy in order to obtain more funding, higher salaries, and greater prestige and they are usually opposed by the departments that rank above them.
3. *Senior faculty versus junior faculty.* Senior faculty (professors) hold most of the power in academic departments and junior faculty (associate and assistant professors) aspire to be professors. However, it is the professors who decide which junior faculty will get promoted. More generally, junior faculty aspire to get a share of the power held by professors who, needless to say, are generally reluctant to share much, if any, of it.
4. *Faculty versus graduate students.* Graduate students are far lower in the status hierarchy than the most junior faculty members who, along with other faculty members, exercise power over them. Graduate students aspire to get the PhDs that they hope will lead them into faculty positions, but existing faculty decide how difficult the process will be and who will or will not get those degrees.
5. *Faculty versus undergraduate students.* Undergraduate students want the time and attention of faculty members, but the latter, especially if they are ambitious, want to devote most of their time to the writing and research that will get them promotions, perhaps even to an elite university.

This far from exhausts the positions, relationships, and struggles in the field of U.S. higher education today, but it does give us at least a sense of it.

Summary

1. Richard Emerson constructed a more integrative exchange theory.
2. He dealt with the psychological basis of exchange as well as exchange relations, networks, and structures at the macro-level.
3. An exchange network is a web of social relationships involving a number of either individual or collective actors; the various actors have a variety of valued resources as well as exchange opportunities and exchange relations with one another.
4. There are a number of these exchange relations and they interrelate with one another to form a single network structure.
5. Power (the potential cost that one actor can induce another to accept) and dependence (the potential cost that an actor will be willing to tolerate within a relationship) are central to Emerson's integrative exchange theory.
6. Anthony Giddens's structuration theory deals with agents and structures as a duality; they cannot be separated from one another.
7. Giddens's approach is distinguished by the power it accords to agents.
8. Structure is defined unconventionally as the structuring properties (specifically rules and resources) that give similar social practices a systemic form.
9. Social systems are reproduced social practices, or relations between actors or collectivities that are reproduced, becoming regular social practices.
10. Structuration is premised on the idea that agents and structures are *not* independent of one another. Rather they are interrelated to such an extent that at the moment they produce action, people produce and reproduce the structures in which they exist.
11. In contrast to Giddens, Archer makes the cases for a dualism in which structure and agency can be distinguished analytically even though they are intertwined in the social world.
12. Archer also argues that culture has been ignored and that we should focus on the relationship between culture and agency.
13. Bourdieu's integrated theory is concerned with the relationship between habitus and field.
14. Habitus is the mental or cognitive structure through which people deal with the social world.
15. The field is a network of relations among the objective positions within it.
16. The positions of agents in the field are determined by the amount of capital—economic, cultural, social, and symbolic—they possess.
17. The field is a site of struggles to gain advantageous positions.

Suggested Readings

KAREN S. COOK and JOSEPH WHITMEYER "Richard Emerson." In George Ritzer, ed., *The Blackwell Companion to Major Social Theorists*. Malden, MA, and Oxford, England: Blackwell, 2000, pp. 486–512. Brief introduction to Emerson's life and work; the senior author is Emerson's most important disciple.

KAREN S. COOK and ERIC RICE "Social Exchange Theory." In George Ritzer, ed., *The Encyclopedia of Social Theory*, 2 volumes. Thousand Oaks, CA: Sage, 2005, pp. 735–740. Examination of the history and current status of exchange theory whose senior author is one of the most important living contributors to that theory.

NOAH FRIEDKIN "Exchange Networks." In George Ritzer, ed., *The Encyclopedia of Social Theory*, 2 volumes. Thousand Oaks, CA: Sage, 2005, pp. 264–265. Entry focused on the concept that gets to the heart of a more integrated exchange theory.

IRA COHEN "Structuration." In George Ritzer, ed., *The Encyclopedia of Social Theory*, 2 volumes. Thousand Oaks, CA: Sage, 2005, pp. 811–814. Readable overview of Giddens's dense and difficult structuration theory by one of its foremost analysts.

IRA COHEN *Structuration Theory*. London: Macmillan, 1989. Makes structuration theory as accessible as possible.

IAN CRAIB *Anthony Giddens*. London: Routledge, 1992. A critical examination of Giddens's work, including structuration theory.

MARGARET ARCHER *Culture and Agency: The Place of Culture in Social Theory*. Cambridge: Cambridge University Press, 1988. The source for Archer's views on Giddens and her own ideas on the integration of culture and agency.

DAVID SWARTZ *Culture and Power: The Sociology of Pierre Bourdieu*. Chicago: University of Chicago Press, 1997. Excellent overview of the contributions of Pierre Bourdieu to social theory.

CRAIG CALHOUN "Pierre Bourdieu." In George Ritzer, ed., *The Blackwell Companion to Major Social Theorists*. Malden, MA, and Oxford, England: Blackwell, 2000, pp. 696–730. Much briefer review of Bourdieu's work and contributions.

RICHARD JENKINS "Pierre Bourdieu." In George Ritzer, ed., *The Encyclopedia of Social Theory*, 2 volumes. Thousand Oaks, CA: Sage, 2005, pp. 66–71. Broad overview of the person and his work that includes a discussion of the relationship between habitus and field.

RICHARD JENKINS "Habitus." In George Ritzer, ed., *The Encyclopedia of Social Theory*, 2 volumes. Thousand Oaks, CA: Sage, 2005, pp. 352–353. More detailed examination of the best-known and most influential of Bourdieu's concepts.

CHAPTER 8

Contemporary Feminist Theories

Patricia Madoo Lengermann
The George Washington University

Gillian Niebrugge
American University

The Basic Theoretical Questions
The Classical Roots
Contemporary Feminist Theories
Toward a Feminist Sociological Theory
Summary
Suggested Readings

Feminist theory is a generalized, wide-ranging system of ideas about social life and human experience developed from a woman-centered perspective. It is woman-centered in two ways. First, the starting point of all its investigation is the situations and experiences of women in society. Second, it seeks to describe and critically evaluate the world from the distinctive vantage points of women. Feminist theory differs from most sociological theories in that it is the work of an interdisciplinary community. Feminist sociologists seek to broaden and deepen sociological knowledge by incorporating discoveries being made by this interdisciplinary community.

This chapter has four main sections: an overview of the basic questions that guide feminist theory; a sketch of the classical roots of contemporary feminist theory; a description of the various types of contemporary feminist theory, emphasizing the contributions of sociologists to those theories; and an integrated statement of a general feminist sociological theory developed out of these various theoretical traditions. The theoretical traditions are presented in terms of basic questions of feminism.

---

feminist theory   A generalized, wide-ranging system of ideas about social life and human experience developed from a woman-centered perspective.

THE BASIC THEORETICAL QUESTIONS

Historically feminist theory has developed in relation to feminist activism, which is usually described in terms of "waves" of collective mobilization. The classic roots of contemporary feminist theory are in first-wave feminist activism (ca. 1848–1920), which centered on women's struggle for the vote and for admission to the political process. Contemporary feminist theory began with second wave activism (1960–1990), which worked to translate basic political rights into tangible economic and social equality with men, and is continued in third-wave activism (1990–present), which will be determined by those of you who will spend the majority of your life in the 21st century.

The impetus for contemporary feminist theory begins in a deceptively simple question: *And what about the women?* In other words: Where are the women in any situation being investigated? If they are not present, why? If they are present, what exactly are they doing? How do they experience the situation? What do they contribute to it? What does it mean to them?

A half century of posing this question has produced some general conclusions. Women are present in most social situations. Where they are not present, the reason is not because of their lack of ability or interest but because there have been deliberate efforts to exclude them. Where they are present, women have played roles very different from the popular conception of them (e.g., as passive wives and mothers). Indeed, as wives and as mothers and in a series of other roles, women have, along with men, actively created the social world. Yet though women are actively present in most social situations, academics and people in general, both male and female, have often been blind to their presence. Moreover, women's roles in most social situations, although essential, have been different from and less privileged than those of men. Their invisibility is only one indicator of this inequality.

Feminism's second basic question, then, is *"Why is all this as it is?"* In answering this question, feminist theory has produced a general social theory with broad implications for sociology. One of feminist sociological theory's major contributions to answering this question has been the development of the concept of *gender.* Beginning in the 1970s, feminist theorists made it possible for people to see the distinctions between biologically determined attributes associated with male and female and the socially learned behaviors associated with masculinity and femininity by designating the latter as "gender." The essential qualities of gender remain a point of theoretical debate in feminism and these debates offer one way to distinguish among some of the varieties of feminist theories. But a starting point of agreement among nearly all varieties of feminist theory is an understanding of gender as a social construction, something not emanating from nature but created by people as part of the processes of group life.

The third question for all feminists is: *How can we change and improve the social world to make it a more just place for all people?* This commitment to social transformation in the interest of justice is the distinctive characteristic of critical social theory. This commitment is shared in sociology by feminism, Marxism, neo-Marxism, and social theories being developed by racial, ethnic and sexual minorities and in postcolonial societies. The commitment to critical theory requires that feminist theorists ask how their work will improve the lives of the people they study.

As the circle of feminists exploring these questions has become more inclusive of people from diverse backgrounds, both in the United States and internationally, feminist theorists have raised a fourth question: *And what about the differences among women?* Exploring this question leads to a general conclusion that the invisibility, inequality, and role differences in relation to men, which generally characterize women's lives, are profoundly affected by a woman's social location—that is, by her class, race, age, affectional preference, marital status, religion, ethnicity, and global location.

But feminist theory is not just about women, nor is its major project the creation of a middle-range theory of gender relations. Posing and answering feminist theory's basic questions has produced a theory of social life universal in its applicability and comparable to the revolution in thought produced by Marx. Marx, more than a century ago, showed social scientists that the knowledge people assumed to be an absolute and universal statement of truth about society in fact reflects the experiences of those who economically and politically rule the social world and that it is possible to view the world from the vantage point of the world's workers, the economically and politically subordinate. Today, feminism's basic theoretical questions are producing a similar radical transformation of our understanding of the world. What we have taken as universal and absolute knowledge is in fact knowledge derived from the experiences of a powerful section of society, men as masters. That master's knowledge is relativized if we rediscover the vantage point of women who though subordinated have been indispensable in sustaining and recreating the society we live in.

Feminism not only relativizes established knowledge, but also deconstructs such knowledge. Feminism deconstructs established systems of knowledge by showing their masculinist bias and the gender politics framing and informing them. But feminism itself is now experiencing two relativizing and deconstructionist pressures. First, women of color, women in postcolonial societies, working-class women, lesbians are confronting the white, privileged-class, heterosexual status of many leading feminists. These women, speak from what bell hooks calls margin to center and question whether there is a unitary woman's standpoint. Second, a growing postmodernist literature (see Chapter 9) raises questions about the reality of gender and of the individual self and hence challenges the validity of talking about a standpoint of women. Nevertheless, the practice of doing theory from the standpoint of women remains vital in sociology because empirically one half of the world's population in their daily lives know themselves, are interacted with by others, and defined by macrostructures as "women."

THE CLASSICAL ROOTS

Posing the question "And what about the women?" has resulted in studies like our own work in the history of women in sociology, *The Women Founders: Sociology and Social Theory, 1830–1930.* This work shows within the discipline of sociology itself the ways that women can be major players in the creation and

Harriet Martineau
Biographical Vignette (1802–1876)

Born on June 12, 1802 in Norwich, England to a Unitarian manufacturing family, Harriet Martineau received a good education for a woman in her times because of the family's religious principles which emphasized human reason as the way to transcendental experience. But she was left penniless with the failure of the father's textile business in 1829 and had to choose, as she later said, between making her living by the needle or by the pen. She had written for Unitarian publications in her youth with success in the form of monetary prizes and so she turned to writing. She became a household name in England, outselling even Charles Dickens, with the publication of *Illustrations of Political Economy* (1832–1834), a series of novels designed to teach the general public the principles of what was then economics. The effort left her with enough financial independence to be able to choose her new project and at the same time disillusioned with the possibilities of economics. She turned to the new science of sociology and to a test of this new science in the new world, the United States, where she felt she would be able to view a society in the making (a view shared by her contemporary Alexis de Tocqueville (see Chapter 1), whose time in America overlapped with hers). On her way to the U.S. in 1835, she drafted the first methods text in sociology, *How to Observe Morals and Manners*. She used many of the principles therein as a guide to the field research that produced *Society in America* in 1836/37. In 1853, she published her translation, reorganization, and abridgement of Auguste Comte's six-volume *Positive Philosophy*, a version Comte liked so much that he had it retranslated into French, where it became a standard version. Long-recalled only for this last work, Martineau is now being studied for her original work of the 1830s and recognized as being, along with Comte, one of the inventors of sociology. Martineau was a prolific writer in many genres of literature, publishing some seventy books and over 1500 newspaper articles. Deaf from her early teens, she was the first sociologist to write about illness and disability. She died on June 27, 1876.

development of a field and yet have their contributions remain invisible—a process we call "erasure." Women were active creators of both sociology and social theory in the first century of the discipline. Indeed, the claim can be made that in the founding generation, it was the work of a woman, Harriet Martineau (1802–1876), along with Auguste Comte (see Chapter 2), that produced the first formal mapping of sociology as a way of thinking and as a method (see Biographical Vignette). Later, in the classic generation (1890–1930), at the same time that Durkheim, Weber, Simmel and Mead were creating what would become the academic field of sociology, a group of women who formed a broad and connected network of social reformers were also developing pioneering sociological theories.

These women included Jane Addams (1860–1935), Anna Julia Cooper (1858–1964), Charlotte Perkins Gilman (1860–1935), Florence Kelley (1859–1932), Beatrice Potter Webb (1858–1943), Marianne Weber (1870–1954), and

Ida B. Wells-Barnett (1862–1931). With the possible exception of Cooper, they can all be connected through their relationship to Jane Addams—and Cooper was influenced by Addams. That they have not been known or recognized in conventional histories of the discipline as sociologists or sociological theorists is dramatic evidence of the power of gender politics within sociology. Although the sociological theory of each of these women is a product of individual theoretical effort, when they are read collectively, they represent a coherent statement of early feminist sociological theory.

The chief hallmarks of their theories are characteristics they share with contemporary feminist sociological theory and are also the very qualities which may account for their being passed over in the development of professional academic sociology. First, they practice a critical rather than a descriptive or even simply explanatory analysis. They understand sociology as part of the general progressive movement of the late nineteenth and early twentieth centuries and claim that the purpose of sociology is social amelioration and that the main problem to be ameliorated is social inequality. Second, they emphasize women's experience and women's lives and works as being equal in importance to men's. A third hallmark is a conscious awareness that they—like all people—speak from a situated and embodied standpoint and that this understanding must be central to sociological method. And, fourth, they have a concern with *domination* as the chief practice by which inequality is maintained in the world; domination is the power relation in which the superordinate makes the subordinate an instrument of his will, denying the subordinate's individual capacity for thought and opinion.

What distinguishes the classical women theorists from each other is the nature of and the remedy for the inequality on which they focused—gender, race, or class, or the intersection of these factors. But all these women translated their views into social and political activism and helped shape and change the North Atlantic societies in which they lived. This activism was as much a part of their sense of practicing sociology as was creating theory. They believed in social science research as part of both the theoretical and activist practices of sociology. They were, consequently, highly creative innovators of social science method. As the developing discipline of sociology marginalized these women as sociologists and sociological theorists, it often incorporated their research methods into its own practices, while using the women's activism as an excuse to define them as "not sociologists." Thus, the women are remembered as social activists, community organizers, and social workers rather than sociologists. Their heritage is a sociological theory that is a call to action as well as to thought.

CONTEMPORARY FEMINIST THEORIES

In this section we look at how feminist sociologists have incorporated the insights of feminist theory into the theory and practice of sociology. The first basic point is that feminist theory takes several forms. One map of this variety is given by sociologist Judith Lorber in terms of how the theories approach gender inequality. She identifies three approaches: theories that aim to "reform" the gender system by equalizing opportunities for women and men—including liberal and socialist theories; theories that aim to "resist" the gender system by actively promoting the value of women's ways of being—including radical, cultural, and psychoanalytic theories; and theories that "rebel" against the gender system by challenging the existence of gender itself—including postmodern and queer theories. We offer a somewhat different mapping from Lorber—but the important first point is that while there is variety within feminist theory, there is an underlying unity based in a dedication to understanding and improving women's position in society.

Our typology classifies the various feminist theories in terms of their answer to feminism's most basic question, "And what about the women?" In our mapping, there are four basic answers to this question.

1. Women's location in, and experience of, most situations is *different* from that of the men in those situations.
2. Women's location in most situations is not only different from but also less privileged than or *unequal* to that of men.
3. Women's situation also has to be understood in terms of a direct power relationship between men and women. Women are *oppressed:* that is, restrained, subordinated, molded, and used and abused by men.
4. Women's experiences of difference, inequality, and oppression vary according to their total location within societies' arrangements of *structural oppression* or vectors of oppression and privilege: class, race, ethnicity, age, affectional preference, marital status, and global location.

These general answers can be further broken down in terms of the second basic question of feminist theory, "Why is all this as it is?" (see Table 8.1).

Table 8.1 needs to be read with the following cautions in mind. One caution is that the typology outlines theoretical positions, not the location of specific theorists; a given theorist may write over the course of a career from several of these positions. A second caution is that feminist theory and feminist sociological theory are dynamic enterprises that change over time. Over the last few years, there has been a steady movement toward synthesis, toward seeing how elements of these various theories complement each other. There has also been a shift in the focus of much feminist theorizing from women's oppression to oppressive practices and structures that impact the lives of the majority of the world's population, men and women. A major line of tension has developed between interpretations that emphasize culture and meaning and those that emphasize the material consequences of power. Part of this debate over what explains most—meaning or materiality—has focused on problematizing gender. Theorists are exploring and deconstructing the taken-for-granted meanings of gender. And finally, the theories identified in the chart do not exist on a level playing field: at this moment, some are relatively dormant, that is, have made significant contributions in the past but are not now being elaborated—most notably psychoanalytic feminism but also to some degree radical feminist

TABLE 8.1 Overview of Varieties of Feminist Theory

Basic varieties of feminist theory—answers to the descriptive question: What about the women?	Distinctions within theories—answers to the explanatory question: Why is women's situation as it is?
Gender Difference	
Women's location in, and experience of, most situations is *different* from those of men in the situation.	Cultural feminism Phenomenological Institutional Interactional
Gender Inequality	
Women's location in most situations is not only different but also less privileged than or *unequal* to that of men.	Liberal feminism Rational Choice feminism
Gender Oppression	
Women are *oppressed*, not just different from or unequal to, but actively restrained, subordinated, molded, and used and abused by men.	Psychoanalytic feminism Radical feminism
Structural Oppression	
Women's experiences of difference, inequality, and oppression vary by their social location within capitalism, patriarchy, and racism.	Socialist feminism Intersectionality theory

theory; other theories are currently dynamic and expanding—most notably, ethnomethodology and intersectionality.

Gender Difference

By "theories of gender difference," we mean theories that describe, explain, and trace the implications of ways men and women are or are not the same in behavior and experience. Theories of gender difference have to confront the problem of "the essentialist argument." The essentialist argument is the thesis that the fundamental differences between men and women are givens that cannot be changed. That immutability is traced to three factors: biology, the needs of social institutions for men and women to perform different roles, and the mental need humans have to think in terms of a category of "Otherness" as part of defining the self. The closest feminist theory and feminist sociological theory come to the essentialist argument is in theories of sociobiology. Sociologist Alice Rossi has explored the thesis that human biology determines many social differences between men and women. But overall the feminist response to sociobiology has been oppositional. We will look at theories of gender difference in terms of general feminist theory, first, and then sociological theories of gender difference.

General Feminist Theories of Difference

There are two major theories of gender difference in general feminist theory: cultural feminism and existential (or phenomenological) feminism.

Cultural feminism is unique among theories analyzed here because it does not focus on explaining the origins of difference but rather it explores (and celebrates) the social value of women's distinctive ways of being, that is, of the ways in which women are different from men. This approach allows cultural feminism to sidestep rather than resolve problems posed by the essentialist thesis. The essentialist thesis was first used against women in male patriarchal discourse to claim that women are inferior to men. But that argument was reversed by some First Wave feminists who created cultural feminism. Cultural feminism extols the positive qualities of what it defines as "the female character" or "personality." Theorists such as Margaret Fuller, Frances Willard, Jane Addams, and Charlotte Perkins Gilman argued that the governing of society needed women's virtues like cooperation, pacifism, and nonviolence in the settling of disputes. This tradition has continued in the present day in arguments about women's distinctive standards for ethical judgment, mothers' particular quality of consciousness, female communication style, women's capacity for openness to emotion, women's lower level of aggression than men. The best-known contemporary work of this type is psychologist Carol Gilligan's thesis that women make their moral decisions based on "an ethic of care" which is different from what she sees as the typical male ethic, an ethic of rights derived from abstract principles. Cultural feminism suggests that women's ways of being may be a healthier template for producing a just society than those of an androcentric (or male-centered) culture.

Existential or phenomenological feminism has developed one of the most enduring themes of feminist theory: that women are marginalized as "Other" in a male-created culture. This theme is given its classic formulation in Simone de Beauvoir's analysis in *The Second Sex*. The theme has also been developed by Mary Daly in *Beyond God the Father: Toward a Philosophy of Women's Liberation*, a text widely used in the sociology of religion. Existential or phenomenological feminism sees people being born into a world that is shaped by a culture that reflects male experience and ignores or marginalizes women's experience. De Beauvoir argues that human thought and culture tend to organize around

---

cultural feminism   A feminist theory that explores and celebrates the social value of women's distinctive ways of being.

existential or phenomenological feminism   A feminist theory of difference that sees people born into a world shaped by culture that reflects male experience and ignores or marginalizes women's experience.

a binary opposition—an either/or logic. A major binary opposition is male/female. One is either male or female. But de Beauvoir says, in a world built on male experience, woman is not just part of either/or, she is "Other." Woman is assigned all the "other" qualities that are the opposite of the agentic male subject. She is seen as passive where he is active, as timid where he is brave, as simple where he is complex, etc. Women's difference from men results in part from this fact of cultural construction which excludes them. It also results in part from their internalizing this "otherness" so that they do not experience themselves as actors in the world but as objects that wait for men to desire them. Existential or phenomenological feminism raises crucial questions about difference: can women liberate themselves from the status of object/other? Must they become like men to do so? One answer being asserted in French feminism by thinkers like Hélène Cixous and Luce Irigaray is that liberation will come for women only when they develop a consciousness and culture that is uniquely theirs.

Sociological Theories of Difference

Feminist institutional theory posits that gender differences result from the different roles that women and men play within various institutional settings. A major source of difference is the sexual division of labor in the family to which all people are socialized both as children and adults. This sexual division of labor links women to the functions of wife, mother, and household worker; to the private sphere of home and family; and thus to a lifelong series of events and experiences very different from those of men. Women's roles as mothers and wives in producing and reproducing a female personality and culture have been analyzed by theorists like Jessie Bernard in *The Future of Marriage* (see Liberal Feminism below), Nancy Chodorow in *The Reproduction of Mothering*, and Miriam Johnson in *Strong Mothers, Weak Wives*. Repeated experience in these settings is pictured as a carrying over into other institutions and producing differences between women and men in political behavior (e.g., the gender gap in voting), in choice of careers (e.g., the caring professions for women), in styles of corporate management, and in possibilities for advancement (e.g., the "mommy track"). Institutional placement theories have been subject to two criticisms. First, they do not account for the persistence of gender difference when men and women occupy the same institutional position. Second, many sociologists see these theories as presenting too static and deterministic a model.

    Feminist interactionist theory is currently the most elaborated sociological understanding of the origins of gender difference. It is anchored in

---

feminist institutional theory   A feminist theory that sees gender differences as resulting from the different roles that women and men play within various institutional settings.

feminist interactionist theory   A feminist theory that views gender as an accomplishment by skilled actors in interaction with others who hold them accountable for conforming to appropriate gender behavior.

ethnomethodology's analysis of gender as an *accomplishment*. Ethnomethodology (see Chapter 6) claims that institutional order, culture, and stratification are maintained by the ongoing activities of individuals in interaction. When this idea is applied by them to gender, it produces the understanding that "people do gender"—or what is called in shorthand "doing gender." West and Zimmerman's 1987 article "Doing Gender" distinguishes among sex, sex category, and gender. A baby is born with some configuration of biological sex (though this may be more or less clear); on the basis of what the adults attending to the birth interpret as its sex, the baby is assigned to a sex category; after that assignment, everyone around the child and the child itself over time begin to do gender, to act in ways considered appropriate to the sex category designations. The question of how they know what is appropriate is resolved in ethnomethodology by the principle of *accountability*—people do not just act any way they choose; people in interactions hold other people "accountable" for behaving in ways that are expected, or useful, or understandable.

Thus, gender is constantly being produced by people in interaction with each other as a way of making sense of and letting the world work. For instance, using the "right" public restroom is a way of avoiding all sorts of potential embarrassments; it is a method of getting through the day okay—and it is one so taken for granted that the person doing it hardly considers it doing gender. Ways of hugging, laughing, complaining—conveying the whole range of human emotions—are deeply gendered and are situationally enacted by people as they attempt to communicate with other people. Indeed, one question that emerges from the doing gender perspective is whether it is possible *not* to do gender.

While the elemental understanding of "doing" holds constant for women and men, interactionist theorists recognize that a part of the substance of the doing in gender is "doing difference," is acting to make distinctions, to distinguish oneself as masculine not feminine or, conversely, as feminine not masculine. These acts of distinction are repeated from situation to situation to maintain gender identity.

The major criticism of this approach is the sense—felt about much ethnomethodology—that it is not clear where the standards for accountability come from, that it is perhaps too voluntaristic in its orientation because people in individual interactions do for the most part produce remarkably similar behaviors in doing gender. Other sociologists have argued that the approach is too concerned with how gender gets reproduced and does not account enough for moments of resistance.

"Doing gender" as a theory has gained additional attention because of its similarities with the thesis of postmodernist philosopher Judith Butler that gender is a "performance." Everyday meanings of "doing" and "performance" have led to a confusion about whether the two ideas are really the same. Three differences are important. First, there is the difference in the beginning points of the two theories: the ethnomethodologists begin from an attempt to understand how gender is produced in everyday life; Butler begins from an unease with the most basic categories of feminism—"woman" and "gender." For Butler, the category of woman arises out of the process that produces gender, a process she names "performativity." The concept of "performativity" comes from speech act theory where a performative is an act of speaking that makes something happen. For instance, according to this theory, when a minister says, "I now pronounce you man and wife," the act of speaking makes the marriage happen. Butler sees gender as arising as people perform it in interaction with each other. In Butler's thinking, people do not begin life with an internal identity as man or woman; rather they get hold of certain understandings of man and woman depending on their personal biographies and their locations in history. These meanings suggest ways of acting and as people look around they can see other people engaged in similar ways of acting. Thus, gender is created as people imitate other people trying to act in accord with culturally given ideas about masculinity and femininity. These ideas so effectively bring into being what they name that people take as real the idea of a core gendered self—even though all that is really there is an ongoing chain of imitative performances.

A second difference between ethnomethodology and Butler's performativity is that ethnomethodology, like nearly all sociology, does believe in a unified, basically rational self—there is a being behind the doing (or the imitating) and that being makes choices. Butler like other postmodernists calls the existence of this unified self into question. A third difference is that ethnomethodology has in its principle of accountability a way of understanding what controls the particular "imitations" that a person undertakes to achieve.

In seeking to bring about change, theorists of difference demand that women's ways of being be recognized as viable alternatives to male modes and that public knowledge, academic scholarship, and the organization of social life be adjusted to take serious account of female ways of being. At its most militant, this theoretical approach makes the centuries-old feminist claim: When a major infusion of women's ways becomes part of public life, the world will be a safer, more just place for us all.

Gender Inequality

Four themes characterize feminist theories of gender inequality. Men and women are situated in society not only differently but also unequally. Women get less of the material resources, social status, power, and opportunities for self-actualization than do men who share their social location—whether it is a location based on class, race, occupation, ethnicity, religion, education, nationality, or any other socially significant factor. This inequality results from the organization of society, not from any significant biological or personality differences between women and men. All human beings are characterized by a deep need for freedom to seek self-actualization and by a fundamental malleability that leads them to adapt to the constraints or opportunities of the situations in which they find themselves. To say that there is gender inequality, then, is to claim that women are situationally less empowered than men to realize the need they share with men for self-actualization. All inequality theories assume that both women and men will respond fairly easily and naturally to more egalitarian social structures and situations. They affirm, in other words, that it is possible to change the situation. In this belief, theorists of gender inequality contrast with the theorists of gender difference, who present a picture of social life in which gender differences are, whatever their cause, more durable, more penetrative of personality, and less easily changed.

Liberal Feminism   The major expression of gender inequality theory is liberal feminism, which argues (1) that women may claim equality with men on the basis of an essential human capacity for reasoned moral agency, (2) that gender inequality is the result of a sexist patterning of the division of labor, and (3) that gender equality can be produced by transforming the division of labor through the repatterning of key institutions—law, work, family, education, and media. The basic ideas of liberal feminist theory have been so intertwined with the history of U.S. feminist activism, realized and elaborated in practice, and successfully incorporated into the daily life of the society, that its foundational principle now seems unremarkable. That principle is that women and men are equal, an idea now so taken-for-granted, that it may be hard to envision it as the starting point of a theory. But in 1848, at the time of the first women's rights convention in world history, at Seneca Falls, New York, women were only barely even second class citizens: They could neither vote nor serve on juries (even if the defendant was a woman) nor hold public office nor practice medicine or law or theology. If married, the woman could not hold property in her own name, claim her wages from work outside the home as her own, have a right to custody of her children in the case of divorce, or even sign her own will; her husband had the right and—many, including judges, held—the duty to physically chastise her, that is, to beat her in order to preserve order in the commonwealth. The Seneca Falls convention concluded with the adoption of "the Declaration of Sentiments," which opens by revising the Declaration of Independence: "We hold these truths to be self-evident: that all men and women are created equal" ("and women" is added). This was a radical claim, both politically and conceptually. It situated the women's quest for justice in the intellectual discourses of the Enlightenment, the American and French revolutions, and the Abolitionist Movement, and it conceptualized the woman not in the context of home and family but as an autonomous individual with rights in her own person. These rights empower women to enter the political process to secure full equality through organized appeals to a reasonable public and the use of the state.

Liberal feminism, thus, rests on the beliefs that (1) all human beings have certain essential features—capacities for reason, moral agency, and self-actualization; (2) the exercise of these capacities can be secured through legal

---

liberal feminism   A feminist theory of inequality that argues that women may claim equality with men on the basis of an essential human capacity for reasoned moral agency, that gender inequality is the result of a patriarchal and sexist patterning of the division of labor, and that gender equality can be produced by transforming the division of labor through the repatterning of key institutions—law, work, family, education, and media.

recognition of universal rights; (3) the inequalities between men and women assigned by sex are social constructions having no basis in "nature"; and (4) social change for equality can be produced by an organized appeal to a reasonable public and use of the powers of government.

Where cultural feminism (see Gender Difference above) argued that women had a duty to bring from home and family their ways of knowing to the running of the state, classical liberal feminism argued that women, like men, carried in their human personhood the right to participate in the government of society on their own behalf.

Contemporary liberal feminism has become the foremost theoretical proponent of gender as a social construction, divorced from biology. It is the ideas and practices associated with gender that lead to differences in the treatment of men and women. All such practices of differential treatment are seen as unjust, unfair, and disadvantageous to women.

The fact that such barriers existed and that attempts to remove them met with intense resistance is explained by liberal feminists in terms of **sexism,** which is defined as a system of discriminatory attitudes and practices connected by a theme of privileging male experience and devaluing female experience. Contemporary feminist theory has expanded to include a global feminism which confronts racism in North Atlantic societies and works for the human rights of women everywhere.

In sociology, contemporary liberal feminism is in part focused on the intellectual project of defining gender as a structure. Barbara Risman contrasts this approach with past analyses that have explained gender in terms of social structure (such as those of institutional placement discussed above under Gender Difference). Risman argues that gender must be understood as a highly complex structure in its own right; a structure that patterns human behavior at three levels—individual, cultural/interactional, and institutional—and creates a system of stratification. Liberal feminism sees that gender as a system of stratification produces a gendered division of labor, an organization of society into public and private spheres, and a cultural dimension of sexist ideology.

The sexual division of labor in modern societies divides production in terms of genders and areas of life called "spheres" which are denoted as "public" and "private." Women are given primary responsibility for the private sphere. Men are given privileged access to the public sphere, which liberal feminists see as the sphere that offers the major rewards of social life—money, power, status, freedom, opportunities for growth, and self-worth. The fact that women have the access to the public sphere that they do is one of the achievements of liberal feminism. The two spheres interact in the lives of women more than they do in men's, and both spheres are shaped by patriarchal ideology and sexism which are pervasive in mass culture.

---

sexism   A system of discriminatory attitudes and practices connected by a theme of privileging male experience and devaluing female experience.

One feature of contemporary liberal feminist sociology is the attempt to understand the interactions of these spheres in women's lives. Arlie Hochschild in *The Second Shift* and *The Time Bind* has been the primary theorist naming the tensions women face. On the one hand, women find their experience within the public sphere of education, work, politics, and public space still limited by practices of discrimination, marginalization, and harassment. On the other hand, in the private sphere, they find themselves in a "time bind" as they return home from paid employment to a "second shift" of home and child care infused by an ideology of intensive mothering. Women's ability to compete in career and profession is hindered by the demands of the private sphere and by what Joan Williams calls "the ideal worker norm" of the public sphere. The ideal worker norm assumes the life schedule available to the typical male worker as the basis for organizing and evaluating all work; this assumption puts women workers, who carry "the second shift," at an ongoing disadvantage.

A recurring theme in liberal feminist analysis is the problem of achieving equality in marriage. This theme is given its classic formulation in Jessie Bernard's *The Future of Marriage*, which addresses the recurring topic of the problem of achieving equality in marriage. Bernard analyzes marriage as at one and the same time a cultural system of beliefs and ideals, an institutional arrangement of roles and norms, and a complex of interactional experiences for individual women and men:

1. Culturally, marriage is idealized as the destiny and source of fulfillment for women; a mixed blessing of domesticity, responsibility, and constraint for men; and for American society as a whole, an essentially egalitarian association between husband and wife.
2. Institutionally, marriage empowers the role of husband with authority and with the freedom, indeed, the obligation, to move beyond the domestic setting; it meshes the idea of male authority with sexual prowess and male power; and it mandates that wives be compliant, dependent, self-emptying, and essentially centered on the activities and demands of the isolated domestic household.
3. Experientially then there are two marriages in any institutional marriage:
   - The man's marriage, in which he holds to the belief of being constrained and burdened, while experiencing what the norms dictate: authority; independence; and a right to domestic, emotional, and sexual service by the wife.
   - The wife's marriage, in which she affirms the cultural belief of fulfillment, while experiencing normatively mandated powerlessness and dependence, an obligation to provide domestic, emotional, and sexual services, and a gradual dwindling away of the independent young person she was before marriage.

The results of all this are to be found in the data that measure human stress: Married women, whatever their claims to fulfillment, and unmarried men, whatever their claims to freedom, rank high on all stress indicators, including heart palpitations, dizziness, headaches, fainting, nightmares, insomnia, and

---

Jessie Bernard (1903–1996)
A Biographical Vignette

Bernard's life is marked by a series of transitions, or "outgrowths," from old to new ways of being. Born Jessie Ravitch on June 8, 1903, in Minneapolis, she made her first outgrowth when she moved from her Jewish immigrant family to the University of Minnesota at the age of 17. At the university, she studied with Pitirim Sorokin, who later founded the Harvard sociology department, and with L. L. Bernard, who helped found the *American Sociological Review* and whom she married in 1925. Her study with Bernard gave her a grounding in positivistic sociology that showed in her later work in her ability to integrate quantitative research into increasingly qualitative and critical studies. She completed her Ph.D. at Washington University in St. Louis in 1935.

By the mid-1940s, the Bernards were at Pennsylvania State University, and Jessie was in the midst of outgrowing positivism. The Nazi Holocaust destroyed her faith that science could know and produce a just world, and she moved toward a sense of knowledge as contextualized rather than objective. She also began to establish an independent academic reputation. Her husband died in 1951, but she remained at Penn State until about 1960, teaching, writing, and raising her three children. In the 60s, she moved to Washington, D.C., to devote herself fully to writing and research.

The most dramatic outgrowth was in the last third of her life, from 1964 to her death in 1996. This period is significant for both Bernard's extraordinary output and what it says about career patterns in women's lives.

---

fear of nervous breakdown; unmarried women, whatever their sense of social stigma, and married men rank low on all the stress indicators. Marriage then is good for men and bad for women and will cease to be so unequal in its impact only when couples feel free enough from the prevailing institutional constraints to negotiate the kind of marriage that best suits their individual needs and personalities. Recent studies have suggested that Bernard's analysis still holds for most marriages but that some couples are achieving, through dedicated effort, the liberal feminist ideal of egalitarian marriage.

Liberal feminism's agenda for change is consistent with its analyses of the basis for claiming equality and the causes of inequality: They wish to eliminate gender as an organizing principle in the distribution of social goods, and they are willing to invoke universal principles in their pursuit of equality. They pursue change through law—legislation, litigation, and regulation—and through appeal to the human capacity for reasoned moral judgments, that is, the capacity of the public to be moved by arguments for fairness. They argue for:

- Equal educational and economic opportunities.
- Equal responsibility for the activities of family life.
- The elimination of sexist messages in family, education, and mass media.
- Individual challenges to sexism in daily life.

For liberal feminists, the ideal gender arrangement is one in which each individual acting as a free and responsible moral agent chooses the lifestyle most suitable to her or him and has that choice accepted and respected, whether it be for housewife or househusband, unmarried careerist or part of a dual-income family, childless or with children, heterosexual or homosexual. Liberal feminists see this ideal as one that enhances the practice of freedom and equality—central cultural ideals in America. Liberal feminism, then, is consistent with the dominant American ethos in its basic acceptance of democracy and capitalism; its reformist orientation; and its appeal to the values of individualism, choice, responsibility, and equality of opportunity.

Rational choice feminist theory has been little developed since its original potential was suggested by Debra Friedman and Carol Diem in 1993 and reinforced by Janet Chafetz in 1997. We explore it briefly here because it offers a conceptual framework for refining the study of gender inequality proposed in liberal feminism. As its name suggests, rational choice theory (see Chapter 6) conceives of the human being as a rational decision-maker and it seeks to study social outcomes as the result of decisions by such people. Rational choice theory understands the rational decision-maker as a purposive actor who makes decisions based on the best information available to her and in terms of external and internal constraints. There are two kinds of external constraints—institutional constraints and opportunity costs. Institutional constraints are the ways that social structures function to limit one's agency. Opportunity costs are the benefits a person has to give up when deciding to pursue one course of action over another; the course of action not pursued is an opportunity cost—to do A, one must forego doing B. Internal restraints take the form of preferences—there are things that people would like or feel are necessary or good. In the context of explaining why women's condition is as it is, rational choice theory urges sociologists to consider women as rational decision-makers who labor under more institutional constraints and more pressing opportunity costs than do men. For instance, for women the "ticking of the biological clock" is a constant opportunity cost that they have to weigh as they make decisions about marriage and career. These opportunity costs may combine with institutional constraints to produce an outcome—when both are weighed by a purposive actor. For instance, a woman in medical school may be more influenced than a man by the need in her future to balance her medical practice with childcare responsibilities and this may affect her choice of specialty. Her understanding of the institutional constraints of some specialties may lead her to feel that dermatology is a better specialty than cardiology because of the absence of emergencies in the former.

Rational choice theory also offers possibilities for explaining collective outcomes like political action groups. Friedman and Diem look at Kristen Luker's

---

rational choice feminist theory　Rational choice feminist theory sees women as rational decision-makers who labor under more institutional constraints and more pressing opportunity costs than men.

study of antichoice women and argue that the women in her study have bene-fitted from the traditional role of wife and mother. The presence of on-demand abortion makes it more possible for women to compete in the economic job market and reduces the difference in the positions of men and women. But the antichoice women have chosen not to so compete and have made the insti-tutional constraints of gender difference a part of their life choice equations. Introducing the possibility of such competition alters those equations and can be seen as hurting rather than helping these women.

The major contributions of rational choice theory are to give a way to ana-lyze the specific mechanisms by which gender inequality is produced and to conceptualize women as actors whose choices are guided by a desire to pro-duce the outcome that is most beneficial to them, given their preferences. "Pref-erence" is an open concept and is not in anyway limited to wealth or material goods; it may as easily be marriage or children or a day to oneself. Feminist rational choice theory valorizes women's preferences by treating them as part of the actions of autonomous moral agents.

Gender Oppression

Theories of gender oppression describe women's situation as the consequence of a direct power relationship between men and women in which men have fun-damental and concrete interests in controlling, using, subjugating, and oppress-ing women: that is, in the practice of domination. By **domination,** oppression theorists mean any relationship in which one party (individual or collective), the dominant, succeeds in making the other party (individual or collective) the subordinate, an instrument of the dominant's will, refusing to recognize the subordinate's independent subjectivity. Conversely, from the subordinate's viewpoint, it is a relationship in which the subordinate's assigned significance is solely as an instrument of the will of the dominant. Women's situation, then, for theorists of gender oppression, is centrally that of being used, controlled, subjugated, and oppressed by men.

This pattern of gender oppression is incorporated in the deepest and most pervasive ways into society's organization, a basic structure of domination most commonly called patriarchy. Patriarchy is not the unintended and sec-ondary consequence of some other set of factors, like biology or socialization or sex roles or the class system. It is a primary power structure sustained by strong and deliberate intention. Indeed, to theorists of gender oppression, gen-der differences and gender inequality are by-products of patriarchy.

Two major variants of oppression theory are psychoanalytic feminism and radical feminism.

---

domination   To oppression theorists, any relationship in which one party (individual or collective), the *dominant,* succeeds in making the other party (individual or col-lective) the *subordinate,* an instrument of the dominant's will, and refuses to recog-nize the subordinate's independent subjectivity.

Psychoanalytic Feminism **Psychoanalytic feminism** attempts to explain patriarchy by reformulating the theories of Freud and his intellectual heirs. These theories, broadly speaking, map and emphasize the emotional dynamics of personality, focusing on emotions often deeply buried in the subconscious or unconscious areas of the psyche; they also highlight the importance of infancy and early childhood in the patterning of these emotions. In attempting to use Freud's theories, however, feminists undertake a fundamental reworking of his arguments. They follow through on directions implied by Freud's theories while rejecting his gender-specific conclusions, which are sexist and patriarchal.

Psychoanalytical feminists operate with a particular model of patriarchy. Like all oppression theorists, they view **patriarchy** as a system in which men subjugate women. It is universal, pervasive in its social organization, durable over time and space, and triumphantly maintained in the face of occasional challenge. Distinctive to psychoanalytic feminism, however, is the view that this system is one that all men, in their individual daily actions, work continuously and energetically to create and sustain. Women resist only occasionally but are to be discovered far more often either acquiescing in or actively working for their own subordination. The puzzle that psychoanalytical feminists set out to solve is why men bring everywhere enormous, unremitting energy to the task of sustaining patriarchy and why there is an absence of countervailing energy on the part of women.

In searching for an explanation to this puzzle, these theorists give short shrift to the argument that a pragmatic calculation of practical benefits is sufficient for the intense energy that men invest in patriarchy, especially because men may not always and everywhere be certain that patriarchy is of unqualified value to them. Moreover, an argument anchored in the cognitive pursuit of self-interest suggests that women would as energetically mobilize against patriarchy. Instead, these theorists look to those aspects of the psyche so effectively mapped by the Freudians: the zone of human emotions, of half-recognized or unrecognized desires and fears, and of neurosis and pathology. Here they find a clinically proven source of extraordinary energy and debilitation, one springing from psychic structures too deep to be recognized or monitored by individual consciousness. In searching for the emotional underpinnings of patriarchy, psychoanalytical feminists have identified as one possible explanation for male domination of women the socioemotional environment in which the personality of the young child takes form.

Two important explorations by sociologists of early childhood development from a psychoanalytic perspective are Nancy Chodorow's *The Reproduction of Mothering* and Jessica Benjamin's *The Bonds of Love*. These works focus

---

psychoanalytic feminism   An effort to explain patriarchy through the use of reformulated theories of Freud and his successors in psychoanalytic theory.

patriarchy   A system in which men subjugate women. It is universal, pervasive in its social organization, durable over time and space, and triumphantly maintained in the face of occasional challenge.

on two facets of early childhood development: (1) the assumption that human beings grow into mature people by learning to balance a never-resolved tension between the desire for freedom of action—individuation—and the desire for confirmation by another—recognition; and (2) the observable fact that in all societies infants and children experience their earliest and most crucial development in a close, uninterrupted, intimate relationship with a woman, their mother or mother substitute.

As infants and young children, for considerable periods lacking even language as a tool for understanding experience, individuals experience their earliest phases of personality development as an ongoing turbulence of primitive emotions: fear, love, hate, pleasure, rage, loss, desire. The emotional consequences of these early experiences stay with people always as potent but often unconscious feeling memories. Central to that experiential residue is a cluster of deeply ambivalent feelings for the woman/mother/caregiver: need, dependence, love, possessiveness, but also fear and rage. Children's relationship to the father/man is much more occasional, secondary, and emotionally uncluttered.

From this beginning, the male child, growing up in a culture that positively values maleness and devalues femaleness and increasingly aware of his own male identity, attempts to achieve an early, rapid individuation and emotional separation from the woman/mother. This culturally induced separation is not only partial but also destructive in its consequences. In adulthood the emotional carryover from early childhood toward women—need, love, hate, possessiveness—energizes the man's quest for a woman of his own who meets his emotional needs and yet is dependent on and controlled by him: that is, he has an urge to dominate and finds mutual recognition difficult.

The female child, bearing the same feelings toward the woman/mother, discovers her own female identity in a culture that devalues women. She grows up with deeply mixed positive and negative feelings about herself and about the woman/mother and in that ambivalence dissipates much of her potential for mobilized resistance to her social subordination. She seeks to resolve her emotional carryover in adulthood by emphasizing her capacities for according recognition—often submissively with males in acts of sexual attraction and mutually with females in acts of kinship maintenance and friendship. And rather than seeking mother substitutes, she recreates the early infant-woman relationship by becoming a mother.

Psychoanalytical feminist theorists have extended the analyses beyond individual personality to Western culture. The emphases in Western science on a distinct separation between man and nature, on man as the dominator of nature, and on a scientific method derived from these attitudes and promising objective truth have been challenged and reinterpreted as the projection by the overindividuated male ego of its own desire for domination and its own fear of intersubjective recognition. Motifs in popular culture, such as the repeated positioning in both plot and image of the male as dominant over the female, are interpreted by psychoanalytical theorists as a sign of a breakdown in the requisite tensions between a need for individuation and a need for recognition. When this breakdown reaches, in a culture or personality, severe enough proportions, two pathologies result: the overindividuated dominator, who recognizes the other only through acts of control, and the underindividuated subordinate, who relinquishes independent action to find identity only as a mirror of the dominator.

Psychoanalytical feminists, then, explain women's oppression in terms of men's deep emotional need to control women, a drive arising from near-universal male neuroses centering on ambivalence toward the mothers who reared them. Women either lack these neuroses or are subject to complementary neuroses, but in either case they are left psychically without an equivalent source of energy to resist domination. Much clinical psychiatric evidence supports the argument that these neuroses are in fact widespread in Western societies. But these theories, in drawing a straight line from universal human emotions to universal female oppression, fail to explore the intermediate social arrangements that link emotion to oppression and fail to suggest possible lines of variation in emotions, social arrangements, or oppression. Several theorists have discussed the unacknowledged ethnic, class, and nationality assumptions in these theories—their generalization from white, upper-middle-class, North Atlantic family experience. Moreover, and partly because of these omissions, psychoanalytic feminist theory suggests very few strategies for change, except perhaps that we restructure our childbearing practices. These theories thus give us some provocative insights into and deepen our understanding of the roots of gender oppression, but they require a great deal more elaboration of both sociological factors and change strategies.

Radical Feminism   **Radical feminism** is based on two emotionally charged central beliefs: (1) that women are of absolute positive value as women, a belief asserted against what they claim to be the universal devaluing of women; and (2) that women are everywhere oppressed—violently oppressed—by the system of patriarchy. From this passionate mixture of love and rage, radical feminists elaborate a theory of social organization, gender oppression, and strategies for change. The classic statement of radical feminism is Adrienne Rich's "Compulsory Heterosexuality and Lesbian Existence." Sociological contributions to this perspective include Pauline Bart and Eileen Moran's *Violence Against Women: The Bloody Footprints,* and Diane Scully's *Understanding Sexual Violence: A Study of Convicted Rapists.*

Radical feminists see in every institution and in society's most basic structures—heterosexuality, class, caste, race, ethnicity, age, and gender—systems of oppression in which some people dominate others. Of all these systems of domination and subordination, the most fundamental structure of oppression is gender, the system of patriarchy. Not only is patriarchy historically

---

radical feminism   A theory of social organization, gender oppression, and strategies for change that affirms the positive value of women and argues that they are everywhere oppressed by violence or the threat of violence.

the first structure of domination and submission, but it continues as the most pervasive and enduring system of inequality, the basic societal model of domination. Through participation in patriarchy, men learn how to hold other human beings in contempt, to see them as nonhuman, and to control them. Within patriarchy, men see and women learn what subordination looks like. Patriarchy creates guilt and repression, sadism and masochism, manipulation and deception, all of which drive men and women to other forms of tyranny. Patriarchy, to radical feminists, is the least noticed and yet the most significant structure of social inequality.

Central to this analysis is the image of patriarchy as violence practiced by men and by male-dominated organizations against women. Violence may not always take the form of overt physical cruelty. It can be hidden in more complex practices of exploitation and control:

- In standards of fashion and beauty.
- In tyrannical ideals of motherhood, monogamy, chastity, and heterosexuality.
- In sexual harassment in the workplace.
- In the practices of gynecology, obstetrics, and psychotherapy.
- In unpaid household drudgery and underpaid wage work.

Violence exists whenever one group controls in its own interests the life chances, environments, actions, and perceptions of another group, as men do women.

But the theme of violence as overt physical cruelty lies at the heart of radical feminism's linking of patriarchy to violence: rape, sexual abuse, femicide, enforced prostitution, spouse abuse, incest, sexual molestation of children, hysterectomies and other excessive surgery, the sadism in pornography, the historic and cross-cultural practices of witch burning, the stoning to death of adulteresses, the persecution of lesbians, female infanticide, Chinese footbinding, the abuse of widows, and the practice of clitorectomy.

Patriarchy exists as a near-universal social form because men can muster the most basic power resource, physical force, to establish control. Once patriarchy is in place, the other power resources—economic, ideological, legal, and emotional—also can be marshaled to sustain it. But physical violence always remains its base, and in both interpersonal and intergroup relations, that violence is used to protect patriarchy from women's individual and collective resistance.

Men create and maintain patriarchy not only because they have the resources to do so but because they have real interests in making women serve as compliant tools. Women are a uniquely effective means of satisfying male sexual desire. Their bodies are essential to the production of children, who satisfy both practical and prestige needs for men. Women are a useful labor force. They can be ornamental signs of male status and power. As carefully controlled companions to both the child and the adult male, they are pleasant partners, sources of emotional support, and useful foils who reinforce the male's sense of central social significance. These useful functions mean that men everywhere seek to keep women compliant. But differing social circumstances give different rank orders to these functions and therefore lead to cross-cultural variations in the patterning of patriarchy. Radical feminists give us both an explanation of universal gender oppression *and* a model for understanding cross-cultural variations in this oppression.

How is patriarchy to be defeated? Radicals hold that this defeat must begin with a basic reworking of women's consciousness, so that each woman recognizes her own value and strength; rejects patriarchal pressures to see herself as weak, dependent, and second-class; and works in unity with other women, regardless of differences among them, to establish a broad-based sisterhood of trust, support, appreciation, and mutual defense. With this sisterhood in place, two strategies suggest themselves: a critical confrontation with any facet of patriarchal domination whenever it is encountered; and a degree of separatism as women withdraw into women-run businesses, households, communities, centers of artistic creativity, and lesbian love relationships. Lesbian feminism, as a major strand in radical feminism, is the practice and belief that erotic and emotional relationships with other women are a form of resistance to patriarchal domination.

How does one evaluate radical feminism? Emotionally each of us will respond to it in light of our own degree of personal radicalism, some seeing it as excessively critical and others as entirely convincing. But in attempting a theoretical evaluation, one should note that radical feminism incorporates arguments made by both socialist and psychoanalytical feminists about the reasons for women's subordination and yet moves beyond those theories. Radical feminists, moreover, have done significant research to support their thesis that patriarchy ultimately rests on the practice of violence against women. They have a reasonable, though perhaps incomplete, program for change. They have been faulted in their exclusive focus on patriarchy. This focus seems to simplify the realities of social organization and social inequality and thus to approach the issues of ameliorative change somewhat unrealistically.

Structural Oppression

Structural oppression theories, like gender oppression theories, recognize that oppression results from the fact that some groups of people derive direct benefits from controlling, using, subjugating, and oppressing other groups of people. These theories analyze how those interests in domination are enacted through mechanisms of social structure, that is, through recurring and routinized large-scale arrangements of social interaction. Structural oppression theorists see that these arrangements are always arrangements of power that have arisen over time. They focus on the structures of patriarchy, capitalism, racism, and heterosexism; and they locate enactments of domination and experiences of oppression in the interplay of these structures, that is, in the way they mutually enforce each other. Structural oppression theorists do not absolve individuals who engage in domination of responsibility for their actions, but they examine how those individual actions are the product of structural arrangements. This section deals with two types of structural oppression theory: socialist feminism and intersectionality theory.

Socialist Feminism   Socialist feminism attempts to achieve a critique of the distinctive yet interrelated oppressions of patriarchy and capitalism from a standpoint in women's experience. To do this, socialist feminists develop methods for social analysis out of an expanded understanding of Marxist historical materialism (Chapter 2). Socialist feminists seek to bring together what they perceive as the most valuable feminist traditions: Marxian and radical feminist thought.

Radical feminism, as discussed previously, is a critique of patriarchy. Marxian feminism like Marxian theory is a critique of capitalism that focuses on class oppression. The problematic part of the Marxian analysis is that it makes patriarchy a by-product of economic relations. Socialist feminists accept the radical feminist argument and proof that patriarchy, while interacting with economic conditions, is an independent structure of oppression.

Socialist feminism sets out to bring together these dual knowledges—knowledge of oppression under capitalism and of oppression under patriarchy—into a unified explanation of all forms of social oppression. One term used to try to unify these two oppressions is **capitalist patriarchy.** But the term perhaps more widely used is *domination* (defined previously). Socialist feminism's explanations of oppression present domination as a large-scale structural arrangement, a power relation between groups or categories of social actors. This structure of domination both patterns and is reproduced by the agency, the willful and intentional actions, of individual actors. Women are central to socialist feminism in two ways. First, as with all feminism, the oppression of women remains a primary topic for analysis. Second, women's location and experience of the world serve as the essential vantage point on domination in all its forms. Ultimately, though, these theorists are concerned with all experiences of oppression, either of women or of men. They also explore how some women, themselves oppressed, may yet actively participate in the oppression of other women, as, for example, privileged-class women in American society who oppress poor women. Indeed, one strategy of all socialist feminists is to confront the prejudices and oppressive practices *within* the community of women itself.

Both the focus on capitalist patriarchy and that on domination are linked to a commitment, either explicit or implicit, to historical materialism as an

---

socialist feminism   An effort to develop a unified theory that focuses on the role of capitalism and patriarchy in creating a large-scale structure that oppresses women.

capitalist patriarchy   A term that indicates that the oppression of women is traceable to a combination of capitalism and patriarchy.

analytical strategy. **Historical materialism,** a basic principle in Marxian social theory, refers to the claim that:

- The material conditions of human life, inclusive of the activities and relationships that produce those conditions, are the key factors that pattern human experience, personality, ideas, and social arrangements.
- Those conditions change over time because of dynamics immanent within them.
- History is a record of the changes in the material conditions of a group's life and of the correlative changes in experiences, personality, ideas, and social arrangements.

In linking historical materialism to their focus on domination, socialist feminists attempt to realize their goal of a theory that probes the broadest of human social arrangements, domination, and yet remains firmly committed to precise, historically concrete analyses of the material and social arrangements that frame particular situations of domination.

But in their use of the principle of historical materialism, socialist feminists move beyond the Marxians in three crucial ways.

First, they broaden the meaning of the concept of the "material conditions of human life." Marxians typically mean by this idea the economic dynamics of society, particularly the ways in which goods of a variety of types are created for and exchanged in the market. In these various exploitative arrangements, which make some wealthy and others poor, they locate the roots of class inequality and class conflict. Socialist feminist analysis includes economic dynamics but also other conditions that create and sustain human life: the human body, its sexuality and involvement in procreation and child rearing; home maintenance, with its unpaid, invisible round of domestic tasks; emotional sustenance; and the production of knowledge. In *all* these life-sustaining activities, exploitative arrangements profit some and impoverish others. This redefinition of the concept of material conditions transforms the Marxian assumption that human beings are producers of goods into a theme of human beings as creators and sustainers of all human life.

Second, socialist feminism emphasizes the role of ideas, which some Marxians dismiss as mere byproducts of economic life. The emphasis on ideas includes consciousness, motivation, ideas, social definitions of the situation, knowledge, texts, ideology, the will to act in one's interests or acquiesce to the interests of others. To socialist feminists all these factors deeply affect human

---

historical materialism   The Marxian idea that the material conditions of human life, inclusive of the activities and relationships that produce those conditions, are the key factors that pattern human experience, personality, ideas, and social arrangements; that those conditions change over time because of dynamics immanent within them; and that history is a record of the changes in the material conditions of a group's life and of the correlative changes in experiences, personality, ideas, and social arrangements.

personality, human action, and the structures of domination that are realized through that action. Moreover, these ideas are produced by social structures that are inextricably intertwined with, and as elaborate and powerful as, those that produce economic goods. Within all these structures, too, exploitative arrangements enrich and empower some while impoverishing and immobilizing others.

Third, socialist feminist analysis is not primarily concerned with class inequality but with the complex intertwining of a wide range of social inequalities. Socialist feminism develops a portrait of social organization in which the public structures of economy, polity, and ideology interact with the intimate, private processes of human reproduction, domesticity, sexuality, and subjectivity to sustain a multifaceted system of domination. The workings of this system are discernible both as enduring and impersonal social patterns and in the more varied subtleties of interpersonal relationships. To analyze this system, socialist feminists shuttle between a mapping of large-scale systems of domination and a situationally specific, detailed exploration of the mundane daily experiences of oppressed people.

A contemporary socialist feminist classic, Chrys Ingraham's *White Weddings*, explores how capitalism, patriarchy, and racism play out in the institution of the wedding as an increasingly mandatory and enormously costly public ceremony marking two people's private intentions. Ingraham demonstrates the importance of the wedding for capitalism with raw financial data—this is a billion-dollar industry, part of the profits arising from the exploitation of workers around the world—about diamond mine workers in Africa, honeymoon resort workers in the Caribbean, sweatshop sewers of wedding gowns in Southeast Asia. She shows capitalism's ideological practices as it sells persistently the image of the wedding fantasy through toys, films, TV shows, and women's magazines. She also demonstrates how this ideological appeal is deeply intertwined with patriarchy. The ritual of the white wedding has become the sacred ceremony of what Adrienne Rich earlier termed "compulsory heterosexuality" and Ingraham calls heteronormativity. Heteronormativity lies at the heart of patriarchy. It is the collectively enforced belief that adult needs for family, security, and intimacy must only be satisfied in a relation between a man and a woman, that is, between two people who within patriarchy's gender stratification are unequal in power, rights, status. Ingraham shows how the white wedding is passionately desired by brides and their families because it encodes the "heterosexual imaginary": the idealized image of romantic love between a man and a woman that obscures and erases from the mind all knowledge of the work required to maintain a relation between unequals, the risks of noncommunication, and ultimately divorce. To be told, as women are, that one's wedding day is "the happiest day of one's life" is to say that one's significance as a human being is not in accomplishment but in being chosen as an object of desire.

Socialist feminists' program for change calls for a global solidarity among women to combat the abuses capitalism works in their lives, the lives of their communities, and the environment. They call on the feminist community to

---

Patricia Hill Collins (1948–   )
A Biographical Vignette

Collins writes that her experiences of educational success were permeated by the counterexperience of being the first, or only, African-American (or woman, working-class person, etc.) in various social settings. She learned that educational success seemed to demand that she distance herself from her black working-class background. This created for her a loss of voice.

Her response to these tensions has been to formulate an alternative understanding of social theory and an alternative way of doing theory. This project led her to discover the theoretical voice of her community and to reclaim her own voice by situating it in that community. It culminated in *Black Feminist Thought: Knowledge, Consciousness, and Empowerment* (1990), a landmark text in feminist and social theory. *Black Feminist Thought* presents social theory as the understandings of a specific group, black women; to this end, Collins draws on a wide range of voices—some famous; others obscure. What she presents is a community-based social theory that articulates that group's understanding of its oppression by intersections of race, gender, and class—and its historic struggle against that oppression. In 2009 Collins served as the first African-American Woman President of the American Sociological Association.

---

be ever vigilant about the dangers of their own co-optation into a privileged intelligentsia that serves capitalist interests. Their project is to mobilize people to use the state as a means for the effective redistribution of societal resources through the provision of an extensive safety net of public services like publicly supported education, health care, transportation, child care, housing; a progressive tax structure that reduces the wide disparities of income between rich and poor; and the guarantee of a living wage to all members of the community. They believe that this mobilization will be effective only if people become aware of and care about the life conditions of others as well as their own. The feminist social scientist's duty is to make visible and experientially real the material inequalities that shape people's lives.

Intersectionality Theory   **Intersectionality theory** begins with the understanding that women experience oppression in varying configurations and in varying degrees of intensity. The explanation for that variation (and this explanation is the central subject of intersectionality theory) is that while all women potentially experience oppression on the basis of gender, women are, nevertheless, differentially oppressed by the varied intersections of other arrangements of social inequality. We may describe these arrangements of inequality

---

intersectionality theory   The view that women experience oppression in varying configurations and in varying degrees of intensity.

as **vectors of oppression and privilege** (or in Patricia Hill Collins's phrase, "the matrix of domination" [1990]), which include not only gender but also class, race, global location, sexual preference, and age. The variation of these intersections qualitatively alters the experience of being a woman; and this alteration, this diversity, must be taken into account in theorizing the experiences of women. The argument in intersectionality theory is that the pattern of intersection itself produces a particular experience of oppression—not merely the salience of any one variable, the working out of one vector. Kimberly Crenshawe, for example, shows that black women frequently experience discrimination in employment because they are black women, but courts routinely refuse to recognize this discrimination—unless it can be shown to be a case of what is considered general discrimination, sex discrimination (read "white women") or race discrimination (read "black men"). In characterizing these as vectors of oppression and privilege, we wish to suggest a fundamental insight of intersectionality theories—that the privilege exercised by some women and men turns on the oppression of other women and men. Theories of intersectionality at their core understand these arrangements of inequality as hierarchical structures based in unjust power relations. The theme of injustice signals the consistent critical focus of this analysis.

Intersectionality theory recognizes the fundamental link between ideology and power that allows dominants to control subordinates by creating a politics in which difference becomes a conceptual tool for justifying arrangements of oppression. In social practice, dominants use differences among people to justify oppressive practices by translating difference into models of inferiority/superiority; people are socialized to relate to difference not as a source of diversity, interest, and cultural wealth but evaluatively in terms of better or worse. These ideologies operate in part by creating what Audre Lorde calls a mythical norm (in the United States, examples include white, thin, male, and heterosexual) against which people evaluate others and themselves. This norm not only allows dominants to control social production (both paid and unpaid), but it also becomes part of individual subjectivity—an internalized rejection of difference that can operate to make people devalue themselves; reject people from different groups; and create criteria within their own group for excluding, punishing, or marginalizing group members. Gloria Anzaldua describes this last practice as **othering,** an act of definition done within a subordinated group to establish that a group member is unacceptable, an "other," by some criterion. This definitional activity, she points out, erodes the potential for coalition and resistance.

---

vectors of oppression and privilege   The varied intersections of a number of arrangements of social inequality (gender, class, race, global location, sexual preference, and age) that serve to oppress women differentially. Variation in these intersections qualitatively alters the experience of being a woman.

othering   An act of definition within a subordinated group to establish that a group member is unacceptable, an "other," by some criterion; this erodes the potential for coalition and resistance.

The intersection of vectors of oppression and privilege creates variations both in the forms and the intensity of people's experience of oppression. Much of the writing and research done out of an intersectionality perspective presents the concrete reality of people's lives as those lives are shaped by the intersections of these vectors. The most studied intersections by feminists are of gender and race, gender and class, and race, gender, class. Other analyses include gender and age, gender and global location, and gender and sexual preference.

In response to their material circumstances, women create interpretations and strategies for surviving and resisting the persistent exercise of unjust power. One part of the project of intersectionality theory is to give voice to the group knowledges worked out in specific life experiences created by historic intersections of inequality and to develop various feminist expressions of these knowledges, for example, black feminist thought or chicana feminism.

Intersectionality theory develops a critique of earlier feminist writings in which it sees that work reflecting the experience and concerns of white privileged-class feminists in North Atlantic societies. Some of this work of critique is paralleled by work done in postmodernism, but this parallelism should not be overstated. Intersectionality theory is one of the oldest traditions in feminism. This critique has produced questions about what we mean by categories such as woman, gender, race, and sisterhood. It has focused on the diversity of experience in such seeming universals as mothering and family and has reinterpreted theoretical works like the sociological-psychoanalytic studies of Chodorow. This critique has prompted a repositioning of the understandings of whiteness by white feminists who seek to understand whiteness as a construction, the ways that whiteness results in privilege, what they can actively do to reduce racism, and how they can contribute to producing a more inclusive feminist analysis.

This process of theory-building, research, and critique has brought intersectionality theory to one of its central themes and one of the central issues confronting feminism today: how to allow for the analytic principle and empirical fact of diversity among women, while at the same time holding to the valuational and political position that specific groups of women share a distinctive standpoint. Explaining **standpoint** (see the Key Concept box titled Standpoint), Patricia Hill Collins proposes that it is the view of the world shared by a group characterized by a heterogeneous commonality. Thus, Collins concludes that a group's standpoint is constituted not out of some essentialism but out of a recognition that everyone is in the same boat. Although vectors of oppression and privilege—race, class, gender, age, global location, sexual preference—intersect in all people's lives, these theorists argue that the way they intersect markedly affects the degree to which a common standpoint is affirmed. Among factors facilitating this affirmation are the group's existence over time, its sense of its own history as a group, its location in relatively segregated identifiable spaces,

---

standpoint   The perspective of embodied actors within groups that are differentially located in social structure.

and its development of an intragroup system of social organizations and knowledges for coping with oppression. But a group standpoint is never monolithic or impermeable; the very fact that the group is constituted out of intersections of vectors means that group members can pivot between varying senses of self. Group members frequently move from the home group into the larger society where their experience is that of **the outsider within.** Moreover, the home group is subject to permeation by outside ideas and is not undifferentiated; it has its own internal dynamics of difference and may even be constituted by its existence at what Anzaldua names a cultural borderland. Intersectionality theorists warn that, although it is easy to locate the experience of intersection and of standpoint in individuals, this reductionism is theoretically and politically dangerous, erasing the historic structures of unequal power that have produced the individual experience and obscuring the need for political change.

In developing an agenda for change, intersectionality theory turns to the knowledge of oppressed people and their long-held evaluative principles of faith and justice. The theory argues for the need to bear witness, to protest, and to organize for change within the context of the oppressed community; for only within community can one keep faith in the eventual triumph of justice—a justice understood not in the narrow framing of legal rationality but as the working out within social institutions and social relations of the principles of fairness to, and concern for, others and oneself.

TOWARD A FEMINIST SOCIOLOGICAL THEORY

Drawing on all the lines of feminist argument reviewed above, feminist sociologists have begun to create a general theory that addresses the key concerns of all sociological theories: the relation between social structure and individual action (or agency), the relation between macrosocial and microsocial, the nature of power, the causes of inequality, and the origins of change.

This emergent feminist theory views human agents as living and acting within a complex field of power that they are determined by and that in their agency they both reproduce and contest. Social life is presented as an ongoing series of enactments of oppression by agents who cannot be absolved from their responsibility for the reproduction of domination even when we can explain the social structures framing those enactments. Social life can also be understood as an ongoing series of individual and group responses to oppression, responses like coping, challenging, witnessing, subverting, rebelling, resisting—a politics of resistance in which individual and collective agency oppose structures and agents of domination. Significant to oppositional politics are the existence and persistence of group *standpoints* (see Key Concept box); these group standpoints are ways of understanding society that develop out of social structural

---

the outsider within   The frequent experience of group members when they move from the home group into the larger society.

Key Concept
Standpoint

Much of feminist theory is premised on the idea that people operate from a particular **standpoint** in the social world, from the perspective of the positions of embodied actors within groups that are differentially located in social structure. As a result, what everyone sees and knows is always partial and interested, never total and objective. Knowledge is produced in and varies among groups and, to some degree, among actors within groups. That knowledge is always affected by power relations—whether it is formulated from the standpoint of dominant or subordinate groups.

A feminist sociological theory begins here because feminists attempt to describe, analyze, and change the world from the standpoint of women, and because, working from women's subordinated position in social relations, feminist sociological theorists see that knowledge is part of the system of power governing the production of knowledge, as it governs all production in society. Feminist sociological theory attempts to alter the balance of power within sociological discourse—and within social theory—by establishing the standpoint of women as one of the standpoints from which social knowledge is constructed.

In attempting to do sociology from the standpoint of women, feminist sociological theorists have to consider what constitutes a standpoint of women. A standpoint is the product of a social collectivity with a sufficient history and commonality of circumstance to develop a shared knowledge of social relations. All women under patriarchy have been assigned to the tasks of social reproduction (childbearing, child-rearing, housekeeping, food preparation, care of the ill and dependent, emotional and sexual service); hence, this work, which is done without material compensation, is exploitative. This shared and historic relation to social reproduction in circumstances of subordination is the basis for the feminist claim of the standpoint of women, but the intersection of gender inequality with race inequality, class inequality, geo-social inequality, and inequalities based on sexuality and age produces a complex system of unequally empowered standpoint groups relating through shifting arrangements of coalition and opposition. These intersectionalities are now an integral part of the feminist description and analysis of women's standpoint.

---

arrangements and that serve as motivations for individual and group reproduction of or resistance to domination. Even though the structural determinist may argue that standpoints are the product of social structures, feminist analysis points to the human capacity to hope and act for better things even in circumstances of the most brutal oppression. Feminist analysis emphasizes the emotional responsiveness of embodied human subjects to structures, their capacity to respond in anger and to turn anger to constructive uses. The emotional response of anger—and the willingness to turn that anger into a stand against injustice or a demand for justice—cannot be accounted for by the structures

---

standpoint   The perspective of embodied actors within groups that are differentially located in social structure.

of oppression that produce it. In this affirmation, feminism bases its hope for liberationist politics and offers a solution to the theoretical problematic of the structure versus agency debate.

Feminist theorists have also been developing a vocabulary for talking about the various and simultaneous realities of macro- and micro-relations. Dorothy Smith has introduced the concepts of relations of ruling; generalized, anonymous, impersonal texts; and local actualities of lived experience.

1. **Relations of ruling** refers to the complex, nonmonolithic but intricately connected social activities that attempt to control human social production.
2. Human social production must by its material nature occur at some moment in the **local actualities of lived experience**: that is, the places where some actual person sits while writing or reading a book (or plants food or produces clothing).
3. The relations of ruling in late capitalist patriarchy manifest themselves through **texts** that are characterized by their essential anonymity, generality, and authority. These texts are designed to pattern and translate real-life, specific, individualized experience into a language form acceptable to the relations of ruling. This criterion of acceptability is met when the text imposes the dominants' definition on the situation. The texts may range from contracts to police reports to official boards-of-inquiry statements to school certificates to medical records. Everywhere they alter the material reality—reinterpreting what has occurred, determining what will be possible. Thus, in seeking to interact with the relations of ruling, even at a fairly local level, a given individual (such as a student applying for a summer job in a restaurant owned by a family friend) finds that she or he must fill out some texts (e.g., tax forms) that have been established not by the employer face-to-face but by part of the apparatus of ruling. These texts continuously create intersections between the relations of ruling and the local actualities of lived experience. It is important to observe that this intersection works both ways: At some series of moments in historic time, embodied actors, situated in absolutely individual locations, sit at desks or computer workstations or conference tables generating the forms that will become part of the apparatus of ruling.

All three aspects of social life—relations of ruling, local actualities of lived experience, and texts—are widespread, enduring, constant features of the organization

---

relations of ruling The complex, nonmonolithic but intricately connected social activities that attempt to control human social production.

local actualities of lived experience The places where actual people act and live their lives.

texts "Written documents issued out of the relations of ruling, having the power to organize relations of production in the everyday life world and having the quality of generality and anonymity so that they may be seen as applicable in various everyday life circumstances; texts include licenses, diplomas, contracts, purchasing orders, laws, college catalogues, etc."

Dorothy E. Smith (1926–   )
A Biographical Vignette

Dorothy E. Smith explained that her sociological theory derived from her life experiences as a woman, moving between the male-dominated academic sphere and the female life experience which she describes the single parent. Remembering herself studying for a doctorate in sociology as "not so much . . . a career as a series of contingencies, of accidents." This theme of contingency is an important hallmark of her sociology of women.

Whether they occurred by accident or design, the following events appear to the outsider as significant stages in Smith's development. She was born in 1926 in Great Britain. She earned her bachelor's degree in sociology from the University of London in 1955 and her Ph.D. in sociology from the University of California at Berkeley in 1963. During this same period, she had "the experience of marriage, of immigration [to Canada] closely following marriage, of the arrival of children, of the departure of a husband rather early one morning, of the jobs that became available." These events, Smith stresses, "were moments in which I had in fact little choice and certainly little foreknowledge." The jobs that became available included research sociologist at Berkeley; lecturer in sociology at Berkeley; lecturer in sociology at the University of Essex, Colchester, England; associate professor and then professor in the department of sociology at the University of British Columbia; and professor of sociology in education at the Ontario Institute for Studies in Education, Toronto.

Smith's ideas are foundational to feminist macro-theory, integrated feminist-theory, and socialist feminism.

of social life and of domination. All three features at the same time can and must be studied as the actions, relationships, and work of embodied human subjects. Each dimension has its distinctive internal dynamic: the drive for control in the relations of ruling, the drive for production and communication in the local actualities, and the drive toward objectification and facticity in the generalized texts. This world is both gendered and racialized. Thus, although no one can totally escape life in the local actuality—everyone has to be physically somewhere in time and space—women are much more deeply implicated in the never-ending maintaining of the local actualities, and men are much freer to participate as dominants in the relations of ruling; these same divisions are repeated for economic and racial subordinates and dominants. The texts that strive for objectification and facticity are drawn in ways that make it impossible for all to share equally in the activity the text organizes. Those inequalities are created along lines of race, gender, class, age, global location; that is, difference is an organizational principle of the texts of the relations of ruling. Through this lens the elements of structure and interaction are fused. Domination and production become the problematic, and their manifestations involve and thus absorb the age-old sociological distinctions of micro-macro and agency-structure.

Feminist sociological theorists describe a micro-social order in which there is a radical difference in the world of everyday life experienced by society's dominants and society's subordinates, of whom women compose the overwhelming majority worldwide. In other words, micro-social life experience is shaped and pervaded by relations of power and inequality in macro-social structures. This vision of micro-social life is at odds with that of traditional mainstream sociology that tends to see the micro-social world as operating in a kind of democratic ethos of equals trying to work things out together or at least of situations in which any individual could emerge as the "winner" or "definer." But feminist sociological theory argues that the ongoing social experiences of action, interaction, self, and consciousness are radically different for women and other subordinates from those same experiences for dominants.

Action, for someone with some configuration of the various forms of privilege—conferred by patriarchy, capitalism, and racism in the macro-social order—involves the purposive setting of goals, and the pursuit of those goals through linear courses of action in which one can compartmentalize and focus on the project at hand. In contrast, women's lives have a quality of incidentalism, as women find themselves caught up in agendas that shift and change with the vagaries of marriage, husbands' courses of action, children's unpredictable impact on life plans, divorce, widowhood, and the precariousness of most women's wage-sector occupations. In their daily activities, women find themselves not so much pursuing goals in linear sequences as responding continuously to the needs and demands of others, oriented not so much to their own goals as to the task of monitoring, coordinating, facilitating, and moderating the wishes, actions, and demands of others.

For society's dominants the experience of *interaction* with others may involve a mutuality of orientation, a pressure to arrive at common understandings, and the freedom to move in and out of interactional settings. Any interpersonal equality or dominance that women as individuals may achieve is effectively offset, with the interactive process itself. The macrostructural patterning of gender inequality affects the broad division of labor, that is, who sets and who implements projects. It also affects details like the enactment of authority and deference in seating and seating-standing arrangements, forms of address and conversation, eye contact, and the control of space and time. This assumption of inequality as a feature in interactive situations is intensified and complicated when factors of race and class are included in the feminist analytic frame.

Persons with power arrive at a knowledge of *self* by learning to see themselves as others like them see them. Women are socialized to see themselves through the eyes of men—the genuine other. Feminist theory calls into question the existence for the socially disempowered of a unified generalized other. The subordinate has to pivot between a world governed by a dominant generalized other, or meaning system, and locations in home groups that offer alternative understandings and generalized others.

Contemporary Applications
Domestic Violence

Domestic violence has reached epidemic proportions in the United States, with some estimates running as high as three women a day being killed by a husband or boyfriend and over 3 million reports of physical abuse yearly. This macrosocial trend is fleshed out in newspapers daily with dramatic stories of violence and pain inflicted by men on women in primary relationships of intimacy. One such story that haunted readers in Washington, D.C. involved Yvette Cade, 32, whose request for the extension of a protective order against her estranged husband Roger B. Hargave was denied by Prince Georges County Judge Richard Palumbo; three weeks later Hargave attacked Cade at work, doused her with gasoline and set her afire. He was charged with attempted murder; she was left horribly burned but determined to become an advocate for victims of domestic violence; Judge Palumbo was forced to retire because of his contemptuous attitude toward women complainants.

As the figures suggest, that story is repeated in some form almost daily in the U.S.—vivid evidence for the validity of radical feminist claims. Here, however, we look at domestic violence from the perspective of Dorothy E. Smith's feminist sociology. The world of domestic violence, like the world in general, can be divided into the local actuality of lived experience—the place where Cade is doused with gasoline and set afire—and the extralocal relations of ruling—the place where texts like protective orders are issued by male judges like Palumbo, who regularly trivialized the life experiences of women whom he described in court as being like buses, "if you miss one, there'll be another one along in a few minutes." The protective order is one of the weapons that liberal feminists have worked to put in place to try to help women. But its success depends on its being issued and on police officers taking its enforcement seriously. The ability to successfully navigate the court system, to make the relations of ruling act in your favor, is affected by the intersection of vectors of oppression and privilege; gender, race, class, age, sexual preference all influence judges and police.

And none of these operate in a vacuum. The news media, which report these incidents with such regularity and attention to detail, at the same time also create an atmosphere in which women's suffering is defined not as suffering caused by gender as an unjust social structure but as suffering arising out of the strange workings of the human heart. As domestic violence was racking up millions of victims a year, 95 percent of them women, a white male columnist, Hendrik Hertzberg, writing in *The New Yorker* at the time of Barack Obama's defeat of Hillary Clinton, declared that justice had been done because while "not [to] belittle the oppressions of gender . . . in America the oppressions of race have cut deeper . . . [T] there is no gender equivalent of the nightmare of disenfranchisement, lynching, apartheid, and peonage." As Hertzberg notes, but then ignores, it does little good to compare oppressions; yet, from the standpoint of feminist theory, it is clear that someone must speak in response to his column: three women dying every day in domestic violence is close to a gender equivalent. And it is the practice of sexist and patriarchal ideology to dismiss it (but trivialization remains a chief weapon of sexism). The slick commentary of *The New Yorker* is another form of text issuing from the relations of ruling and controlling the lives of women in the local actuality of lived experience.

For women, the most pervasive feature of the cognitive style of everyday life is what Dorothy Smith calls a **bifurcated consciousness,** developing along a line of fault between their own personal, lived, and reflected-on experience and the established types available in the social stock of knowledge to describe that experience. A feminist sociology of subjectivity asks, how do people survive when their own experience does not fit the established typifications of that experience? We know already that some do so by avoiding acts of sustained reflection, some by cultivating their own series of personal types to make sense of their experience, some by seeking community with others who share this bifurcated reality, and some by denying the validity of their own experience. But it is out of this line of fault, this division between what one knows from living and what a world organized by capitalist racist patriarchy says, that the possibility of change emerges, that one learns to see through and question the taken-for-granted and to believe that things can be different because one knows from living that they are different.

Summary

1. Feminist theory is a generalized, wide-ranging system of ideas about social life and human experience developed from a woman-centered perspective.
2. Feminist theory raises several basic questions: What about the women? Why is all this as it is? How can we change and improve the social world to make it a more just place for women and all people? What about the differences among women?
3. Contemporary feminist sociology has its historical roots in the work of earlier generations of women theorists, who, in the nineteenth and early twentieth centuries made important contributions to the formulation of sociology, but whose accomplishments were erased from the record by a politics of gender.
4. One type of feminist theory focuses on gender difference.
5. Cultural feminism extols the positive aspects of being female.
6. Explanatory theories locate the source of gender differences in biology, institutional roles, socialization, and social interaction.
7. The second type of feminist theory focuses on gender inequality.
8. Liberal feminism argues that women may claim equality with men on the basis of an essential human capacity for reasoned moral agency, that gender inequality is the result of a patriarchal and sexist patterning of the division of labor, and that gender equality can be produced by transforming the division of labor through the repatterning of key institutions: law, work, family, education, and media.
9. Theories of gender oppression describe women's situation as the consequence of a direct power relationship between men and women in which men have fundamental and concrete interests in controlling, using, subjugating, and oppressing women: that is, in the practice of domination.

---

bifurcated consciousness   A type of consciousness characteristic of women that reflects the fact that, for them, everyday life is divided into two realities: the reality of their actual, lived, reflected-on experience and the reality of social typifications.

10. Psychoanalytic feminism maps and emphasizes the emotional dynamics of personality, emotions often deeply buried in the subconscious or unconscious areas of the psyche; it also highlights the importance of infancy and early childhood in the patterning of these emotions.
11. Radical feminism is based on the belief that women are of absolute positive value as women, a belief asserted against what they claim to be the universal devaluing of women, and that women are everywhere oppressed—violently oppressed—by the system of patriarchy.
12. Structural oppression theories recognize that oppression results from the fact that some groups of people derive direct benefits from controlling, using, subjugating, and oppressing other groups of people. These theories analyze how those interests in domination are enacted through mechanisms of social structure: that is, through recurring and routinized large-scale arrangements of social interaction.
13. Socialist feminists seek to bring together Marxian and radical feminist thought.
14. Intersectionality theory begins with the understanding that women experience oppression in varying configurations and in varying degrees of intensity. The explanation for that variation is that, although all women potentially experience oppression on the basis of gender, women are, nevertheless, differentially oppressed by the varied intersections of other arrangements of social inequality.
15. Feminist sociological theory links structure and agency, micro-social and macrosocial, through the concepts of standpoint, extra-local relations of ruling, local actualities of lived experience, texts, incidentalism, responsive action, and bifurcated consciousness.

Suggested Readings

PATRICIA MADOO LENGERMANN and JILL NIEBRUGGE-BRANTLEY *The Women Founders: Sociology and Social Theory 1830–1930*. New York: McGraw-Hill, 1998. Excellent treatment of the theories of the long-neglected early female contributors to sociology. Includes very useful selections from these thinkers.

ARLIE HOCHSCHILD with ANNE MACHUNG. *The Second Shift*. London: Penguin Books, 2003. This is a new edition of the 1989 classic, honored as a *New York Times* notable book, with a new introduction by Hochschild.

PATRICIA HILL COLLINS *Black Feminist Thought: Knowledge, Consciousness, and Empowerment*. Boston: Unwin Hyman, 1990. Fast becoming a contemporary classic on the black feminist perspective and standpoint theory.

PATRICIA HILL COLLINS *Fighting Words: Black Women and the Search for Justice*. Minneapolis: University of Minnesota Press, 1998. Later theorizing by the author of *Black Feminist Thought*.

BETTY FRIEDAN *The Feminine Mystique*. New York: Dell, 1963. A modern classic within the tradition of liberal feminism.

NANCY CHODOROW *The Reproduction of Mothering: Psychoanalysis and the Sociology of Gender*. Berkeley: University of California Press, 1978. A book that gave great impetus to psychoanalytic feminism.

CHRYS INGRAHAM *White Weddings*. New York: Routledge, 2008. A classic of socialistic materialist feminism.

JOAN WILLIAMS *Unbending Gender*. New York: Oxford University Press, 2000. Explores problems of balancing work and family.

DOROTHY E. SMITH *The Everyday World as Problematic*. Boston: Northeastern University Press, 1987. Smith's major theoretical statement.

CHAPTER 9

Postmodern Grand Theories

Chapters 4 and 5 dealt with a variety of modern grand theories. Most grand theories that deal with the contemporary world have been created by theorists who consider themselves to be modernists. This chapter discusses a series of grand theories (postmodern theorists have done comparatively little work on everyday life) that either deal with the postmodern world and/or were created by thinkers associated with postmodern social theory. The irony is that postmodern theorists are often critical of modern grand theories, although they themselves have created such perspectives.

THE TRANSITION FROM INDUSTRIAL TO POSTINDUSTRIAL SOCIETY

The work of Daniel Bell (1919–   ) on the coming of the postindustrial society represents something of a transition from Chapters 4 and 5 on modern grand theories to this one on postmodern grand theories. Even though he is decidedly a modernist, many commonalities exist between what he has to say on industrial-postindustrial societies and what the postmodernists argue about modern/postmodern societies. However, although grand theories seem to emerge unintentionally in the work of postmodernists, as a modernist, Bell has no hesitation about consciously offering a theory of the great sweep of recent history. Bell is also eager to criticize at least some aspects of postindustrial society; most postmodernists are inclined to depict that society in more positive terms, at least in comparison to modern society.

What Bell has to say on the industrial-postindustrial relationship is embedded in a broader scheme of social change that also includes preindustrial society. He sees a transition from preindustrial (most of Asia and Africa), industrial (some of Western Europe, Russia), to postindustrial (the United States was considered the sole postindustrial society at the time Bell wrote [the early 1970s]). Of course, much has happened in the nearly three decades since Bell wrote. The United States is a far more pronounced postindustrial society and other nations have moved further in that direction (e.g., several Western European nations and Japan).

Postindustrial Society　Bell's primary concern is postindustrial society and to analyze it he divides society into three realms: social structure, polity, and culture. The coming of the postindustrial society primarily affects social structure and several of its major components: the economy, the work world, science, and technology. However, changes in social structure do have implications for the political system (polity) and culture.

The following is an enumeration of the major changes in social structure associated with the transition to **postindustrial society:**

1. Within the economy, there is a transition from goods production to the provision of services. Production of such goods as clothing and steel declines and services such as selling hamburgers and offering advice on investments increase. Although services predominate in a wide range of sectors, health, education, research, and government services are the most decisive for a postindustrial society.
2. The importance of blue-collar, manual work (e.g., assembly line workers) declines and professional (lawyers) and technical work (computer programmers) come to predominate. Of special importance is the rise of scientists (e.g., medical and genetic) and engineers.
3. Instead of practical know-how, theoretical knowledge is increasingly essential in a postindustrial society. Such knowledge is seen as the basic source of innovations (e.g., the knowledge created by those scientists involved in the human genome project is leading to new ways of treating many diseases). Advances in knowledge also lead to the need for other innovations such as ways of dealing with ethical questions raised by advances in cloning technology. All of this involves an emphasis on theoretical rather than

---

postindustrial society　A society characterized by the provision of services rather than goods; professional and technical work rather than blue-collar, manual work; theoretical knowledge rather than practical know-how; the creation and monitoring of new technologies; and new intellectual technologies to handle such assessment and control.

empirical knowledge and on the codification of knowledge. The exponential growth of theoretical and codified knowledge, in all its varieties, is central to the emergence of the postindustrial society.

4. Postindustrial society seeks to assess the impacts of new technologies and, where necessary, to exercise control over them. The hope is, for example, to better monitor things like nuclear power plants and to improve them so that accidents like that at Three-Mile Island or Chernobyl can be prevented in the future. The goal is a surer and more secure technological world.

5. To handle such assessment and control, and more generally the sheer complexity of postindustrial society, new intellectual technologies are developed and implemented. They include cybernetics, game theory, and information theory.

6. A new relationship is forged in postindustrial society between scientists and the new technologies they create. Scientific research has come to be institutionalized, and new science-based industries have come into existence. The fusion of science and innovation, as well as systematic technological growth, lies at the base of postindustrial society. This leads to the need for more universities and university-based students. In fact, the university is crucial to postindustrial society. The university produces the experts who can create, guide, and control the new and dramatically changing technologies.

Differences among Types of Societies   Given this depiction of postindustrial society, Bell outlines a number of differences between it and preindustrial and industrial societies:

1. Occupationally, preindustrial society is dominated by farmers, miners, fishermen, and unskilled workers; industrial society, by semiskilled workers and engineers; and postindustrial society, by professional and technical scientists.

2. The three types of society involve different types of challenges. The challenge to preindustrial society is to be able to extract things from nature in the realms of mining, fishing, forestry, and agriculture. The challenge in industrial society is to deal with machines through more sophisticated coordination, scheduling, programming, and organization. Finally, the main challenge in postindustrial society is other people. Some people are providing services to other people and those who provide the services generally have more information and knowledge (they are the experts) than those to whom the service is being provided. This gives them a great advantage in dealing with their clients.

3. In preindustrial societies, the landowners and the military hold the power, and they exercise it through the direct use of force. In industrial society, businesspeople have the lion's share of power, although they exercise it indirectly by influencing politicians. Scientists and researchers come to the fore as the dominant figures in postindustrial society, and they seek to balance technical and political forces.

Culture All of these factors focus on changes in social structure in postindustrial society, but Bell, as we've seen, is also interested in the polity and, especially, the culture. Of great interest to Bell is the fact that fundamentally different principles lie at the base of social structure and culture in postindustrial society. Although social structure, with its focal concern with economic issues, is dominated by a concern for rationality and efficiency, culture is dominated by notions of irrationality, self-realization, and self-gratification. Thus, in postindustrial society the old-fashioned ideas of self-discipline, restraint, and delayed gratification predominate in social structure and conflict with the hedonism that characterizes the cultural domain.

In this context Bell explicitly attacks postmodernism, which he associates with such irrational and hedonistic ideas as impulse, pleasure, liberation, and eroticism. Clearly, a culture characterized in this way is at odds with a social structure dominated by efficiency and rationality. In Bell's terms, this leads to a disjuncture between social structure and culture, and this situation can create the conditions needed for a social revolution.

Although he is at odds with the postmodernists on this and other grounds, Bell, like the postmodernists, does accord central importance to the rise of consumer society. Hedonism has replaced frugality and asceticism, at least in part, because of the mass production and sale of all sorts of goods. Traditional values are being eroded and being replaced by a focal interest in things like pleasure, play, fun, and public display. As a modernist, and a conservative at that, Bell is alarmed by these postmodern developments and the threats they pose to society.

INCREASING GOVERNMENTALITY (AND OTHER GRAND THEORIES)

To some, Michel Foucault is a forerunner of postmodern social theory, while to others he is one of its foremost practitioners. In either case, he created an important grand theory that needs to be considered by every serious student of social theory.

One thing that especially distinguishes Foucault's grand theories from modern grand theories is that he does not see, or at least does not emphasize, the continuities over time that are integral to most modern grand narratives. Foucault does not view history unfolding in a unilinear and unidirectional fashion as Weber, among others, does in his theory of rationalization. The following are several differences between Foucault's grand theories and those of modernists:

1. Modernists often search for the source or the origin of social developments, while Foucault seeks to describe and analyze social realities at various points in time. Finding the origin is akin to finding the answer, but postmodernists reject the idea of finding an answer. They are more interested in raising questions than in finding answers; they are more interested in keeping the intellectual dialogue alive than they are in the modernist search for

answers (or origins). After all, once a theorist purports to have found the answer or origin, the issue is presumably closed.

2. While modernists emphasize coherence, Foucault focuses on incoherence. To put it another way, while modernists focus on what holds things together over time, Foucault is interested in the internal contradictions that exist at any given point in time.

3. In contrast to the modernists who emphasize continuity in developments over time, Foucault emphasizes the discontinuities, the ruptures, the sudden reversals that characterize social history. Historical developments do not occur uniformly, consistently, unidirectionally, and without ebbs and flows; there are movements backward, sideward, and sometimes even forward.

Increasing Governmentality

Within the context of such general views on change, Foucault was interested in the changing nature of what he called **governmentalities**, or the practices and techniques by which control is exercised over people. The most obvious form of governmentality is that exercised by the state over its citizens. Although Foucault is interested in this, what distinguishes his approach is his interest in the way governmentality is practiced by agencies and agents unrelated to the state (including the social sciences and social scientists). Also distinctive in his work is a concern for the way people govern themselves. No directionality is implied in this conceptualization, but it is found in some of Foucault's specific works.

Discipline and Punish   The best example of Foucault's interest in non-state-related governmentality is in his book, *Discipline and Punish*. His main concern in this work is the period between 1757 and the 1830s, specifically within the prison system, where he sees a historical process by which the torture of prisoners is replaced by control by prison rules. Characteristically, he views this change as developing in fits and starts, not unidirectionally. Nonetheless, there is general trend from one form of punishment to the other. Not only was there such a change, but it was viewed (by modernists) as a progressive development. The transition from torture to rule-based control was seen by most observers as involving a progressive humanization of the treatment of criminals. In general, punishment was viewed as growing more kind, less painful, and less cruel. However, the reality from Foucault's perspective was that the system had greatly enhanced its ability to punish criminals.

For one thing, the new ability to punish had fewer negative side-effects. Earlier, prisoners had been subjected to public torture, but the problem was that this treatment tended to incite the masses viewing the spectacle to criminal acts, riots, and perhaps even rebellion. Excited by the scenes of public torture, people were prone to all sorts of behavior that those in power viewed as antisocial and

---

governmentalities   The practices and techniques by which control is exercised over people.

threatening to them and their position. In contrast, the imposition of rules on prisoners generally occurred behind prison walls and, even if it didn't, it was unlikely to incite a crowd.

Imposing rules carried with it many more advantages over torture. First, the ability to impose rules can occur much earlier in the deviance process than torture; people can be taught the rules before they even think of engaging in a deviant act, or they can have those rules reinforced at the first sign of a tendency toward deviance. In contrast, torture is only likely to be undertaken when an act, and more likely a series of acts, of deviance has occurred.

In addition, the imposition of rules can take place far more often than torture; rules can be taught and retaught. However, torture cannot be practiced repeatedly on the same deviant because it is likely to badly injure, maim, or even kill the deviant. Furthermore, the more often acts of torture are practiced, the more likely it is that those who witness them will engage in deviant acts of their own.

Third, rule imposition is closely associated with rationalization and bureaucratization. Among other things, that means it is more efficient, more impersonal, more sober, and more invariable than torture. In other words, torture is likely to be inefficient (it may anger the prisoner rather than bringing him under greater control); it could get very personal (the person using a whip could take out personal animosity on the victim); it could become very emotional for the torturer, the tortured, and those who witness the whole thing; and it could be highly variable with one user of the whip being far more aggressive than another.

Finally, and perhaps most importantly, imposition of rules has much broader ramifications. It is almost impossible to torture an entire population, but rule-based control can be exercised over a population. This ability to control an entire population is based on the ability to exercise surveillance over it on a regular basis. However, power and surveillance are not, in Foucault's view, part of a single overarching power system, but are exercised in a number of seemingly independent local settings. Thus, there are innumerable points in which power and surveillance are exercised over people, *and* there is always the possibility within Foucault's theoretical perspective for opposition to this to occur at every one of those points. Three basic instruments are available to those who seek to exercise control and observe a population.

Instruments of Observation and Control   The first is **hierarchical observation** or the ability of officials at or near the top of an organization to oversee all that they control with a single gaze. In this context is found Foucault's famous discussion of a panopticon. A **panopticon** is a structure that allows someone in power (e.g., a prison officer) the possibility of complete observation of a group

---

hierarchical observation   The ability of officials at or near the top of an organization to oversee all that they control with a single gaze.

panopticon   A structure that allows someone in power (e.g., a prison officer) the possibility of complete observation of a group of people (e.g., prisoners).

of people (e.g., prisoners). In fact, the official need not necessarily be present in the structure; the mere possibility that the official might be there constrains people and forces them to behave as they are expected to behave. For example, a panopticon might take the form of a tower surrounded by a circular prison. Guards in the tower, who may or may not be visible to the prisoners, can see into all of the cells that are open to view from the tower. The tower gives guards the possibility of total surveillance if the guards are on duty and observing what is transpiring around them. More importantly, it gives the guards enormous power even if they are not present in the tower or observing what is transpiring in the cells. The reason is that the inmates cannot see into the tower and therefore cannot tell whether they are being watched. However, because of an ever-present possibility that they are being watched, they are likely to behave as expected even though guards may be absent or inattentive for long periods of time. Guards need not do anything; prisoners will control themselves because they fear they *might* be observed by the guards. The panopticon, and variations on it, are the base of what Foucault calls the **disciplinary society**.

His point is that there are many places from which, and many ways in which, we can be observed, with the result that we exert control over ourselves and prevent ourselves from engaging in acts that might cause us trouble if they are seen. Take the case of the computer. There are various ways in which our behavior on the Internet can be monitored, with the result that we monitor ourselves and prevent ourselves from, for example, visiting certain Web sites (e.g., those that allow access to pornography). In the workplace, we might be tempted to log on to an e-tail site and do some shopping, but we do not do so because we think there is a possibility that our boss may be monitoring our use of the computer and the Web sites we visit.

The panopticon is a specific example of hierarchical power, involving those in official, high-ranking positions who are in a position to have constructed the panopticon and to occupy, or to have subordinates occupy, the lookout positions in it. They are also the ones who initiate and control newer technologies, like those associated with the Internet, that monitor what subordinates are doing. Most generally, hierarchical observation involves the ability of superiors to oversee all they control with a single gaze.

A second instrument of disciplinary power is the ability to make **normalizing judgments** and to punish those who violate the norms. Those in power can decide what is normal and what is abnormal on a variety of dimensions. Those who violate the norms, who are judged abnormal, can then be punished by officials or their agents. For example, officials may focus on time and make normalizing judgments about those who are late. Or they may concentrate on

---

disciplinary society   A society in which control over people is pervasive.

normalizing judgments   Those in power can decide what is normal and what is abnormal on a variety of dimensions. Those who violate the norms, who are judged abnormal, can then be punished by officials or their agents.

behavior and penalize those who do not behave as expected. For example, students are supposed to be attentive in class; those who are inattentive may be punished.

Finally, officials can use **examinations** as a way of observing subordinates and judging what they are doing. This involves the other two methods (hierarchical observation and normalizing judgments). An examination is a way of checking up on subordinates and assessing what they have done. It is employed by those in authority in a given setting and involves normalizing judgments about what is and is not an adequate score. We usually associate examinations with schools, but we also find examinations of the kind being discussed by Foucault in psychiatrist's offices and psychiatric hospitals, in physician's offices and in hospitals, and in various work settings.

Increasing Disciplinary Power   Foucault's most general point is that because of the creation of new and better methods of disciplinary power, our ability to punish people has increased, not decreased. Torture may have been cruel, but it was limited to the moment of torture. The disciplinary power previously discussed affects us all the time and in all settings. We are constantly watched and judged. If we misbehave in the eyes of those in power, we will be punished. Thus, there has not been a liberalization and humanization of punishment. Rather, it has become more pervasive and more insidious.

However, in rejecting one grand theory Foucault seems to be replacing it with another. This is true to some degree. Here and elsewhere in his work Foucault does offer grand theories, but he is also wary of them and tempers them in ways that would not be found in the grand theories of modernists. For example, although a modernist would tend to see various changes affecting parts of society in a rather uniform way, Foucault writes about discipline "swarming" through society. This is meant to imply that the process affects some parts of society and not others, or it may affect some parts at one time and other parts at another time. Thus, instead of creating something like Weber's iron cage, it creates more of a patchwork of centers of discipline amidst a world in which other settings are less affected or unaffected by the spread of the disciplinary society. One term that gets at this is the notion of a **carceral archipelago**. Foucault views various islands of discipline amidst a sea in which discipline is more or less absent.

---

examination   A way of observing subordinates and judging what they are doing. It involves checking up on subordinates and assessing what they have done; it is employed in a given setting by those in authority who make normalizing judgments about what is and is not an adequate score.

carceral archipelago   An image of society that results from the idea that discipline is swarming through society. This means that the process affects some parts of society and not others, or it may affect some parts at one time and other parts at another time. Thus, it creates a patchwork of centers of discipline amidst a world in which other settings are less affected or unaffected by the spread of the disciplinary society.

Michel Foucault (1926–1984)
A Biographical Vignette

Among Foucault's last works was a trilogy devoted to sex: *The History of Sexuality (1976)*, *The Care of the Self (1984)*, and *The Use of Pleasure (1984)*. These works reflected Foucault's lifelong obsession with sex. A good deal of Foucault's life seems to have been defined by this obsession, in particular his homosexuality and his sadomasochism. During a trip to San Francisco in 1975, Foucault visited and was deeply attracted to the city's flourishing gay community. Foucault appears to have been drawn to the impersonal sex that flourished in the infamous bathhouses of that time and place. His interest and participation in these settings and activities were part of a lifelong interest in "the overwhelming, the unspeakable, the creepy, the stupefying, the ecstatic." In other words, in his life (and his work) Foucault was deeply interested in "limit experiences" (where people, including himself, purposely push their minds and bodies to the breaking point) like the impersonal sadomasochistic activities that took place in and around those bathhouses. It was Foucault's belief that it was during such limit experiences that great personal and intellectual breakthroughs and revelations became possible.

Sex was related to limit experiences, and both, in turn, were related in his view of death: "I think the kind of pleasure I would consider as *the* real pleasure would be so deep, so intense, so overwhelming that I couldn't survive it . . . Complete total pleasure . . ., for me, it's related to death." Even in the fall of 1983, when he was well aware of AIDS and the fact that homosexuals were disproportionately likely to contract the disease, he plunged back into the impersonal sex of the bathhouses of San Francisco: "He took AIDS very seriously . . . When he went to San Francisco for the last time, he took it as a 'limit-experience.'"

Foucault also had a limit experience at Zabriskie Point in Death Valley in the spring of 1975. There Foucault tried LSD for the first time, and the drug pushed his mind to the limit: "The sky has exploded . . . and the stars are raining down upon me. I know this is not true, but it is the Truth." With tears streaming down his face, Foucault said, "I am very happy . . . Tonight I have achieved a fresh perspective on myself . . . I now understand my sexuality . . . We must go home again."

The roots of the disciplinary society lie in the prison, but the theories, practices, and technologies developed there are seen by Foucault as swarming into many other sectors of society—schools, hospitals, and military barracks, for example. The result is that he sees more and more settings coming to resemble prisons. This is the creation of the carceral archipelago and carceral society that are central to Foucault's grand theory of the changing nature of, and increase in, governmentality.

Microphysics of Power Another aspect of Foucault's grand theory differentiates it from that of the modernists: Foucault is ever attuned to oppositional forces within each of these settings as well as those that operate against the process in general. There are innumerable points of opposition, confrontation, and resistance. These settings and the overall process are always being contested and being reshaped by that constant testing. This is another reason why we cannot view these settings as iron cages. Constant contestation is altering these structures on a continuing basis. His interest in these processes is part of his interest in what he calls the **microphysics of power**.

Other Grand Theories

Madness and Civilization   In spite of these and other refinements, one senses a grand theory not only in *Discipline and Punish* but in other works of Foucault. For example, in *Madness and Civilization*, Foucault studies the history of the relationship between madness and the psychiatry. Similar to his critique of the increasingly humane treatment of criminals, Foucault takes on the modern grand theory that because of the rise of psychiatry and psychiatric facilities, we have witnessed, over the last several centuries, the growth of scientific, medical, and humanitarian treatment of those who are mad. Instead, he sees an increase in the ability of the sane and their agents to separate out the insane from the rest of the population and to oppress and repress them (and this implies a serious questioning of the whole idea of mental illness). Writing in the 1960s, Foucault was certainly thinking of the then widespread mental hospitals and institutions to which the mentally ill were sent and in which they were often treated abysmally. He was also thinking of the control psychiatrists, psychologists, and other mental health workers exercised over those with psychological problems.

Since the 1960s we have witnessed a **deinstitutionalization** of the mentally ill. Many psychiatric institutions have closed and much of the type of oppression that existed in the 1960s has disappeared. However, it has been replaced by other forms. For example, many mentally ill people have been left free to roam the streets, becoming what we think of today as homeless or streetpeople. Second, many of those freed from mental hospitals, or who were never sent to such hospitals in recent years as a result of deinstitutionalization, have been put on heavy-duty psychotropic drugs that exert great control over their mental and, often, physical functioning. Finally, as Foucault anticipated, many of the mentally ill (and many others) have been forced to judge themselves and their own mental condition. In many senses, such internalized control is the most repressive form of control. For example, people have far more access to their innermost thoughts than do outside agents like psychiatrists. And, while

---

microphysics of power   The idea that power exists at the micro-level and involves efforts to exercise it as well as efforts to contest its exercise.

deinstitutionalization   The process, begun in the 1960s and made possible by new drug treatments, involving the closing of many psychiatric institutions and the release of the vast majority of patients who were left to their own devices to survive in the larger society.

psychiatrists may make occasional negative judgments, individuals are able to judge themselves ceaselessly. Overall, we find in *Madness and Civilization* the same pattern as in *Discipline and Punish*—a critique of a modern grand theory and its replacement, perhaps unintentionally, by another more critical and postmodern form of that type of theory.

A Grand Theory of Sexuality A somewhat different pattern appeared in Foucault's later work on sexuality. *The History of Sexuality* critiques the modern grand theory that Victorianism had led to the repression of sexuality, especially discourse about sexuality. Although he continued to view sex as repressed, he took the opposite position on discourse, arguing that Victorianism had led to an explosion of discourse on sexuality. As a result of Victorianism, there was more analysis, stocktaking, classification, specification, and causal and quantitative study of sexuality. Once again, Foucault was criticizing one grand narrative and seemingly putting another in its place. However, although in previous cases the modern position emphasized greater freedom, and Foucault's position greater constraint, in this case the modern position focuses on increased repression and Foucault sees greater freedom (of discourse on sexuality).

In addition to arguing that we are experiencing more discourses on sexuality we are also witnessing increased efforts to exercise power over sexuality, as well as resistance to that power in a number of specific settings. Beginning in the 18th century an effort was made by society to shift from control over death to control over life, especially sex. This took two forms. The first, focusing on the individual, involved an effort to exert great discipline over the human body, especially the sexual practices associated with it. The second, focusing on the population as a whole, involved efforts to control and regulate population growth, health, life expectancy, and so forth. By controlling sex society was able to control both the individual and the species. Although Foucault was concerned about this oppression, he also saw hope in bodies, sexuality, and pleasure. He believed that through them people can overcome efforts to control not only their sexuality, but their lives.

Thus, in spite of his rejection of the modern grand theory about the increasing repression of sexuality, the outlines of several grand theories appear in Foucault's work.

POSTMODERNITY AS MODERNITY'S COMING OF AGE

Zygmunt Bauman has been a perceptive analyst of the modern world, *and* he has offered many insights into the advent of the postmodern world. Relatedly, he has dealt with the issue of modern sociology as well as what a postmodern sociology and a sociology of postmodernity might look like (see the Key Concepts box: Postmodern Sociology; Sociology of Postmodernity). Depending on

Key Concepts
Postmodern Sociology; Sociology of Postmodernity

Despite some sympathy for it, Bauman is generally opposed to the development of what he calls **postmodern sociology**. One reason for his opposition is the fear that a radically different postmodern sociology would give up on the formative questions that lay at the foundation of the discipline. Bauman also opposes a postmodern sociology because it would, by its very nature, be in tune with the culture of postmodernity. Since postmodern culture is very different from modern culture, postmodern sociology would have to be very different from modern sociology. For example, the difference between rational modern culture and nonrational postmodern culture would be reflected in the respective sociologies. Bauman is not ready for a nonrational sociology; he wants a sociology that is, to a large extent, continuous with its origins.

Bauman feels that what we really need to develop is a **sociology of postmodernity**. Although postmodern sociology breaks sharply with modern sociology, a sociology of postmodernity is continuous with modern sociology by, for example, being characterized by rational and systematic discourse and by an effort to develop a model of postmodern society. Even though it is continuous with modern sociology, the sociology of postmodernity accepts postmodern society as a distinctive and unique type and not as an aberrant form of modern society.

Bauman offers a number of major tenets of a sociological theory of postmodernity including:

1. The postmodern world is complex and unpredictable.
2. The postmodern world is complex because it lacks a central goal-setting organization and it contains a great many large and small, mainly single-purpose agencies. No one of these agencies is large enough to subsume or control the others, and each is resistant to centralized control. Although the agencies may be partially dependent on one another, the nature of that dependence cannot be fixed, with the result that each of these agencies is largely autonomous. Thus, agencies are largely free to pursue their own institutionalized purposes.
3. Even though they are likely to be well ordered internally, when they operate in the larger world, agencies face an arena that appears as a space of chaos

which aspects of his work one wishes to emphasize, he can be thought of as *either* a modern or a postmodern social theorist. Bauman's works on postmodernism occupy our attention here.

---

postmodern sociology A type of sociology that is heavily influenced by postmodern ideas and that would adopt a nonrational approach to the study of society.

sociology of postmodernity A type of sociology that is continuous with modern sociology by being characterized by rational and systematic discourse and by an effort to develop a model of postmodern society. However, the sociology of postmodernity accepts postmodern society as a distinctive and unique type and does not see it as an aberrant form of modern society.

Key Concept—Continued

and chronic indeterminacy and ambivalence, a territory subjected to rival and contradictory meanings. The various states of the postmodern world appear equally contingent. That is, any given state has no overwhelming reason to be what it is, and it could be very different if other agencies operated differently. Agencies need to be cognizant of the fact that what they do affects the world in which they are operating.

4. The existential situation of agents is quite fluid. The identity of agents needs to be self-constituted continually, largely on the basis of trial and error. Identity is permanently changing but not developing in any clear direction. At any given time, the constitution of identity involves the disassembly of some existing elements and the assembly of new elements.

5. The only constant in all of this is the body, but even here agents devote continual attention to the cultivation of the body. People engage in a series of self-controlling and self-enhancing activities (jogging, dieting) that they would have resented were they imposed on them by some external organization. Thus, these activities are seen as the product of free human agents and not resented as externally imposed regimens. More generally, we can say that agents are no longer coerced; rather, they are seduced.

6. Lacking a predesigned life-project, agents need a series of orientation points to guide their moves throughout their lifespans. These are provided by other agencies (real or imagined). Agents are free to approach or abandon these other agencies.

7. Accessibility to resources varies among agents depending on their personal assets, especially knowledge. Those with more knowledge can choose among a wider range of assembly patterns. Variations in freedom to choose among resources is the main basis of social standing and social inequality in postmodern society. Knowledge is also the main stake in any kind of conflict aimed at the redistribution of resources. This emphasis on knowledge and the fact that information is a key resource tends to further enhance the status of experts.

Learning to Live with Ambivalence?

Ambivalence is a distinctive product of modernity, but postmodernism offers at least the possibility of overcoming that problem by simply accepting and learning to live with ambivalence. In fact, Bauman defines postmodernity in opposition to modernity and its need to eliminate ambivalence. However, even if it is successful in learning to live with ambivalence, and thereby eliminating it as a source of problems (and that is by no means assured), postmodernism is fully capable of producing a range of other problems. Thus, Bauman concludes that postmodernity is both worrying and exhilarating; it opens both new possibilities and new dangers. It should be noted that most postmodernists have a far more pessimistic view of postmodern society. For example, barbarism (e.g., ethnic cleansing in the former Yugoslavia) is associated with postmodernism.

Rather than seeking to eliminate ambivalence, postmodernity accepts the messiness of the world; it is *not* determined to impose order on it. For example, the postmodern world is more accepting of the stranger. Generally, it is a more tolerant world, one that tolerates differences. However, tolerance brings with it even more ambiguity. Thus, the postmodern world is destined to be a far more uncertain world than modernity, and those who live in it need to have strong nerves.

Ambivalence about Postmodernity   Although Bauman generally sees postmodernity as preferable to modernity, he is, quite characteristically, ambivalent about it. He argues that postmodernity shares with modernity a fear of the void. Postmodernity has not succeeded in eliminating those fears, but it did serve to privatize them. Faced with private fears, postmodern individuals are also doomed to try to escape those fears on their own. Not surprisingly, they have been drawn to communities as shelters from these fears. However, this raises the possibility of conflict between communities. Bauman worries about these hostilities and argues that we need to put a brake on them through the development of solidarity.

Although the modern world sought to eliminate distinct communities and assimilate them into the whole, postmodernity can be seen as the coming of age of community. In fact, Michel Maffesoli has dubbed this the age of **neotribalism**. These new tribes, or communities, are the refuge for strangers and more specifically for a wide range of ethnic, religious, and political groups. These communities, and their groups, are tolerated by the larger society. Those living in the postmodern world have overcome the hubris of modernity and are therefore less likely to be cruel to others and to have the need to humiliate them. However, this is not enough as far as Bauman is concerned. Each of these communities needs to be respected by all other communities as well as by the society as a whole.

Although it offers hope against ambivalence, the latter does not totally disappear in postmodernity. There is still popular disaffection and discontent, but the postmodern state no longer feels the need to control it. Rather, it may be that scattered ambivalence can be used to help society reproduce itself.

However, the tolerance of postmodernity does not necessarily lead to solidarity. Because it is characterized by a lack of concern, playfulness, and self-centeredness, postmodernity could make it easier to engage in massive acts of cruelty.

Life in postmodern society is not easy. It is a life without clear options and with strategies that are always open to question. However, one thing that is clear in the postmodern world is that consumerism and the freedom associated with it are not enough to satisfy people in that society. The paradox here is that postmodern society is, above else, a consumer society. Therefore, we seem to be doomed to the knowledge that the world we live in is inadequate to our needs.

---

neotribalism   A postmodern development characterized by the coming of age of a wide array of communities that are refuges for strangers and more specifically for ethnic, religious, and political groups.

Postmodern Ethics

Bauman is interested in the status of an ethical code in a postmodern era that is inherently antagonistic to the idea of a coherent set of rules that any moral person ought to obey. In postmodernity the old ethical systems are no longer seen as adequate. This has opened up the possibility of a radical new understanding of moral behavior. Thus, as usual, Bauman sees postmodernity as offering an opportunity, in this case, in the realm of ethics. It may be a time of the renaissance of morality, or, on the other hand, of the twilight of morality.

It is clear that postmodern ethics must reject much of what passed for modern ethics. Postmodern ethics must reject things like coercive normative regulation and the search for things like foundations, universals, and absolutes. Also to be rejected is modernity's search for an ethical code that is nonambivalent and lacking in contradictions. Despite such rejections, clearly, the great issues in ethics have not lost their importance. Even in a postmodern world we are confronted with such issues as human rights, social justice, the conflict between peaceful cooperation and individual self-assertion, and the confrontation between individual conduct and the collective welfare. These issues persist, but they must be dealt with in a novel manner.

The moral code, looked at from a postmodern perspective, is rife with ambivalence and contradictions. Among the aspects of the moral condition viewed from a postmodern perspective are the following:

1. People are neither good nor bad but morally ambivalent, and it is impossible to find a logically coherent ethical code that could accommodate such moral ambivalence.
2. Moral phenomena are not regular and repetitive. Therefore, no ethical code can possibly deal with moral phenomena in an exhaustive fashion.
3. Morality is inherently laden with contradictions that cannot be overcome, with conflicts that cannot be resolved.
4. There is no such thing as a universal morality.
5. From a rational point of view, morality is, and will remain, irrational.
6. Since Bauman rejects coercive ethical systems emanating from society as a whole, he argues for an ethical system that emanates from the self. It is based on the idea that one has to be *for* the Other before it is possible to be *with* the Other.
7. Although the postmodern perspective on morality rejects the modern coercive form of morality, it does *not* accept the idea that anything goes—the idea of complete relativism. Among the ideas central to a postmodern orientation to ethics is the view that the world would fall apart without the nation-state (and the tribe), that the autonomous self will ultimately be emancipated, and that the moral self will ultimately stand up to the inherent and inevitable ambivalence.

Irresolvable Moral Dilemmas Despite the ideas just discussed, neither Bauman nor postmodernism can offer an ethical code to replace the modern ethical code that is being dismantled. As a result, we are destined to a life of irresolvable moral dilemmas. Without an overarching ethical code, people are left with their own individual moralities. Given the innumerable moral voices in today's world, the only ultimate ethical authority lies in the subjectivities of individuals. The challenge of the postmodern world is how to live morally in the absence of an ethical code and in the presence of a bewildering array of seemingly equal moralities. Without such an overarching code, life in the postmodern world is not likely to grow any easier, although it is at least possible that life will become more moral with the dismantling of the oppressive and coercive ethical code associated with modernity. After all, Bauman associates the most heinous of crimes (e.g., the Holocaust) with the modern ethical code. At the minimum, we will be able to face moral issues directly without the disguises and deformities that came with the modern ethical code.

Instead of the coercive and deforming ethical codes of modernity, there is hope in the conscience of the moral self, especially its need to be *for* the Other. The Other is the responsibility of the moral self. Being for the Other does not determine goodness and evil. That will be worked out in the course of the relationship. It will be worked out in a world devoid of certainty, where there will never be a clear dividing line between good and evil. Thus, it does matter what we do and do not do, but that must be worked out in individual conscience and not in some collective moral code. In this way, Bauman adopts a postmodern position *without* surrendering to relativism and nihilism. Nonetheless, there is a fundamental tension between the unconditional need to be for the Other and the discontinuity and fragmentariness that Bauman associates with postmodernity.

The postmodern world is simultaneously one of great moral hope and great personal discomfort: People have full moral choice, but they have it without the guidance of an overarching moral code once promised by modernity. To put it another way, morality, like much else in the postmodern world, has been privatized. Without a larger ethical system to guide people, ethics for individuals become matters of individual decision, involve risks, and involve chronic uncertainty. Postmodernity may be either our bane or our chance. Which it will be is far from determined at this juncture in history.

THE RISE OF CONSUMER SOCIETY, LOSS OF SYMBOLIC EXCHANGE, AND INCREASE IN SIMULATIONS

The social thinker Jean Baudrillard is most associated with postmodern social theory even though he disliked being labeled in such a way. Baudrillard was radical not only in his ideas, but in his style of writing, especially in his later work. Like other postmodernists, he rejected the idea of a grand theory and the style of his later work—books that include a series of seemingly unrelated aphorisms—seem to militate against the creation of grand theory. Yet it is possible to identify several such theories in the body of his work.

From Producer to Consumer Society

In his early work, Baudrillard was heavily influenced by the thinking of Karl Marx and various branches of neo-Marxian theory. However, although Marx and most neo-Marxists focused on issues relating to production, Baudrillard concerned himself with the emergence of consumer society. In doing so, Baudrillard was ahead of his time, since the consumer society with which we have now grown so accustomed was, at the time Baudrillard wrote his book on that society (the late 1960s), still in its infancy.

Although Baudrillard was later to break with Marxian theory, he was still heavily influenced by that theory when he analyzed the consumer society. For example, despite his focus on consumption, he took the traditional Marxian position of according ultimate importance to production; that is, the forces of production control and orchestrate the world of consumption. Thus, Toyota can be seen as controlling the consumption of automobiles, just as Microsoft can be viewed as orchestrating the purchase of computer software. Baudrillard does not go far enough here in terms of his emphasis on consumption. The forces of consumption (e.g., advertisers, shopping malls, McDonald's, Disney World) play their own important role in consumption. Although they are not totally separable from the forces of production, these entities are crucial in their own right in the realm of consumption. Baudrillard is unable to see this at this point in his career because he has not yet made his break with a Marxian view of the world.

Consumption as Language   Baudrillard was also influenced by linguistics, which led him (and others) to think of the consumption of objects as a kind of language. Within that language, each consumer object has a sign associated with it. For example, in today's automobile market the purchase of a Lexus is a sign of wealth, while buying a Kia indicates humble economic circumstances. Similarly, going to an Ashlee Simpson concert is a sign of youth, while attending a performance of *Madame Butterfly* is a sign of being middle-aged, if not elderly. In a real sense, when we purchase cars or tickets, we are purchasing signs as much or more than we are the ability to drive a car or attend a performance. To Baudrillard, consumption is most importantly about signs, not goods.

But how do we know what all these signs mean? Baudrillard argues that we are able to interpret these signs because we all understand the code and are controlled by it. The **code** is basically a system of rules that allows us to understand signs and, more importantly, how they relate to one another. Thus, the code allows us to understand the meaning of Lexus and Kia and, most importantly, the fact that the Lexus yields far higher status than the Kia. Because we all understand and are controlled by the code, we all are able to have similar understandings of the meaning of signs and how those meanings relate to one

---

code   A system of rules that allows us to understand signs and, more importantly, how they relate to one another.

another. In fact, consumption is based on the fact that others will understand the meaning of what we consume in the same way that we do. Thus, the main reason for buying a Lexus is the assumption that others will understand the meaning of that sign and will approve of it, as well of us, for buying a Lexus.

This leads to the point that in consuming objects we are, in the process, serving to define ourselves. Categories of objects define categories of people. One of the ways in which we find our place in the social order is in terms of what we consume. Thus, a Lexus helps give us a higher position in the social order than a Kia. Furthermore, we can alter our position in that order by consuming differently. For example, if we want to move up the stratification ladder, we can go into debt and buy a Honda rather than a Kia. Such purchases allow us, at least to some extent, to manipulate the trajectory of our movement through the stratification system. Of course there are limits on this. We may know that if we really wanted to alter our position, we would need to buy a Lexus, but no matter how far we stretch, many of us may never be able to afford such a car. In this way, the stratification system often acts to keep people in their place within the system. Overall, in a very real sense, people are what they consume; they define themselves, and are defined by others, on that basis.

Consequently, the motivation for consumption is not what we often assume it to be. We generally believe that the cause of consumption is human **needs**. We buy various things because we need them: food to survive, clothes to keep us warm, cars to transport us. However, Baudrillard sees grave problems with such an explanation. How can needs explain why some of us buy the much more expensive Lexus rather than the modestly priced Kia? Both vehicles get us from one point to another quite nicely. How can needs explain the extraordinarily high level of consumption—the **hyperconsumption**—that characterizes the developed world today? Many of us are clearly consuming far more than we need and in many cases far more than we could ever use (or at least we did until the beginning of the 2007 recession; see the Contemporary Applications box "The Death of Consumer Culture? If so, What Next?).

Thus, Baudrillard rejects the theory of needs, at least in our affluent society, and argues that such a consumption pattern is better explained by **difference** than by needs. We consume in order to be different from other people, and such differences are defined by what and how we consume. Buying CDs of operas like *Madame Butterfly* differentiates us from those who buy Ashlee Simpson CDs. Since differences are infinite in number, there is no end to consumption; there are an endless number of things (in addition to those mentioned before, CDs by

---

needs   Those things that people require in order to survive and to function at a minimal level in the contemporary world. Often used to explain why we consume what we do.

hyperconsumption   An extraordinary level of consumption associated with the contemporary world.

difference   An alternate explanation of consumption favored by postmodernists. We consume, not because of needs, but in order to be different from other people; such differences are defined by what and how we consume.

Frank Sinatra, The Grateful Dead, Pete Seeger, and so on, speak to additional differences) that we can buy to differentiate ourselves from others. Thus, the need for difference can never be satisfied; we end up with a continuous, lifelong need to differentiate ourselves from those who occupy other positions in society. This means that consumption is a form of communication. When we consume things, we are communicating a number of things to others, including what groups we do or do not belong to. They understand what we are "saying" because they, too, know the code and therefore understand the meaning of signs.

But that brings us back to the question: How do we know what to buy in order to signify difference? The answer is that such guidelines are inscribed in the code, and because we know the code, we know what to consume. However, this means that the code does more than simply inform our choices; it controls our selections. Thus, what we think of as needs on a day-to-day basis are determined by the code. We end up needing what the code tells us we need. Individual needs exist because the code needs them to exist.

Another key point made by Baudrillard is that consumption has little or nothing to do with what we conventionally think of as reality. When we buy a Big Mac at McDonald's, we are not just, or mainly, buying something to eat, but rather we are obtaining what dining at McDonald's and eating a Big Mac say about us. We are more consuming signs—Big Mac, McDonald's—than we are consuming food to keep us alive. In consuming a Big Mac we are differentiating ourselves from those who eat not only Whoppers at Burger King, but also filet mignon at Morton's. Thus, we are not consuming the reality of the food, but the unreality of the signs associated with them and the code that defines and controls them.

Another key point is that in a society controlled by signs and the code, we are coming to relate far more to consumer objects and the settings in which they are sold, especially the consumption of those objects and settings, than we are to other human beings. Relationships with objects and settings have tended to replace human relationships. We are increasingly oriented to spending more time consuming things in these settings than we are in relationships with other people. Ironically, we do so for what it says about us and our relationship to such people, but we spend less and less time actually relating to them. This is clearest in the settings in which we consume. In those settings, we increasingly are asked to do things ourselves (pump our own gasoline, obtain money on our own from ATMs) rather than to obtain those things from other human beings. Even when we do relate to other human beings in those settings, the relationship is very likely to be an inhuman one in which employees act like automatons and interact with us on the basis of scripts ("Would you like apple pie with your Big Mac?" "Have a nice day.") taught to them by the employing organization. In a McDonald's restaurant, for example, we relate far more to the restaurant and the objects (including the toys that are forever being promoted in such settings) than we do to the people who work there or to the others dining there.

From Production to Consumption   Embedded in all of this is a grand theory. Most generally it involves the argument that we are moving from a society dominated by production to one that focuses on consumption. More specifically,

Contemporary Applications:
The Death of Consumer Culture? If So, What Next?

The focus in the current economic downturn is, as it should be, on closed businesses, shuttered factories, and disappearing jobs. There is also considerable attention to the decline in shopping and, as a result, of retail businesses and even chains. Lost in all of this is the demise of a consumer culture that had become central to many Americans and to many others in the developed and developing world.

Consumer culture emerged and exploded in the second half of the 20th, and early 21st, centuries. In that culture, consumption was no longer something people had to do, but had become something many enjoyed doing. For those who could afford it, consumption of more than the basics needed for survival came to be valued in its own right. More than that, many came to feel compelled to consume and to feel guilty if they did not, or did not consume "enough." Something of a peak in this epoch was reached when after 9/11 both the Mayor of New York and the President of the United States urged Americans to go out and shop. Some wondered when it had become the "duty" of Americans to shop, but in fact consumption for many had come to feel like something they not only liked to do, but felt they had to do. Culture in general, and consumer culture in particular, not only expresses that which we value, but it also constrains our actions.

For about a half century, the growth of consumer culture and the expansion of consumption came to seem inexorable. However, all of that came to an abrupt halt in the severe economic downturn that began in late 2007. Driven by a decline in their economic resources, many individuals are finding, perhaps regretfully, that they cannot consume as much as they once did and they feel less pressure to do so. The culture of consumption is changing; consumer culture is in retreat.

What is not clear is whether this is a temporary development or whether it represents a cultural and economic sea change. The disappearance of some of the titans of the consumer society and the decline of others points to at least a longer-term change. Also pointing in that direction is the decline in the availability of credit and the willingness, let alone eagerness, of consumers to obtain and use it. Amazingly, there appears to be the beginning of a reversal of the long-running decline in the savings rate.

Baudrillard outlines a change from a society in which capitalists focused on controlling their workers to one in which the focus shifts to control over consumers. In the early days of capitalism consumers could be left largely on their own. However, more recently capitalists came to the realization that consumers could no longer be allowed to decide for themselves whether or not to consume or how much or what to consume. Capitalism has increasingly come to need to be sure that people participate, and participate actively, in the consumer society. Specific capitalistic organizations (McDonald's, Lexus) must try to convince people to be active and regular consumers of their products.

In a way, from the perspective of capitalists, consumers, like workers, perform a kind of labor that must be controlled. Going to the mall and buying a

---

Contemporary Applications—Continued

In many ways, this seems to be a welcome, even healthy, development. Less deficit spending, less debt, less of an obsession with the consumption of unneeded goods and services, all seem to be good things. However, if we are witnessing the early stages of a decline in consumer culture and the many businesses and jobs that depend on it, the issue is: What is going to take its place at the center of the U.S. economy?

It seems unlikely that early centers of the economy can fill the void. While the United States is a global agricultural powerhouse, technological and organizational advances mean that it requires ever fewer workers. The "heavy" industry that the United States relied on for so long has long been in decline, and the current catastrophe in the auto industry augurs further declines in those industries and the jobs available in them. Other countries have taken the technological lead in many industries and it seems unlikely that the United States will invest in a whole new generation of smokestack industries. Further, workers remain unlikely to accept wages and working conditions that would make their industries competitive globally, although this should not be ruled out entirely if the economy deteriorates over a long period of time.

With this off the table, what choice is there but a resuscitation of consumer culture in the United States and redoubled efforts, once the current downturn abates, to export it and its components to the rest of the world? While this offers some hope of economic recovery, it also promises in the longer term a recurrence of our current economic difficulties. What would seem to be needed is thinking about the "next new thing" in the economy. Several possibilities exist—new developments on the Internet, alternative forms of energy (solar, wind, biomass), rebuilding the infrastructure of the United States. While all may be desirable in themselves, they do not seem to offer the possibility of economic success, within the United States and globally, that was the case in earlier economic epochs. The implication may well be that the United States experienced unprecedented economic success for more than a century and a half, but it is going to need to adjust to less comparatively at home and to a smaller role in the global economy. Adjusting to less in the current economic downturn may be just the beginning of a long-term trend and may actually help Americans adjust to coming global economic realities.

---

range of goods and services is as much a form of labor as putting hubcaps on cars on an automobile assembly line. When we look at consumers in this way, it is not a stretch for capitalists to think of them as a group that must be exploited in order to enhance the capitalist's profits. This was (and is) the way capitalists think about workers; such thinking has now been extended to consumers. Consumers need to be lured into such things as buying what they do not need, what they cannot afford, and what they may well need to go into debt for in order to acquire. In addition, capitalists are interested in preventing a social revolution and, just as the proletariat were kept from revolting by being kept hard at work, consumers are less likely to become rebellious if they are busy not only consuming but also working in order to afford all those consumables.

The Loss of Symbolic Exchange and the Increase in Simulations

A more general and historically far-reaching grand theory in Baudrillard's work involves his views on the differences between primitive and contemporary society. Basically, he argues that primitive societies characterized by symbolic exchange have tended to be superseded by contemporary societies defined by their simulations.

Symbolic Exchange   By **symbolic exchange** Baudrillard means a reversible process of giving and receiving—a cyclical exchange of gifts and counter-gifts. He praises this type of exchange and the primitive societies in which it occurs. Take, for example, the case of death. In primitive societies, exchanges with people do not end with their death. People continue to engage in exchanges with the dead by bringing offerings to the grave site, integrating cemeteries into the life of the community, and engaging in periodic rituals involving the dead, often at their grave sites. In other words, the dead are integrated into the life of a primitive community. Baudrillard contrasts this to the contemporary situation in which the dead, their grave sites, and cemeteries are segregated from the rest of society. Although there might be a few perfunctory offerings here or there (e.g., bringing flowers to the grave site), in the main, the living have little to do with the dead. Overall, Baudrillard argues that primitive societies are characterized by symbolic exchanges with the dead, but such exchanges have all but disappeared in the contemporary world.

This, for Baudrillard, is emblematic of what has happened throughout society. Thus, in the economic realm symbolic exchange has tended to be replaced by economic exchange. In primitive society the exchange of goods tended to be strictly limited. Gifts and counter-gifts were given, but eventually the parties were satisfied and the cycle associated with that particular exchange ended. However, in the contemporary world of economic exchange, there is no end to the exchange of goods: There is no end to purchasing goods for one's self and others. The idea is to keep the process of economic exchange through consumption going on continually and forever. This, of course, serves to increase production and, ultimately, the wealth of those who control production (today, the capitalists).

Work can also be examined from this perspective. In primitive societies work involved a symbolic exchange between workers and other workers, raw materials, tools, and so forth. For example, workers took from nature (e.g., raw materials), but they also returned to nature (e.g., by replanting that which they had taken). In contemporary societies, work is dominated by economic exchange. Raw materials derived from nature may be purchased, but there is little sense (unless it is coerced by outside forces) that the buyer needs to renew

---

symbolic exchange   A reversible process of giving and receiving; a cyclical exchange of gifts and counter-gifts, associated with primitive society.

what has been taken from nature. In addition, in contemporary society a worker gives the owner labor time and in exchange the worker is paid. There is *no* symbolic exchange between worker and owner. Moreover, in primitive society there were no owners in the contemporary sense of the term; there was simply continual symbolic exchange between people involved in the work process.

Simulations Relatedly, Baudrillard views a transformation from primitive societies characterized by genuine cultural worlds, such as symbolic exchange, to contemporary worlds characterized by their lack of genuineness—by simulations. **Simulations** are fakes and Baudrillard envisions a world increasingly dominated by them. He also views genuine cultural worlds such as those characterized by symbolic exchange as being enchanted, magical. However, over time the social world has lost its enchantment (its magic). The simulations that characterize the contemporary world do not have the capacity for magic and enchantment, at least in the sense that Baudrillard uses the term. Thus, this simulated world is totally disenchanted and is almost shameful in comparison to the primitive, genuine world.

Baudrillard offers several examples of what he means. The Indian tribe, the Tasaday, was real, or genuine, during its existence in primitive times. The tribe that continues to exist today is nothing more than a simulation of its primitive form. It is protected by authorities, frozen artificially in time, and sterilized to eliminate some of its most distinctive characteristics. It exists for anthropologists to study and tourists to ogle, but it is no longer really the Tasaday.

One of Baudrillard's favorite examples of a simulation is Disney World. This contemporary theme park encompasses many simulations of what were at one time genuine social realities. For example, one enters and leaves Disney World through Main Street, a thinly disguised shopping mall that is a simulation of the kinds of main streets that characterized many American towns at the turn of the century. But it is not just the past that is simulated at Disney World; there is also a simulated submarine ride to which people flock in order to view simulated undersea life. Strikingly, many tourists prefer to go there rather than to the more genuine aquarium (itself, however, a simulation of the sea) down the road, to say nothing of actual ocean and its sealife not much further away from the doors of Disney World.

The widespread existence of simulations is a major reason for the erosion of the distinction between the real and the imaginary, the true and the false. Virtually every aspect of the contemporary world is a mixture of the real and the imaginary. Thus, real tribespeople exist among the Tasaday, but their behavior has been altered, made into an imaginary image of how such tribespeople should behave, by government officials, tourists, and so on. Nothing is real at Disney World except for the people who work there, and even they behave in unreal ways by donning costumes (Mickey Mouse, Donald Duck, Snow White,

---

simulations Fakes; to Baudrillard the contemporary world is coming to be increasingly dominated by the inauthentic.

Key Concepts
The Prosumer and Prosumption

The Industrial Revolution marked the beginning of an era in which the focus in the economy was on production (e.g., in the factory) and producers (e.g., workers and owners). In the decades after World War II, especially in the United States, production at first rose and then began to decline (in steel, tires, and more recently automobiles). In its place arose a society increasingly dominated by consumption (e.g., shopping) and consumers. However, in the late 20th and early 21st centuries we have entered an era in which "prosumption" rather than either production or consumption has become pre-eminent. The term prosumption is a fusion of production ("pro") and consumption ("sumption"). That is, we increasingly produce and consume more or less simultaneously. Furthermore, there is a growing realization that we are not only increasingly likely to be prosumers, but that people have *always* been prosumers.

In fact, the clear distinction between production and consumption is relatively recent. On the farm, for example, those who were (and still are) the producers of food (the farmers) were also the consumers of much of what they produced. In the Industrial Revolution and with the emergence of the factory, *all* industrial production simultaneously involved consumption. For example, an enormous range of things are consumed in the production of automobiles, including raw materials, the workers' labor time, and energy of various types.

Recent trends have tended to reduce further whatever separation between the two continues to exist, at least in the developed West. For example, the rise of the modern fast food restaurant was instrumental in the trend toward putting the consumer to work (creating a prosumer). The "diner" at a fast food restaurant, the consumer of fast food, is also, at least to some degree, a producer of that meal. Diners are, for example, expected to serve as their own waiters carrying their meals to their tables and as bus persons (by disposing of their own debris after the meal is finished).

This trend toward putting the consumer to work has accelerated since the birth of the fast food restaurant. Among the examples are: pumping one's own gasoline at filling stations; serving as a bank teller at the ATM machine; working at the checkout counter at the supermarket by scanning one's own food, bagging it, and paying

---

etc.) and speaking and acting in accord with preset scripts. In fact, the real and the true are harder and harder to find and may even be said to have disappeared in an avalanche of simulations. This can make it dangerous to try to get to the bottom of things, to try to probe beneath and behind the simulations. It is increasingly likely that we will find that there is nothing beneath the simulations but other simulations. In other words, in the contemporary world, there is *no* truth; there is *no* reality. Without truth and reality it could be argued that we live in one huge simulation.

Baudrillard views the United States as being in the forefront of this development—the most unreal, false, and simulated society on earth. It is setting

---

Key Concept—Continued

for it by credit card; using electronic kiosks to check into a hotel and at the airport, to purchase movie tickets, etc.; co-creating a variety of experiences such as moving oneself through Disney World and its many attractions or serving as an "actor" in the theatre "staged" by Starbucks designed to create the image of an old-fashioned coffee house.

Medicine is increasingly characterized by do-it-yourself (DIY) technologies (e.g., blood pressure monitors, blood glucose monitors, pregnancy tests) that allow patients to perform tasks without recompense formerly performed by paid medical professionals. In the entertainment industry there is the recent proliferation of "reality TV shows," in which members of the audience become performers, perhaps for an entire season. In pornography, the once-booming "professional" porn industry finds itself in difficulty because of competition from amateurs. Cell phones now allow "amateurs" to photograph dramatic events and then send the photos to TV networks and local stations that show them on air almost immediately.

Much of what transpires on the Internet in terms of content generated by the user (the consumer) needs to be seen in this context and as among the latest developments in this long-term trend. For example, it is the users who generate and constantly edit the articles on Wikipedia; create the profiles (composed of videos, photos, text) and the interaction that creates communities on You Tube, MySpace and Facebook; create the characters and virtual environments in the massively popular Second Life game; are the "blogosphere" where weblogs, personal blogs and the comments on them are produced by those who consume them; create the market on eBay, craigslist, etc.; are the mostly "amateur" photographers who upload and download the photographs on Flickr; and not only do all the work involved in ordering products on sites like Amazon.com., but also do things like write the "reviews" that appear there.

It is on the Internet, especially Web 2.0 (all of the examples in the previous paragraph are examples of Web 2.0), that the prosumer has come of age. Web 1.0 (e.g., the websites for the *New York Times* and the New York Yankees) was, and still is, dominated by distinct producers and consumers of content. What distinguishes Web 2.0 from 1.0 is user-generation; it is the users (consumers) who also generate (produce) most, if not all, of the content.

---

the standard here, but the rest of the world is sure to follow. Thus, America is the home of some of the world's best-known and most popular simulations. Another major example is Las Vegas, especially its hotels that simulate other worlds: New York, New York; Paris; Venetian; Mandalay Bay; Bellagio; and Luxor, to mention just a few. But Baudrillard goes beyond the obvious examples to discuss whole cities (e.g., Los Angeles) and even the entire nation in terms of simulations. Thus, in New York City today, one can discuss the Disneyization of the Times Square area. Disney's renovation of an old theater led to a dramatic change in the entire area as the old pornographic theaters and cheap shops have been closed and replaced by a number of franchises found throughout the United States. One could say that the real Times Square has

---

Jean Baudrillard (1929–2007)
A Biographical Vignette

Jean Baudrillard was an unusual social theorist, even in France, which specializes in producing unique theorists (e.g., Michel Foucault). He was trained in sociology, but soon moved away from it. He taught at the university level, but gave it up rather quickly. One of his early publications was a critique of Foucault, who was then a leading figure in French scholarly life. Foucault dismissed Baudrillard as easily forgotten and Baudrillard subsequently had a difficult time advancing in French scholarly and academic circles. He was a radical strongly influenced by Marxian ideas. Over the years he grew less politically engaged and, even more quickly, he abandoned Marxian theory. One of the reasons for the latter was the fact that Marx and the Marxists focused on production, while Baudrillard quickly came to recognize the increasing centrality of consumption in the contemporary world. In the late 1960s Baudrillard published pioneering work on consumption, work that continues to influence this growing area of sociological interest.

In the 1970s and beyond, Baudrillard published a series of innovative and startling works that led to him being considered the pre-eminent postmodern social theorist. Characteristically, Baudrillard had disdain for the postmodern label and refused to allow himself to be labeled a postmodernist. Yet many students of Baudrillard's work and postmodern theory more generally view him as being at the very heart of that new theoretical orientation. His general perspectives, as well as many of his more specific ideas (e.g., symbolic exchange, simulations, implosion), have powerfully influenced not only postmodern social theory, but more mainstream work in theory.

Baudrillard's influence is not restricted to social theory; many artistic fields have been affected by his ideas. For example, in the movie *The Matrix* there is a closeup of a book entitled *Simulations*. Thus, even pop culture has been influenced by Baudrillard who, himself, has become something of a pop icon. Few thinkers can be considered *both* a pop icon and a serious social theorist.

---

been eliminated and a simulated, sterilized reality, not much different from that found elsewhere, has taken its place. New York is in the process of losing its distinctiveness and coming to look like many other places.

The United States is also the home of other key centers of simulation. The United States dominates the world's movie industry and all of what one sees in the movies is simulation. Similarly, the world's television programming is dominated by the United States and that, too, is entirely within simulation. In addition, the Internet and the various cybersites are all simulations. For example, people increasingly visit cybershops and cybermalls that are simulations of the real things that exist throughout the United States. Of course, they, too, are increasingly simulated so that people find it relatively easy to move smoothly from a cybermall to some real setting like the Park Meadows Retail Resort in suburban Denver, a shopping mall (although it refuses to call itself one) that is a simulation of the rustic Timberline Lodge (itself the model for the simulation of it in the movie, *The Shining*) on Mount Hood in Colorado.

Baudrillard describes such developments as being **hyperreal**, that is, entirely simulated and, as a result, more real than real, more beautiful than beautiful, truer than true. This is certainly true of Disney World, Las Vegas, and even the "new" Times Square in New York. For example, Disney World is cleaner than the world outside its gates and its employees are far friendlier than those we are likely to meet in our daily lives. To take another example, think of the luxury gated communities springing up throughout the United States, especially in states with hospitable climates like Arizona, Florida, and California. In those communities one finds foliage that is not necessarily indigenous to the area. In addition, even that which is indigenous has been nurtured so that it appears far more lush than that which exists in nature. The result is the production of a tropical paradise that is far more real than the surrounding environment, which may well be dry, dusty, and populated by an occasional undernourished palm tree. The tropical paradise of these luxury communities is clearly hyperreal.

Another example, in an entirely different realm, is pornography. The female pornographic film star with her implants, additional cosmetic surgery, tatoos, body makeup, and other alterations can be viewed as a simulated temptress. She is a hyperreal sex object more real than the women most men are ever likely to encounter in real life. The same can be said of the sex acts depicted in these movies; few people attempt, or are even able, to go through the gyrations and manipulations that are seen on the screen. And, if people try, they are turning their own sex lives into simulations. Since the sex acts seen on the screen are hyperreal, people do try to emulate them, with the result that their day-to-day sex lives themselves become simulations. People may also seek to live up to these hyperreal images by transforming themselves so that they look more like porn stars. Thus, women have breast implants and even surgery to beautify their vaginas, while men may undergo surgery to increase the length and breadth of their penises. In this way, they come to be simulated lovers, if not simulated people.

It could be argued that not only are these simulated realities important in themselves, but also because they are serving as the models for transformations beyond their immediate confines. Under the influence of these hyperreal models, the rest of the world is itself becoming increasingly simulated, increasingly hyperreal. Thus, Disney World's influence is not restricted behind its walls or even restricted to Times Square in New York. Many communities are being built on the Disney model in order to simulate America of the turn of the 20th century. In fact, Disney itself has built such a model community, Celebration, on its grounds in Florida. Furthermore, new communities around the country are using it and Disney World as models for their own development. Thus, according to Baudrillard, reality is increasingly contaminated by these simulations.

---

hyperreal   Entirely simulated and, as a result, more real than real, more beautiful than beautiful, truer than true, and so on.

Overall, Baudrillard offers a grand theory of the change from primitive societies characterized by real, human symbolic exchange, through the less real and fully human economic exchange, to the contemporary world increasingly characterized by unreal, inhuman technologies. The sense is that while the United States lies at the heart of all of this, the rest of the world is destined to move in the same simulated direction. Furthermore, even in the United States we are clearly just at the beginning of the process of simulation. The future will bring not only increasingly extraordinary, but increasingly pervasive, simulations.

THE CONSUMER SOCIETY AND THE NEW MEANS OF CONSUMPTION

Strongly influenced by several of Baudrillard's postmodern ideas, as well as other ideas drawn from modernists like Marx and Weber, I have created a grand theory that involves the settings in which we consume. More generally, it depicts a world of increasing consumption leading to contemporary society, which can be seen as being characterized by hyperconsumption.

Means of Consumption: Old and New   Following Marx, I have labeled consumption sites *means of consumption.* Marx uses this term, but he does so in a way that is inconsistent with the way he uses his far better known concept, means of production. To Marx, the **means of production** are those things (tools, machines, raw materials, etc.) that make production possible in a capitalist society. However, as he defines them, the means of consumption are simply consumer goods. To be consistent with the definition of means of production, the **means of consumption** should be defined as those things that make consumption possible. Just as the factory makes production possible, the shopping mall enables the consumer and consumption. Others who have used the concept in this way include Baudrillard, who viewed the Parisian drugstore, among other settings, as a means of consumption.

Part of my grand theory involves movement from what can be termed *old* means of consumption such as taverns, cafes, and diners to the *new* means of consumption to be discussed next. The older, more traditional means of consumption were (and are) all quite material, involving physical structures, face-to-face interaction among customers and employees, consumption of things like food and drink, and payment almost exclusively in cash. Although they were material structures, these sites had, or produced, a number of immaterial

---

means of production   Those things that are needed for production to take place (including tools, machinery, raw materials, and factories).

means of consumption   To Marx, these are simply consumer goods, but to Ritzer, paralleling Marx's sense of the means of production, these are the things that make consumption possible. Just as the factory makes production possible, the shopping mall enables the consumer and consumption.

effects such as feelings of *gemeinschaft,* or community, among those who fre-
quented them. Of course, there are even older means of consumption such as
the bazaar, arcade, department store (see the box, Phantasmagoria and Dream
Worlds), general store, and county fair.

What I am calling the **new means of consumption** are a set of sites that
came into existence largely after 1950 in the United States and have served to
revolutionize consumption. The following are the major new means of consumption with notable examples and the year in which they began operations:

- Franchises (McDonald's, 1955).
- Shopping malls (the first indoor mall, Edina, Minnesota, 1956).
- Megamalls (West Edmonton Mall, 1981; Mall of America, 1992).
- Superstores (Toys 'R' Us, 1957).
- Discounters (Target, 1962).
- Theme parks (Disneyland, 1955).
- Cruise ships (Sunward, 1966).
- Casino-hotels (Flamingo, 1946).
- Eatertainment (Hard Rock Cafe, 1971).

These, too, are material structures, but they also can be seen as phantasmagoria or dream worlds. In fact, over the last half century these have become
increasingly fantastic and spectacular in order to enchant consumers and to
lure them in greater numbers and with increasing frequency into their lairs in
order to heighten progressively the level of consumption—to produce hyperconsumption. They have all been enormously successful in their efforts, and,
through what Joseph Schumpeter called the process of **creative destruction**
(older structures destroyed to make way for newer ones that function more
effectively), have largely replaced the older means of consumption such as diners, arcades, and expositions.

Yet the pace of change is so rapid that many of these new means of consumption are already being threatened by other, even newer, dematerialized
means of consumption such as home shopping television (born in 1985) and
especially cybercommerce of all types (made possible by the coming of the
Internet in 1988). These combine a dematerialized form with the capacity to
produce, and to a far greater extent, phantasmagoria and dream worlds. Their
greater immateriality (both perceptual and real) gives them enormous advantages over the material means of consumption in terms of both what they are
able to do and the effect they are able to create. As a result, they pose a profound threat to several of the more material new means of consumption, especially shopping malls, megamalls, and superstores.

---

new means of consumption   The set of consumption sites that came into existence largely after 1950 in the United States and that served to revolutionize
consumption.

creative destruction   The idea that older structures are destroyed to make way for
newer ones that function more effectively.

Key Concepts
Phantasmagoria and Dream Worlds

An examination of older means of consumption is found in the work of Walter Benjamin, who was concerned with both their physical structure and the immaterial feelings they were designed to evoke. Best known is Benjamin's arcades project (*Passagen-Werk*), a fragmentary, unfinished undertaking focusing on the 19th-century Parisian arcades. The arcades were old means of consumption even when Benjamin wrote about them (roughly 1920–1940) since he used them as a lens to gain greater insight not only into his day but the era in which they flourished. Benjamin saw himself examining the debris or residue of the mass culture of the 1800s. The arcades were essentially privately owned covered city streets lined on both sides with shops of various sorts. The streets were closed to vehicular traffic, allowing consumers to wander from shop to shop in order to buy or merely to window shop.

Benjamin views the arcade as the original temple for the consumption of capitalist commodities. It was the immediate precursor of other temples for the consumption of commodities—expositions and the department stores. (The arcades themselves, of course, had predecessors such as the church [arcades were often shaped like a cross] and Oriental bazaars.)

What were originally confined to the arcades later burst out of those confines and flooded Paris with grander and more pretentious commodity displays. Benjamin accords an important role here to the architect Baron Georges-Eugene Haussmann, who created in Paris a series of physical structures, including railroad stations, museums, wintergardens, sport palaces, department stores, exhibition halls (as well as the boulevards to get to them) that not only dwarfed the original arcades but served to eclipse them. All of these structures related wholly or in part to consumption. However, Benjamin recognized that not only the arcades, but all of

---

Why venture out of the house, into one's car, onto the thruways, into those cavernous parking lots and those enormous and tiring consumption sites when one can obtain as much, and in many cases even more, from the comfort of one's sofa or seat in front of the computer? For example, amazon.com's million-plus list of books is far larger than the stock in the largest of Borders's and Barnes and Noble's book superstores. Instead of all of those physical acts required to get to and from the superstore, consumption can be accomplished with a few keystrokes. Many other new (and old) material means of consumption face a similar struggle in the future in luring customers out of their homes. Why fly to a Las Vegas casino hotel when one can play the slots and other games of chance online? Why go to the racetrack when one can bet on the races over the Internet? Why go to a men's club when one can view a private lap dance on one's own computer screen?

More importantly, these new dematerialized sites of consumption, especially those associated with the Internet, have a far greater potential to produce phantasmagoria or dream worlds than their more material predecessors. I focus on various processes that serve to make the new means of consumption more spectacular, enchanting, dream-like, phantasmagoric. The fact is that, at

---

Key Concept—Continued

these physical structures, were more than material realities; they produced immaterial effects, most notably Benjamin's famous notion of **phantasmagoria**. In fact, his general argument was that the new urban phantasmagoria traced to Haussmann was replacing arcades and that the once magical arcades that had created such phantasmagoria were in decline.

A similar argument is made by Rosalind Williams about other earlier means of consumption: expositions and department stores. Williams argues that the Paris Expositions, especially of 1889 and 1900, were the first systematically planned mass consumption settings and that they were innovative in the way they combined imagination and goods to be sold. Imagination in concert with a planned environment creates a **dream world** for consumers. (Again, we see here the integration of ideal [imagination] and material [planned environmental] factors.) In this context, Williams discusses the founding of the French department store, especially Bon Marché in 1852. She concentrates on such things as the use of décor to lure customers to the stores and to make the store's merchandise seem glamorous, romantic, and, therefore, appealing to consumers. To Williams, the goal of such department stores was to inflame the desires and feelings of consumers for the merchandise in them. The goal was not necessarily to arouse a desire that would be immediately satisfied, but rather a free-floating desire that would sooner rather than later lead to purchases.

The key point is that the older means of consumption were decidedly physical structures, and while analysts such as Benjamin and Williams recognized that fact and acknowledged its importance, they emphasized the way those structures served to arouse various feelings associated with being in a phantasmagoric setting or a dream world.

---

least potentially, the dematerialized means of consumption have a far greater capacity to use these processes to create an alluring fantasy world to consumers. In other words, greater immateriality is not only an advantage in itself, but also one that can be used to create still further advantages for dematerialized means of consumption.

Spectacle and Implosion   One of the ways that the new means of consumption create spectacles is through the **implosion** (this concept, like others, is

---

phantasmagoria   The fantastic immaterial effects produced by physical structures like the arcades as well as the newer means of consumption.

dream world   Similar to the concept of phantasmagoria; more specifically refers to the use of things like décor to lure customers to means of consumption and to make the goods and services being purveyed seem glamorous, romantic, and, therefore, appealing to consumers. The goal is to inflame the desires and feelings of consumers.

implosion   The decline of boundaries and the collapse of various things into each other; dedifferentiation as opposed to differentiation.

borrowed from Baudrillard and involves the decline of boundaries and the collapse of various things into each other) of once separate means of consumption into one setting: the Mall of America, which is both a mall and an amusement park; the cruise ship encompassing a mall, a casino, and so on. Yet because these are material structures, there are limits to what can be imploded into a mall or a cruise ship. People need to be able to physically navigate a mall or the deck of a cruise ship. If, in order to encompass more means of consumption, malls, amusement parks, and so on, grow too big, people will not be able to work their way through them. For example, it was found that if hypermarkets grew too large, customers, especially older ones, would be turned off by the need to walk so far to get a quart of milk.

There are no such limits in cyberspace. Cyberspace can be as big as the imaginations of those who create, and view, its various components. Of course, as cybersites and cyberspace grow larger, it becomes increasingly difficult getting around, but this is where search engines and other technologies come in and do the work for the consumer. A more specific example of such a technology is a shop bot; it roams through various e-tailers looking for a specific item. There is no need for consumers to switch from amazon.com to barnesandnoble.com to varsitybooks.com in search of a specific book; the shop bot will do it for them. Consumers may get irritated by delays and problems finding what they want as the components of the Internet grow more numerous and diverse, but few of them will be winded by the process.

Many of the means of consumption, new and old, are collapsing into the Internet in one way or another. The incredible spectacle is that with a click of a mouse a person can switch from shopping at the cybermall to gambling at the cybercasino to a virtual tour of Disney World.

Spectacles and Simulations   Another way in which the new means of consumption make themselves spectacular is through the creation of simulations more incredible than reality. For example, the Las Vegas Strip encompasses a series of incredible casino-hotel simulations such as New York, New York. As physical structures, casino-hotels must operate with the limitations imposed by their materiality. For example, New York, New York's attractions are not to scale and they are jumbled together indiscriminately. From the outside, the viewer never loses sight of the fact that he or she is looking at a simulation, and inside the viewer never loses the sense of being in a casino-hotel; the viewer never really feels that he or she is in New York.

Cybersites are by definition simulations. Because they do not have the limitations of physical sites, they are freer to create simulations that are more spectacular and even in some senses truer to reality. Thus, a to-scale model of New York could, at least theoretically, be built in cyberspace. Once we have greater bandwidth and the wedding of virtual reality and cyberspace, we will see even greater ability to place people in simulated worlds that closely approximate reality. They may even be more real than real; in other words, hyperreal (e.g., cybersites lack the crowds and the trash one sees in malls). The point is that because they are not restricted physically, cybersites have a much greater potential to use simulations in order to create far more fantastic worlds than are possible in Las Vegas or the Mall of America.

Spectacles, Time, and Space   Time and space are also manipulated in order to create spectacles in the new means of consumption. Las Vegas hotels freely juxtapose time periods. The Luxor of ancient Egypt stands next to Excalibur [the England of King Arthur], which stands adjacent to a mid-20th century New York, New York. Furthermore, the interiors of casino-hotels are designed so that gamblers have no idea what time it is. This is accomplished by allowing no clocks or windows in casinos. Space is manipulated by, for example, creating huge spaces designed to awe consumers. The Mall of America is large enough to encompass both a shopping mall and an amusement park. The Luxor has the world's largest atrium, one that can hold nine Boeing 747 airplanes. As impressive as these are, they pale in comparison to what can potentially be created in cyberspace where literally there are no limits to what can be done with time and space. The entire universe and the entire expanse of time are at the disposal of the means of consumption that exist in cyberspace.

DROMOLOGY

Paul Virilio is less well known than people like Michel Foucault and Jean Baudrillard. Nonetheless, he has created an innovative and intriguing body of work that is worthy of broader recognition. The best term to describe his work is **dromology** (a concept derived from the suffix *drome,* referring to running or a racecourse), or a focal concern with the crucial importance of speed.

At a broad level, Virilio is concerned with the breakdown of boundaries brought about by a series of technological changes over time in modes of transportation, communication, telecommunication, computerization, and so forth. The early forms of these changes led to changes in spatial arrangements, especially the breakdown in physical boundaries. As a result of the breakdown in spatial arrangements, distinctions between here and there are no longer meaningful. In other words, it makes little or no difference today whether one lives in the city, the suburbs, or a rural area. Similarly, it matters little whether one lives in the United States, England, or Japan.

Time and Speed   However, Virilio is more interested in the issue of time than space largely because time is more important than space in a postmodern world. In fact, he argues that increases in speed are serving to erode spatial distinctions and to make it increasingly difficult to distinguish space from time. As a result of advanced technologies; whether they are found in our television sets or attached to our computers, one can no longer separate spatial dimensions from their rate of transmission. Space and time have become progressively indistinguishable

---

dromology   A focal concern with the crucial importance of speed.

from one another. Furthermore, speed has come to overwhelm distance. Virilio creates the notion of speed distance and argues that it serves to annihilate physical and spatial dimensions. Especially important in this process today are advances in the means of communication and telecommunication.

In addition to obliterating space, speed, especially the speed of the communication of knowledge and information, has created a bewildering world of images and appearances. We are increasingly unable to tell where we are, what time it is, or what we are supposed to do. Visible markers, referents, and standards have disintegrated. As a result, we are faced with a crisis of conceptualization and representation. We have gone from a world of stable images to one in which such images are highly unstable.

Our referents are increasingly less likely to take a material form; increasingly they are little more than fleeting images. We are less and less likely to observe things directly. Rather, we sense things indirectly through mediating technologies like the mass media. Although we are able to sense many more things in this way, it is increasingly difficult to make them intelligible because we lack unmediated knowledge of them. As a result, in Virilio's view, we are faced with a crisis of intelligibility.

Advanced technologies of all types play a central role here as they mediate between us and the things we see. The cinema played a major role in this development when the movie camera came between us and the things we see. This problem also exists, and is greatly extended, with the arrival of television. Technologies like these make it far more difficult for us to truly understand what we are seeing, in part because what we are seeing is filtered through the eyes of the camera person and the camera. In addition, we become far less active interpreters of what we see and more passive telespectators. Furthermore, the spatial and temporal lines between us and these media tend to erode; there are no perceptible limits here, no clear line between where the television image ends and we begin. Furthermore, with the coming of the computer, this is increasingly a problem both at home and on the job.

War   One of the recurrent themes in Virilio's work is the relationship between the kinds of changes discussed here and the changing nature of war. To Virilio, when one is concerned with technical issues, war is always the best model. The development of the various technologies of concern to Virilio (e.g., the computer) is closely linked to military research and technological development. The increased speed that results from these technological advances is affecting all sectors of society, including the military. As in the rest of society, speed leads to the destruction of time for reflection. The rapidity with which weapons can be launched makes it impossible for military officers to reflect on their actions. The launching of enemy missiles, for example, leads automatically to the launching of retaliatory weapons. What results is a war that is completely involuntary. Furthermore, instead of direct encounters between armies, we now have instantaneous interface mediated through computers and television screens. These and other things are associated with what Virilio calls pure war.

Endocolonization   Technology clearly plays a central role in his work. As we have seen, the movie camera and its successor, the television camera, play a central role in mediating experiences and disseminating images. In a more recent book, Virilio explores a new role for technology under the heading of **endocolonization**. Instead of a focus on colonizing the world, technology is being used to colonize the human body; the focus has shifted from the territorial body to the animal body. Endocolonization is concerned with the intrusion of technology and micromachines associated with it into the heart of the human body. The focus has shifted from the creating of megamachines to colonize the world to micromachines (e.g., pacemakers) to colonize the body. Thus, he sees a transplant revolution succeeding the communication revolution. Previously, we mentioned the sedentariness that has resulted from the substitution of teleaction for immediate action. This sedentariness is a product of the creators of postmodern technology who have, in turn, come up with a new set of technologies to counter it. Slowed down to a state of near inertia by the media, people can now be simultaneously speeded up through the implantation of various microtechnologies that can help them to think and act more quickly. The focus is shifting to doing to the human body what has been done to everything else in postmodern society. In a sense, the human body has to be brought up to speed; the speed that characterizes the rest of society now must be brought into human beings.

The implantation of various technologies also raises another familiar issue to Virilio, and other postmodernists: the elimination of the distinction between inside and outside. If there are technologies outside of us, and inside of us, and those outside stimulate those inside us, then where do we as humans end and nonhuman technologies begin?

Another of Virilio's consistent concerns is the issue of control. With endocolonization, control over people is being taken to a whole new level. In the past, control has been exercised almost exclusively from the outside. The prison, and especially Foucault's panopticon, are good examples. However, endocolonization opens up the possibility of control from the inside. Clearly, this brings with it new and frightening possibilities.

Virtual Reality   Control is also central to Virilio's analysis of the coming explosion in virtual reality. With global frontiers being eliminated, science has turned to the conquest of internal frontiers like mental images. Virtual technology is an external technology, but its goal is internal control. Virtual reality technology seeks to channel and control mental images and dominate thought cybernetically. The level of control will, in his view, be unimaginable because people will no longer be free to construct their own mental images. Virtual reality will produce other problems, as well, such as increasing our inability to position ourselves in time and space. We will all find ourselves quite lost in a virtual universe.

---

endocolonization   Technology being used to colonize the human body.

Only a few of Virilio's ideas have been presented here, but it is clear that he is in the process of producing a very interesting variant on French postmodern social theory.

In sum, contemporary sociological theory continues to develop and change. The snapshot of that theory at a particular point in time presented in this book will rapidly become a way of remembering what was true in the past. But we cannot understand what comes next in sociological theory unless we comprehend what was has occurred in its recent, and not-too-recent, past.

FEMINISM AND POSTMODERN SOCIAL THEORY
by Patricia Madoo Lengermann and Gillian Niebrugge

Although feminist academic engagement with postmodernist ideas and vocabulary has gained ground in the early 21st century, postmodernism is used less as a theory of society than an epistemological approach by feminists. Postmodernism has been important to feminist theory primarily as an oppositional epistemology, a strategy for questioning its claims to truth or knowledge.

The question Whose knowledge? has proved to be radically transformative, opening debates not only about the relation of power to knowledge but about the basis of human claims to know. Postmodernists reject the basic principle of modernist epistemology, that humans can, by the exercise of pure reason, arrive at a complete and objective knowledge of the world, a knowledge that is a representation of reality, a mirror of nature.

Feminism and postmodernism have much else in common:

1. Both raise the question of *whose* knowledge or definitions are to count.
2. Contemporary feminist theorists find in postmodernism a reinforcement and legitimation for their own insistence on the epistemological and political necessity for moving away from traditional core concerns in the social sciences and for taking apart traditional theories and concepts.
3. Postmodernist epistemology provides some feminist scholars with an expanded possibility for naming their work and has become part of such accepted practices as the liberal feminist project of deconstructing gender. It has not involved an unthinking takeover of postmodern concepts, but a sophisticated incorporation, sometimes keeping, sometimes blending, sometimes changing the original meanings.
4. Above all, the turn pushes feminism to make reflexivity a permanent feature of theory-building, a way of ensuring that it will not become what it has set out to oppose—a hegemonic discourse that oppresses people through essentialist and universalist categories. This directive has been particularly meaningful because it coincides with the questions raised by women of color, women from societies outside the North Atlantic, lesbians, and working class women about second-wave feminism's essentialist claims regarding sisterhood, woman, third-world women, sexuality, family, mothering, and work (see Chapter 8).

But the feminist relation to postmodernism is marked more strikingly by unease than embrace:

1. Many feminists see postmodernism as exclusive in aspiration and therefore antithetical to the feminist project of inclusion. Evidence for this is postmodernism's arcane vocabulary, its location in the academy rather than in political struggle, and its nonreflexive grab for hegemonic status in that academic discourse.
2. Many feminists also question the innocence of the postmodernist challenge, wondering whether it is truly liberationist or part of a politics of knowledge in which a privileged academic class responds to the challenges of marginalized persons with a technically complex argument, to the effect that no location for speech can claim authority. Nancy Hartsock finds it very suspicious that just when women and many other groups have come to redefine themselves, theorize about themselves, and make progress on various grounds, postmodernists have come to question the nature of the subject, the idea of general theory, and the notion of progress.
3. Another source of uneasiness is that the postmodernist emphasis on an infinite regress of deconstruction and difference leads people away from collective, liberationist politics and toward a radical individualism that may conclude that because everyone is unique, everyone's problems are unique; hence, there are no problems that should concern the collectivity as a whole.
4. Above all, the postmodernist turn takes feminist scholars away from the materiality of inequality, injustice, and oppression and toward a neo-idealist posture that sees the world as discourse, representation, and text. In severing the link to material inequality, postmodernism moves feminism away from its commitment to progressive change—the foundational project of any critical social theory.

Summary

1. Daniel Bell's grand theory focused on the emergence of postindustrial society characterized by a transition from goods-production to service-provision, the decline of blue-collar work and the rise of professional and technical work, theoretical knowledge replacing practical know-how, better assessment of and control over technology, and the development of new intellectual technologies.
2. In postindustrial society a conflict occurs between social structure (especially the economy) dominated by rationality and efficiency and culture dominated by irrationality, self-realization, and self-gratification.
3. Michel Foucault's grand theory differed from those of modernists because of his rejection of finding origins and his focus on incoherence and on discontinuity.
4. The substance of Foucault's grand theory deals with the increase in governmentality, the practices and techniques by which control is exercised over people.
5. Instead of seeing progress and increasing humanization in the treatment of prisoners, Foucault saw an increase in the ability to punish people and to punish them more deeply.
6. Three basic instruments are available to those who seek to exercise control over and observe a population. The first is hierarchical observation or the ability of

officials at or near the top of an organization to oversee all that they control with a single gaze.

7. A panopticon is a structure that allows someone in power (e.g., a prison officer) the possibility of complete observation of a group of people (e.g., prisoners).

8. A second instrument of disciplinary power is the ability to make normalizing judgments and to punish those who violate the norms.

9. The third instrument is the use of examinations as a way of observing subordinates and judging what they are doing.

10. Although he focuses on control, Foucault recognizes that control is constantly contested. This is part of his interest in the microphysics of power.

11. In contrast to the accepted grand theory, Foucault sees an increase in the ability of the sane and their agents to separate out the insane from the rest of the population and to oppress and repress them.

12. In contrast to the accepted grand theory on the relationship between Victorianism and sexuality, Foucault sees more analysis, stocktaking, classification, specification, and causal and quantitative study of sexuality.

13. Zygmunt Bauman associates modernity with an inability to accept ambivalence, but postmodernity promises to be more accepting of ambivalence.

14. Bauman also associates neotribalism with postmodernity. These new tribes, or communities, are the refuge for strangers and more specifically for a wide range of ethnic, religious, and political groups. These communities, and their groups, are tolerated by the larger society.

15. The morality of the postmodern world is dominated by the need to be for the Other.

16. Jean Baudrillard sees a transformation from producer to consumer society.

17. Consumption is better explained by the consumer's search for difference than by the needs of consumers.

18. When we consume, we are really consuming signs rather than goods or services.

19. Since the code determines the meanings of signs, it also controls consumption.

20. Capitalism has shifted from a focus on control over workers to control over consumers.

21. Baudrillard also views a transformation from primitive symbolic exchange (a reversible process of giving and receiving) characterized by its genuineness to today's simulations, or fakes, that are characterized by their lack of genuineness.

22. Ritzer sees a world dominated by hyperconsumption, fostered, at least in part, by the new means of consumption.

23. The process of creative destruction continues and even some of the new material means of consumption are threatened by the even newer nonmaterial means of consumption such as cybermalls and home-shopping television.

24. In order to attract consumers, the new means of consumption use a variety of mechanisms such as implosion, simulation, and the manipulation of time and space. Nonmaterial means of consumption are better able to use these mechanisms than the new material means of consumption.

25. One of the most interesting living social theorists is Paul Virilio. Associated with postmodern theory, he has developed his own variant, dromology, as well as a number of new ideas and unique concepts.

26. An uneasy relationship exists between feminism and postmodern social theory.

27. Feminists are very suspicious of the fact that just as women and many other groups have come to redefine themselves, theorize about themselves, and make progress on various grounds, we have witnessed the rise of postmodern suspicions about the nature of the subject, general theory, and the notion of progress.

Suggested Readings

MALCOLM WATERS   "Daniel Bell." In George Ritzer, ed., *The Blackwell Companion to Major Social Theorists*. Malden, MA, and Oxford, England: Blackwell, 2000, pp. 577–600. Brief overview of the contributions of Daniel Bell to social theory.

MALCOLM WATERS   *Daniel Bell*. London: Routledge, 1996. Much fuller, book-length treatment of Bell and his work.

BARRY SMART   "Michel Foucault." In George Ritzer, ed., *The Blackwell Companion to Major Social Theorists*. Malden, MA, and Oxford, England: Blackwell, 2000, pp. 630–650. Brief overview of the contributions of Michel Foucault.

JAMES MILLER   *The Passion of Michel Foucault*. New York: Anchor Books, 1993. Fascinating biography of this most provocative of social theorists.

ZYGMUNT BAUMAN   *Modernity and the Holocaust*. Ithaca, NY: Cornell University Press, 1989. A provocative modernist work by a theorist who has become one of the best-known postmodernists. Demonstrates why, despite his own ambivalence about it, he prefers postmodernity to modernity.

DENNIS SMITH   *Zygmunt Bauman: Prophet of Postmodernity*. Oxford: Blackwell, 2000. A short book-length introduction to the ideas of Zygmunt Bauman.

PETER BEILHARZ   *Zygmunt Bauman: Dialectic of Modernity*. London: Sage, 2000. Study of Bauman's work from a strong theorist and a great admirer of Bauman's work.

KEITH TESTER   *The Social Thought of Zygmunt Bauman*. London: Palgrave, 2004. More recent, but certainly not the last, overview of Bauman's contributions to social theory.

DOUGLAS KELLNER   "Jean Baudrillard." In George Ritzer, ed., *The Blackwell Companion to Major Social Theorists*. Malden, MA, and Oxford, England: Blackwell, 2000, pp. 731–753. Brief introduction to this provocative and controversial postmodern theorists.

MIKE GANE, ed.   *Baudrillard Live: Selected Interviews*. London: Routledge, 1993. Revealing and fascinating set of interviews with this leading postmodern thinker.

GEORGE RITZER   *Explorations in the Sociology of Consumption: Fast Food, Credit Cards, and Casinos*. London: Sage, 2001. A collection of excerpts from my books and essays, several previously unpublished, on the sociology of consumption.

PAUL VIRILIO   *The Information Bomb*. London: Verso, 2000. Later, English-language, publication from this innovative thinker.

JAMES DER DERIAN, ed.   *The Virilio Reader*. Oxford: Blackwell, 1998. Excellent collection of Virilio's most important works, at least until that date.

SONDRA HARDING   *The Science Question in Sociology*. Ithaca, NY: Cornell University Press, 1986. Key work in the modern boom in feminist theory, especially standpoint theory.

PATRICIA CLOUGH   "Judith Butler." In George Ritzer, ed., *The Blackwell Companion to Major Social Theorists*. Malden, MA, and Oxford, England: Blackwell, 2000, pp. 754–773. Overview of the work of one of the most radical and influential feminist/postmodernist theorists.

GARY T. MARX   "Surveillance." In George Ritzer, ed. *The Encyclopedia of Social Theory*, 2 volumes. Thousand Oaks, CA: Sage, 2005, pp. 816–821. Brief overview of surveillance and surveillance methods in the contemporary world.

WILLIAM STAPLES   *Everyday Surveillance: Vigilance and Visibility in Postmodern Life*. Lanham, MD: Rowman and Littlefield, 2000. Book-length discussion of everyday surveillance in the postmodern world.

Globalization Theory

It is likely that no single topic has received as much popular and academic attention in recent years as globalization. In fact, the academic concern is motivated, in large part, by the extraordinary public importance of, interest in, and worry over, globalization. However, there are also reasons internal to the academic world (e.g., reactions against early and narrow approaches to what is now called globalization) that have led to this near-obsession with this topic. Social theorists, including many of those discussed in this chapter and elsewhere in this book, have been no exception to this trend toward a focal concern with globalization. It is beyond the scope of this chapter to offer anything like a complete overview of the voluminous work of social theorists on this topic, let alone a review of the entire literature on globalization. What follows is a brief overview of some of the most important theoretical work on globalization.

Virtually every nation and the lives of billions of people throughout the world are being transformed, often quite dramatically, by globalization. The degree and significance of its impact can be seen virtually everywhere one looks, most visibly in the now common protests that accompany high-level meetings of such global organizations as the WTO (World Trade Organization) and IMF (International Monetary Fund). As both the magnitude of the issues before these organizations and the level of protest against them make clear, people throughout the world feel strongly that they are confronting matters of great moment.

Globalization theory also emerged as a result of a series of developments internal to social theory, notably the reaction against such earlier perspectives as modernization theory. Among the defining characteristics of this theory were its Western bias, the pre-eminence accorded to developments in the West, and the idea that the rest of the world had little choice but to become increasingly like it. While there are many different versions of globalization theory, there is a tendency in virtually all of them to shift away dramatically from a focus on the West (including and especially the United States) and to examine transnational processes that not only flow in many different directions, but also those that are, at least to some degree, autonomous and independent of any single nation or area of the world (see discussion of Appadurai's work below).

Globalization can be analyzed culturally, economically, politically, and/or institutionally. For each, a key difference is whether one sees increasing homogeneity or heterogeneity. At the extremes, the globalization of culture can be seen as the transnational expansion of common codes and practices (homogeneity) or as a process in which many global and local cultural inputs interact to create a kind of pastiche, or a blend, leading to a variety of cultural hybrids (heterogeneity). The trend toward homogeneity is often associated with **cultural imperialism,** or, the influence of a particular culture on a wide range of other cultures. There are many varieties of cultural imperialism including those that emphasize the role played by American culture, the West, or core countries. Among many others, Roland Robertson, although he doesn't use the term *cultural imperialism,* opposes the idea through his famous concept of glocalization (see below) in which the global is seen as interacting with the local to produce something distinctive—the glocal.

Theorists who focus on *economic* factors tend to emphasize their growing importance and homogenizing effect on the world. They generally see globalization as the spread of the market economy throughout many different regions of the world. For example, some have focused on globalization and the expansion of trade. Recently, George Stiglitz, a Nobel Prize–winning economist and former chairman of the Council of Economic Advisors, issued a stinging attack on the World Bank, the World Trade Organization (WTO), and especially the International Monetary Fund (IMF) for their roles in exacerbating, rather than resolving, global economic crises. Among other things, Stiglitz criticizes the IMF for its homogenizing, "one-size-fits-all" approach that fails to take into account national differences. The IMF in particular, and globalization in general, have worked to the advantage of the wealthy nations, especially the United States (which effectively has veto power over IMF decisions), and to the detriment of poor nations; the gap between rich and poor has actually *increased* as a result of globalization.

While those who focus on economic issues tend to emphasize homogeneity, some differentiation (heterogeneity) is acknowledged to exist at the margins of the global economy. Indeed, Stiglitz argues for the need for more differentiated policies by the IMF and other global economic organizations. Other forms of heterogeneity in the economic realm involve, for example, the commodification of local cultures and the existence of flexible specialization that permits the tailoring of many products to the needs of various local specifications. More

---

cultural imperialism   The influence of a particular culture on a wide array of other cultures.

Key Concept
Globalization

Globalization is increasingly omnipresent. We are living in *a*—or even *the*—"global age." Globalization is clearly a very important change; it could even be argued that it is *the most important change in human history*. This is reflected in many domains, but particularly in social relationships and social structures, especially those that are widely dispersed geographically. **Globalization** can be defined as: a transplanetary *process* or set of *processes* involving growing multidirectional *flows* of increasingly *liquid* people, objects, places, and information and the *structures* they encounter and create that are *barriers* to, or *expedite,* those flows.

On the one hand, the emphasis in this definition is on movement—multidirectional processes and flows of various phenomena that have become increasingly liquid in the contemporary world. People move around the world more easily (as tourists, migrants), objects travel easily and quickly because of companies like Federal Express, places move everywhere (McDonald's in well over one hundred countries in the world), and information moves most easily and quickly of all via the Internet.

On the other hand, there are various structures that are also important globally. Some of those structures help in the flow of various phenomena. For example, established routes for airlines help them move throughout the world (and serve to prevent mid-air collisions) and illegal migrants follow well-established tracks from, for example, Central and South America through Mexico and then to the United State. However, other structures serve to slow down or even stop various global flows. The borders of nation-states and passport and customs controls are examples of such structures.

Overall, in thinking about globalization we need to focus on that which is in motion—processes, flows, liquids—as well as the more stationary structures that either expedite or impede those flows.

---

generally, those who emphasize heterogenization would argue that the interaction of the global market with local markets leads to the creation of unique "glocal" markets that integrate the demands of the global market with the realities of the local market.

Political/institutional orientations, too, tend to emphasize either homogeneity or heterogeneity. For example, some of those who operate with a homogenization perspective in this domain focus on the worldwide spread of models of the nation-state and the emergence of similar forms of governance throughout the globe; in other words, the growth of a more-or-less single model of governance around the world. More broadly, there is a concern with the global influence of a multiplicity of institutions. As we will see, some see the growth of transnational institutions and organizations as greatly diminishing the power of both

---

globalization   A transplanetary *process* or set of *processes* involving growing multidirectional *flows* of increasingly *liquid* people, objects, places, and information and the *structures* they encounter and create that are *barriers* to, or *expedite,* those flows.

Key Concept—Continued

In contrast to many other definitions of globalization, the one offered here does *not* assume that greater global integration is an inevitable component of globalization. That is, globalization *can* bring with it greater integration (especially when things flow easily), but it *can* also serve to reduce the level of integration (when structures are erected that successfully block flows).

A term that is closely related to globalization is *transnationalism,* which involves the interconnection of individuals and social groups across the borders of specific nation-states. This is closely related to the idea of *transnationality,* or the development of communities, identities, and relationships that are not limited to a single nation-state.

Globalization and transnationalism are often used interchangeably. However, transnationalism is limited to interconnections that cross geo-political borders, especially those associated with nation-states, while globalizaton includes such connections, but is not restricted to them and encompasses a far wider range of transplanetary processes. Further, geo-political borders are only one of the barriers encountered, and often overcome, by globalization.

Some phenomena, labor unions for example, are better thought of as transnational rather than as global. That is, the cross-border relationship between labor unions that exist in two or more nation-states is more important than the global labor movement. Transnationalism is most often used in thinking about, and doing research on, immigrants who move from one country to another, but who continue to be involved in various ways with the country from which they came.

---

the nation state and other, more local, social structures to make a difference in people's lives. One of the most extreme views of homogenization in the political realm is Benjamin Barber's thinking on "McWorld," or the growth of a single political[1] orientation that is increasingly pervasive throughout the world.

Interestingly, Barber also articulates, as an alternative perspective, the idea of "Jihad"—localized, ethnic, and reactionary political forces (including "rogue states") that involve an intensification of nationalism and that lead to greater political heterogeneity throughout the world. The interaction of McWorld and Jihad at the local level may produce unique, glocal political formations that integrate elements of both the former (e.g., use of the Internet to attract supporters) and the latter (e.g., use of traditional ideas and rhetoric).

While the issue of homogenization/heterogenization cuts across a broad swath of globalization theory, it is clearly not exhaustive. That will become clear in the following discussion of major theories of globalization that certainly touches in various ways on homogenization/heterogenization, but also highlights a number of other facets of globalization theory. This discussion will be divided into four sections. First, we will look at the perspectives on globalization of some of the major contemporary theorists (Giddens, Beck, and Bauman) encountered earlier in this book. Then, we will turn to three broad categories of theorizing globalization—cultural, economic, and political/institutional.

Key Concept
Civil Society

The major figure in social theory associated with the idea of civil society is Alexis de Tocqueville (see Chapter 1). Tocqueville lauded the early American propensity to form a wide range of associations (e.g., religious, moral) that were *not political* in nature and orientation. Such civil associations allowed people to interact with one another and to develop, renew, and enlarge feelings, ideas, emotions and understandings. These civil associations also allowed people to band together and to act in concert with one another. Without such associations they would be isolated and weak in large-scale contemporary societies.

The United States (and the West more generally) often conquered the world through uncivilized, even violent, means (colonialism, imperialism). However, it also played a major role in creating many of the elements of civil society such as a free press, written constitutions, religious tolerance, human rights, etc. A robust civil society was already in existence by the nineteenth century and early twentieth century (e.g., peace societies, cooperatives, workers[1] movements), but it was soon set back dramatically by the two world wars. It is largely in the aftermath of World War II that modern civil society took shape and expanded dramatically.

Central importance is accorded to the 1970s and 1980s, especially in Latin America and Eastern Europe. In both regions, there was opposition to military dictatorship and efforts to find an autonomous and self-organizing base outside of the state in order to oppose the military. It was also during this period that civil society became increasingly global as improved travel and communication made linkages among various civil society groups throughout the world increasingly possible. These groups mounted appeals to international authorities and were able to create a global political space for themselves where they argued for, and helped bring about, international agreements on such issues as human rights. Of great importance in the 1990s was the emergence of global activists who came together in an effort to deal with land mines, human rights, climate change, and HIV/AIDS.

Civil society is the process through which individuals deal with political and economic authorities in a wide variety of ways. It is a realm in which people can

---

MAJOR CONTEMPORARY THEORISTS ON GLOBALIZATION

Anthony Giddens on the "Runaway World" of Globalization

Giddens' views on globalization are obviously closely related to, and overlap with, his thinking on the juggernaut of modernity (see Chapter 5). Giddens also sees a close link between globalization and risk, especially the rise of what he calls manufactured risk. Much of the runaway world of globalization is beyond our control, but Giddens is not totally pessimistic. We can limit the problems created by the runaway world, but we can never control it completely. He holds

---

Key Concept—Continued

engage each other more or less directly and in which they can, among other things, analyze and criticize their political and economic institutions. People can do this, and thereby act publicly, by acting through a variety of voluntary associations, social movements, political parties, and labor unions. Thus, civil society involves *both* settings and actions that take place within those settings. It also represents an ideal toward which many people and groups aspire—an active, vital, and powerful civil society that can influence, and act as a counterbalance to, the polity and the economy. It is particularly the case that civil society stands as a counterbalance and an alternative to *both* the nation-state and the economic market, especially the neo-liberal capitalist market.

While civil society was linked historically to groups and actions within states, in more recent years it has been associated with more global actions and organizations (e.g., international nongovernmental organizations: INGOs). In other words, we have moved increasingly toward a global civil society, although civil society remains a force within states and societies, as well. Global civil society is nongovernmental, a form of society composed of interlinked social processes, oriented to civility (nonviolence), to being pluralistic (including the strong potential to reduce conflict), and to being global.

A number of factors are involved in the recent rise of civil society in general, and INGOs in particular. Perhaps the most important are various global flows (see Key Concept: Globalization) including flows of both resources (money, information, popular culture, etc.) and threats (e.g., pollution, drugs, sex trafficking). As the power of the nation-state to deal with these flows, and in the case of negative flows, to mitigate or prevent them, has declined, the role of civil society in general, and of myriad INGOS in particular, has grown. Among the most notable of these INGOS are CARE, Worldwide Fund for Nature, Greenpeace, Amnesty International, Friends of the Earth, *Medecins Sans Frontières*, Oxfam, and so on. Perhaps of greatest importance today in civil society are groups that represent the poor, especially those in less-developed countries, and their efforts to improve the position of the poor within the global economy.

---

out some hope for democracy, especially international and transnational forms of democracy such as the European Union.

Giddens emphasizes the role of the West in general, and the United States in particular, in globalization. However, he also recognizes that globalization is a two-way process, with America and the West being strongly influenced by it. Furthermore, he argues that globalization is in the process of becoming increasingly decentered with nations outside the West playing an increasingly large role in it. He also recognizes that globalization has both undermined local cultures *and* served to revive them. And he makes the innovative point that globalization "squeezes sideways" producing new areas that may cut across nations. He offers as an example an area around Barcelona in Northern Spain that extends into France.

A key clash taking place at the global level today is that between funda-mentalism and cosmopolitanism. In the end, Giddens sees the emergence of a "global cosmopolitan society." Yet even the main force in opposition to it—traditionalism—is itself a product of globalization. Furthermore, fundamental-ism uses global forces (e.g., the mass media) in order to further its ends. Funda-mentalism can take various forms—religious, ethnic, nationalist, political—but whatever form it takes, Giddens thinks that it is problematic, both because it is at odds with cosmopolitanism and because it is linked to violence.

Ulrich Beck and the Politics of Globalization

We can get at the essence of Beck's thinking on this issue by discussing his distinction between globalism and globality. **Globalism** is the view that the world is dominated by economics and that we are witnessing the emergence of the hegemony of the capitalist world market and the neoliberal ideology that underpins it. To Beck, this view involves both monocausal and linear thinking. The multidimensionality of global developments—ecology, politics, culture, and civil society—is wrongly reduced to a single economic dimension. And that economic dimension is seen, again erroneously, as evolving in a linear direc-tion of ever-increasing dependence on the world market. Clearly, Beck sees the world in much more multidimensional and multidirectional terms. In addition, he is very sensitive to the problems associated with the capitalist world market including the fact that there are all sorts of barriers to free trade and that there are not just winners in this world market, but also (many) losers.

While Beck is a critic of globalism, he sees much merit in the idea of **global-ity** in which closed spaces, especially those associated with nations, are grow-ing increasingly illusory. They are growing illusory because of globalization, which involves transnational actors, with varying degrees of power, identities, and the like, criss-crossing and undermining nation-states. These transnational processes are not simply economic, but also involve ecology, culture, politics, and civil society. Such transnational processes traverse national borders ren-dering them porous, if not increasingly irrelevant: Nothing is any longer lim-ited to the local. That which takes place locally, including both advances and catastrophes, affects the entire world.

While transnational processes have long existed, globality is new for at least three reasons. First, its influence over geographic space is far more exten-sive than ever before. Second, its influence over time is far more stable; it is of continual influence from one time to another. Third, there is far greater den-sity to its various elements including transnational relationships and networks.

---

globalism   The monocausal and unilinear view that the world is dominated by eco-nomics and that we are witnessing the emergence of the hegemony of the capitalist world market and the neoliberal ideology that underpins it.

globality   The view that closed spaces, especially those associated with nations, are growing increasingly illusory in the era of globalization.

Zygmunt Bauman (1925–   )
A Biographical Vignette

Zygmunt Bauman has had an interesting life and scholarly career. Born in Poland, he escaped the Nazis (he is Jewish) by fleeing with his family to Russia. He fought in the Polish army during World War II and by 1953 had risen to the rank of major before being relieved of his duties during a wave of anti-Semitism. He then turned to the social sciences and by 1968 had risen to become a professor at Warsaw University when he was again forced out of his position by anti-Semitism. He eventually ended up at the University of Leeds in England, where he proceeded to publish widely in English and became one of the leading social theorists of the day.

His first book in English appeared in 1972, and while he achieved significant recognition in the ensuing decades, his career really took off when in 1989 he published the landmark *Modernity and the Holocaust*, a book that argued that the Holocaust was not an aberration, but an expression of the essential nature of modernity. This critique of modernity led Bauman in the direction of postmodernity and postmodern social theory, which he engaged and adapted to his own orientation through the 1990s. More recently, he has increasingly become a public intellectual writing on a wide range of subjects, including globalization, but this has not prevented him from making new and original contributions to the scholarly literature such as his 2000 notion of "liquid modernity."

Beck also lists a number of other things that are distinctive about globality in comparison to earlier manifestations of transnationality:

1. Everyday life and interaction across national borders are being profoundly affected.
2. There is a self-perception of this transnationality in such realms as the mass media, consumption, and tourism.
3. Community, labor, and capital are increasingly placeless.
4. There is a growing awareness of global ecological dangers and actions to be taken to deal with them.
5. There is an increasing perception of transcultural others in our lives.
6. Global culture industries circulate at unprecedented levels.
7. There is an increase in the number and strength of transnational agreements, actors, and institutions.

This leads Beck to refine his previously discussed thinking on modernity and to argue that globality, and the inability to reverse it, is associated with what he now calls "second modernity." Above all, however, what defines the latter is the decline of the power of the nations and the national borders that went to the heart of "first modernity." The central premise of first modernity is (was) that we live in self-enclosed nation-states. (Beck dismisses this as a "container theory" of society.) Thus globality, and second modernity, mean, most importantly, denationalization and, Beck hopes, the rise of transnational organizations and perhaps a transnational state.

Zygmunt Bauman on the Human Consequences of Globalization

Bauman sees globalization in terms of a "space war." In his view, it is mobility that has become the most important and differentiating factor in social stratification in the world today. Thus, the winners of the space war are those who are mobile; able to move freely throughout the globe and in the process to create meaning for themselves. They can float relatively free of space and when they must "land" somewhere, they isolate themselves in walled and policed spaces where they are safe from the losers in the space war. The latter not only lack mobility but are relegated and confined to territories denuded of meaning and even of the ability to offer meaning. Thus, while the elite are likely intoxicated by their mobility opportunities, the rest are more likely to feel imprisoned in their home territories from which they have little prospect of moving. Furthermore, the latter are likely to feel humiliated by the lack of their own mobility and the sight of elites free to move about at will. As a result, territories become battlefields where the losers and winners of the space war face off in a very uneven conflict.

The winners can be said to live in time rather than space; they are able to span virtually every space quickly, if not instantaneously. In contrast, the losers can be seen as living in space. That space is beyond their control, heavy, resilient, resistant, untouchable, able to tie time down. However, it is important to distinguish among those who have at least some mobility. The **tourists** are on the move because they want to be. They are attracted by something, find it irresistible and move toward it. Then there are the **vagabonds** who are on the move because they find their environs unbearable, inhospitable for any number of reasons. The positive aspects of what we applaud as globalization is that which is associated with tourists, while an unavoidable side effect is that many others are transformed into vagabonds. However, most people exist between these two extremes. They are not only unsure exactly where they now stand, but wherever it is, they are not sure they will be in the same place tomorrow. Thus, globalization translates into uneasiness for most of us.

However, even the seeming winners in globalization—the tourists—have their problems. First, there is the burden associated with the impossibility of slowing down; it is hard to be always on the move and at high speed. Second, mobility means an unending string of choices and each choice has a measure of uncertainty associated with it. Third, each of these choices also carries with it a series of risks and dangers. Endless mobility and continual choice eventually become troublesome if not burdensome.

Given the globalization theories of some of today's major social theorists, we turn to the major types of globalization theory, often with examples from other major social thinkers.

---

tourists   Those on the move throughout the globe because they want to be.

vagabonds   Those on the move throughout the globe because they find their environs unbearable, inhospitable for any number of reasons.

CULTURAL THEORY

Jan Nederveen Pieterse has identified three major paradigms in theorizing the cultural aspects of globalization, specifically on the centrally important issue of whether cultures around the globe are eternally different, converging, or creating new "hybrid" forms out of the unique combination of global and local cultures. Let us look at each of these paradigms and a representative example (or examples) of each.

Cultural Differentialism

Those who adopt this paradigm argue that there are lasting differences among and between cultures that are largely unaffected by globalization or any other bi-, inter-, multi-, and transcultural processes. This is not to say that culture is unaffected by any of these processes, especially globalization, but it is to say that at their core they are largely unaffected by them; they remain much as they always have been. In this perspective globalization only occurs on the surface with the deep structure of cultures largely, if not totally, unaffected by it. Cultures are seen as largely closed not only to globalization, but also to the influences of other cultures. In one image, the world is envisioned as a mosaic of largely separate cultures. More menacing is a billiard ball image, with billiard balls (representing cultures) seen as bouncing off others (representing other cultures). This is more menacing because it indicates the possibility of dangerous and potentially catastrophic collisions among and between world cultures.

This paradigm has a long history, but it has attracted increasing attention and adherents (as well as critics) in recent years because of two sets of current events. One is the terrorist attacks of September 11th and the subsequent wars in Afghanistan and Iraq. To many, these events were seen as the product of a clash between Western and Islamic culture and the eternal cultural differences between them. The other is the increasing multiculturalism of both the United States (largely the growth of the Hispanic population) and of Western European countries (largely the growing Muslim populations) and the vast differences, and enmity, between majority and minority populations.

The most famous, and controversial, example of this paradigm is Samuel Huntington's *Clash of Civilizations and the Remaking of the World Order*. Huntington traces the beginnings of the current world situation to the end of the Cold War and the reconfiguring of the world from one differentiated on a political-economic basis (democratic/capitalist vs. totalitarian/communist) to one based on cultural differences. Such cultural differences are nothing new, but they were largely submerged (as in the old Yugoslavia and the differences between, among others, Serbs and Croats) by the overwhelming political-economic differences of the Cold War era. What we have seen resurfacing in the last two decades are ancient identities, adversaries, and enemies. Huntington uses the term **civilization** to describe the broadest level of these cultures

---

civilization The broadest domain of cultures and cultural identities; culture "writ large."

and cultural identities (indeed, to him civilization is culture "writ large"). What he sees is the emergence of fault lines among and between these civilizations, and this is a highly dangerous situation given the historic enmities among at least some of these civilizations.

Huntington differentiates between seven or eight world civilizations—Sinic [Chinese], Japan [sometimes combined with the Sinic as Far Eastern], Hindu, Islamic, Orthodox [centered in Russia], Western Europe, North America, along with the closely aligned Australia, New Zealand, Latin America, and (possibly) Africa. He sees these civilizations as differing greatly on basic philosophical assumptions, underlying values, social relations, customs, and overall outlooks on life. To Huntington, human history is in effect the history of civilizations, especially these civilizations. Civilizations share a number of characteristics including the fact that there is great agreement on what they are (although they lack clear beginnings and there are no clear-cut boundaries between civilizations which, nonetheless, are quite real). They are:

1. Among the most enduring of human associations (although they do change over time),
2. The broadest level of cultural identity (short of humanity in its entirety),
3. The broadest type of subjective self-identification,
4. Usually span more than one state (although they do not perform state functions),
5. Are a totality,
6. Are closely aligned with both religion and race.

Huntington offers a modern grand narrative of the relationships among civilizations. For more than 3000 years (approximately 1500 BC to AD 1500) civilizations tended to be widely separated in terms of both time and space. As a result, contacts among them tended to be nonexistent. When they occurred, they tended to be on a limited or intermittent basis and they were likely quite intense.

The next phase, roughly from 1500 to the close of World War II, was characterized by the sustained, overpowering, and unidirectional impact of Western civilization on all other civilizations. Huntington attributes this to various structural characteristics of the West including the rise of cities, commerce, state bureaucracy, and an emerging sense of national consciousness. However, the most immediate cause was technological especially in ocean navigation and the military, including a superior military organization, discipline and training, and, of course, weaponry. In the end, the West excelled in organized violence and while those in the West sometimes forget this, those in other parts of the world have not. Thus, by 1910, just before World War I, the world came closer, in Huntington's view, than at any other time in history to being one world, one civilization—Western civilization.

The third phase—the multicivilizational system—is traceable to the end of the expansion of the West and the beginning of the revolt against it. The period after World War I to about 1990 was characterized by a clash of ideas, especially capitalist and communist ideologies. With the fall of communism the major clashes in the world now revolve around religion, culture, and ultimately civilizations. While the West continues to be dominant, Huntington foresees its decline. It will be a slow decline, it will not occur in a straight line, and it will involve a decline (at least relatively) in the West's resources—population, economic product, and military capability (traceable to such things as the decline of U.S. forces and the globalization of the defense industries making generally available weapons once available only, or largely, in the West). Other civilizations will increasingly reject the West, but they will embrace and utilize the advances of modernization, which can and should be distinguished from Westernization.

While the West declines, the resurgence of two other civilizations are of greatest importance. The first is the economic growth of Asian societies, especially Sinic civilization. Huntington foresees continuing growth of Asian economies that will soon surpass those of the West. Important in itself, this will translate into increasing power for the East and a corresponding decline in the ability of the West to impose its standards on the East. He sees the economic ascendancy of the East as largely traceable to the superior aspects of its culture(s), especially its collectivism in contrast to the individuality that dominates the West. Also helpful to the economic rise of the East are various other commonalities among the nations of the region (e.g., religion, especially Confucianism). The successes of Asian economies will not only be important in themselves, but also for the role they will play as models for other non-Western societies.

This first of Huntington's arguments is not that surprising or original. After all, we witnessed the dramatic growth of the post-World War II Japanese economy and we are now witnessing the amazing economic transformation of China. Few would disagree with the view that projecting present economic trends, the Chinese economy will become the largest in the world in the not-too-distant future. More controversial is Huntington's second major contention that involves the resurgence of Islam. While the Sinic emergence is rooted in the economy, Islamic growth is rooted in dramatic population growth and the mobilization of the population. This has touched virtually every Muslim society, usually first culturally and then socio-politically. It can be seen as part of the global revival of religion. It also can be seen as both a product of, and an effort to come to grips with, modernization.

Huntington goes beyond pointing to this development to paint a dire portrait of the future of the relations between the West and these other two civilizations, especially Islam. The Cold War conflict between capitalism and communism has been replaced by conflict that is to be found at the "fault lines" among and between civilizations, especially the Western, Sinic, and Islamic civilizations. Thus, he foresees dangerous clashes in the future between the West (and what he calls its "arrogance"), Islam (and its "intolerance"), and Sinic "assertiveness." Much of the conflict revolves around the West's view of itself as possessing "universal culture," its desire to export that culture to the rest of the world, and its declining ability to do so. Furthermore, what the West sees as universalism, the rest of the world, especially Islamic civilization, sees as imperialism. More specifically, the West wants to limit weapons proliferation, while other civilizations want weapons, especially "weapons of mass destruction." The West also seeks to export democracy to, even impose it on, other societies and civilizations that often resist it as part of the West's idea of universal culture. And the West seeks to control and to limit immigration (especially from Islamic civilization), but many from those civilizations have found their way into the West, or want to be there. As this increases, Huntington sees cleft societies developing *within* both Europe and the United States (in the latter, fault lines will develop not only between Westerners and Muslims, but Anglos and Hispanics).[2]

What has earned Huntington numerous criticisms and the greatest enmity is his controversial statements about Islamic civilization and Muslims. For example, he argues that wherever Muslims and non-Muslims live in close proximity to one another, violent conflict and intense antagonism are pervasive. And Huntington puts much of the blame for this on Muslims and their propensity toward violent conflict. He argues that from the beginning, Islam has been a religion of the sword; it glorified military values and there is a history of Islamic conquest.[3] The relationship between Islam and other civilizations has historically been one of mutual indigestibility. Of course, Western imperialism—often with Islam as a target—has played a key role in this. Islam also lacks a strong core state to exert control over the civilization. But of greatest importance to Huntington is the pressures created by the demographic explosion within Islam.

Huntington is concerned about the decline of the West, especially of the United States. He sees the United States, indeed all societies, as threatened by their increasing multicivilizational or multicultural character. For him, the demise of the United States effectively means the demise of Western civilization. Without a powerful, unicivilizational United States, the West is minuscule. For the West to survive and prosper, the United States must do two things. First, it must reaffirm its identity as a Western (rather than multicivilizational) nation. Second, it must reaffirm and reassert its role as the leader of Western civilization around the globe. The reassertion and acceptance of Western civilization (which would also involve a renunciation of universalism), indeed all civilizations, is the surest way to prevent warfare between civilizations. The real danger, for Huntington, is multiculturalism within the West and all other civilizations. Thus, Huntington ultimately comes down on the side of cultural continuity and something approaching cultural purity within civilizations. Thus, for him, at least in some ideal sense, globalization becomes a process by which civilizations continue to exist and move in roughly parallel fashion in the coming years. This constitutes a reaffirmation of the importance of civilization, that is, culture, in the epoch of globalization.

Cultural Convergence

While the previous paradigm is rooted in the idea of lasting differences among and between cultures and civilizations as a result of, or in spite of, globalization, this paradigm is based on the idea of globalization leading to increasing sameness throughout the world. While thinkers like Huntington emphasize the persistence of cultures and civilizations in the face of globalization, those who support this perspective see those cultures changing, sometimes radically, as a result of globalization. The cultures of the world are seen as growing increasingly similar, at least to some degree and in some ways. There is a tendency to see global assimilation in the direction of dominant groups and societies in the world. Those who operate from this perspective focus on such things as "cultural imperialism," global capitalism, Westernization, Americanization, and "McDonaldization." At its extreme, globalization becomes Westernization, Americanization, and McDonaldization writ large.

Next, we will discuss two versions of this basic argument that is closely associated with my own work on this topic. However, a note of warning and clarification. While my work does focus on cultural convergence, it certainly does *not* argue that that is all that is happening in globalization or that local cultures are disappearing completely, or even necessarily being altered in some fundamental way. Rather, the argument is that there are global processes that are bringing the same or similar phenomena (e.g., McDonald's restaurants in 120-plus countries in the world) to many parts of the world and, in that sense, there is cultural convergence. However, side-by-side with such global phenomena exist local phenomena (e.g., local open-air food markets or craft fairs) that continue to be vibrant and important. Furthermore, it may well be that the arrival of these global forms spurs the revival or development of new local forms. While the last two points are certainly meritorious, in accepting them we must not lose sight of the fact that some, perhaps a great deal, of cultural convergence, is also occurring (the spread of Wal-Mart into Mexico and other nations would be another example).

"McDonaldization"   Although it is based on Max Weber's ideas on the rationalization of the West (see Chapter 2), the McDonaldization thesis adopts a different model (Weber focused on the bureaucracy, but I concentrate on the fast-food restaurant), brings the theory into the 21st century, and views rationalization extending its reach into more sectors of society and areas of the world than Weber ever imagined. Of greatest concern in terms of this section is the fact that McDonaldization is, as we will see, a force in globalization, especially increasing cultural homogenization.

McDonaldization is the process by which the principles of the fast-food restaurant are coming to dominate more and more sectors of American society, as well as the rest of the world. The nature of the McDonaldization process may be delineated by outlining its five basic dimensions: efficiency, calculability, predictability, control through the substitution of technology for people, and, paradoxically, the irrationality of rationality.

McDonaldization   The process by which the principles of the fast-food restaurant are coming to dominate more and more sectors of American society, as well as the rest of the world; in the latter sense, a form of cultural imperialism.

First, a McDonaldizing society emphasizes **efficiency,** or the effort to discover the best possible means to whatever end is desired. Workers in fast-food restaurants clearly must work efficiently; for example, burgers are assembled, and sometimes even cooked, in an assembly-line fashion. Customers want, and are expected, to acquire and consume their meals efficiently. The drive-through window is a highly efficient means for customers to obtain, and employees to dole out, meals. Overall, a variety of norms, rules, regulations, procedures, and structures have been put in place in the fast-food restaurant in order to ensure that *both* employees and customers act in an efficient manner. Furthermore, the efficiency of one party helps to ensure that the other will behave in a similar manner.

Second, great importance is given to **calculability,** to an emphasis on quantity, often to the detriment of quality. Various aspects of the work at fast-food restaurants are timed; this emphasis on speed often serves to adversely affect the quality of the work, from the point of view of the employee, resulting in dissatisfaction, alienation, and high turnover rates. Similarly, customers are expected to spend as little time as possible in the fast-food restaurant. In fact, the drive-through window reduces this time to zero, but if the customers desire to eat in the restaurant, the chairs may be designed to impel them to leave after about 20 minutes. This emphasis on speed clearly has a negative effect on the quality of the dining experience at a fast-food restaurant. Furthermore, the emphasis on how fast the work is to be done means that customers cannot be served high-quality food that, almost by definition, requires a good deal of time to prepare.

McDonaldization also involves an emphasis on **predictability,** meaning that things (products, settings, employee, customer behavior, etc.) are pretty much the same from one geographic setting to another and from one time to another. Employees are expected to perform their work in a predictable manner and, for their part, customers are expected to respond with similarly predictable behavior. Thus, when customers enter, employees ask, following scripts, what they wish to order. For their part, customers are expected to know what they want, or where to look to find what they want, and they are expected to order, pay, and leave quickly. Employees (following another script) are expected to thank them when they do leave. A highly predictable ritual is played out in the fast-food restaurant—one that involves highly predictable foods that vary little from one time or place to another.

---

efficiency   The effort to discover the best possible means to whatever end is desired; a dimension of McDonaldization.

calculability   An emphasis on quantity, often to the detriment of quality; a dimension of McDonaldization.

predictability   Things (products, settings, employee, customer behavior, etc.) are pretty much the same from one geographic setting to another and from one time to another; a dimension of McDonaldization.

In addition, great **control** exists in a McDonaldized society and a good deal of that control comes from technologies. Although these technologies currently dominate employees, increasingly they will be replacing them. Employees are clearly controlled by such technologies as french-fry machines that ring when the fries are done and even automatically lift the fries out of the hot oil. For their part, customers are controlled both by the employees who are constrained by such technologies as well as more directly by the technologies themselves. Thus, the automatic fry machine makes it impossible for a customer to request well-done, well-browned fries.

Finally, both employees and customers suffer from the **irrationality of rationality** that seems inevitably to accompany McDonaldization. That is, paradoxically, rationality seems often to lead to its exact opposite—irrationality. For example, the efficiency of the fast-food restaurant is often replaced by the inefficiencies associated with long lines of people at the counters or long lines of cars at the drive-through window. Although there are many other irrationalities, the ultimate irrationality is dehumanization. Employees are forced to work in dehumanizing jobs and customers are forced to eat in dehumanizing settings and circumstances. The fast-food restaurant is a source of degradation for employees and customers alike.

McDonaldization, Expansionism, and Globalization McDonald's has been a resounding success in the international arena. About half of McDonald's restaurants are outside the United States (in the mid-1980s only 25 percent of McDonalds were outside the United States). The vast majority of new restaurants opened each year are overseas. Well over half of McDonald's profits come from its overseas operations. Starbucks has become an increasingly global force and is now a presence in Latin America, Europe (it's particularly visible in London), the Middle East, and the Pacific Rim.

Many highly McDonaldized firms outside of the fast-food industry have also had success globally. In addition to its thousands of stores in the United States, Blockbuster now has just over 2,000 sites in 28 other countries. Although Wal-Mart opened its first international store (in Mexico) in 1991, it now operates over a thousand stores overseas (compared to over 3,000 in the United States, including supercenters and Sam's Club).

Another indicator of globalization is the fact that other nations have developed their own variants of this American institution. Canada has a chain of coffee shops, Tim Hortons (merged with Wendy's a few years ago), that has 2,200 outlets (160 in the United States). Paris, whose love for fine cuisine might lead you to think it would prove immune to fast food, has a large number of fast-food croissanteries; the revered French bread has also been

---

control Domination of technologies over employees and customers; a dimension of McDonaldization.

irrationality of rationality The paradoxical reality that rationality seems often to lead to its exact opposite—irrationality.

George Ritzer (1940–   )
An Autobiographical Vignette

As with a surprising number of other twists and turns in my academic career, I did not set out to write about globalization. When I first wrote about the McDonaldization of society in 1983, and even a decade later when I published the first edition of a book with that title, I was not fully conscious of its relationship to globalization. I was certainly aware of, and described, the spread of McDonald's, and the larger process that it spawned, through both the United States and the world, but the broader issue of globalization was not on my radar and, in fact, was not much on sociology's radar when I first began this work.

My sensitivity to the relationship between McDonaldization and globalization increased in a 1995 book, *Expressing America: A Critique of the Global Credit Card Society*. As the title makes clear, that book took a global orientation and it included a discussion of McDonaldization focusing on the degree to which the credit card industry was McDonaldized. Perhaps, more importantly for my developing orientation, it focused on credit cards as a form of Americanization and the latter was clearly one aspect of a broad process of globalization.

I soon found myself with three interrelated concepts—McDonaldization, Americanization, and globalization—that needed to be sorted out and analyzed on their own and in relationship to one another. It became clear that both McDonaldization and Americanization were subprocesses under the broader heading of globalization. It also became clear that the former needed to be differentiated with McDonaldization not being reducible to one form of Americanization. For one thing, McDonaldization had roots outside the United States and, more importantly, today it has taken root outside the United States and is being exported back into it.

Gradually, my focus has shifted more and more in the direction of globalization. In my most recent work on the topic, I have come to focus on the globalization of "nothing" and to argue that McDonaldization and Americanization are two key contributors to the globalization of nothing. I have also related that form of globalization to several others in an effort to cast light on globalization in general, especially as it relates to culture.

Thus, I embarked on an intellectual voyage that has led me to a focal interest in globalization, although that topic could not have been further from my mind when I began.

McDonaldized. India has a chain of fast-food restaurants, Nirula's, that sells mutton burgers (about 80 percent of Indians are Hindus, who eat no beef) as well as local Indian cuisine. Mos Burger is a Japanese chain with over 1,500 restaurants that, in addition to the usual fare, sells Teriyaki chicken burgers, rice burgers, and Oshiruko with brown rice cake. Russkoye Bistro, a Russian chain, sells traditional Russian fare like pirogi (meat and vegetable pies), blini (thin pancakes), Cossack apricot curd tart, and, of course, vodka. Perhaps the most unlikely spot for an indigenous fast-food restaurant, war-ravaged Beirut of 1984, witnessed the opening of Juicy Burger, with a rainbow instead of golden arches and the J.B. the Clown standing in for Ronald McDonald.

Its owners hoped that it would become the McDonald's of the Arab world. After the 2003 war with Iraq, a number of clones of McDonald's ("Madonal," "Matbax") quickly opened.

Now McDonaldization is coming full circle. Other countries with their own McDonaldized institutions have begun to export them to the United States. The Body Shop, an ecologically sensitive British cosmetics chain, had over 1,900 shops in 50 nations in 2003, of which 300 were in the United States. Furthermore, American firms are now opening copies of this British chain, such as Bath & Body Works. Pollo Campero, a Guatemalan chain specializing in fried chicken, is currently in six countries and is spreading rapidly throughout the United States.

McDonald's, as the model of the process of McDonaldization, has come to occupy a central position throughout the world. At the opening of McDonald's in Moscow, it was described as the ultimate American icon. When Pizza Hut opened in Moscow in 1990, customers saw it as a small piece of America. Reflecting on the growth of fast-food restaurants in Brazil, an executive associated with Pizza Hut of Brazil said that his nation is passionate about things American.

The "Globalization of Nothing"   The globalization of nothing, like McDonaldization, implies increasing homogenization as more and more nations around the world have an increasing number of the various forms of nothing. I am *not* arguing that globalization is nothing; indeed it is clear that the process is of enormous significance. Rather, the argument is that there is an *elective affinity* (using a term borrowed from Weber) between globalization and nothing. That is, one does not cause the other, but they do tend to vary together.

What is central here is the idea of **grobalization** (a companion to the notion of glocalization, see below for a definition), or the imperialistic ambitions of nations, corporations, organizations, and the like and their desire, indeed need, to impose themselves on various geographic areas. Their main interest is in seeing their power, influence, and in some cases profits *grow* (hence the term *gro*balization) throughout the world. Grobalization involves a variety of subprocesses, three of which—capitalism, Americanization, McDonaldization—are not only central driving forces in grobalization, but also of great significance in the worldwide spread of nothingness.

By **nothing,** I mean (largely) empty forms; forms largely devoid of distinctive content. Conversely, **something** would be defined as (largely) full forms; forms rich in distinctive content. Thus, it is easier to export empty forms throughout the globe than it is forms that are loaded with content (something).

---

grobalization   The imperialistic ambitions of nations, corporations, organizations, and the like and their desire, indeed need, to impose themselves on various geographic areas.

nothing   Largely empty forms; forms devoid of most distinctive content.

something   Largely full forms; forms rich in distinctive content.

The latter are more likely to be rejected by at least some cultures and societies because the content conflicts, is at variance with, local content. In contrast, since they are largely devoid of distinctive content, empty forms are less likely to come into conflict with the local. In addition, empty forms have other advantages from the point of view of globalization including the fact that since they are so minimalist, they are easy to replicate over and over. They also have a cost advantage since they are relatively inexpensive to reproduce. A good example of nothing in these terms is the shopping mall (e.g., any of the malls created by the Mills Corporation—Potomac Mills, Sawgrass Mills, etc.), which is an empty (largely) structure that is easily replicated around the world. These malls could be filled with an endless array of specific content (e.g., local shops, local foods, etc.—something!) that could vary enormously from one locale to another. However, increasingly they are filled with chain stores of various types—nothing! Since more and more countries in the world have these malls, this is an example of the grobalization of nothing and of increasing global homogenization.

There are four subtypes of nothing and all of them are largely empty of distinctive content and are being globalized. The four types are "non-places," or settings that are largely empty of content (e.g., the malls discussed above); "non-things" such as credit cards in which there is little to distinguish one from the billions of others and which work in exactly the same way for all who use them anywhere in the world; "non-people," or the kind of employees associated with non-places, for example, telemarketers (who may be virtually anywhere in the world) and who interact with all customers in much the same way, relying heavily on scripts; and "non-services" such as those provided by ATMs (the services provided are identical; the customer does all the work involved in obtaining the services) as opposed to human bank tellers. The grobal proliferation of non-places, non-things, non-people, and non-services is another indication of increasing homogenization.

Cultural Hybridization

The third paradigm emphasizes the mixing of cultures as a result of globalization and the production, out of the integration of the global and the local, of new and unique hybrid cultures that are not reducible to either the local or the global culture. From this perspective, McDonaldization and the grobalization of nothing may be taking place, but they are largely superficial changes. Much more important is the integration of these and other global processes with various local realities to produce new and distinctive hybrid forms that indicate continued heterogenization rather than homogenization. Hybridization is a very positive, even romantic, view of globalization as a profoundly creative process out of which emerges new cultural realities, and continuing if not increasing heterogeneity, in many different locales.

The concept that gets to the heart of cultural hybridization, as well as what many contemporary theorists interested in globalization think about the nature of transnational processes, is glocalization. **Glocalization** can be defined as the interpenetration of the global and the local resulting in unique outcomes in different geographic areas. While grobalization, as discussed above, tends to be associated with the proliferation of nothing, glocalization tends to be tied more to something and therefore stands opposed, at least partially (and along with the local itself), to the spread of nothing.

Following Roland Robertson, the following are the essential elements of glocalization:

1. The world is growing more pluralistic. Glocalization theory is exceptionally sensitive to differences within and between areas of the world.
2. Individuals and local groups have great power to adapt, innovate, and maneuver within a glocalized world. Glocalization theory sees local individuals and groups as important and creative agents.
3. Social processes are relational and contingent. Globalization provokes a variety of reactions—ranging from nationalist entrenchment to cosmopolitan embrace—that feed back on and transform grobalization; that produce glocalization.
4. Commodities and the media are *not* seen as (totally) coercive, but rather as providing material to be used in individual and group creation throughout the glocalized areas of the world.

Those who emphasize glocalization tend to see it as militating against the grobalization of nothing and, in fact, view it as leading to the creation of a wide array of new, "glocal" forms of something. In contrast, those who emphasize grobalization see it as a powerful contributor to the spread of nothingness throughout the world.

A discussion of some closely related terms (and related examples) will be of considerable help in getting a better sense of glocalization, as well as the broader issue of cultural hybridization. Of course, **hybridization** itself is one such term emphasizing increasing diversity associated with the unique mixtures of the global and the local as opposed to the *uniformity* associated with grobalization. A cultural hybrid would involve the combination of two, or more, elements from different cultures and/or parts of the world. Among the examples of hybridization (and heterogenization, glocalization) are Ugandan tourists visiting Amsterdam to watch two Moroccan women engage in Thai boxing, Argentinians watching Asian rap performed by a South American band at a London club owned by a Saudi Arabian, and the more mundane experiences of Americans eating such concoctions as Irish bagels, Chinese

---

glocalization The interpenetration of the global and the local resulting in unique outcomes in different geographic areas.

hybridization A perspective on globalization that emphasizes the increasing diversity associated with unique mixtures of the global and the local as opposed to the *uniformity* associated with grobalization.

tacos, Kosher pizza, and so on. Obviously, the list of such hybrids is long and growing rapidly with increasing hybridization. The contrast of course would be such uniform experiences as eating hamburgers in the United States, quiche in France, or sushi in Japan.

Yet another concept that is closely related to glocalization is **creolization.** The term *creole* generally refers to people of mixed race, but it has been extended to the idea of the creolization of language and culture involving a combination of languages and cultures that were previously unintelligible to one another.

All of the above—glocalization, hybridization, creolization—should give the reader a good feel for what is being discussed here under the heading of cultural hybridization.

Appadurai's "Landscapes"   Arjun Appadurai's *Modernity at Large: Cultural Dimensions of Globalization* emphasizes global flows and the disjunctures among them. These serve to produce unique cultural realities around the world; they tend to produce cultural hybrids.

Appadurai discusses five global flows—*ethnoscapes, mediascapes, technoscapes, financescapes,* and *ideoscapes.* The use of the suffix *scape* allows Appadurai to communicate the idea that these processes have fluid, irregular, and variable shapes and are therefore consistent with the idea of heterogenization and not homogenization. That there are a number of these scapes and that they operate independently of one another to some degree, and are perhaps even in conflict with one another, make this perspective also in tune with those that emphasize cultural diversity and heterogeneity. Furthermore, these scapes are interpreted differently by different agents ranging all the way from individuals, to face-to-face groups, subnational groups, multinational corporations, and even nation-states. And these scapes are ultimately navigated by individuals and groups on the basis of their own subjective interpretations of them. In other words, these are imagined worlds and those doing the imagining can range from those who control them to those who live in and traverse them. While power obviously lies with those in control and their imaginings, this perspective gives to those who merely live in or pass through them the power to redefine and ultimately subvert them.

At the center of Appadurai's thinking are the five landscapes mentioned above:

1. **Ethnoscapes** are the mobile, moving groups and individuals (tourists, refugees, guest workers) that play such an important role in the shifting world in which we increasingly live. This involves actual movement as well as fantasies about moving. Furthermore, in an ever-changing world, people

---

creolization   A combination of cultures that were previously separate from one another; often used interchangeably with hybridization.

ethnoscapes   Mobile groups and individuals (tourists, refugees, guest workers). Can involve actual movement as well as fantasies about moving; one of Appadurai's landscapes.

cannot afford to allow their imaginations to rest too long and thus must keep such fantasies alive.

2. **Technoscapes** are the ever-fluid, global configurations of high and low, mechanical and informational technology and the wide range of material (Internet, e-mail) that now moves so freely and quickly around the globe and across borders that were at one time impervious to such movement (or at least thought to be).

3. **Financescapes** involve the processes by which huge sums of money move through nations and around the world at great speed through commodity speculations, currency markets, national stock exchanges, and the like.

4. **Mediascapes** involve both the electronic capability to produce and transmit information around the world as well as the images of the world that these media create and disseminate. Involved here are global film makers and distributors, television stations (CNN and Al-Jazeera are notable examples), and newspapers and magazines.

5. **Ideoscapes,** like mediascapes, are sets of images. However, they are largely restricted to political images either produced by states and in line with their ideology, or the images and counter-ideologies produced by movements that seek to supplant those in power, or at least to gain a piece of that power.

Three things are especially worth noting about Appadurai's landscapes. First, they can be seen as global processes that are partly or wholly independent of any given nation-state. Second, global flows not only occur through the landscapes, but also increasingly in and through the *disjunctures* among them. Thus, to give one example of such a disjuncture, the Japanese are open to ideas (ideoscapes, mediascapes), but notoriously closed to immigration (at least one of the ethnoscapes). More generally, the free movement of some landscapes may be at variance with blockages of others. Studies in this area must be attuned to such disjunctures and to their implications for globalization. Third, territories are going to be affected differently by the five landscapes and their disjunctures leading to important differences among and between cultures. The

---

technoscapes The ever-fluid, global configurations of high and low, mechanical and informational technology and the wide range of material (Internet, e-mail) that now moves so freely and quickly around the globe and across borders; one of Appadurai's landscapes.

financescapes The processes by which huge sums of money move through nations and around the world at great speed; one of Appadurai's landscapes.

mediascapes The electronic capability to produce and transmit information around the world as well as the images of the world that these media create and disseminate; one of Appadurai's landscapes.

ideoscapes Largely political images either produced by states and in line with their ideology, or the images and counter-ideologies produced by movements that seek to supplant those in power, or at least to gain a piece of that power; one of Appadurai's landscapes.

focus on landscapes and their disjunctures points globalization studies in a set of unique directions. However, it is in line with the idea that globalization is much more associated with heterogenization than homogenization.

ECONOMIC THEORY

While there are many theories of the economic aspects of globalization, the most important perspectives, at least in sociology, tend to be those associated with Marxian theory, that are neo-Marxian in nature. Two major examples are discussed in this section.

Neo-Liberalism

Neo-liberalism is a theory that is particularly applicable to economics (especially the market and trade), as well as politics (especially the need to limit the government's involvement in, and control over, the market and trade). It is not only an important theory in itself, but it has also strongly influenced other thinking and theorizing about both of those domains. This is especially the case with various neo-Marxian economic theories that are highly critical of neo-liberalism. In the following section we will deal with two of the major neo-Marxian alternatives to neo-liberalism.

A number of well-known scholars, especially economists, are associated with neo-liberalism. We will briefly examine some of the ideas of one neo-liberal economist—William Easterly—here in order to give the reader a sense of this perspective from the point of view of one of its supporters.

Easterly is opposed to any form of collectivism and state planning, either as they were espoused and practiced in, for example, the Soviet Union or are today by the UN, other economists, and so on. Collectivism failed in the Soviet Union and, in Easterly's view, it will fail today. It will fail because it inhibits, if not destroys, freedom and freedom, especially economic freedom, is highly correlated with economic success. This is the case because economic freedom allows for searches for success that are decentralized; such searches go the heart of the idea of a free market. Economic freedom and the free market are great favorites of neo-liberal economists.

Easterly offers several reasons why economic freedom is related to economic success. First, it is extremely difficult to know in advance which economic actions will succeed and which will fail. Economic freedom permits a multitude of actions and those that fail are weeded out. Over time, what remains, in the main, are the successful actions and they serve to facilitate a higher standard of living. Central planners can never have nearly as much knowledge as myriad individuals seeking success and learning from their failures and from those of others. Second, markets offer continuous feedback on which actions are succeeding and failing; central planners lack such feedback. Third, economic freedom leads to the ruthless reallocation of resources to those actions that are succeeding; central planners often have vested interests that prevent such a reallocation. Fourth, economic freedom permits large and rapid increases in scale by financial markets and corporate organizations; central planners lack the flexibility to make large-scale changes rapidly. Finally, because of sophisticated contractual protections, individuals and corporations are willing to take great risks; central planners are risk-averse because of their personal vulnerability if things go wrong.

Created by John Locke (1632–1704), Adam Smith (1723–1790), and others, classical *liberal theory* came to be termed neo-liberalism, at least by some, as a result of developments in the 1930s. The term **neo-liberalism** involves a combination of the political commitment to individual liberty with *neo*classical economics devoted to the free market and opposed to state intervention in that market. Entrepreneurs are to be liberated, markets and trade are to be free, states are to be supportive of this and to keep interventions to a minimum, and there are to be strong property rights.

Neo-liberalism emerged during the Depression era, at least in part, in reaction to Keynesian economics and its impact on the larger society. The market, entrepreneurs, and corporations, inspired in part by the then-predominant theories of John Maynard Keynes (1883–1946), came to be limited by a number of constraints (social and political) and a strong regulative environment. In addition, calls for a revitalization of liberal ideas were spurred by the need to counter the collectivism (Marxian theory) that dominated much thinking and many political systems in the early 20th century.

The intellectual leaders of this revitalization were economists, especially members of the Austrian School including Friedrich van Hayek (1899–1992) and Ludwig von Mises (1881–1973). An organization devoted to liberal ideas—the Mont Pelerin Society (MPS)—was created in 1947. Its members were alarmed by the expansion of collectivist socialism (especially in, and sponsored by, the Soviet Union) and the aggressive intervention by liberal governments in the market (e.g., Franklin Roosevelt's "New Deal"). Those associated with MPS, especially the famous and highly influential Chicago economist, Milton Friedman (1912–2006), played a key role in the efforts to protect traditional liberal ideas, to develop neo-liberal theory, and to sponsor their utilization by countries throughout the world.

Neo-liberalism as a theory comes in various forms, but all are undergirded by some or all of the following ideas:

- Great faith is placed in the *free market* and its rationality. The market needs to be allowed to operate free of any impediments, especially those imposed by the nation-state and other political entities. The free operation of the market will in the "long run" advantage just about everyone and bring about both improved economic welfare and greater individual freedom (and a democratic political system). To help bring this about, it is important

---

neo-liberalism A theory that combines the political commitment to individual liberty with *neo*classical economics devoted to the free market and opposed to state intervention in that market.

to champion, support, and expand a wide range of technological, legal and institutional arrangements that support the market and its freedom. The free market is so important that neo-liberals equate it with capitalism. Further, the principles of the free market are not restricted to the economy (and the polity); transactions in every sphere of life (family, education, culture) *should* also be free like those in the economy.

- The key, if not only, actor in the market is the *individual;* neo-liberalism is radically individualistic.
- Related to the belief in the free market is a parallel belief in *free trade.*
- Where there are restraints on the free market and free trade, the theory leads to a commitment to *deregulation* to limit or eliminate such restraints. Free markets and free trade are linked to a *democratic political system.* Thus the political system, especially the freedom of democracy, is associated with economic well-being and with the freedom of individuals to amass great individual wealth.
- There is a commitment to *low taxes* and to *tax cuts* (especially for the wealthy) where taxes are deemed too high and too burdensome. Low taxes and tax cuts are believed to stimulate the economy by encouraging people to earn more and ultimately to invest and to spend more.
- *Tax cuts for business and industry* are also encouraged with the idea that they would use the tax savings to invest more in their operations and infrastructure, thereby generating more business, income and profits. This is seen as benefiting not only business and industry, but society as whole. Higher profits would "trickle down" and benefit most people in society.
- Spending on *welfare should be minimized* and the *safety net* for the poor should be *greatly reduced.* Such spending and such a welfare system are seen as hurting economic growth and even as harming the poor. Cuts in welfare are designed to reduce government expenditures and thereby to allow the government to cut taxes and/or to invest in more "productive" undertakings. It also is presumed that without the safety net more poor people would be forced to find work, often at minimum wage or with low pay. More such workers presumably allow companies to increase productivity and profits. Reduction of the safety net also creates a larger "reserve army" that business can draw on in good economic times in order to expand its workforce.
- There is a strong and generalized belief in *limited government.* The theory is that no government or government agency can do things as well as the market (the failure of the Soviet Union is seen as proof of that). Among other things, this leaves a government that is, at least theoretically, less able, or unable, to intervene in the market. It also presumably means a less expensive government, one that would need to collect less in taxes. This, in turn, would put more money in the hands of the public, especially the wealthier members of society who, in recent years, have benefited most from tax cuts. The state must not only be limited, but its job is to cooperate with open global markets.

- There is great belief in the need for the *global capitalist system to continue to expand*. It is presumed that such expansion would bring with it increased prosperity (but for which members of society?) and decreased poverty.

While most of the above deals with the neo-liberal economy, a few ideas apply to the closely linked neo-liberal state. More concretely and directly, the neo-liberal state should:

- Provide a climate that is supportive of business and its ability to accumulate capital. This should be done even if certain actions (e.g., raising interest rates by the Federal Reserve) lead to higher unemployment for the larger population.
- Focus on furthering, facilitating and stimulating (where necessary) the interests of business. This is done in the belief that business success will benefit everyone. However, many believe that neo-liberalism has benefited comparatively few people and areas of the world.
- Privatize sectors formerly run by it (e.g., education, telecommunications, transportation) in order to open up these areas for business and profit-making. It seeks to be sure that those sectors that cannot be privatized are "cost effective" and "accountable."
- Work to allow the free movement of capital among and between economic sectors and geographic regions.
- Extol the virtues of free competition, although it is widely believed that the state actually works in support of the monopolization of markets by business interests.
- Work against groups (e.g., unions, social movements) that operate to restrain business interests and their efforts to accumulate capital.
- Work to reduce barriers to the free movement of capital across national borders and to the creation of new markets.
- Bail out financial institutions if they are in danger of collapse (as in the 2007–8 cases of Bear Stearns, Fannie Mae and Freddie Mac, AIG, Citibank).

Overall, critics argue that the neo-liberal state favors elites, but seeks to conceal that fact by seeming to be democratic; in fact, it is in the eyes of many deeply antidemocratic. Its emphasis on things like freedom and liberty is largely restricted to the market.

Contrary to the established view, neo-liberalism has not made the state irrelevant. Rather, the institutions and practices of the state have been transformed to better attune them to the needs and interests of the neo-liberal market and economy.

However, the neo-liberal state is riddled with internal contradictions. For one thing, its authoritarianism co-exists uncomfortably with its supposed interest in individual freedom and democracy. For another, while it is committed to stability, its operations, especially in support of financial (and other) speculation, lead to increased instability. Then there is commitment to competition while it operates on behalf of monopolization. Most generally, there is the contradiction that its public support for the well-being of everyone is given the lie by its actions in support of the economic elites.

Critiquing Neo-Liberalism

The Early Thinking of Karl Polanyi   Much of the contemporary critique of neo-liberalism, especially as it relates to economics, is traceable to the work of Karl Polanyi (1886–1964), especially his 1944 book, *The Great Transformation: The Political and Economic Origins of Our Time*. He is the great critic of a limited focus on the economy, especially the focus of economic liberalism on the self-regulating, or unregulated, market, as well as on basing all on self-interest. In his view, these are not universal principles, but rather were unprecedented developments associated with the advent of capitalism. Polanyi shows that the *laissez-faire* system came into existence with the help of the state and it was able to continue to function as a result of state actions. Furthermore, if the *laissez-faire* system was left to itself, it threatened to destroy society. Indeed, it was such threats, as well as real dangers, that led to counter-reactions by society and the state (e.g., socialism, communism, the New Deal) to protect themselves from the problems of a free market, especially protection of the products of, and those who labored in, it. The expansion of the laissez-faire market and self-protective reaction against it by the state and society is called the **double movement.** While economic liberalism saw such counter-reactions (including any form of protectionism) as "mistakes" that disrupted the operation of the economic markets, Polanyi saw them as necessary and desirable reactions to the evils of the free market. Polanyi saw the self-regulating market as an absurd idea. He also described as mythical the liberal idea that socialists, communists, New Dealers, and so on were involved in a conspiracy against liberalism and the free market. Rather than being a conspiracy, what took place was a natural, a "spontaneous," collective reaction by society and its various elements that were threatened by the free market. In his time, Polanyi saw a reversal of the tendency for the economic system to dominate society. This promised to end the evils produced by the dominance of the free market system, and also to produce *more*, rather than less, freedom. That is, Polanyi believed that collective planning and control would produce more freedom, more freedom for all, than was then available in the liberal economic system.

   It is interesting to look back on Polanyi's ideas with the passage of more than sixty years since their publication and especially with the rise of a global economy dominated by the kind of free market system he so feared and despised. Polanyi's hope lay with society and the nation-state, but these have been rendered far less powerful with the rise of globalization, especially the global economy. Very telling here is Margaret Thatcher's (in)famous statement: "There is no such thing as society." Without powerful social and political influences, one wonders where collective planning and social control over the market are to come from. Clearly, such planning and control are more inadequate than ever in the global age. Beyond that, one wonders whether the creation of truly global

---

double movement   The expansion of the laissez-faire market and the self-protective reaction against it by the state and society.

planning and control is either possible or desirable. Nevertheless, it is likely that were he alive today, the logic of Polanyi's position would lead him to favor global planning and control because of his great fears of a free market economy, now far more powerful and dangerous because it exists on a global scale.

The great global economic crisis of 2007–2009 underscores the importance of Polanyi's ideas. The market had come to be allowed unprecedented freedom; restraints on it turned out to be limited or nonexistent. The result was a series of excesses (mortgage loans to those who should not have qualified for them; excessively risky undertakings by financial institutions; financial instruments that were opaque [e.g., "derivatives"] and that diffused responsibility for bad loans [mortgage-backed securities], etc.) that led to the collapse of the American housing market, the credit crunch and eventually a global economic meltdown. Polanyi would have said that the cause of all of this was a lack of state control over the market. In fact, in wake of the crisis we are witnessing a resurfacing of interest in regulating the market and the economy.

(More) Contemporary Criticisms of Neo-Liberalism.   Among the problems with neo-liberalism as a theory is the fact that it assumes that everyone in the world wants very narrow and specific types of economic well-being (to be well-off economically, if not rich) and political freedom (democracy). The fact is, there are great cultural differences in the ways in which well-being (e.g., to not have to work very hard) and freedom (e.g., to be unfettered by the state even if it is not democratically chosen) are defined. Neo-liberalism very often comes down to the North, the United States, and/or global organizations (e.g., International Monetary Fund), seeking to impose *their* definitions of well-being and freedom on other parts of the world. Furthermore, there is great variation on this among individuals in each of these societies with the result that these definitions are different from at least some of theirs, but are nonetheless imposed on them.

Another problem lies in the fact that the theory conceals or obscures the social and material interests of those who push such an economic system with its associated technological, legal, and institutional systems. These are *not* being pursued because everyone in the world wants them or will benefit from them, but because *some*, usually in the North, are greatly advantaged by them and therefore push them.

Among the other criticisms of neo-liberalism are the fact that it has produced financial crises in various countries throughout the world (e.g., Mexico, Argentina), its economic record has been dismal since it has redistributed wealth (from poor to rich) rather than generating new wealth, it has sought to commodify *everything*, it has helped to degrade the environment, and so on. Furthermore, there are signs that it is failing such as deficit financing in the United States and China, signs of more immediate crisis (e.g., burgeoning budget deficits, the bailout of financial institutions), and evidence that U.S. global hegemony is crumbling.

The Death of Neo-Liberalism?   It is arguable that the economic crisis of 2007–9 spelled the beginning of the end of neo-liberalism (see box). In a speech in late 2008 French President Sarkozy said: "The idea of the absolute power of the

Contemporary Application
Is Global Neo-Liberal Capitalism Dead?

The deep economic recession that began in the United States in late 2007 deepened in the ensuing months and years and spread rapidly throughout much of the world threatening globalization, in particular neo-liberal economic globalization. There have been prior epochs of globalization (e.g., the late 1800s until 1914) and they were ended by abrupt changes such as war (e.g., World War I) and a recession/ depression. A frequent reaction in such times is for nations to begin to close their borders and to turn inward, especially economically; to engage in "protectionism." The goal is to husband remaining resources and protect the nation as much as possible from the disastrous effects of negative global flows of all types (e.g., military invasion, a run on stock markets and banks). However, such protectionism is anathema to capitalism in general, but especially neo-liberal global capitalism, which is premised on free markets and free trade. The partially or completely closed borders that result from protectionism serve to block, at least in part, the flow of goods, money and the like that is the lifeblood of neo-liberal global capitalism. During the global economic crisis that began in late 2007, the dangers posed by protectionism to global capitalism led to warnings being raised, most notably by the President of the United States (the major source and the center of neo-liberalism and capitalism), that nations should not react to it by resorting to protectionism.

However, a broader issue may have been raised by this most recent global economic crisis and that is the future of global capitalism, especially in its neo-liberal form. The crisis commenced in the United States and began because of the lack of restraints on, and regulations over, capitalist enterprises, especially financial institutions and their highly risky investments. Many institutions throughout the world had bought some of these high-risk investments (not fully understanding how risky they were) and losses cascaded around the world. Losses across the world led to other kinds of losses and a growing lack of confidence in the global economic system led to deep declines in many stock markets, and economies in general, throughout

markets that should not be constrained by any rule, by any political intervention, was a mad idea. The idea that markets are always right was a mad idea."[4] Referring implicitly to the global economic system dominated to that point by neo-liberalism, Sarkozy argued that "we need to rebuild the whole world financial and monetary system from scratch."[5] In other words, we need to scuttle the remnants of the global neo-liberal economic system, just as the Keynesian system was scuttled as neo-liberalism gained ascendancy, and replace it with some as yet undefined alternative. Where and how far this goes remains to be seen, but believers in neo-liberalism have not disappeared and their ideas, perhaps in some new form, are likely to resurface when the dust of the current economic crisis settles.

If nothing else, this economic crisis has reminded us of the importance of not only the neo-Marxian critique of neo-liberalism, but also of neo-Marxian alternatives to it. We turn now to two major examples of neo-Marxian thinking.

Contemporary Applications—Continued

the world. Job losses accelerated, poverty increased, and fear and worry over the economy mounted. Many, including the President of France, Nicolas Sarkozy, blamed American-style, risk-taking, neo-liberal capitalism and began a search for global alternatives to it.

The issue is: Is there a viable alternative to a neo-liberal global economy? There are, of course, many ways to run an economy (e.g., socialism), including a global economy, but the most likely alternative seems to be some efforts to reform neo-liberalism both in terms of the way it operates in the United States (and elsewhere), as well as globally. Thus, global neo-liberal capitalism does *not* seem to be dead. Rather, what is likely to happen once the immediate crisis passes is a wide range of efforts to reform the system so that its worst inadequacies and abuses are limited or eliminated. What this will mean is the creation of a variety of regulations and restraints on capitalism and its enterprises both nationally and globally. After all, many blamed the crash that began in December, 2007 on the relaxation, or inadequacy of, restraints on the system, especially in the United States.

So, we will see an era of "restrained" neo-liberal global capitalism. At a general level, neo-liberalism regards any form of restraint as anathema to its basic principles. More concretely, if history is any guide, capitalistic businesses will find those restraints objectionable and in their pursuit of ever-higher profits will seek, and eventually find, ways to circumvent them. Without constant vigilance, the world will find itself faced with a renewal of economic excess and the possibility of yet another global economic meltdown in the not-too-distant future. From the point of view of Marxian and neo-Marxian theory, this is just another example of the "boom and bust" character of capitalism. The big question is whether the great gains in boom periods (which tend to go to a relatively small portion of the population) are worth the disastrous consequences of the busts (especially for those least able to afford an economic setback). If not, then an alternative to neo-liberal global capitalism is needed.

Neo-Marxian Theoretical Alternatives to Neo-Liberalism

We have already presented, at least implicitly, critiques of neoliberalism from a neo-Marxian perspective, but neo-Marxists have done more than critique neoliberalism, they have developed their own perspectives on, and theories of, capitalism. While neoliberalism is supportive of capitalism, the neo-Marxists are, needless to say, critical of it. In this section we offer two examples of a neo-Marxian approach that are explicitly and implicitly critical of the neo-liberal theory outlined in this chapter. However, they are not only of interest as critiques; they are important in their own right.

Transnational Capitalism

Leslie Sklair distinguishes between two systems of globalization. The first—the capitalist system of globalization—is the one that is now predominant. The other is the socialist system that is not yet in existence, but is foreshadowed by current antiglobalization movements, especially those oriented toward greater human rights throughout the world. The antiglobalization movements, and the possibility of a socialist form, are made possible by the problems in the current system of globalization, especially class polarization and the increasing ecological unsustainability of capitalist globalization.

While the nation-state remains important, it is the case that Sklair focuses on transnational practices that are able to cut across boundaries—including those created by states—with the implication that territorial boundaries are of declining importance in capitalist globalization. As a Marxist, Sklair accords priority to economic transnational practices and it is in this context that one of the central aspects of his analysis—**transnational corporations**—predominate. Underlying this is the idea that capitalism has moved away from being an international system (since the nation [-state] is of declining significance) to a globalizing system that is decoupled from any specific geographic territory or state.

The second transnational practice of great importance is political and here the **transnational capitalist class** predominates. However, it is not made up of capitalists in the traditional Marxian sense of the term. That is, they do not necessarily own the means of production. Sklair differentiates among four " fractions" of the transnational capitalist class. The first is the *corporate fraction* made up of executives of transnational corporations and their local affiliates. Second, there is a *state fraction* composed of globalizing state and interstate bureaucrats and politicians. The third, *technical fraction,* is made up of globalizing professionals. Finally, there is the *consumerist fraction* encompassing merchants and media executives. This is obviously a very different group than Marx thought of in conceptualizing the capitalist.

The transnational capitalist class may not be capitalist in a traditional sense of the term, but it is transnational in various ways. First, its "members" tend to share global (as well as local) interests. Second, they seek to exert various types of control across nations. That is, they exert economic control in the workplace, political control in both domestic and international politics, and culture-ideological control in everyday life across international borders. Third, they tend to share a global rather than a local perspective on a wide range of issues. Fourth, they come from many different countries, but increasingly they see themselves as citizens of the world and not just of their place of birth. Finally,

---

transnational corporations   Corporations that dominate the contemporary capitalist global economy and whose actions are largely unconstrained by the borders of nation-states.

transnational capitalist class   Not made up of capitalists in the traditional Marxian sense of the term; its members do not necessarily own the means of production. Includes four "fractions"—*corporate,* made up of executives of transnational corporations and their local affiliates; *state,* composed of globalizing state and interstate bureaucrats and politicians; *technical,* made up of globalizing professionals; *consumerist,* encompassing merchants and media executives.

wherever they may be at any given time, they share similar lifestyles, especially in terms of the goods and services they consume.

The third transnational practice is culture-ideology and here Sklair accords great importance to the **culture-ideology of consumerism** in capitalist globalization. While the focus is on culture and ideology, this ultimately involves the economy by adding an interest in consumption to the traditional concern with production (and the transnational corporations) in economic approaches in general, and Marxian theories in particular. It is in this realm that the ability to exert ideological control over people scattered widely throughout the globe has increased dramatically primarily through the greater reach and sophistication of advertising, the media, and the bewildering array of consumer goods that are marketed by and through them. Ultimately, they all serve to create a global mood to consume that benefits transnational corporations, as well as the advertising and media corporations that both are examples of such corporations and profit from them.

Ultimately, Sklair is interested in the relationship among the transnational social practices and institutions that dominate each by arguing that transnational corporations utilize the transnational capitalist class to develop and solidify the consumerist culture and ideology that is increasingly necessary to feed the demands of the capitalist system of production. Indeed, it is this relationship that defines global capitalism today and it is the most important force in ongoing changes in the world.

As a Marxist, Sklair is not only interested in critically analyzing capitalist globalization, but in articulating an alternative to it and its abuses. He sees some promising signs in the protectionism of some countries that see themselves as exploited by transnational corporations. Also hopeful are new social movements such as the green movement seeking a more sustainable environment and the various anti-globalization groups that have sprung up in recent years. He is particularly interested in various human rights movements in which, he believes, can be found the seeds of the alternative to capitalist globalization, that is socialist globalization. He predicts that these and other movements will gain momentum in the 21st century as they increasingly resist the ways in which globalization has been appropriated by transnational corporations. In fact, in good Marxian dialectical terms, he sees the success of capitalist globalization sowing the seeds of its own destruction. That is, its expansion tends to provide the opponents with resources (derived from the economic success of transnational capitalism), organizational forms (copied from the successful organizations in global capitalism), and most obviously a clarity of purpose. That is, as the transnational corporations grow more successful, so do their abuses and the need to supplant them as the central players in the global system.

---

culture-ideology of consumerism   An ideology that affects people scattered widely throughout the globe with the greater reach and sophistication of advertising, the media, and consumer goods. Ultimately, a global mood to consume is created that benefits transnational corporations, as well as the advertising and media corporations.

Empire   The most important and widely discussed and debated Marxian approach to globalization is Michael Hardt and Antonio Negri's *Empire*. Although they have reservations about postmodern social theory, they analyze the postmodernization of the global economy. They associate modernity with **imperialism**, the defining characteristic of which is a nation(s) at the center that controls and exploits, especially economically, a number of areas throughout the world. In a postmodern move, they "decenter" this process thereby defining empire as a postmodern reality in which such dominance exists, but *without* any single nation (or any other entity) at its center. To put this another way, modern sovereignty can be traced to a *place*, but in its postmodern form as empire sovereignty exists in a nonplace. That is, there is no center, it is deterritorialized, it is virtual in the form of communication (especially through the media), and, as a result, the spectacle of the empire is everywhere; it is omnipresent.

Empire does not yet exist fully; it is in formation at the moment, but we can already get a sense of its parameters. Empire governs the world with a single logic of rule, but there is no single power at the heart of empire. Instead of a single source of command, in empire power is dispersed throughout society and the globe. Even the United States, in spite of its seeming hegemony in the world today, is not an empire in these terms and does not lie at the heart of Hardt and Negri's sense of an empire. However, the sovereignty of the United States does constitute an important precursor to empire and the United States continues to occupy a privileged position in the world today. However, it is in the process of being supplanted by empire.

Empire lacks (or will) geographic or territorial boundaries. It can also be seen as lacking temporal boundaries in the sense that it seeks (albeit unsuccessfully) to suspend history and to exist for all eternity. It also can be seen as lacking a lower boundary in that it seeks to expand down into the depths of the social world. This means that it seeks control not only of the basics of the social world (thought, action, interaction, groups), but to go further in an effort to use biopower to control human nature and population; both peoples' brains and their bodies. In a way, empire is far more ambitious than imperialism in that it seeks to control the entirety of life down to its most basic levels.

The key to the global power of **empire** lies in the fact that it is (or seeks to be) a new juridical power. That is, it is based on such things as the constitution of order, norms, ethical truths, and a common notion of what is right. This

---

imperialism   The control and exploitation, especially economically, of a number of areas throughout the world by a nation(s) at the center.

empire   A decentered, postmodern Marxian perspective on globalization and the exertion of power around the world based on new juridical power such as the constitution of order, norms, ethical truths, and a common notion of what is right. It can, in the name of what is "right," intervene anywhere in the world in order to deal with what it considers humanitarian problems, to guarantee accords, and to impose peace on those who may not want it or even see it as peace.

juridical formation is the source of power of empire. Thus, it can, in the name of what is "right," intervene anywhere in the world in order to deal with what it considers humanitarian problems, to guarantee accords, and to impose peace on those who may not want it or even see it as peace. More specifically, it can engage in "just wars" in the name of this juridical formation; the latter legitimates the former. Such wars become a kind of sacred undertaking. The enemy is anyone or anything that the juridical formation sees as a threat to ethical order in the world. Thus, the right to engage in just war is seen as boundless, encompassing the entire space of civilization. The right to engage in it is also seen as boundless in time; it is permanent, eternal. In a just war, ethically grounded military action is legitimate and its goal is to achieve the desired order and peace. Thus, empire is not based on force, but on the ability to project force in the service of that which is right (precursors of this can be seen in the two U.S. wars against Iraq, as well as the incursion into Afghanistan).

Empire is based on a triple imperative. First, it seeks to incorporate all that it can. It appears to be magnanimous and it operates with a liberal facade. However, in the process of inclusion, it creates a smooth world in which differences, resistance, and conflict are eliminated. Second, empire differentiates and affirms differences. While those who are different are celebrated culturally, they are set aside juridically. Third, once the differences are in place, empire seeks to hierarchize and to manage the hierarchy and the differences embedded in it. It is hierarchization and management that are the real powers of empire.

Empire is, then, a postmodern Marxian perspective on globalization and the exertion of power around the world. However, instead of capitalists, or capitalist nations, exerting that power, it is the much more nebulous empire that is in control. If there are no more capitalists in empire, what about the proletariat? To Hardt and Negri, the time of the proletariat is over. But if the proletariat no longer exists to oppose empire, where is the opposition to it to come from? After all, operating from a Marxian perspective, Hardt and Negri must come up with an oppositional force. In fact, they do not disappoint on this score and label that oppositional group the multitude. This is an interesting choice of terms for many reasons. For one thing it is much more general and abstract than the proletariat and also moves us away from a limited focus on the economy. Secondly, it is clear that there are lots of at least potential opponents of the empire; indeed, those in control in the empire constitute only a small minority vis-à-vis the multitude.

The **multitude** is that collection of people throughout the world that sustains empire in various ways, including, but *not* restricted to, its labor (it is the real productive force in empire). Among other ways, it also sustains it by buying into the culture-ideology of consumption and, more importantly, in actually consuming a variety of its offerings. Like capitalism and its relationship to the

---

multitude   A collection of people throughout the world that sustains empire in various ways, including, but not restricted to, its labor (it is the real productive force in empire), but it also has the power, at least potentially, to overthrow empire.

proletariat, empire is a parasite on the multitude and its creativity and produc-tivity. Like Marx's proletariat (which all but disappears in this theory), the mul-titude is a force for creativity in empire. Also like the proletariat, the multitude is capable of overthrowing empire through the autonomous creation of a counter-empire. The counter-empire, like empire, is, or would be, a global phenomenon created out of, and becoming, global flows and exchanges. Globalization leads to deterritorialization (and the multitude itself is a force in deterritorialization and is deterritorialized) and the latter is a prerequisite to the global liberation of the multitude. That is, with deterritorialization social revolution can, as Marx predicted, occur, perhaps for the first time, on a global level.

Thus, while Hardt and Negri are certainly critics of globalization, whether it be modern capitalist imperialism or postmodern empire, they also see a utopian potential in globalization. Thus, globalization is *not* the problem, but rather the form that it has taken, or takes, in imperialism and empire. That utopian potential has always been there, but in the past it has been smothered by modern sovereign powers through ideological control or military force. Empire now occupies, or soon will, that controlling position, but its need to suppress that potential is counterbalanced by the need of the multitude to manifest and express it. Ultimately, it is in globalization that there exists the potential for universal freedom and equality. Further, globalization prevents us from fall-ing back into the particularism and isolationism that has characterized much of human history. Those processes, of course, would serve to impede the global change sought by the multitude. More positively, as globalization progresses, it serves to push us more and more in the direction of the creation of counter-empire. This focus on the global serves to distinguish Hardt and Negri from other postmodernists and post-Marxists who tend to focus on the local and the problems and potential that exists there. In contrast, in their view, a focus on the local serves to obscure the fact that the sources of both our major problems and our liberation exist at the global level, in empire.

While Hardt and Negri foresee counter-empire, they, like Marx in the case of communism, offer no blueprint for how to get there or what it might look like. Like communism to Marx, counter-empire will arise out of actual prac-tice (*praxis*), especially that of the multitude. Counter-empire must be global, it must be everywhere, and it must be opposed to empire. Counter-empire is made increasingly likely because empire is losing its ability to control the multitude. Thus, it must redouble its efforts (e.g., through police power) and this serves to mobilize the multitude and make counter-empire more likely. As postmodernists, Hardt and Negri reject a focus on the agent of the type found in Marxian theory, specifically the centrality accorded to the proletarian rev-olutionary agent who is increasingly conscious of exploitation by capitalism. Instead, they focus on such nonagential, collective actions by the multitude as desertion, migration, and nomadism. In accord with their postmodern orienta-tion and the latter's focus on the body, Hardt and Negri urge a new "barba-rism" involving new bodily forms of the kind that are now appearing in the realm of gender, sexuality, and esthetic mutations (such as tattooing and body piercing). Such bodies are less likely to submit to external control and more

Contemporary Applications
The Great Global Economic Meltdown of 2008

If there was any lingering doubt about the reality of globalization, it was put to rest by the global economic crisis that began in 2007 and reached a crescendo (at least for the moment) in late 2008. It began as a largely U.S. problem relating specifically to its housing market, bad mortgage loans, and accelerating foreclosures on those unable to keep up with their mortgage payments. What was at first seen as a small and manageable American problem soon grew out of control in the United States and ultimately spread throughout much of the world.

It turned out that many of these bad mortgages has been carved up into little pieces and packaged as financial instruments (they had been "securitized," turned into mortgage-backed securities) that had been sold to many financial institutions not only in the United States but throughout the world. They had bought them because of faith in the U.S. economy, in the safety of mortgage loans (backed by real estate), and ultimately because small pieces of so many mortgages in any given financial instrument seemed to mean that the failure of a few mortgages would have little impact on the instrument as a whole.

However, as the number of bad mortgages increased dramatically, these financial instruments were increasingly threatened and they declined significantly in value. Soon major American financial institutions came under increasing pressure and a number failed (e.g., Lehman Brothers, Indy Mac and Washington Mutual banks), or were bailed out by the U.S. government (Fannie Mae, Freddie Mac, AIG). These developments put at risk financial institutions throughout the world which found themselves holding financial instruments whose value was in freefall.

Prior to this, there had been much talk that the global economy had "decoupled" from, was no longer closely tied, to the American economy. Many areas (EU) and nations (China, India, Brazil) had become so successful economically that it was believed that they could withstand a decline in the U.S. economy by either trading more with each other and/or increasing consumption of their products, as well as those of other successful economies. To many, it seemed that the economic crises that had previously befallen the world (e.g., the Asian financial crisis of the late 1990s) were a thing of the past.

However, it turned out this was not the case and what was an American economic problem rapidly became a global economic problem. Banks and other financial institutions throughout much of the world came under increasing pressure; some failed and others were bailed out by their governments. Many governments also injected large sums of money into their economies to keep them afloat. Some nations failed almost completely (e.g., Iceland) or experienced severe economic problems and in some cases (e.g., Hungary, Pakistan) had to be helped by financial aid from the International Monetary Fund (IMF). Consumption declined globally and, as a result, production declined in response to lower demand. Global oil prices, which had risen to almost $150 a barrel, declined to almost $40 a barrel because of reduced demand as global economies slowed. The demand for other commodities (e.g., copper) also fell and their prices also declined precipitously.

These and other aspects of the economic crisis of 2007–8 indicated how tightly intertwined the world had become and how easily economic problems flowed throughout the world. There was little that any given region or nation-state could do to protect itself from these negative economic flows and from globalization more generally. Of course, this cuts both ways and when the global economy improves those improvements, like the problems, will flow throughout much of the world.

likely to create a new life; the basis of counter-empire. Thus, the revolutionary force is not a conscious agent, but new bodily, corporeal forms.

While Hardt and Negri retain a Marxian interest in production, they do recognize a new world of production and work in which immaterial, intellectual, and communicative labor is increasingly central. Thus, control over those engaged in such work—a key element and increasing proportion of multitude—is of increasing importance. However, while they are controlled through global communication and ideology (especially via the media), it is also through communication and ideology that the revolutionary potential of the multitude will be expressed. The key thing about communication is that it flows easily and effectively across the globe. This makes it easier for empire to exert control, to organize production globally, and to make its justification of itself and its actions immanent within that communication. Conversely, of course, it is also the mechanism by which the multitude can ultimately create counter-empire.

POLITICAL THEORY

There are several theories, most of which are deeply rooted in political science rather than sociology that deal with globalization. **International relations** (IR) focuses on the relations among and between the nation-states of the world. They are viewed as distinct actors in the world, occupying well-defined territories, and as sovereign within their own borders. There is also an emphasis on a distinct and well-defined inter-state system.

Within IR, **political realism** begins with the premise that international politics is based on power, organized violence and ultimately war. It assumes that nation-states are the predominant actors on the global stage; that they act as coherent units in the global arena; that force is not only a usable, but also an effective, method by which nation-states wield power on the global stage; and that military issues are of utmost importance in world politics.

Complex interdependence sees nation-states relating to one another through multiple channels; formally and informally; through normal channels and so-called "back channels." Where complex interdependence differs from realism is in the importance accorded to these informal channels where,

---

international relations (IR)   A political theory that focuses on the relations among and between the nation-states of the world.

political realism   A political theory that operates on the premise that international politics is based on power, organized violence, and ultimately war.

complex interdependence   A political theory that sees nation-states relating to one another through multiple channels and that emphasizes informal channels where, for example, entities (e.g., MNCs) other than the state connect societies to one another.

for example, entities (e.g., MNCs) other than the state connect societies to one another. There is no clear hierarchy of interstate relationships and it is certainly not the case that military issues always, or even often, predominate. Coalitions arise within and between nation-states on these issues. Conflict may or may not arise and, if conflict arises, it varies greatly in terms of degree of intensity. Complex interdependence tends to lead to the decline in, or even the disappearance of, the use of military force by one nation-state against other(s) within a given region or alliance, although military action may continue to occur outside that region or bloc. While international organizations have only a minor role to play in the realist view of the world, they play an expanded role from the perspective of complex interdependence. Such organizations bring together representatives from various countries, set agendas, serve as catalysts for the formation of coalitions, serve as arenas from which political initiatives arise, and are helpful to weak states in playing a larger role in the international arena. Thus, the complex interdependence perspective continues to focus on relationships among nation-states, but takes a much wider and broader view of the nature of those relationships.

There is also a variety of positions that are at variance with IR and its derivatives and that offer fundamental challenges to it. Among these are a wide range of other scholars associated with IPE (international political economy) that challenge IR. Among other things, they focus more on power and critique the state-centrism of IR, which ignores other entities with political and economic power, especially the corporation.

An over-riding interest in the literature on globalization and politics is the fate of the nation-state in the age of globalization. Many see the nation-state as threatened by various global processes, especially global economic flows. Some go so far as to argue that the state is now a minor player globally in comparison to a huge and growing borderless global economy that nation-states are unable to control. While nation-states once controlled markets, it is now the markets that often control the nation-states.

There is a variety of other factors threatening the autonomy of the nation-state, including flows of information, illegal immigrants, new social movements, terrorists, criminals, drugs, money (including laundered money, and other financial instruments), sex-trafficking, and much else. Many of these flows have been made possible by the development and continual refinement of technologies of all sorts. The nation-state has also been weakened by the growing power of global and transnational organizations (e.g., the EU) that operate largely free of the control of nation-states. Another factor is the growth of global problems (AIDs, TB) that cannot be handled, or handled very well, by a nation-state operating on its own. A more specific historical factor is the end of the Cold War, which had been a powerful force in unifying, or at least holding together, some nation-states. One example is Yugoslavia and its dissolution at the end of the Cold War, but the main one, of course, is the dissolution of the Soviet Union into a number of independent nation-states (Russia, Ukraine, Georgia, etc). Then there are "failed states" (e.g., Somalia) where there is, in effect, no functioning national government as well as states that are in the process of breaking down. Clearly, failed states, and states that are disintegrating, are in no position to maintain their borders adequately.

One way of summarizing much of this is to say that the nation-state has become increasingly *porous*. While this seems to be supported by a great deal of evidence, the fact is that no nation-state has *ever* been able to control its borders completely. Thus, it is not the porosity of the nation-state that is new, but rather what is new is a dramatic *increase* in that porosity and of the kinds of flows that are capable of passing through national borders.

There are at least some who contest the position taken above. A variety of arguments is made, including that the nation-state continues to be *the* major player on the global stage, that it retains at least some power in the face of globalization, that nation-states vary greatly in their efficacy in the face of globalization, and that the rumors of the demise of the nation state are greatly exaggerated.

There are even scholars who see the role of the state as not only enduring, but even increasing in the world today. There are greater demands being placed on the state because of four major sources of collective insecurity: terrorism, economic globalization leading to problems such as outsourcing and pressures toward downsizing, threats to national identity due to immigration, and the spread of global diseases such as AIDs. Further, the state does not merely respond to these threats; it may actually find it in its interest to exaggerate or even create dangers and thereby make its citizens more insecure. A good example is the United States and British governments' arguments prior to the 2003 war with Iraq that Saddam Hussein had Weapons of Mass Destruction (WMDs) that posed a direct threat to them. The United States even claimed that Iraq could kill millions by using offshore ships to lob canisters containing lethal chemical or biological material into American cities. The collective insecurity created by such outrageous claims helped foster public opinion in favor of invading Iraq and overthrowing Saddam Hussein.

The other side of this argument in support of the nation-state is that global processes of various kinds are just not as powerful as many believe. For example, global business pales in comparison to business *within* many countries, including the United States. For another, some question the porosity of the nation-state by pointing, for example, to the fact that migration to the United States and other countries has *declined* substantially since its heights in the late 19th and early 20th centuries.

A related point is that it would be a mistake simply to see globalization as a threat to, a constraint on, the nation-state; it can also be an *opportunity* for the nation-state. For example, the demands of globalization were used as a basis to make needed changes (at least from a neo-liberal point of view) in Australian society, specifically allowing it to move away from protectionism and in the direction of (neo-)liberalization, to transform state enterprises into private enterprises, and to streamline social welfare. In this, the rhetoric of globalization, especially an exaggeration of it and its effects, was useful to those politicians who were desirous of such changes. In other words, Australian politicians used globalization as an ideology in order to reform Australian society.

OTHER THEORIES

The preceding, of course, only gives the reader a sense of a few of the types of theorizing about globalization and a few examples of each. There are many other well-known theories of globalization (e.g., ones that draw on network theory and complexity theory, or that focus on religion, sport, or the city). However, the preceding gives the reader at least a sense of the most important broad types of theorizing on, and specific theories of, globalization. Of course, the process of globalization continues, is expanding, and is constantly changing. As a result, we can expect the continuing development of theorizing about globalization, including new and innovative approaches to the topic.

Summary

1. Globalization theory emerged as a result of developments and changes in both the world as a whole as well as within academia.
2. Globalization can be analyzed culturally, economically, politically, and institutionally. A concern for homogenization/heterogenization cuts across work in all of these areas.
3. Central to the work of Giddens on globalization is losing control over the juggernaut of modernity and creating a runaway world.
4. Beck sees hope in globality with the decline of the nation-state and in transnational organizations and possibly a transnational state.
5. To Bauman, what defines the global world is a "space war" between those who have and those who do not have mobility. However, even those with mobility face grave problems.
6. Cultural theories of globalization may be divided into three paradigms—cultural differentialism, cultural convergence, and cultural hybridization.
7. Cultural differentialism adopts the view that there are lasting differences among and between cultures that are largely unaffected by globalization.
8. Huntington offers the best-known example of cultural differentialism with his focus on civilizations, the major civilizations of the world, and the likelihood of economic conflict between Sinic and Western civilization and warfare between Islamic and Western civilization.
9. Cultural convergence takes the view that globalization is leading to increasing sameness around the world.
10. Two examples of cultural convergence are the McDonaldization thesis and the idea that the world is increasingly dominated by the "grobalization" of "nothing".
11. Cultural hybridization adopts the perspective that globalization is bringing with it the mixing of cultures; the production of new and unique cultures that are not reducible to either global or local.
12. A number of theoretical ideas are associated with cultural hybridization including glocalization, hybridization, and creolization.
13. A major theory included under the heading of cultural hybridization is Appadurai's thinking on landscapes and the disjunctures among and between them.
14. Neo-liberalism is the dominant economic theory of globalization. It combines a commitment to individual liberty with the economic ideas of the free market and an opposition to state intervention in that market.
15. The excesses of neo-liberalism in the economy and the polity led to counter-reactions to it, including the work of Karl Polanyi on the "double movement," which

involves the expansion of the laissez-faire market and the self-protective reaction against it by the state and society.

16. Leslie Sklair develops a neo-Marxian economic theory of globalization that focuses on transnational capitalism, especially transnational corporations, the transnational capitalist class, and the culture-ideology of consumerism.
17. Sklair argues that transnational capitalism is providing the basis for the emergence of socialist globalization.
18. To Hardt and Negri, we are in the midst of a transition from capitalist imperialism to the dominance of empire. Empire lacks a center and is based on juridical power.
19. The multitude sustains empire, but it also has, at least potentially, the power to overthrow empire and create counter-empire.
20. There are several political theories that relate to globalization, including international relations, political realism, and complex interdependence.
21. A central issue in the study of political globalization is the degree to which the nation-state is being weakened by globalization.

Suggested Readings

ANTHONY GIDDENS   *Runaway World: How Globalization Is Reshaping Our Lives.* New York: Routledge, 2000. Perhaps today's most famous and influential contemporary theorist relates his ideas on the juggernaut of modernity to the possibility that globalization is bringing with it a runaway world.

ARJUN APPADURAI   *Modernity at Large: Cultural Dimensions of Globalization.* Minneapolis: University of Minnesota Press, 1996. An important anthropological take on globalization that is best known for its discussion of various "scapes "and the disjunctures among and between them.

BENJAMIN BARBER   *Jihad vs. McWorld.* New York: Times Books, 1995. Popular and influential work by a political scientist that sees a global split between the forces of McWorld and Jihad. However, it is likely that in order to succeed in the long term, Jihad will need to use more of the tools of McWorld (e.g., Internet, television).

GEORGE RITZER   *The Globalization of Nothing 2.* Thousand Oaks, CA: Pine Forge Press, 2007. A theory of globalization that emphasizes both heterogenization (glocalization) and homogenization (grobalization), although its most important argument is that increasing homogenization is occurring through the grobalization of nothing.

GEORGE RITZER   *The McDonaldization of Society 5.* Thousand Oaks, CA: Pine Forge Press, 2008. Develops both a theory of contemporary society building on Max Weber's theory of rationalization and a theory of increasing global homogenization as a result of the worldwide proliferation of McDonaldized forms.

GEORGE RITZER   *Globalization: A Basic Text.* Malden, MA: Blackwell, 2010.

JAMES N. ROSENAU   *Distant Proximities: Dynamics Beyond Globalization.* Princeton: Princeton University Press, 2003. A political scientist analyzes global political trends through a variety of developments that produce both "distant proximities" and increasing "fragmegration."

JAN NEDERVEEN PIETERSE   *Globalization and Culture: Global Melange.* Lanham, MD: Rowman and Littlefield, 2004. Develops a useful way of looking at three paradigms in the analysis of the relationship between culture and globalization, as well as further developing the idea of hybridization.

JOHN TOMLINSON   *Globalization and Culture.* Chicago: University of Chicago Press, 1999. Excellent overview of work on the relationship between culture and globalization, especially that which emphasizes heterogenization.

JOHN URRY   *Global Complexity.* Cambridge: Polity, 2003. Unique look at globalization through the lens of complexity or chaos theory.

JOSEPH E. STIGLITZ   *Globalization and Its Discontents.* New York: W.W. Norton, 2002. Important critique of globalization and the role played by the United States and key international organizations (e.g., IMF) in structuring globalization to the advantage of the United States and the West.

LESLIE SKLAIR   *Globalization: Capitalism and Its Alternatives.* Oxford: Oxford University Press, 2002. A neo-Marxian economic treatise that emphasizes the importance of transnational corporations, the transnational corporate class, and the culture ideology of consumerism.

MANUEL CASTELLS   *The Rise of the Network Society.* Malden, MA: Blackwell, 1996. Highly processual view of globalization that focuses on global flows and networks.

MICHAEL HARDT and ANTONIO NEGRI   *Empire.* Cambridge: Harvard University Press, 2000. Highly influential and controversial neo-Marxian approach to globalization that sees a more nebulous empire replacing capitalist imperialism and multitude taking the role of the proletariat in traditional Marxian theory.

MICHAEL HARDT and ANTONIO NEGRI   *Multitude: War and Democracy in the Age of Empire.* New York: Penguin, 2004. Important, more popularly oriented, follow-up to *Empire* that among other things further develops the elusive idea of multitude.

SAMUEL P. HUNTINGTON   *The Clash of Civilizations and the Remaking of World Order.* New York: Simon and Schuster, 1996. Perhaps *the* most controversial book on globalization. It focuses on culture "writ large," that is, civilizations, but its arguments on Islam led to the most heated critiques.

ULRICH BECK   *World Risk Society.* Cambridge: Polity Press, 1999. Beck develops further his theory of risk society, its relationship to globalization, as well as offering further insights into the latter.

ZYGMUNT BAUMAN   *Globalization: The Human Consequences.* New York: Columbia University Press, 1998. One of the most famous theorists of the day expounds on his thoughts on globalization, especially on the "space war" and the advantages that accrue to those who can move easily across space over the immobile.

Endnotes

[1]Barber's view of McWorld is not restricted to politics; he sees many other domains following the model of McWorld.

[2]For more on this, see Samuel Huntington, "The Hispanic Challenge," *Foreign Policy* March/April 2004.

[3]However, this clearly pales in comparison to the history of Western conquest.

[4]www.france24.com/en/20080926.

[5]www.france24.com/en/20080926.

Glossary

absolute spaces   are natural spaces (e.g., "green" areas) that are not colonized, rendered inauthentic, or smashed by elite economic and political forces (Lefebvre).

abstract space   This is space from the point of view of a theoretician such as an urban planner or an architect, but it is not just about ideas; it involves real, material spaces that actually replace historical spaces (which are erected on the base of absolute spaces) (Lefebvre).

accounting   The process by which people offer accounts in order to make sense of the world (ethnomethodology).

accounting practices   The ways in which one person offers an account and another person accepts or rejects that account (ethnomethodology).

accounts   The ways in which actors explain (describe, criticize, and idealize) specific situations (ethnomethodology).

act   The basic concept in Mead's theory, involving an impulse, perception of stimuli, taking action involving the object perceived, and using the object to satisfy the initial impulse.

action   Things that people do that are the result of conscious processes.

actual social identity   What a person actually is (Goffman).

adaptation   One of Parsons's four functional imperatives. A system must adjust to its environment and adjust the environment to its needs. More specifically, a system must cope with external situational dangers and contingencies.

affectual action   Nonrational action that is the result of emotion (Weber).

agency   Actions that are perpetrated by actors; what occurs would not have occurred in that way were it not for the fact that the actor intervened and took the action in question.

agents   Actors who have the ability to make a difference in the social world; they have power.

alienation   The breakdown of, the separation from, the natural interconnection between people and their productive activities, the products they produce, the fellow workers with whom they produce those things, and with what they are potentially capable of becoming (Marx).

310

altruistic suicide When people are too well integrated into the collectivity they are likely to kill themselves in greater numbers because the group leads them, or even forces them, to (Durkheim).

anomic suicide People are more likely to kill themselves when they do not know what is expected of them, where regulation is low, and they are largely free to run wild. This mad pursuit is likely to prove unsatisfying and, as a result, a higher percentage of people in such a situation are apt to commit this type of suicide (Durkheim).

anomie A sense, associated with organic solidarity, of not knowing what one is expected to do, of being adrift in society without any clear and secure moorings (Durkheim). To Merton, a situation in which there is a serious disconnection between social structure and culture; between structurally created abilities of people to act in accord with cultural norms and goals and the norms and goals themselves.

appearance The way the actor looks to the audience; especially those items that indicate the performer's social status (Goffman).

association The relationships among people, or interaction (Simmel).

autopoietic systems Systems that produce their own basic elements, establish their own boundaries and structures, are self-referential, and are closed (Luhmann).

back stage Where facts suppressed in the front stage or various kinds of informal actions may appear. A back stage is usually adjacent to the front stage, but it is also cut off from it. Performers can reliably expect no members of their front audience to appear in the back (Goffman).

base To Marx, the economy, which conditions, if not determines, the nature of everything else in society.

behavior Things that people do that require little or no thought.

behavioral organism One of Parsons's action systems, responsible for handling the adaptation function by adjusting to and transforming the external world.

behaviorism The study, largely associated with psychology, of behavior.

bifurcated consciousness A type of consciousness characteristic of women that reflects the fact that, for them, everyday life is divided into two realities: the reality of their actual, lived, reflected-on experience and the reality of social typifications (feminist theory).

boomerang effect Risks strike back on the upper classes and rich nations most responsible for their production (Beck).

breaching experiments Experiments in which social reality is violated in order to shed light on the methods by which people construct social reality (ethnomethodology).

bureaucracy A modern type of organization in which the behavior of officers is rule bound; each office has a specified sphere of competence and has obligations to perform specific functions, the authority to carry them out, and the means of compulsion to get the job done; the offices are organized into a hierarchical system; technical training is needed for each office; those things needed to do the job belong to the office and not the officer; the position is part of the organization and cannot be appropriated by an officer; and much of what goes on in the bureaucracy (acts, decisions, rules) is in writing (Weber).

business A pecuniary approach to economic processes, in which the dominant interests are acquisition, money, and profitability rather than production and the interests of the larger community (Veblen).

calculability   The emphasis on quantity, often to the detriment of quality (Ritzer).

capitalism   An economic system composed mainly of capitalists and the proletariat, in which one class (capitalists) exploits the other (proletariat) (Marx).

capitalist patriarchy   A term that indicates that the oppression of women is traceable to a combination of capitalism and patriarchy (feminist theory).

capitalists   Those who own the means of production under capitalism and are therefore in a position to exploit workers (Marx).

carceral archipelago   An image of society that results from the idea that discipline is swarming through society. This means that the process affects some parts of society and not others, or it may affect some parts at one time and other parts at another time. Thus, it creates a patchwork of centers of discipline amidst a world in which other settings are less affected or unaffected by the spread of the disciplinary society (Foucault).

center-periphery differentiation   Differentiation between the core of a system and its peripheral elements (Wallerstein).

charisma   The definition by others that a person has extraordinary qualities. A person need not actually have such qualities in order to be so defined (Weber).

charismatic authority   Authority legitimated by a belief by the followers in the exceptional sanctity, heroism, or exemplary character of the charismatic leader (Weber).

civilization   The broadest domain of cultures and cultural identities; culture "writ large" (Huntington).

civilizing process   The long-term change in the West in manners as they relate to daily behavior. Everyday behaviors once acceptable have, over time, become increasingly unacceptable. We are more likely to observe the everyday behaviors of others, to be sensitive to them, to understand them better, and, perhaps most importantly, to find an increasing number of them embarrassing. What we once found quite acceptable now embarrasses us enormously. As a result, what was once quite public is now hidden from view (Elias).

class consciousness   The ability of a class, in particular the proletariat, to overcome false consciousness and attain an accurate understanding of the capitalist system (Marx).

code   A system of rules that allows us to understand signs and, more importantly, how they relate to one another (Baudrillard). A way of distinguishing elements of a system from elements that do not belong to the system; the basic language of a functional system (Luhmann).

collective conscience   The ideas shared by the members of a collectivity such as a group, a tribe, or a society (Durkheim).

colonization of the lifeworld   As the system and its structures grow increasingly differentiated, complex, and self-sufficient, their power grows and with it their ability to direct and control what transpires in the lifeworld (Habermas).

communism   The social system that permits, for the first time, the expression of full human potential (Marx).

complex interdependence   A political theory that sees nation-states relating to one another through multiple channels and that emphasizes informal channels where, for example, entities (e.g., MNCs) other than the state connect societies to one another.

conflict group A group that actually engages in group conflict (Dahrendorf).

conspicuous consumption The consumption of a variety of goods, not for subsistence but for higher status for those who consume them and thereby to create the basis for invidious distinctions between people (Veblen).

conspicuous leisure The consumption of leisure; the nonproductive use of time; the waste of time as a way of creating an invidious distinction between people and elevating the social status of those able to use their time in this way (Veblen).

constructivist perspective The view that schemes of perception, thought, and action create structures (Bourdieu).

consummation Final stage of the act involving the taking of action that satisfies the original impulse (Mead).

control Domination by technologies over employees and customers (Ritzer).

conversation of gestures Gestures by one party that mindlessly elicit responding gestures from the other party (Mead).

core The geographical area that dominates the capitalist world-economy and exploits the rest of the system (Wallerstein).

cost Rewards lost in adopting a specific action and, as a result, in forgoing alternative lines of action (exchange theory).

creative destruction The idea that older structures are destroyed to make way for newer ones that function more effectively (Schumpeter).

creolization A combination of cultures that were previously separate from one another; often used interchangeably with hybridization.

cultural capital The various kinds of legitimate knowledge possessed by an actor (Bourdieu).

cultural feminism A feminist theory that explores and celebrates the social value of women's distinctive ways of being.

cultural imperialism The influence of a particular culture on a wide array of other cultures.

cultural system The Parsonsian action system that performs the latency function by providing actors with the norms and values that motivate them for action.

culture-ideology of consumerism An ideology that affects people scattered widely throughout the globe with the greater reach and sophistication of advertising, the media, and consumer goods. Ultimately, a global mood to consume is created that benefits transnational corporations, as well as the advertising and media corporations (Sklair).

culture industry To the critical theorists, industries such as movies and radio that were serving to make culture a more important factor in society than the economy.

debunking Looking beyond stated intentions to real effects (Berger).

definition of the situation The idea that if people define situations as real, then those definitions are real in their consequences (Thomas and Thomas).

deinstitutionalization   The process, begun in the 1960s and made possible by new drug treatments, involving the closing of many psychiatric institutions and the release of the vast majority of patients who were left to their own devices to survive in the larger society.

dependence   The potential cost that an actor will be willing to tolerate within a relationship (exchange theory).

dependency chains   The chain of relationships involving those people that a person is dependent on as well as those people's dependency on the person (Elias).

difference   An alternate explanation of consumption favored by postmodernists. We consume, not because of needs but in order to be different from other people; such differences are defined by what and how we consume.

differential space   A hoped-for space that accentuates difference and freedom from control; it would restore the natural unity that is broken by abstract space (Lefebvre).

differentiation   The system copying within itself the difference between it and the environment (Luhmann).

disciplinary society   A society in which control over people is pervasive (Foucault).

discreditable stigma   The stigma is neither known by audience members nor discernible by them (Goffman).

discredited stigma   The actor assumes that the stigma is known by the audience members or is evident to them (Goffman).

discrimination   The tendency to manifest behavior only under the specific circumstances that proved successful in the past (exchange theory).

discursive consciousness   The ability to describe our actions in words (Giddens).

distanciation   The tendency for various components of the modern juggernaut to grow quite distant from us in space and time (Giddens).

domination   To (feminist) oppression theorists, any relationship in which one party (individual or collective), the *dominant,* succeeds in making the other party (individual or collective), the *subordinate,* an instrument of the dominant's will, and refuses to recognize the subordinate's independent subjectivity.

double hermeneutic   The social scientist's understanding of the social world may have an impact on the understandings of the actors being studied, with the result that social researchers can alter the world they are studying and thus lead to distorted findings and conclusions (Giddens).

double movement   The expansion of the laissez-faire market and the self-protective reaction against it by the state and society (Polanyi).

dramaturgy   A view of social life as a series of dramatic performances akin to those that take place in the theater (Goffman).

dream world   Similar to the concept of phantasmagoria; more specifically refers to the use of things like decor to lure customers to means of consumption and to make the goods and services being purveyed seem glamorous, romantic, and, therefore, appealing to consumers. The goal is to inflame the desires and feelings of consumers (Williams).

dromology   A focal concern with the crucial importance of speed (Virilio).

dualism   Structure (and culture) and agency can be distinguished for analytic purposes, although they are intertwined in social life (Giddens, Archer).

duality   All social action involves structure and all structure involves social action. Agency and structure are inextricably interwoven in ongoing human activity or practice (Giddens, Archer).

dyad   A two-person group (Simmel).

dynamic density   The number of people and their frequency of interaction. An increase in dynamic density leads to the transformation from mechanical to organic solidarity (Durkheim).

dysfunctions   Observable consequences that have an adverse effect on the ability of a particular system to adapt or adjust (Merton).

economic capital   The economic resources possessed by an actor (Bourdieu).

economy   To Parsons, the subsystem of society that performs the function of adapting to the environment.

efficiency   The effort to discover the best possible means to whatever end is desired (Ritzer).

egoistic suicide   When people are not well integrated into the collectivity and largely on their own, they feel a sense of futility, meaninglessness, and more of them feel that they are morally free to kill themselves (Durkheim).

empire   A decentered, postmodern Marxian perspective on globalization and the exertion of power around the world based on new juridical power such as the constitution of order, norms, ethical truths, and a common notion of what is right. It can, in the name of what is "right," intervene anywhere in the world in order to deal with what it considers humanitarian problems, to guarantee accords, and to impose peace on those who may not want it or even see it as peace (Hardt and Negri).

endocolonization   Technology being used to colonize the human body (Virilio).

ethnomethodology   The study of ordinary members of society in the everyday situations in which they find themselves and the ways in which they use commonsense knowledge, procedures, and considerations to gain an understanding of, navigate in, and act on those situations.

ethnoscapes   Mobile groups and individuals (tourists, refugees, guest workers) can involve actual movement as well as fantasies about moving; one of Appadurai's landscapes.

evolution   The process of selection from variation (Luhmann).

examination   A way of observing subordinates and judging what they are doing. It involves checking up on subordinates and assessing what they have done; it is employed in a given setting by those in authority who make normalizing judgments about what is and is not an adequate score (Foucault).

exchange network   A web of social relationships involving a number of either individual or collective actors and the various actors have a variety of valued resources as well as exchange opportunities and exchange relations with one another. A number of these exchange relations exist and interrelate with one another to form a single network structure (Emerson).

existential or phenomenological feminism   A feminist theory of difference that sees people born into a world shaped by culture that reflects male experience and ignores or marginalizes women's experience.

exploitation   In capitalism, the capitalists get the lion's share of the rewards and the proletariat get enough to subsist even though, based on the labor theory of value, the situation should be reversed (Marx).

false consciousness   In capitalism, both the proletariat and the capitalists have an inaccurate sense of themselves, their relationship to one another, and the way in which capitalism operates (Marx).

fatalistic suicide   In situations of excessive regulation (e.g., slavery) people are often so distressed and depressed by their lack of freedom that they take their own lives more frequently than otherwise (Durkheim).

feminist institutional theory   A feminist theory that sees gender differences as resulting from the different roles that women and men play within various institutional settings.

feminist interactionist theory   A feminist theory that views gender as an accomplishment by actors in interaction with others who hold them accountable for conforming to appropriate gender behavior.

feminist theory   A generalized, wide-ranging system of ideas about social life and human experience developed from a woman-centered perspective.

fiduciary system   To Parsons, the subsystem of society that handles the pattern maintenance and latency function by transmitting culture (norms and values) to actors and seeing to it that it is internalized by them.

field   A network of relations among objective positions (Bourdieu).

fieldwork   A methodology used by symbolic interactionists and other sociologists that involves venturing into the field (the day-to-day social world) to observe and collect relevant data.

figurations   Social processes involving the interweaving of people who are seen as open and interdependent. Power is central to social figurations; they are constantly in flux. Figurations emerge and develop, but in largely unseen and unplanned ways (Elias).

financescapes   The processes by which huge sums of money move through nations and around the world at great speed; one of Appadurai's landscapes.

formal rationality   The choice of the most expedient action is based on rules, regulations, and laws that apply to everyone. This form of rationality is distinctive to the modern West (Weber).

forms   Patterns imposed on the bewildering array of events, actions, and interactions in the social world both by people in their everyday lives and by social theorists (Simmel).

front stage   That part of a dramaturgical performance that generally functions in rather fixed and general ways to define the situation for those who observe the performance (Goffman).

functional differentiation   The most complex form of differentiation and the form that dominates modern society. Every function within a system is ascribed to a particular unit (Luhmann).

functions   Consequences that can be observed and that help a particular system adapt or adjust (Merton).

game stage   The second stage in the genesis of the self (the first is the play stage): Instead of taking the role of discrete others, the child takes the role of everyone involved in a game. Each of these others plays a specific role in the overall game (Mead).

gender   Socially constructed male and female roles, relations, and identities.

generalization   The tendency to extend behavior to similar circumstances (exchange theory).

generalized other   The attitude of the entire community or of any collectivity in which the actor is involved (Mead).

genetic structuralism   Bourdieu's approach, which involves the study of objective structures that cannot be separated from mental structures, that, themselves, involve the internalization of objective structures.

gestures   Movements by one party (person or animal) that serve as stimuli to another party (Mead).

globalism   The monocausal and unilinear view that the world is dominated by economics and that we are witnessing the emergence of the hegemony of the capitalist world market and the neoliberal ideology that underpins it.

globality   The view that closed spaces, especially those associated with nations, are growing increasingly illusory in the era of globalization.

globalization   A transplanetary *process* or set of *processes* involving growing multidirectional *flows* of increasingly *liquid* people, objects, places, and information and the *structures* they encounter and create that are *barriers* to, or *expedite*, those flows.

glocalization   The interpenetration of the global and the local resulting in unique outcomes in different geographic areas (Robertson).

goal attainment   The second of Parsons's functional imperatives involving the need for a system to define and achieve its primary goals.

governmentalities   The practices and techniques by which control is exercised over people (Foucault).

grand theory   A vast, highly ambitious effort to tell the story of a great stretch of human history.

grobalization   The imperialistic ambitions of nations, corporations, organizations, and the like and their desire, indeed need, to impose themselves on various geographic areas (Ritzer).

habitus   The mental or cognitive structures through which people deal with the social world (Bourdieu).

hierarchical observation   The ability of officials at or near the top of an organization to oversee all that they control with a single gaze (Foucault).

historical materialism   The Marxian idea that the material conditions of human life, inclusive of the activities and relationships that produce those conditions, are the key factors that pattern human experience, personality, ideas, and social arrangements; that those conditions change over time because of dynamics immanent within them; and that history is a record of the changes in the material conditions of a group's life and of the correlative changes in experiences, personality, ideas, and social arrangements.

hybridization   A perspective on globalization that emphasizes the increasing diversity associated with unique mixtures of the global and the local as opposed to the *uniformity* associated with grobalization (Pieterse).

hyperconsumption   An extraordinary level of consumption associated with the contemporary world (Ritzer).

hyperreal   Entirely simulated and, as a result, more real than real, more beautiful than beautiful, truer than true, and so on (Baudrillard).

hysteresis   The condition that results from having a habitus that is not appropriate for the situation in which one lives (Bourdieu).

I   The immediate response of the self to others; the incalculable, unpredictable, and creative aspect of the self (Mead).

ideal speech situation   A speech situation that is free of all distorting influences, especially power; one in which the better argument wins out rather than the one that is backed by the most powerful individual or group. A consensus arises out of this contest of ideas as to what is the truth; truth arises from consensus and not because it is a copy of reality (Habermas).

ideal type   A one-sided, exaggerated concept, usually an exaggeration of the rationality of a given phenomenon, used to analyze the social world in all its historical and contemporary variation. The ideal type is a measuring rod to be used in comparing various specific examples of a social phenomenon either cross-culturally or over time (Weber).

ideoscapes   Largely political images either produced by states and in line with their ideology, or the images and counter-ideologies produced by movements that seek to supplant those in power, or at least to gain a piece of that power; one of Appadurai's landscapes.

imperatively coordinated associations   Associations of people controlled by a hierarchy of authority positions (Dahrendorf).

imperialism   The control and exploitation, especially economically, of a number of areas throughout the world by a nation(s) at the center.

implosion   The decline of boundaries and the collapse of various things into each other; dedifferentiation as opposed to differentiation (Baudrillard).

impression management   The techniques actors use to maintain certain impressions in the face of problems they are likely to encounter and the methods they use to cope with these problems (Goffman).

impulse   First stage of the act, in which the actor reacts to some external stimulus and feels the need to do something about it (Mead).

individual culture   The capacity of the individual to produce, absorb, and control the elements of objective culture (Simmel).

industry   The understanding and productive use, primarily by the working classes, of a wide variety of mechanized processes on a large scale (Veblen).

integration   The third of Parsons's functional imperatives, this one requiring that a system seek to regulate the interrelationship of its component parts. Integration also involves the management of the relationship among the other three functional imperatives (AGL).

interest group Unlike quasi groups, interest groups are true groups in the sociological sense of the term, possessing not only common interests, but also a structure, a goal, and personnel. Interest groups have the capacity to engage in group conflict (Dahrendorf).

interests Concerns, usually shared by groups of people (Dahrendorf).

international relations A political theory that focuses on the relations among and between the nation-states of the world.

intersectionality theory The view that women experience oppression in varying configurations and in varying degrees of intensity (feminist theory).

irrationality of rationality The idea that rational systems inevitably spawn a series of irrationalities (Weber). Various unreasonable things associated with rationality (and McDonaldization), especially dehumanization in which employees are forced to work in dehumanizing jobs and customers are forced to eat in dehumanizing settings and circumstances (Ritzer).

juggernaut Giddens's metaphor for the modern world as a massive force that moves forward inexorably riding roughshod over everything in its path. People steer the juggernaut, but it always has the possibility of careening out of control.

knowledge industry To the critical theorists, those entities in society concerned with knowledge production and dissemination, especially research institutes and universities. Like the culture industry, these settings achieved a large measure of autonomy within society, which allowed them to redefine themselves. Instead of serving the interests of society as a whole, they have come to focus on their own interests, and this means that they are intent on expanding their influence over society.

labor theory of value Marx's theory that *all* value comes from labor and is therefore traceable, in capitalism, to the proletariat.

latency One aspect of Parsons's fourth functional imperative involving the need for a system to furnish, maintain, and renew the motivation of individuals.

latent functions Unintended positive consequences (Merton).

latent interests Unconscious interests that translate, for Dahrendorf, into objective role expectations.

levels of functional analysis Functional analysis can be performed on any standardized repetitive social phenomenon ranging from society as a whole, to organizations, institutions, and groups (Merton).

liberal feminism A feminist theory of inequality that argues that women may claim equality with men on the basis of an essential human capacity for reasoned moral agency, that gender inequality is the result of a patriarchal and sexist patterning of the division of labor, and that gender equality can be produced by transforming the division of labor through the repatterning of key institutions—law, work, family, education, and media.

lie A form of interaction in which a person intentionally hides the truth from others (Simmel).

lifeworld The commonsense world, the world of everyday life, the mundane world; that world in which intersubjectivity takes place (Schutz). Habermas is more concerned with interpersonal communication in the lifeworld.

local actualities of lived experience The places where actual people act and live their lives (feminist theory).

looking-glass self The idea that we form our sense of ourselves by using others, and their reactions to us, as mirrors to assess who we are and how we are doing (Cooley).

lumpenproletariat The mass of people who stand below even the proletariat in the capitalist system (Marx).

manifest functions Positive consequences that are brought about consciously and purposely (Merton).

manifest interests Latent interests of which people have become conscious (Dahrendorf).

manipulation Third stage of the act involving manipulating the object, once it has been perceived (Mead).

manner The way an actor conducts himself; tells the audience what sort of role the actor expects to play in the situation (Goffman).

mass culture The culture (e.g., radio quiz shows) that has been made available to, and popular among, the masses (Critical Theory).

material social facts Social facts that take a material form in the external social world (e.g., architecture) (Durkheim).

McDonaldism The continuing existence of many characteristics of Fordism in industries like fast food: homogeneous products, rigid technologies, standardized work routines, deskilling, and homogenization of workers and consumers (Ritzer).

McDonaldization The process by which the principles of the fast-food restaurant are coming to dominate more and more sectors of American society, as well as the rest of the world. Its five basic dimensions are efficiency, calculability, predictability, control through the substitution of technology for people, and, paradoxically, the irrationality of rationality (Ritzer).

me The individual's adoption and perception of the generalized other; the conformist aspect of the self (Mead).

means-ends rational action The pursuit of ends that the actor has chosen for himself; that choice is affected by the actor's view of the environment in which he finds himself, including the behavior of people and objects in it (Weber).

means of consumption To Marx, these are simply consumer goods, but to Ritzer, paralleling Marx's sense of the means of production, these are the things that make consumption possible. Just as the factory makes production possible, the shopping mall enables the consumer and consumption.

means of production Those things that are needed for production to take place (including tools, machinery, raw materials, and factories) (Marx).

mechanical solidarity In Durkheimian theory, the idea that primitive society is held together by the fact there is little division of labor and, as a result, virtually everyone does essentially the same things.

mediascapes The electronic capability to produce and transmit information around the world as well as the images of the world that these media create and disseminate; one of Appadurai's landscapes.

methodological holists Those social scientists who focus on the macro-level and view it as determining the micro-level.

methodological individualists Those social scientists who focus on the micro-level and view it as determining the macro-level.

methodological relationists Those social scientists who focus on the relationship between macro- and micro-level phenomena (Ritzer).

microphysics of power The idea that power exists at the micro-level and involves efforts to exercise it as well as efforts to contest its exercise (Foucault).

middle-range theories Theories that seek a middle ground between trying to explain the entirety of the social world and a very minute portion of that world (Merton).

mind To Mead, the conversations that people have with themselves using language.

multitude A collection of people throughout the world that sustains empire in various ways, including, but not restricted to, its labor (it is the real productive force in empire), but it also has the power, at least potentially, to overthrow empire (Hardt and Negri).

mystification An effort by actors to confound their audience by restricting the contact between themselves and the audience, concealing the mundane things that go into their performance (Goffman).

need-dispositions To Parsons, drives that are shaped by the social setting.

needs Those things that people require in order to survive and to function at a minimal level in the contemporary world. Often used to explain why we consume what we do.

neoliberalism A theory that combines the political commitment to individual liberty with *neo*classical economics devoted to the free market and opposed to state intervention in that market.

neotribalism A postmodern development characterized by the coming of age of a wide array of communities that are refuges for strangers and more specifically for ethnic, religious, and political groups.

net balance The relative weight of functions and dysfunctions (Merton).

new means of consumption The set of consumption sites that came into existence largely after 1950 in the United States and that served to revolutionize consumption (Ritzer).

nonfunctions Consequences that are irrelevant to the system under consideration (Merton).

nonmaterial social facts Social facts that are external and coercive, but which do not take a material form; they are nonmaterial (e.g., norms and values) (Durkheim).

normalizing judgments Those in power can decide what is normal and what is abnormal on a variety of dimensions. Those who violate the norms, who are judged abnormal, can then be punished by officials or their agents (Foucault).

nothing Largely empty forms; forms devoid of most distinctive content (Ritzer).

objective culture The objects that people produce—art, science, philosophy, and so on—that become part of culture (Simmel).

observation A methodology closely related to fieldwork, in which the symbolic interactionist (and other sociologists) studies the social world by observing what is transpiring in it. In the case of symbolic interactionism, this enables researchers to engage in sympathetic introspection and put themselves in the place of actors in order to understand meanings and motives and to observe the various actions that people take.

one-dimensional society   To Herbert Marcuse, the breakdown in the dialectical relationship between people and the larger structures so that people are largely controlled by such structures. Lost is the ability of people to create and to be actively involved in those structures. Gradually, individual freedom and creativity dwindle away into nothingness, and people lose the capacity to think critically and negatively about the structures that control and oppress them.

operant conditioning   The learning process by which the consequences of behavior serve to modify that behavior (exchange theory).

opportunity costs   The costs of forgoing the next most-attractive action when an actor chooses an action aimed at achieving a given end (rational choice theory).

organic solidarity   To Durkheim, the idea that because of the substantial division of labor in modern society, solidarity comes from differences; that is, people need the contributions of an increasing number of people in order to function and even to survive.

othering   An act of definition within a subordinated group to establish that a group member is unacceptable, an "other," by some criterion; this erodes the potential for coalition and resistance (feminist theory).

outside   Neither front nor back; literally outside the realm of the performance (Goffman).

outsider within, the   The frequent experience of group members when they move from the home group into the larger society (feminist theory).

panopticon   A structure that allows someone in power (e.g., a prison officer) the possibility of complete observation of a group of people (e.g., prisoners).

patriarchy   A system in which men subjugate women. It is universal, pervasive in its social organization, durable over time and space, and triumphantly maintained in the face of occasional challenge (feminist theory).

pattern maintenance   The second aspect of Parsons's fourth functional imperative involving the need to furnish, maintain, and renew the cultural patterns that create and sustain individual motivation.

perception   Second stage of the act, in which the actor consciously searches for and reacts to stimuli that relate to the impulse and the ways of dealing with it (Mead).

periphery   Those areas of the capitalist world-economy that provide raw materials to the core and are heavily exploited by it (Wallerstein).

personal front   Those items of expressive equipment that the audience identifies with the performers and expects them to carry with them into the setting (Goffman).

personality   To Parsons, the individual actor's organized system of orientation to, and motivation for, action.

personality system   The Parsonsian action system responsible for performing the goal-attainment function by defining system goals and mobilizing resources to attain them.

phantasmagoria   The fantastic immaterial effects produced by physical structures like the arcades as well as the newer means of consumption (Benjamin).

play stage   The first stage in the genesis of the self, in which the child plays at being someone else (Mead).

political realism A political theory that operates on the premise that international politics is based on power, organized violence, and ultimately war.

polity To Parsons, the subsystem of society that performs the function of goal attainment by pursuing societal objectives and mobilizing actors and resources to that end.

postindustrial society A society characterized by the provision of services rather than goods; professional and technical work rather than blue-collar, manual work; theoretical knowledge rather than practical know-how; the creation and monitoring of new technologies; and new intellectual technologies to handle such assessment and control (Bell).

postmodern sociology A type of sociology that is heavily influenced by postmodern ideas and that would adopt a nonrational approach to the study of society (Bauman).

poststructuralist A theorist, like Bourdieu, who has been influenced by a structuralist perspective, but has moved beyond it to synthesize it with other theoretical ideas and perspectives.

power To Emerson, the potential cost that one actor can induce another to accept.

practical consciousness Involves actions that the actors take for granted, without being able to express in words what they are doing (Giddens).

practical rationality On a day-to-day basis, we deal with whatever difficulties exist and find the most expedient way of attaining our goal of getting from one point to another (Weber).

practice To Bourdieu, actions that are the outcome of the dialectical relationship between structure and agency. Practices are not objectively determined, nor are they the product of free will.

praxis The idea that people, especially the proletariat, must take concrete action in order to overcome capitalism (Marx).

predictability The idea that goods or services will be essentially the same from one time or place to another (Ritzer).

primary group An intimate face-to-face group that plays a crucial role in linking the individual to the larger society. Of special importance are the primary groups of the young, mainly the family and friendship groups (Cooley).

profit The greater number of rewards gained over costs incurred in social exchange (exchange theory).

proletariat Those who, because they do not own means of production, must sell their labor time to the capitalists in order to get access to those means (Marx).

Protestant ethic Because of their belief in predestination, the Calvinists could not know whether they were going to heaven or hell or directly affect their fate. However, it was possible for them to discern signs that they were either saved or damned and one of the major signs of salvation was success in business (Weber).

psychoanalytic feminism An effort to explain patriarchy through the use of reformulated theories of Freud and his successors in psychoanalytic theory.

punishments Actions with negative values; an increase in such actions means that the actor is less likely to manifest undesired behaviors (exchange theory).

quasi group A number of individuals who occupy positions that have the same role interests (Dahrendorf).

radical feminism   A theory of social organization, gender oppression, and strategies for change that affirms the positive value of women and argues that they are everywhere oppressed by violence or the threat of violence.

rational-legal authority   A type of authority in which the legitimacy of leaders is derived from the fact that there are a series of codified rules and regulations, and leaders hold their positions as a result of those rules (Weber).

rationalization   To Giddens, this means the development of routines that not only give actors a sense of security but enable them to deal efficiently with their social lives.

reason   People assess the choice of means to ends in terms of ultimate human values such as justice, freedom, and happiness (critical theory).

recursive   The idea that social practices are neither created mentally (or any other way) by actors, nor are they created by the structural social conditions in which actors find themselves. Rather, as people are expressing themselves as human actors, they are creating their consciousness and the structural conditions that make these practices possible; practices, consciousness, and structure are created simultaneously by the actor (Giddens).

reflexive sociology   The use by sociologists of their own theoretical and empirical tools to better understand their discipline (Bourdieu).

reflexivity   The ability to put ourselves in others' places: think as they think, act as they act (Mead).

reify   To endow social structures, which are created by people, with a separate and real existence (Marx).

relations of ruling   The complex, nonmonolithic, but intricately connected social activities that attempt to control human social production (feminist theory).

representational spaces   are ideas about, representations of, space that flow from the lived experiences of people, especially from those who are poor, silent, underground, or clandestine (Lefebvre).

representations of space   involve space as it is conceived by societal elites such as urban planners and architects; it overlies and ultimately dominates spatial practice (Lefebvre).

repressive law   Characteristic of mechanical solidarity, this is a form of law in which offenders are likely to be severely punished for any action that is seen by the tightly integrated community as an offense against the powerful collective conscience (Durkheim).

restitutive law   Characteristic of organic solidarity and its weakened collective conscience. In this form of law offenders are likely simply to be asked to comply with the law or to repay (make restitution to) those who have been harmed by their actions (Durkheim).

rewards   Actions with positive values; an increase in such actions is more likely to elicit the desired behavior (exchange theory).

role   What an actor does in a status, seen in the context of its functional significance for the larger system (Parsons).

role distance   The degree to which individuals separate themselves from the roles they are in (Goffman).

routinization of charisma Efforts by disciples to recast the extraordinary and revolutionary characteristics of the charismatic leader so that they are better able to handle mundane matters. This is also done in order to prepare for the day when the charismatic leader passes from the scene and to allow the disciples to remain in power (Weber).

secrecy As defined by Simmel, the condition in which one person has the intention of hiding something while the other is seeking to reveal that which is being hidden.

segmentary differentiation The division of parts of the system on the basis of the need to fulfill identical functions over and over (Luhmann).

self The ability to take oneself as an object. To Goffman, a sense of who one is that is a dramatic effect emerging from the immediate dramaturgical scene being presented.

semiperiphery A residual category in the capitalist world-economy that encompasses a set of regions somewhere between the exploiting and the exploited (Wallerstein).

setting The physical scene that ordinarily must be there if the actors are to engage in a dramaturgical performance (Goffman).

sexism A system of discriminatory attitudes and practices connected by a theme of privileging male experience and devaluing female experience.

significant gestures Gestures that require thought before a response is made; only humans are capable of this (Mead).

significant symbols Symbols that arouse in the person expressing them the same kind of response (it need not be identical) as they are designed to elicit from those to whom they are addressed (Mead).

simulations Fakes; to Baudrillard the contemporary world is coming to be increasingly dominated by the inauthentic.

social capital The extent of the valued social relations possessed by an actor (Bourdieu).

social facts To Durkheim, social facts are the subject matter of sociology. They are to be treated as things that are external to, and coercive over, individuals and they are to be studied empirically.

social stratification To the structural functionalist, a structure involving a hierarchy of positions that has the function of leading those people with the needed skills and abilities to do what is necessary to move into the high-ranking positions that are most important to society's functioning and survival.

social system The Parsonsian action system responsible for coping with the integration function by controlling its component parts; a number of human actors who interact with one another in a situation with a physical or environmental context. To Giddens, reproduced social practices, or relations between actors or collectivities, that are reproduced, becoming regular social practices.

socialist feminism An effort to develop a unified theory that focuses on the role of capitalism and patriarchy in creating a large-scale structure that oppresses women.

societal community To Parsons, the subsystem of society that performs the integration function; coordinating the various components of society.

societal functionalism A variety of structural functionalism that focuses on the large-scale social structures and institutions of society, their interrelationships, and their constraining effects on actors.

society   To Parsons, a relatively self-sufficient collectivity.

sociological theory   A set of interrelated ideas that allow for the systematization of knowledge of the social world, the explanation of that world, and predictions about the future of the social world.

sociology of postmodernity   A type of sociology that is continuous with modern sociology by being characterized by rational and systematic discourse and by an effort to develop a model of postmodern society. However, the sociology of postmodernity accepts postmodern society as a distinctive and unique type and does not see it as an aberrant form of modern society (Bauman).

something   Largely full forms; forms rich in distinctive content (Ritzer).

spatial practice   involves the actions (including and especially the actions of the masses) that produce and continually reproduce space (Lefebvre).

spirit of capitalism   In the West, unlike any other area of the world, people were motivated to be economically successful, not by greed, but by an ethical system that emphasized the ceaseless pursuit of economic success. The spirit of capitalism had a number of components, including the seeking of profits rationally and systematically, frugality, punctuality, fairness, and the earning of money as a legitimate end in itself (Weber).

standpoint   The perspective of embodied actors within groups that are differentially located in the social structure (feminist theory).

status   A structural position within the social system (Parsons).

stigma   A gap between virtual and actual social identity (Goffman).

stranger   One of Simmel's social types defined by distance: One who is neither too close nor too far.

stratificatory differentiation   Vertical differentiation according to rank or status in a system conceived as a hierarchy (Luhmann).

structural functionalism   A sociological theory that focuses on the structures of society and their functional significance (positive or negative consequences) for other structures.

structuralist perspective   The view that there are hidden or underlying structures that determine what transpires in the social world.

structuration   Agents and structures are interrelated to such an extent that at the moment they produce action, people produce and reproduce the structures in which they exist; the dialectical relationship between structure and agency. Structure and agency are a duality; neither can exist without the other (Giddens).

structure   To Giddens, the structuring properties (specifically, rules and resources) that give similar social practices a systemic form.

structures   In society, patterned social interaction and persistent social relationships (structural functionalism).

subsistence wage   The wage paid by the capitalist to the proletariat that is just enough for the worker to survive and to have a family and children so that when the worker falters, he can be replaced by one of his children (Marx).

substantive rationality   The choice of the most expedient action is guided by larger values rather than by daily experiences and practical thinking (Weber).

superstructure To Marx, secondary social phenomena, like the state and culture, that are erected on an economic base that serves to define them. Most extremely, the economy determines the superstructure.

surplus value The difference between the value of a product when it is sold and the value of the elements consumed in production of the product (including worker's labor) (Marx).

symbolic capital The amount of honor and prestige possessed by an actor (Bourdieu).

symbolic exchange A reversible process of giving and receiving; a cyclical exchange of gifts and counter-gifts, associated with primitive society (Baudrillard).

symbolic interactionism The school of sociology that, following Mead, focused on symbolic interaction; the distinctive human ability to relate to one another not only through gestures, but also through significant symbols.

symbolic violence A soft form of violence (the agent against whom it is practiced is complicit in its practice) that is practiced indirectly, largely through cultural mechanisms (Bourdieu).

sympathetic introspection The methodology of putting oneself in the places and the minds of those being studied. Researchers do so in a way that is sympathetic to who others are and what they are thinking, and they try to understand the meanings and the motives that lie at the base of peoples' behavior.

system To Habermas, the structures (such as the family, the legal system, the state, and the economy) that have their source within the lifeworld, but which come to develop their own distinctive existence and to grow distant and separated from the lifeworld.

team Any set of individuals who cooperate in staging a single performance (Goffman).

technocratic thinking Concern with being efficient, with simply finding the best means to an end without reflecting on either the means or the end (critical theory).

technoscapes The ever-fluid, global configurations of high and low, mechanical and informational technology and the wide range of material (Internet, e-mail) that now moves so freely and quickly around the globe and across borders; one of Appadurai's landscapes.

texts Written documents issued out of the relations of ruling, having the power to organize relations of production in the everyday life world and having the quality of generality and anonymity so that they may be seen as applicable in various everyday life circumstances; texts include licenses, diplomas, contracts, purchasing orders, laws, college catalogues, etc.

theoretical rationality An effort to master reality cognitively through the development of increasingly abstract concepts. The goal is to attain a rational understanding of the world rather than to take rational action within it (Weber).

theories of everyday life Theories that focus on such everyday and seemingly mundane activities as individual thought and action, the interaction of two or more people, and the small groups that emerge from such interaction.

tourists Those on the move throughout the globe because they want to be (Bauman).

traditional action Action taken on the basis of the ways things have been done habitually or customarily (Weber).

traditional authority　Authority based on the belief by followers that certain people (based on their family, tribe, or lineage) have exercised sovereignty since time immemorial. The leaders claim, and the followers believe in, the sanctity of age-old rules and powers (Weber).

tragedy of culture　Stems from the fact that over time objective culture grows exponentially while individual culture and the ability to produce it grow only marginally. Our meager individual capacities cannot keep pace with our cultural products. As a result, we are doomed to increasingly less understanding of the world we have created and to be increasingly controlled by that world (Simmel).

transnational capitalist class　Not made up of capitalists in the traditional Marxian sense of the term; its members do not necessarily own the means of production. Includes four "fractions"—*corporate,* made up of executives of transnational corporations and their local affiliates; *state,* composed of globalizing state and interstate bureaucrats and politicians; *technical,* made up of globalizing professionals; *consumerist* encompassing merchants and media executives (Sklair).

transnational corporations　Corporations that dominate the contemporary capitalist global economy and whose actions are largely unconstrained by the borders of nation-states (Sklair).

triad　A three-person group (Simmel).

types　Patterns imposed on a wide range of actors by both laypeople and social scientists in order to combine a number of them into a limited number of categories.

utilities　Actor's preferences, or values.

vagabonds　Those on the move throughout the globe because they find their environs unbearable, inhospitable for any number of reasons (Bauman).

value-rational action　Action that occurs when an actor's choice of the best means to an end chosen on the basis of the actor's belief in some larger set of values. This may not be the optimal choice, but it is rational from the point of view of the value system in which the actor finds herself (Weber).

vectors of oppression and privilege　The varied intersections of a number of arrangements of social inequality (gender, class, race, global location, sexual preference, and age) that serve to oppress women differentially. Variation in these intersections qualitatively alters the experience of being a woman (feminist theory).

verstehen　A methodological technique involving an effort to understand the thought processes of the actor, the actor's meanings and motives, and how these factors led to the action (or interaction) under study (Weber).

virtual social identity　What a person ought to be (Goffman).

world-system　A broad economic entity with a division of labor that is not circumscribed by political or cultural boundaries. It is a social system, composed internally of a variety of social structures and member groups, that is largely self-contained, has a set of boundaries, and has a definable life span (Wallerstein).

Permission and Source Acknowledgments

Chapter 2

p. 17. Excerpt from Steven Lukes, *Emile Durkheim: His Life and Work* (New York: Harper & Row, 1972), pp. 345, 347. © 1972 by Steven Lukes. Used by permission.

p. 26. Excerpt from "Communism and the Augsburger Allgemeine Zeitung," in D. McLlellan (ed.), *Karl Marx: Selected Writings* (New York: Oxford University Press, 1844/1972, p. 20. By permission of Oxford University Press.

Chapter 3

p. 56. Excerpt cited in Rick Tilman, *Thorstein Veblen and His Critics, 1891–1963: Conservative, Liberal, and Radical Perspectives* (Princeton University Press, 1992), pp. 9–10.

p. 61. Excerpts from Leonard S. Cottrell Jr., "George Herbert Mead: The Legacy of Social Behaviorism," in R. K. Merton and M. W. Riley (eds.), *Sociological Traditions from Generation to Generation: Glimpses of the American Experience* (Norwood, NJ: Ablex, 1980), pp. 40–50. Copyright © 1980 by Ablex Publishing Company. Reproduced with permission of Greenwood Publishing Group, Inc., Westport, CT.

Chapter 4

p. 73. Figure 4.1: "Structure of the General Action System." Reprinted by permission of the publisher from *The American University* by Talcott Parsons and Gerald Platt, p. 15, Cambridge, MA: Harvard University Press, Copyright © 1973 by The President and Fellows of Harvard College.

p. 74. Figure 4.2: "Parson's Action Schema" from Talcott Parsons, *Societies: Evolutionary and Comparative Perspective*, 1st ed., © 1966. Adapted by permission of Pearson Education, Inc., Upper Saddle River, NJ.

p. 81. Excerpts from Robert Merton, "Remembering the Young Talcott Parsons" from *American Sociologist* 15 (1980), pp. 69, 70, 71. © 1980 by the American Sociological Association.

p. 84. © Robert Merton. Used by permission.

Chapter 5

p. 124. Excerpt from Stephen Mennell, *Norbert Elias: An Introduction* (Oxford: Blackwell, 1992), p. 23. Used by permission of Blackwell Publishing.

p. 128. Excerpts cited in Rolf Wiggershaus, *The Frankfurt School: Its History, Theories, and Political Significance* (Cambridge, MA: MIT Press, 1994). Used by permission.

p. 132. Excerpt from Ian Craib, *Anthony Giddens* (London: Routledge, 1992), p. 12. Used by permission.

Chapter 6

p. 140. Excerpt from Robert E. Park, "Life History" (1927/1973), in *American Journal of Sociology*, 79:253.

p. 148. Excerpt from Randall Collins, "The Passing of Intellectual Generations: Reflections on the Death of Erving Goffman," in *Sociological Theory* 4 (1986):106–113, p. 112. © 1986 by the American Sociological Association.

p. 153. Figure 6.1: "Breaching in Tic-Tac-Toe" from Michael Lynch, "Pictures of Nothing? Visual Constructs in Social Theory," from *Sociological Theory* 9 (1991). © 1991 by the American Sociological Association. Reprinted with the permission of the author and the American Sociological Association.

p. 157. Reprinted with the permission of George Homans.

p. 164. Excerpts from James S. Coleman, "A Vision for Sociology," in *Society* 32 (1994): 32–33. © 1994 by Transaction Publishers. Reprinted by permission of the publisher.

Chapter 8

p. 224. Excerpts from Dorothy E. Smith, "A Sociology for Women," in J. A. Sherman and T. Beck (eds.), *The Prism of Sex: Essays in the Sociology of Knowledge* (Madison: University of Wisconsin Press, 1979), p. 151. © 1979. Reprinted by permission of The University of Wisconsin Press.

Chapter 9

p. 237. Excerpts from Michel Foucault in James Miller, *The Passion of Michel Foucault* (New York: Anchor Books, 1993).

Index